SQL For Analytics with MS Access 365

Pindaro E. Demertzoglou, Ph.D.

Alpha Press – Stratford, Connecticut 2025

ISBN-13: 978-1-958272-02-2

Printed in the United States of America

Library of Congress Control Number: 2024924141

About the Author

Pindaro's relationship with databases started with dBase III back in 1991, continuing with all versions of MS Access since 1993, and working with MS SQL Server, MySQL, Oracle, IBM DB2, and other database engines. From then on, he is still in love with all of them. After more than thirty two years, he still works with data and databases.

Pindaro is currently an Associate Professor of Practice at the University of New Haven and the founder of AlphaPress Publishing, a company that focuses on data analytics books, webinars, and datasets for artificial intelligence models. Pindaro has worked and taught at the University level for 26 years with amazing feedback from his students. He developed multiple data and business intelligence labs for experiential learning, and he collaborated on a myriad of database projects for organizations in collaborative efforts between the University and various corporations.

Pindaro's interests in information science, data systems, and analytics focus on creating more efficient and flexible organizations. The idea is to accomplish more with fewer resources and in less time leaving a small footprint on the environment. Pindaro's education includes a BS from the American College in Thessaloniki Greece, an MS, MBA, and a PhD in the United States.

Most of the author's experience came from participating in a multitude of industry projects. There, everything must work efficiently, reliably and above all be acceptable by the people of the corporation. Theoretical knowledge, though useful, takes a second place.

Dedication

This book is dedicated to all the educators around the world for their continuous efforts which keep the learning processes going for all of us.

Acknowledgments

I would like to express my gratitude and say a big thank you to all the teachers around the globe for their effort, patience, and time they devote to their students.

I would like to thank the faculty and staff of the American College of Thessaloniki, Greece who made this college a prestigious and internationally recognized institution. Specifically, I would like to express my deepest appreciation to the former president of the college, Dr. William McGrew and the head librarian Mrs. Pat Kastritsis for their decisive and unrelenting guidance and help to their students. Pat is no longer with us today but the difference she made in my life is propagated to the thousands of students. She will live through my own students and the students of my students who receive the same values and attention as the ones I received from Dr. McGrew and Mrs. Kastritsis.

Moreover, I would like to express my deepest appreciation to the staff and faculty of the University of New Haven, New Haven, CT, United States for the collegiate atmosphere and continuous support in my efforts. Finally, I really want to thank all my students who, with their tens of thousands of questions on databases over the years, gave me the spark to think and rethink a multitude of points from different perspectives and learn a lot as a result.

BRIEF TABLE OF CONTENTS

DETAILED TABLE OF CONTENTS

PREFACE: HOW TO USE THIS BOOK

How to download the practice database

To download the practice database for this book, go to https://www.alphapresspublishing.com, click on "Books", and then click on the image of the book.

To obtain the instructor resources, send an email to demerp@alphapresspublishing.com and upon verification of instructor status all resources will be available to you.

How to start working with the book examples

Start Microsoft Access and open the practice database. Click "Create" in the main menu and then from the group "Queries" click on "Query Design".

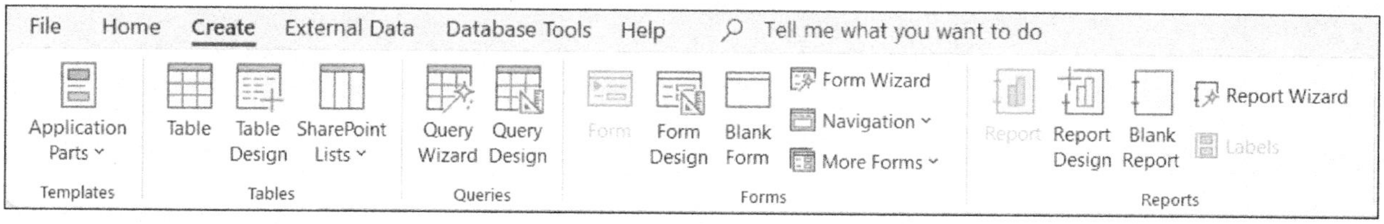

Click the "SQL" button in the "Results" group below:

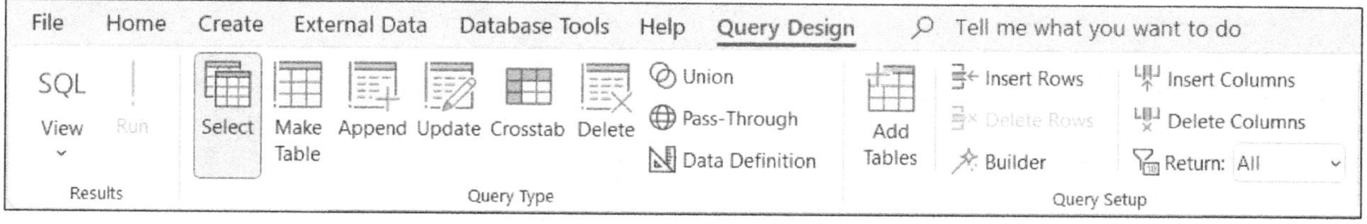

The following window will come up where you can write your SQL code. To run your SQL statement and see the result, click the "Run!" button in the "Results" group.

CHAPTER 1
FUNDAMENTAL CONCEPTS ON SQL

SQL stands for Structured Query Language, and it is the standard for manipulating relational databases. It was developed by IBM in the mid-seventies and at that point it was named SEQUEL standing for Standard English Query Language.

SQL is based on the Relational Database Model officially defined in June 1970 by E. F. Codd in his amazing paper "A Relational Model of Data for Large Shared Data Banks." In his article, Dr. Codd explained the need for a new relational model and language for maximum independence from specific programs and system platforms. To this end the goal set more than 50 years ago has been achieved and SQL is used in a multitude of platforms and database servers.

IBM continued its work on SQL throughout the 1970s and introduced SQL/DS in 1981, and DB2 in 1983. The problem was that Oracle was successful in releasing a relational RDBMS in 1979 beating IBM in its own game by two years. Sybase and Microsoft formed a partnership to produce their own RDBMS and they worked together up until version 4 of their product. After that, Sybase and Microsoft continued to produce their own databases with Sybase working on their SYSTEM products and Microsoft on their SQL Server versions. Today all commercial vendors face severe competition from open-source relational databases like PostgreSQL.

A tribute to Dr. Codd

Dr. Codd joined IBM in 1949 and he worked on numerous projects such the logical design of computers and operating systems. He will be remembered for his creation and work on the relational model of databases in 1970 and relational algebra in 1972. Dr. Codd continued his work on SQL and in 1981 received the extremely prestigious Turing Award for his work on database

SQL is endorsed by the American National Standards Institute (http://www.ansi.org) which periodically publishes versions of the SQL standard such as SQL-89, SQL-92, SQL 2006, SQL 2011, and SQL:2016 which is the latest one. However, the constructs and expressions used in a particular environment might be different because commercial vendors introduce proprietary features to gain a competitive edge.

Why SQL?

SQL is the most popular language for data management and analytics and amongst the top ones overall. Learning to work with SQL enables us to produce intricate and accurate analytics that are necessary for any business professional who works with data. Currently, a big portion of this analysis need is covered with Excel but with SQL new and unlimited horizons open for amazing insight and decision making. In a 2020 survey from Stack Overflow with 65,000 developers, SQL was the third most popular tool just behind JavaScript and HTML, and well above such popular tools like C (and variants), Python, Java, PowerShell, R, and PHP.

SQL is a fourth generation, non-procedural computer programming language. By non-procedural we mean that we are looking at the result and not the sequence of lines of code. In traditional programming, lines of code execute in sequence, one after the other, to produce the end result. In SQL, a section of code at the end of the SQL statement might execute before a section of code in the beginning of the SQL statement.

After you go through this book, you will not get stuck with a particular tool or vendor. Almost 100% of your SQL skills will be applicable and can be used in other relational databases such as MySQL, PostgreSQL, Oracle, IBM DB2, SQLite, SQL Server, and others. Consequently, if at your company you are using a different database server such as Oracle for example, your SQL skills are 100% applicable.

Beyond operational databases, your knowledge of SQL is applicable to information generation and analytics, data warehouses, big data platforms and applications, data lakes, ETL systems, XML data exchanges, web scripting languages, data linking and sharing, business process automation, OLAP platforms, data mining, machine learning, and artificial intelligence. In this chapter we will explore the specifics of all these SQL applications.

The value of SQL in the Enterprise

As you can see from Figure 1 below, an organization consists of three hierarchical levels. First, the strategic level, where the top management sets the strategic objectives of the corporation. Strategic objectives are specific goals, not general ambitions such as "increase sales of product A by 5% in the state of New York in a period of five years". Executives at the strategic level of the corporation need information to make decisions and formulate strategic objectives. These pieces of information come from data at the operational level of the company where all the business activity, such as sales, sourcing, marketing, replenishing, accounting, and other business transactions, take place.

Second, the tactical level of the corporation is where managers make sure that the company stays on course to achieve its strategic objectives. For example, if for a period of two-months, sales are not materializing as forecasted, the tactical managers will take action to bring sales back on track and compensate for lost sales. The tactical managers need information to make these tactical adjustments. These pieces of information also come from the transactional level of the corporation.

The third level of the corporation is the transactional/operational level. This is the place where the daily business activity takes place. For example, taking an order from a customer is a transaction, processing a quotation for a customer is a transaction, updating accounts payable is a transaction, hiring a new employee and creating a new HR record is a transaction, preparing a shipment for a customer is a transaction, fulfilling an order is a transaction, and processing payment for an order is a transaction. All these transactions might aggregate to hundreds, thousands, or even hundreds of thousands of transactions per day. Consequently, we have a lot of data generated daily in various parts of the corporation typically in multiple functional areas such as accounting, sales, human resources, and marketing. This is the transactional data that we want to convert to information and direct it to the tactical and strategic levels for decision making. This is where SQL constitutes the tool of choice to aggregate, summarize, sort, group by, calculate, concatenate, and pivot data to generate the information the corporation needs to set its tactical and strategic directions.

Figure 1: Organizational Hierarchical Levels

In Figure 2, we present a real-life corporate transaction processing system. As you can see, this company has a functional design and it is divided in four departments: Finance/Accounting, Sales/Marketing, Human Resources, and Production. We also notice that the transactional/operational system has two layers: an application layer and a data layer. The application layer consists of the actual front-end applications which corporate employees use to process transactions. A front-end application is usually made up by a collection of forms which employees use to enter, edit, delete, and update data. This front-end is also commonly called the user interface. Notice an additional couple of items: Departmental applications do not communicate with each other. But even within the department itself, the departmental units are using different applications. For instance, in the Finance/Accounting department, the accounts receivable, accounts payable, and investment management are all using different applications. This results in longer communication times among departments and units which in turn leads to higher cycle times for order processing, fulfillment, accounting debits/credits, and other corporate transactions.

These higher cycle times lead to increased transactional costs and thus in higher operational expenses and a corresponding decrease in our operating margin. Even worse, higher operational expenses result in increased risk for the corporation which means that in difficult times this company will be the one to have trouble first. To explain this further, the operational cost of a corporation is not directly related to production output. This means that we will incur operational cost independently of the level of business turnover we have. In times of booming business this is not a problem because the added and unnecessary operational cost we experience becomes lower when measured by unit of output. In times of recession however, this operational cost increases by unit of output and its weight shows in full in the income statement.

It is exactly in these suppressed business conditions that managers make their biggest mistakes as well. Instead of trying to make the corporation more efficient, that is, look at cycle times, transactional cost, operating expenses, and risk, they look at the usual culprit: the employee of the corporation. This trend needs to stop at some point and one of the ways to do it is for management to understand how data processing, analysis, and dissemination affects their business. Therefore, SQL represents a crucial technology for our business.

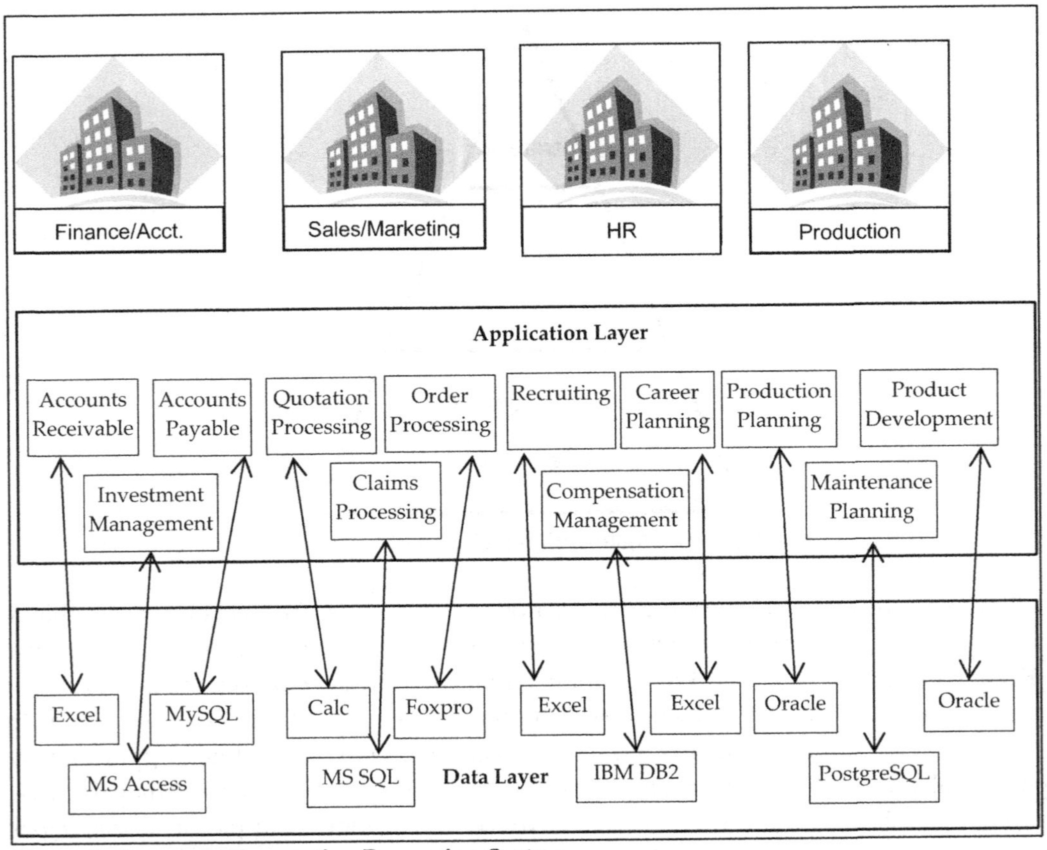

Figure 2: Corporate Transaction Processing System

The second operational layer, which we see in Figure 2, is the data tier of the corporation. In most businesses, the data layer consists of many heterogeneous data sources. In theory, books, and ERP (Enterprise Resource Planning) pitches, an idealized solution is offered where the data layer consists of a single database management system. This is very far from the truth and what actually happens is what you see in Figure 2 where not only departments but also departmental units use different data systems. For instance, the Career Planning and Compensation Management units in Human Resources use different and separate data sources. Career Planning is using Excel to store and process its data while Compensation Management uses an IBM DB2 relational database. It will take time, effort, and expensive integration packages to move data among these heterogeneous departmental data sources. It is possible but get ready for the ensuing political conflict that will lead to a quagmire and finally a compromise to a higher or lesser degree. The main problem here is that in the data layer of the corporate transaction processing system we have multiple and heterogeneous data sources. This of course leads to inefficient data exchange. What is inefficient? By inefficient we mean we need more time to exchange data and we are more prone to mistakes when we do the exchange. This practically means increased cycle times to process business transactions accompanied by increased transactional cost which in turn will lead to higher operational cost for the corporation with resulting decreases in the operating margin and net profits for the business. In addition, there will be an increased perceived risk for the corporation which is always the case for corporations with high levels of operational cost with respect to revenue. An inefficient corporation can cover its high operational expenses in high revenue but when one of the two constituents of revenue goes down (either price or units sold), then this type of business will be among the first to go belly up.

Now, the question is how do we use SQL to help in the above situations? In the next pages, we will list specific instances on how SQL is used throughout the corporation. The list, though not exhaustive, it is comprehensive enough for a very deep understanding of the role of SQL.

SQL for database management - Data Definition Language(DDL)

A major usage of SQL is to create, manage, and manipulate the properties of tables, indexes, relationships, user accounts, security rules, backup plans, referential constraints, and other database objects and settings we need to manage the database. SQL DDL has three statements:

CREATE (to create objects)
ALTER (to modify objects)
DROP (to delete objects)

Now, one might question the practicality of learning how to work with DDL statements since we can perform all the DDL tasks using the user interface from the specific database. However, knowing how to manipulate databases using SQL makes our knoeledge portable since we can accomplish the tasks we want in multiple databases without having to learn the particularities of the user interface of each one of them. In addition, we use SQL DDLstatements in many more cases than databases. For instance, we use DDL in server-side web pages such as java server pages, PHP, and ASPX to add, delete, and modify tables in the back-end database. The same is true for applications developed with hard-coded languages like C variants and Java. In addition, we use SQL DDL a lot in extraction, transformation, and loading (ETL) applications to move data from one database to another or from a relational database to a data warehouse. Consequently, SQL DDL is a tool that must exist in the belt of any SQL professional.

Below, I provide a couple of examples on DDL statements and in this book, I have devoted three chapters on SQL DDL statements for table, relationships, and indexes manipulation. All the other chapters focus on SQL for data analytics. If you want to delve on SQL DDL statements, this is not the appropriate book to use; there are many excellent books in the market written by amazing authors which focus entirely on SQL DDL.

The following is an example of a DDL statement which we use to create a new table with CustomerID as its primary key and two text fields for storing the customer's first and last name.

```
CREATE TABLE TempCustomer (
[CustomerID] Counter Primary key not null,
[LastName] text(50),
[FirstName] text(50))
```

The following SQL DDL statement will alter the structure of the existing table "TempCustomer" and add one more field called "City". Notice how we can define the data type of the field we are adding as well as its length.

```
ALTER TABLE TempCustomer
ADD City varchar(25)
```

Open the table in design view to have a look at its structure.

Finally, we can delete the table "TempCustomer" by using the DROP DDL statement:

```
DROP TABLE TempCustomer
```

SQL for Analytics - Data Manipulation Language (DML)

We use SQL DML statements to manipulate data and produce analytics for the corporation. The DML language includes four statements:

SELECT (to retrieve records from tables and queries)
UPDATE (to edit records in tables)
DELETE (to delete records in tables)
INSERT (insert records in tables)

We use these statements to retrieve, aggregate, sort, group, filter, pivot, update, and delete records in the database. The SELECT statement is the most popular one followed by the UPDATE and DELETE statements. We use less the INSERT statement in SQL per se. Usually, it is used at the application level to insert a multitude of records at once in the database. This whole book focuses on SQL for business analytics, that is on SQL DML statements that produce information for the business.

Below, we see a basic SQL DML statement that retrieves fields from the customers table, filters for customers with silver membership, and then sorts the results by LastName ascending.

```
SELECT Firstname, Lastname, City, State, MembershipType, BonusPoints
FROM Customers
WHERE MembershipType = 'Silver'
ORDER BY LastName asc
```

SQL for Business Transaction Processing

In Figure 3, we have a conceptual view of how SQL is used for transaction processing at the operational/transactional level of the corporation. A business user can process transactions such as entering an order, updating an order, or deleting an order. Business users use front-end applications, usually a set of forms (Access, Oracle, Visual Basic, Java, web etc.), to work on these transactions. These forms contain "add", "edit", "delete", and other buttons that initiate the requested transactions. The business user does not see the SQL statements behind these forms and but has the expertise to work with the front-end application forms.

Behind the scenes, it is the actual SQL developer who writes the SQL statements so that business users can do their job. This developer is needed constantly because the SQL statements she develops will not stay constant but will change as the business conditions change. That is, as the business engages in activities to acquire market share, to reduce cost, to increase revenue, to increase profit, to launch new products, or respond to competitors, the business requirements for the application will change. This means that the SQL code of the application needs to change to accommodate the new logic for processing transactions. Consequently, the role of the SQL developer is ongoing to help the corporation achieve its strategic and tactical objectives.

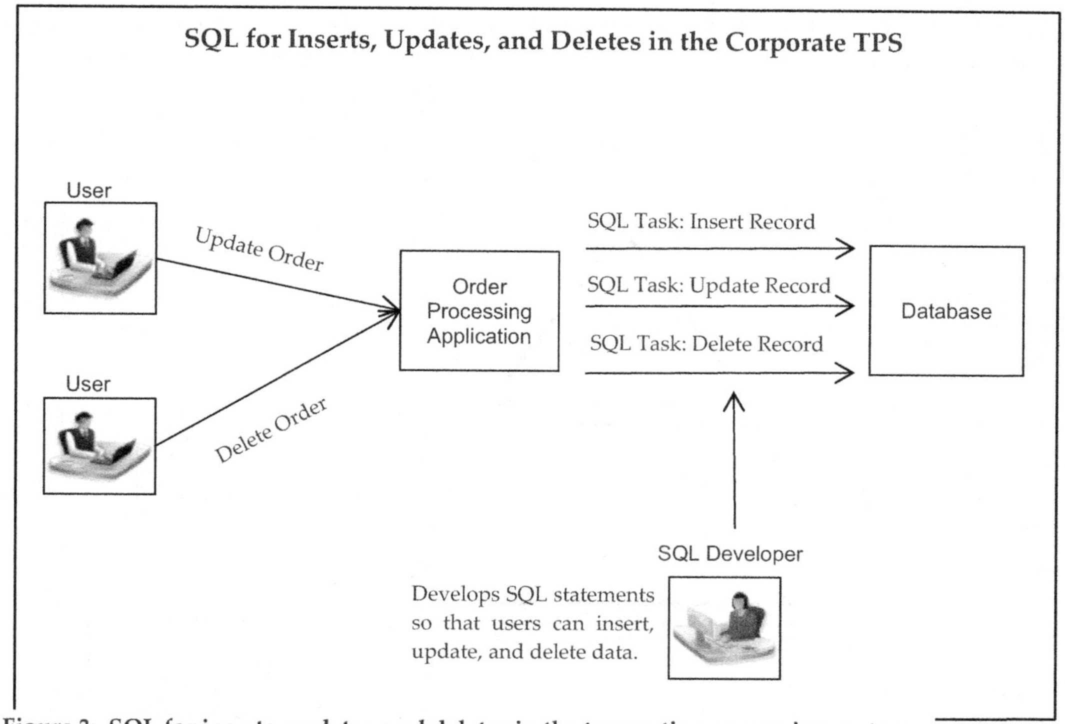

Figure 3: SQL for inserts, updates, and deletes in the transaction processing system

The SQL developer in this role is not the technical person who writes code all day long. Most of her time will be spent communicating with the users of the corporation so that she can understand in detail the business expectations behind her code. Consequently, the SQL developer becomes a businessperson and an integral part of the business operations of the company.

SQL for Information generation at the operational, tactical, and strategic levels of the business

In this scenario, we visualize how SQL is used to convert data to information in a corporation. As you can see from Figure 4, we use multiple SQL statements such as GROUP BY, aggregate functions, conditions, crosstab queries, and a multitude of other techniques to generate information out of data that is stored in tables and has been generated from corporate transactions. A lot of data is generated at the operational/transactional level as business departments interact with customers, suppliers, partners, distributors, and the government.

It is the job of the SQL professional to provide intelligence to the operational, tactical and strategic levels of the corporation. This process has two tasks: As you can see from Figure 4, the data in the data layer of the corporation is stored in multiple heterogeneous formats and we need to retrieve it from multiple different databases such as MySQL , PostgresSQL, SQL Server and data sources such as Excel, text files, and XML files. This is because the corporation does not use a single database as the basis for its transaction processing system.

But even in the case where corporations engaged in ERP implementations, databases in departmental units, and even personal databases emerge like mushrooms. Consequently, we need to accept a degree of heterogeneity of data sources in any corporate environment. The consequence is that the SQL developer needs to do some staging in the first place. That is, he or she needs to import data from various sources into a relational database so that he or she can manipulate this data to extract information. This staging procedure might be something as simple as a single import or something as intricate as the development of multiple Extraction Transformation and Loading (ETL) packages. ETL has become an expertise area itself and a whole book can be devoted to it. In any case, a SQL developer who augments his or her portfolio with ETL knowledge, positions himself or herself very strongly in the market.

SQL for information generation – from the TPS to the tactical and strategic levels

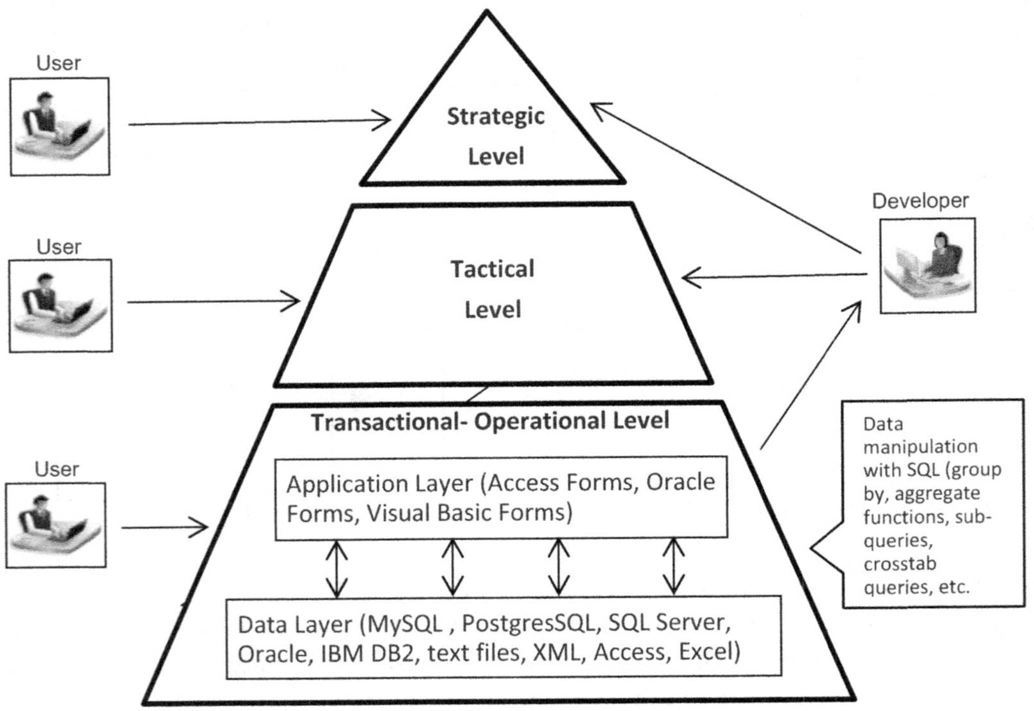

Figure 4: SQL for information generation – from the TPS to tactical and strategic levels

Once the transactional data is in a common (usually relational) format, then we can work with SQL statements to convert this data to information. Specifically, we can use calculated fields, concatenated fields, string functions, date functions, group by, cross tabbing, union operators, aggregate functions, and other techniques to convert pieces of data to information that makes sense and is needed by the strategic, tactical, and operational levels of the corporation. This information is usually provided in the form of web-based reports for larger corporations. No matter what the reporting platform is, the SQL professional has a central role in the provision of intelligence to the corporation and on many occasions, this is a full-time job with important responsibilities for the medium and long-term planning of the company.

SQL in Data Warehousing

Beyond operational databases, your knowledge of SQL will be thoroughly applicable in data warehouse environments on premise or on the cloud. On premise data warehouses are built in many cases using traditional relational databases like the ones listed above but there are many cloud-based data warehouses with which you can work to compile analytics using your SQL skills. For instance, Amazon Redshift, Google BigQuery, Snowflake Cloud Data Platform, Azure Synapse Analytics, IBM Db2 Warehouse, Oracle Autonomous Data Warehouse, Panoply Data Warehouse, SAP Data Warehouse, Teradata Cloud Data Warehouse, and Yellowbrick Data Warehouse are all examples of cloud based data warehouses with which you can work using your SQL skills and apply to related job positions.

SQL in Big Data Platforms

Even with Big Data platforms like Hadoop, SQL is the most popular tool for data analytics and you will be able to apply your SQL knowledge with Big Data tools such as Apache Hive, Facebook Presto, IBM Big SQL, Apache Spark, Impala, Oracle Big Data SQL, and others. Years ago, I was very excited to learn about these new Big Data Analytics applications, all brand-new concepts back then. I went ahead and downloaded and setup Impala to check how these new tools worked for data analytics. To my surprise, the SQL code I have used in my books on relational databases was working perfect with Impala. Obviously, the big data interface and the platform setup is quite different from traditional relational databases, but this is also the case when we switch environments such as from SQL Server to Oracle which are two traditional relational databases! The main point is your knowledge of SQL from this book will be 100% applicable to big data environments.

SQL in NoSQL databases

SQL is also used in NoSQL databases such as document based big data databases which use documents to store data. These documents can be JSON files. Multiple related JSON documents form collections which can become sub-collections to higher level collections. In one sentence, NoSQL databases use sets and subsets of documents to store data instead of tables used in relational databases. My conclusion is that both relational and NoSQL databases are excellent tools when applied to support the business function for which they have been developed and your knowledge on SQL is relevant to both types of databases.

SQL in Data Pipelines and Data Integration (ETL)

These tools automate the transfer and transformation of data to facilitate corporate transactional processes as well as processes that produce analytics. Although vendors say you can work with visual tools, it is close to impossible to work effectively with ETL systems if you do not know how to work with SQL. Such ETL tools include SSIS, Informatica, IBM Data Stage, Hitachi Vantara-Pentaho, Talend, Boomi, AWS Glue, and Azure Data Factory.

This area has a lot of potential for work or consulting since all corporations need to move data for transaction processing or for business intelligence. We can define ETL as the general process of extracting data from one or more data sources, transforming this data to appropriate formats, and load it in one or more data destinations. An ETL process might involve extracting data from a transaction processing system and load it to a data warehouse (see Figure 5). This is the most common scenario for which ETL is known but it is not the only one. ETL might involve the exchange of data between two transaction processing databases, an Excel file to an XML file, or an XML file to a data warehouse. The important point is that ETL is a process that brings tremendous efficiency in any data integration scenario and should be included in system planning.

One of the major differences between ad hoc data moves and rigorous ETL processes is the notion of the timing and complexity of data exchanges. A simple import of data from an Excel spreadsheet into a database cannot be described as an ETL process. However, when we retrieve data from ten heterogeneous data sources, process transformations automatically, incorporate workflow and error checking, run the package automatically every week, every day, or even every hour, then we can say we have an ETL process in place.

Data sources might be homogeneous or heterogeneous. For example, let us assume we have an ETL process in place which takes data from ten data sources. These data sources are two Oracle databases, one PostgreSQL database, one MySQL database, three XML files, an Excel spreadsheet, two text files, and an ODBC connection to our own DB2 database system. The two Oracle databases are homogeneous data sources, but XML files and MySQL tables are heterogeneous data sources. In a data warehouse scenario, we will usually have to work with a number of heterogeneous data sources so that we can have all the data needed for advanced business analytics.

Such a scenario is shown in figure 9, where we get data from multiple heterogeneous data sources from our suppliers, partners, and our own transaction processing system. The goal is to integrate all this data into a data warehouse which will function as the basis of our business intelligence system. A data warehouse is a historical data repository, or in other words, a repository of completed historical transactions. We will use this data to generate information using tools such as Data Mining, Online Analytical Processing (OLAP), and reporting tools such as Power BI, Tableau, or SSRS.

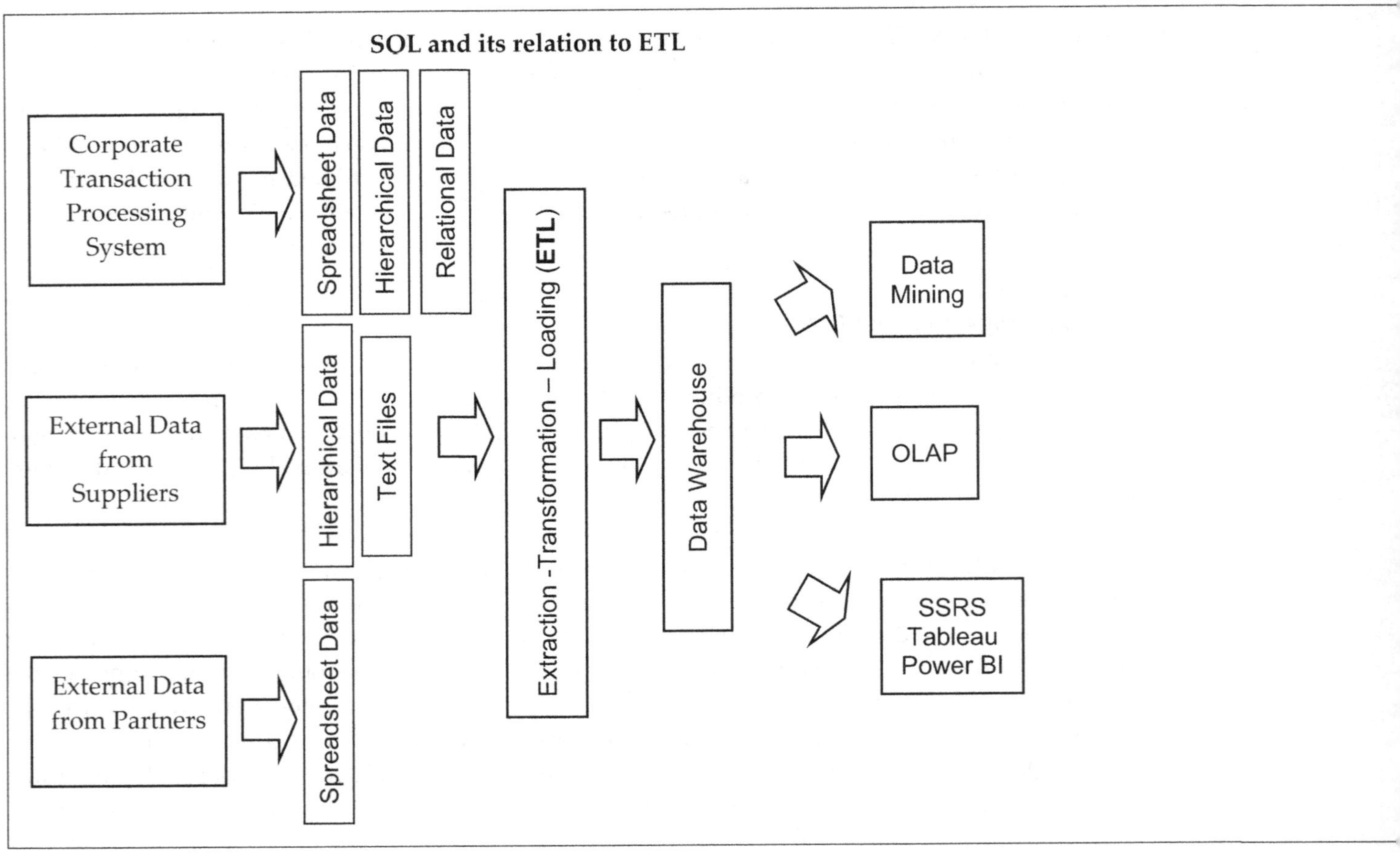

Figure 5: SQL and ETL

The job of the SQL developer is to provide his or her expertise in designing, developing, and implementing the ETL packages. He or she needs to be able to connect to data sources (databases or others), write SQL code, develop queries, concatenate fields, write functions to alter existing data, convert data from text to numeric formats, write criteria, and a host of additional tasks that require real command of the SQL language. This is ongoing work as we might have tens or even hundreds of ETL packages. Moreover, ETL packages are repetitive, and they need editing as business conditions change. For instance, we might need to include a new supplier, delete a partner, include one more data source, delete a field, change scrubbing rules, and a myriad of other tasks. We see at this point how important the role of the SQL developer becomes at any level of the company.

SQL in XML and Data Exchange

The business example in this scenario is to outsource inventory replenishment. We would like our suppliers to assume the cost of re-supplying us with inventory because we want to reduce the people and financial resources we devote to this process, so that we can reduce our operational cost and decrease our replenishing cycles. The suppliers will be willing to do this because it concerns their sales and revenue. Incurring minimal cost for inventory replenishment is an excellent idea and, in this example, we discuss one way to achieve this in technical terms.

As you can see from Figure 6, an MS SQL server database contains a Products table in which we keep our product inventory quantities. The data in this table is in relational format. The SQL developer will write SQL statements to retrieve the inventory quantities from every supplier. Then, automated ETL packages will send the data from these SQL statements to XML files on the web server. For illustration purposes we named such a file Inventory.xml. Today's database servers support the automated importing and exporting of XML data with easily set procedures. Then, the suppliers can access these XML files through the Internet. They check to see what they need to send us from each product, and they replenish our inventory themselves which allows us to keep our operational cost down. This process is automated and repeatable which means that every day, every three days, or every week we replace the XML files on the web server so that the suppliers have access to all the latest data about the status of our inventory.

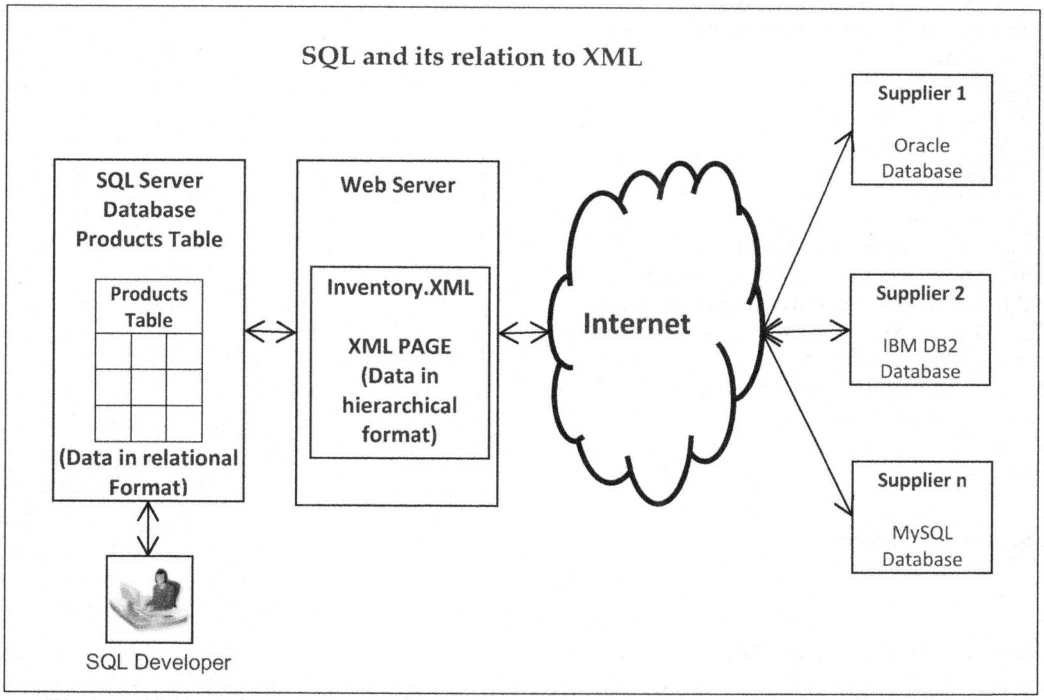

Figure 6: SQL and its relation to XML

On a more technical level, when we export data from a relational database to an XML file there are a couple of items we need to know. First, databases follow the relational data model which means we have a set of related entities (tables) to store data. This for a business task of exchanging data is a problem since the data we need to send to our suppliers might be in four, five or even more related tables and there is no way to send those tables and their relationships across the web. Consequently, what we do is use SQL to get the data we need from those tables in a single view and then we export the result of this view to an XML file which follows the hierarchical data model. But what is an XML file? XML files are text documents containing elements. An element can be a book, an employee, a product etc. This single element contains sub-elements and these sub-elements contain additional elements down the hierarchy. Have you noticed the word hierarchy?

In Figure 7, we see a simple XML file. Notice that this file contains information about two employees. In a relational database they would represent two records in the employee table. In this XML file we notice that we have a root element called <Employees> which contains two instances of the sub- element <Employee> or in other words information about two employees of ours. We also notice that in the sub-element <Employee> there are additional sub-elements like LastName, FirstName, Title, etc. We see that between the element tags we have the actual name, title, and address for each employee. Consequently, this single XML file contains both the data and the description of this data. When we receive a file like this, it is very easy to make sense of the data it contains. Consequently, when our suppliers connect to a file like this through the Internet, they can read it, they understand its meaning, import it into their database for processing, and finally send us the products we need to do our work with no or minimal cost to us.

```
<?xml version="1.0" encoding="UTF-8" ?>
<Employees>
  <Employee>
  <LastName>Smith</LastName>
  <FirstName>George</FirstName>
  <Title>Sales Representative</Title>
  <Address>507 - 20th Ave. E. Apt. 2A</Address>
  <City>Seattle</City>
  <Region>WA</Region>
  <PostalCode>98122</PostalCode>
  <Country>USA</Country>
</Employee>
  <Employee>
  <LastName>Fuller</LastName>
  <FirstName>Andrew</FirstName>
  <Title>Vice President, Sales</Title>
  <Address>908 W. Capital Way</Address>
  <City>Tacoma</City>
  <Region>WA</Region>
  <PostalCode>98401</PostalCode>
  <Country>USA</Country>
 </Employee>
</Employees>
```

Figure 7: Sample XML file

SQL in Web Scripting Languages

Another area where SQL is needed is the web. Specifically, in server-side web pages like active server pages.net (ASP.net), Jakarta server pages (JSP), and hypertext preprocessor (PHP) pages. These web pages contain code in languages like java script, VB script, vb.net, c#, and others. They also contain HTML code. However, in many cases they also contain SQL code used to communicate with back-end databases. In these cases, you might be called to write the SQL part of the page since web developers might not have the depth required to write complex SQL statements.

In Figure 8, you see a scenario of a web site that contains multiple php pages. Specifically, there are four php pages: SubmitOrder.php, UpdateOrder.php, ReviewOrder.php, and DeleteOrder.php. These four pages constitute an application to which customers connect through the web to place and manage orders. Notice that each customer uses a dissimilar browser as the client to connect to the web site on the web server. The beauty of server-side pages is that they are browser independent. Consequently, we do not need to worry about the browser type used by the customer. In addition, the php pages connect to a database in the back-end database server. Now, on most occasions, the web server and the database server are different machines, but it might be the case that both the web server software and the relational database server software are installed on the same machine. For our purposes, the fundamental point is that php pages use SQL to connect to back-end databases.

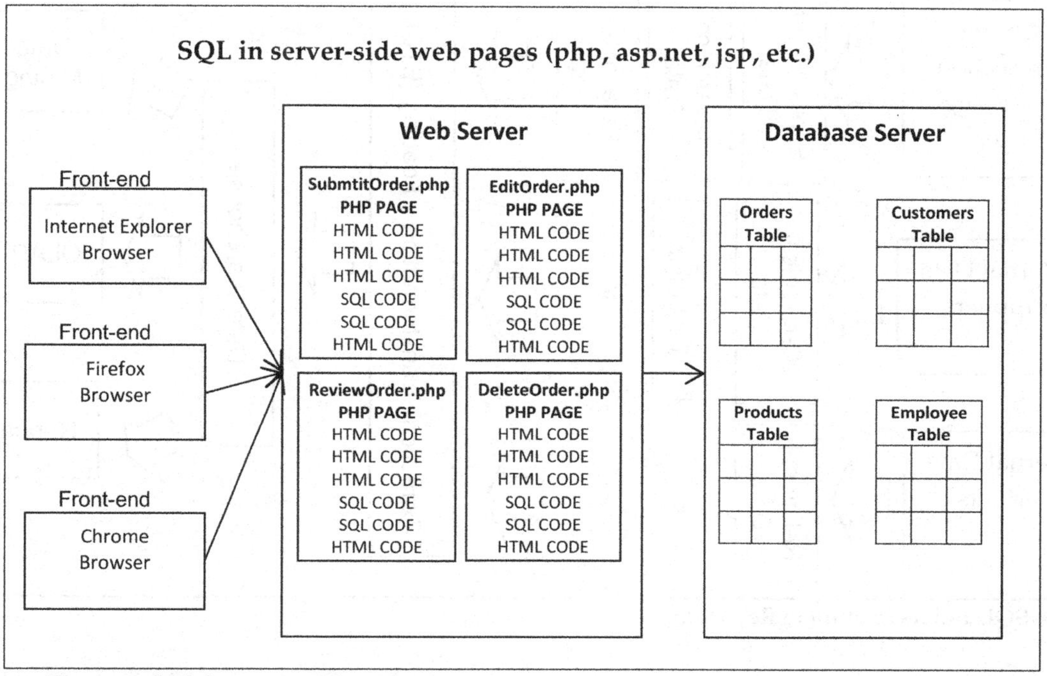

Figure 8: SQL in server-side web pages

SQL in Reporting Applications

The next area where SQL is a must for the enterprise is for its reporting applications. Reporting tools such as Power BI, Tableau, and Qlik are very popular with corporations because they allow the generation and propagation of analytics to almost everyone in the company. Employees who consume these reports do not need to be data experts although knowledge of data processing would help a lot. However, the people who build these reports must know how to work with SQL. In Tableau for example, to join data sets, to create calculated fields, concatenate fields, use aggregate functions you need to know how to work with SQL. This is the case for traditional page-based reports like Crystal reports, MS Access reports, and SSRS reports, as well as cross-tabulation based reports like Tableau, QlikView, PowerBI, and Excel Pivot Tables.

No matter the type of report or tool, SQL is not an option but a requirement for report writers. First, they should be able to retrieve data from multiple and in many cases heterogeneous data sources within or outside the corporation using SQL statements. Second, they must know how to combine all these heterogeneous and sometimes geographically dispersed data sources into one unified data source. It is this unified data source that they will use as the basis for their reports. Third, they should know how to manipulate fields at the data source level, like for example, concatenating fields, using string and date functions to extract text or date parts, write conditional statements, and create calculated fields. Fourth, even within the report itself they might need to use calculated fields, conditional functions, aggregate functions, string functions and date functions. Reporting tools provide us with amazing functionality, but they cannot surpass the breadth and wealth of SQL statements and their unique ability in data manipulation.

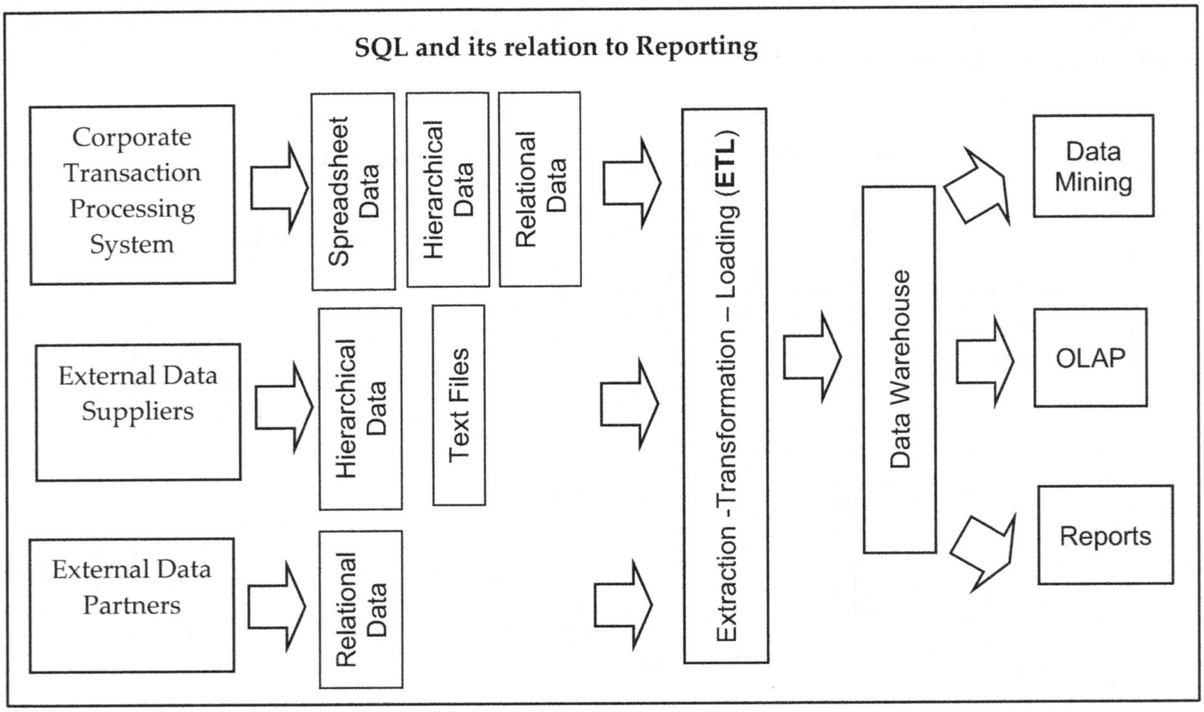

Figure 9: SQL and its relation to Reporting

SQL in OLAP

An OLAP cube constitutes an analytics solution for the company. It is an object that contains data retrieved from a transactional database or from a data warehouse database as you can see in Figure 11. An OLAP cube is a data container itself, that is, it does not need to be linked to a data source to produce data analytics; it only connects to the source data to be updated with the latest records. In addition, an OLAP object does not contain all the records from the source database; it only contains the data necessary to meet the business analytics requirements of the business. For instance, in the source database, we might have fifteen hundred fields and the OLAP cube might contain only fifty. This way OLAP cubes produce fast responses, and they are used extensively in the market for fast, easy, and interactive production of analytics.

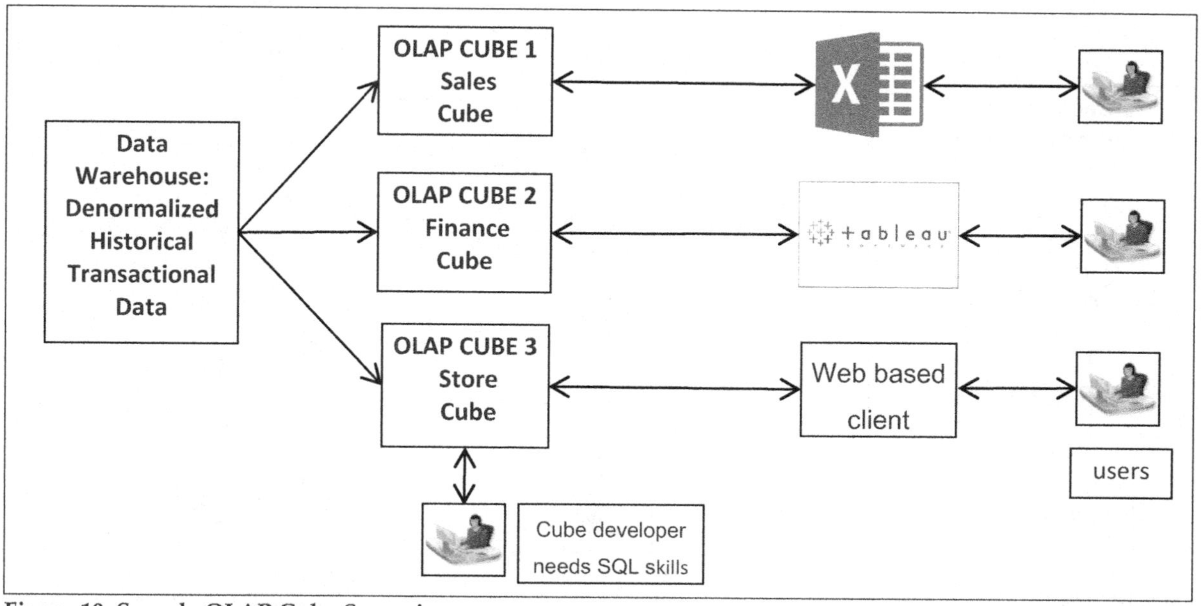

Figure 10: Sample OLAP Cube Scenario

Platforms on which we can create OLAP cubes can be premise based like Microsoft SQL Server Analysis Services (SSAS), Pentaho Mondrian OLAP Server, IBM Cognos OLAP Server, MicroStrategy OLAP Services, Apache Kylin Big Data OLAP engine, Jedox OLAP Server, and cloud based such as Amazon Web Services (AWS) OLAP, Google Big Query OLAP, Azure Analysis Services, and others. We also have an array of client tools which we need to connect to the OLAP engines. Such tools include Excel, Tableau, PowerBI, Qlik, IBM Cognos client app, MicroStrategy client app, and others.

An OLAP cube contains two major types of fields: attributes (descriptors) and measures (numbers). For example, numeric fields can be Price, QuantitySold, UnitsOnHand, UnitsOnOrder, and TotalSales. Descriptors can be StoreName, ProductName, City, State, County, and Zip. Then, we use OLAP cube clients like Excel, Tableau, Power BI, and Qlik to create very dynamic crosstab reports very fast, see Figure 10. In these reports, we analyze numbers by descriptors. For example, we calculate the QuantitySold by City, the UnitsOnHand by StoreName, the TotalSales by State, or the SalesTax by City. It is imperative to know how to use SQL in OLAP because in every cube we create additional calculated fields, groupings, filters, date fields, and concatenations that might not exist in the original data source.

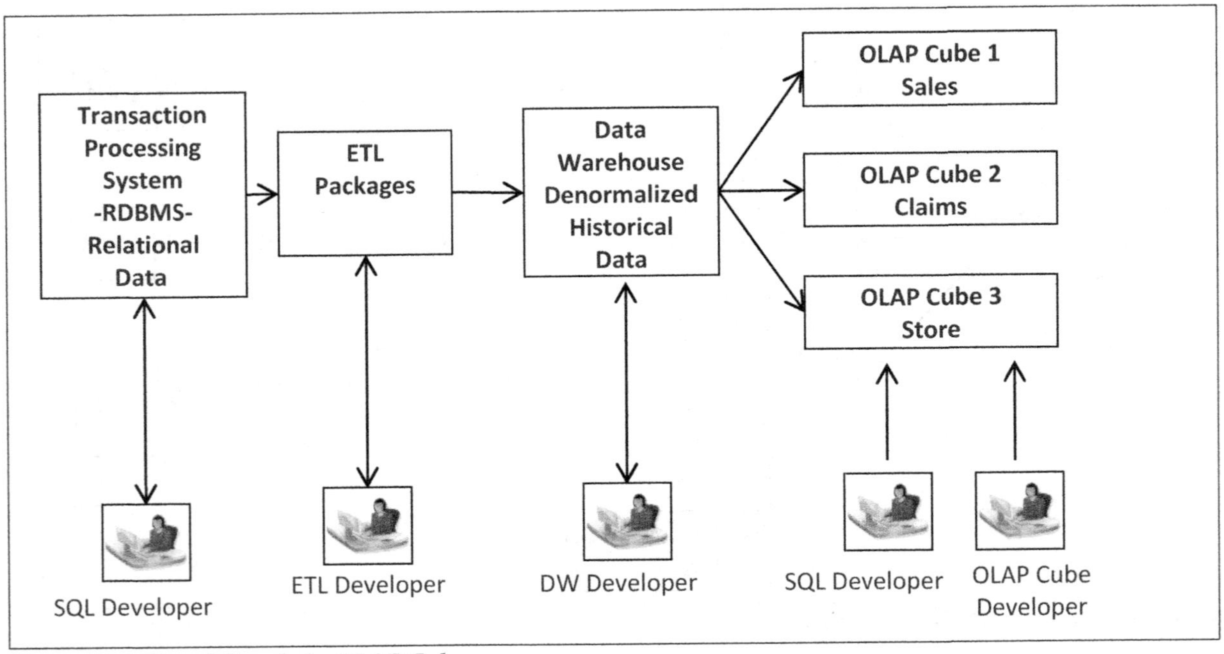

Figure 11: SQL and its role in OLAP Cubes

SQL in Data Mining

In the area of Data Mining (DM), Machine Learning (ML), and Artificial Intelligence (AI) SQL is also an absolute must have knowledge tool. For instance, your team might be working to develop a prediction model to increase your marketing campaign efficiency and you use a Decision Trees or Neural Networks algorithm to develop this model. In this case, there is a very high probability that you will need SQL to prepare your data for the model and most importantly you will need SQL to manipulate the output of the model which is again a data set.

For those of you who plan to work on data mining models for business analytics, you should expect to need SQL for their development. In most scenarios, structured corporate data is stored in relational databases. To build data mining models, you need to have access to these historical transactions such as customer orders, shipments, quotations, and inventory quantities. You will need SQL to create calculations, aggregations, cross-tabulations, concatenations and apply data and string functions, to create the additional fields, filters, and functions to develop your data mining models and to make sure their predictive ability is as high as possible. You will also need SQL after you have built your models to manipulate the data output from the models. For example, if a model has identified the best eight hundred customers out of ten thousand original customer records, you will need to manipulate this dataset of prospective customers by further excluding customers based on location, income, distance, education, and marital status. Consequently, in data mining, you need SQL twice. First, to manipulate historical data to develop and test your models, and second to manipulate data sets produced by these mining models.

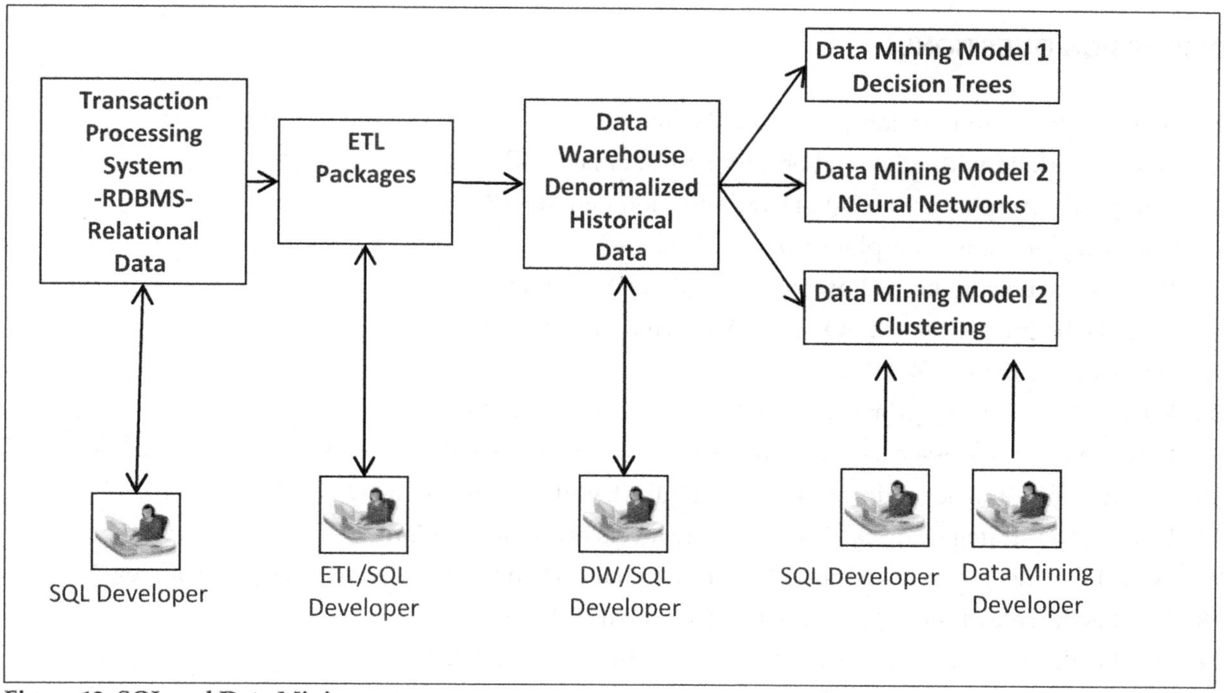

Figure 12: SQL and Data Mining

SQL in Artificial Intelligence

Even with Artificial Intelligence (AI) software tools like the Google ML toolkit which contains multiple Machine Learning (ML) technologies, you will need SQL to move data around and manipulate it either directly or through Google Big Query. The same is true for multiple Cloud based AI tools from Google, AI tools from Azure, AI tools from IBM, and AI tools from Amazon Web Services. At the writing of this book, these vendors are at the top of the AI market according to the Gartner Magic Quadrant for Cloud Based AI tools.

Since Artificial Intelligence models, human emulators, and robots need data to function, the role of SQL is primary in this field as well. Today's relational, NoSQL (not only SQL), big data, on premise, and cloud databases, can store multiple data types such as text, numbers, images, spreadsheet files, XML files, sound files, binary data, and others. SQL is an imperative skill to access this data, filter it, discard useless points, include what is important, aggregate it, group it, sort it, integrate it, format it, and in general perform a multitude of actions to make the data available to the AI models and relevant for their algorithms and their outputs. We have a great set of tools to develop algorithms and prediction models using AI but who prepares the data? It is the role of the SQL professional to prepare the right data, in the right format, with the right joins for the development of those models.

.

DISCUSSION QUESTIONS

1. Is SQL a procedural or non-procedural language?
2. Is SQL working with relational or hierarchical databases?
3. What is the purpose of the SQL Data Definition Language?
4. Can you give some examples of DDL statements?
5. Why do we need to know how to work with DDL statements?
6. What is the purpose of the SQL Data Manipulation Language (DML)?
7. What are the main SQL DML statements?
8. Why SQL is working primarily with highly normalized databases?
9. Is SQL a language associated with a particular database product or vendor?
10. At what corporate level do we use SQL to insert, edit, and delete data?
11. Why do the strategic and tactical corporate levels need information?
12. Why do we need to pay attention to transactional cycle times from a business point of view?
13. What is the role of the SQL professional in web development?
14. What is the difference between relational and hierarchical data?
15. Why do we want to export relational data in hierarchical (XML) format?
16. What is the role of extraction, transformation, and loading (ETL) packages in the corporation?
17. Can the SQL developer help with the development of ETL packages?
18. What is the role of SQL in developing data mining models?
19. Why do we need SQL when we build OLAP cubes?
20. Why do we need SQL with reporting applications such as SAP Crystal Reports?

CHAPTER 2
SELECTING AND RETRIEVING DATA

The SELECT statement is the most widely used keyword in any relational database, and it constitutes the basis for SQL statements. We will go through examples of how to use the SELECT statement alone or in combination with its various clauses like WHERE, GROUP BY, HAVING, and ORDER BY. The general structure of the SELECT statement appears below:

```
SELECT field1, field2, field3
FROM table
[WHERE]
[GROUP BY]
[HAVING]
[ORDER BY]
```

1. Retrieve all columns and rows from a table - SELECT with *

Retrieve all columns and rows from the customer table

Discussion:

The * wildcard character will retrieve all columns and all rows from a table. Records will be retrieved in the order they are stored in the table.

Code:

```
SELECT *
FROM Customers
```

Result:

CustomerID	FirstName	LastName	Address	City	State	Zip	Country
1	John	Demarco	11 Lark Street	New York	NY	12189	USA
2	Mary	Demania	12 Madison Ave	New York	NY	12189	USA
3	George	Demers	23 New Scotland Ave	New York	NY	12189	USA
4	Phillip	Demetriou	22 Academy Road	New York	NY	12189	USA

(There are more records in the result set than the ones shown in this image)
(There are more columns in the result set than the ones shown in this image)
(201 row(s) returned)

2. Retrieve only the field names from a table

Provide documentation for the Orders table by retrieving a list of its fields

Discussion:

If we want to retrieve only the filed names, for documentation purposes, or to just have a look at them before we write a query, we can use the code below.

Code:

```
SELECT * FROM Customers
WHERE 0=1
```

Result:

CustomerID	FirstName	LastName	Address	City	State	Zip	Country

(There are more columns in the result set than the ones shown in this image)
(0 row(s) returned)

3. Retrieve specific columns from a table

Create a customer list for mailing labels

Discussion:

In most cases, we need to retrieve only a subset of columns from a table. In this example, we retrieve address related fields.

Code:

```
SELECT LastName, FirstName, Address, City, State, Zip
FROM Customers
```

Result:

LastName	FirstName	Address	City	State	Zip
Demarco	John	11 Lark Street	New York	NY	12189
Demania	Mary	12 Madison Ave	New York	NY	12189
Demers	George	23 New Scotland Ave	New York	NY	12189
Demetriou	Phillip	22 Academy Road	New York	NY	12189

(There are more records in the result set than the ones shown in this image)
(201 row(s) returned)

4. Retrieve specific records from a table

Create a report of customers in Boston

Discussion:

SQL statements provide great flexibility for filtering records. For instance, we can retrieve all columns from a table, all rows, some columns and all rows, some rows and all columns, or some rows and some columns. In this example, we retrieve all the columns from the customer table, but we limit the rows by selecting only customers from Boston.

Code:

```
SELECT *
FROM Customers
WHERE city = 'Boston'
```

Result:

CustomerID	FirstName	LastName	Address	City	State	Zip	Country
163	Arnold	Cormack	31 2nd Street	Boston	MA	22459	USA
164	Carolyn	Currier	58 Holmes CT	Boston	MA	22459	USA
165	Catherine	Davis	87 Coral Street	Boston	MA	22459	USA
166	Cristopher	Geisler	93 Kate Street	Boston	MA	22459	USA

(There are more columns in the result set than the ones shown in this image)
(There are more records in the result set than the ones shown in this image)
(14 row(s) returned)

5. Retrieve specific columns and specific rows from a table

Create a list of suppliers from NY state, but do not display the state field

Discussion:

In this example, we are retrieving only the company name and the contact name of suppliers who operate in New York. Notice that although we use the state as a criterion field, the state itself will not appear in the result set since it is not included in the SELECT statement.

Code:

```
SELECT CompanyName, ContactName, ContactTitle
FROM Suppliers
WHERE state = 'NY'
```

Result:

CompanyName	ContactName	ContactTitle
America's Greatest Snacks	Andrew Daves	Sales Manager
Berkley Bakery	Frank Baker	Marketing Manager
Mediterranean Foods	Nick Papadopoulos	Owner
BayLine Farms	Lisa Anderson	Sales Representative
Nature's Food	Tony Lebrant	Purchasing Director

(5 row(s) returned)

6. Column aliases – Select AS

Retrieve data from the suppliers table but change the column titles

Discussion:

In many cases, table fields have names that make sense to the database developer but not the end user. For example, Cust_LN and Cust_FN might make sense to the developer because they represent naming conventions for the customer's last name and first name fields. However, if we use them as titles for queries or reports, no one will be able to discern their meaning.

In these cases, we use the SELECT AS statement to assign field aliases or column titles that make sense for all of us. We can do this on the fly in a SELECT statement. In the example below, we change the titles of the fields CompanyName, and ContactName in the suppliers table. Notice we enclose the second alias [Supplier Contact] in brackets because we have a space between the two words. If we forget the brackets, the SQL statement will not run.

Code:

```
SELECT CompanyName AS Company, ContactName AS [Supplier Contact]
FROM suppliers
```

Result:

Company	Supplier Contact
Home of Snacks	Pedro Adkins
American Foods	John Marrey
American Imports	Maria Hopkins
America's Greatest Snacks	Andrew Daves

(There are more records in the result set than the ones shown in this image)
(10 row(s) returned)

7. Concatenate fields

Create a letter for the customers

Discussion:

SQL enables us to combine field data with plain text. In this example, we are writing a letter to our customers right in the database! The cool thing about letters from the database is that they are very dynamic as we can change the filtering criteria and the respective audience at will. Notice that we enclose plain text in single quotes (' '). In addition, note that the characters (+ ' ' +) add spaces between fields and plain text. Finally, the whole statement below is just one concatenated field named "CustomerLetter."

Code:

```
SELECT 'Dear' + ' ' + firstname + ' ' + 'We would like you to know that our full product catalog is on
sale in the city of'  + ' ' + city + ' ' + 'Please visit our website for details' As CustomerLetter
FROM customers
```

Result:

CustomerLetter
Dear John We would like you to know that our full product catalog is on sale in the city of New York Please visit our website for details
Dear Mary We would like you to know that our full product catalog is on sale in the city of New York Please visit our website for details
Dear George We would like you to know that our full product catalog is on sale in the city of New York Please visit our website for details
Dear Phillip We would like you to know that our full product catalog is on sale in the city of New York Please visit our website for details

(There are more records in the result set than the ones shown in this image)
(201 row(s) returned)

8. Sorting records – ORDER BY

Sort a customer list by last name

Discussion:

In this example, we select the fields LastName, FirstName, Address, City, State, and Zip, and all rows from the Customers table and then, sort this data on last name. To sort data in SQL, we use the ORDER BY clause. Specifically, to sort in ascending order, we use ORDER BY ASC, and to sort in descending order, we use ORDER BY DESC. If no ASC or DESC keyword is used, then the ORDER BY clause will sort in ascending order by default.

Code:

```
SELECT LastName, FirstName, Address, City, State, Zip
FROM Customers
ORDER BY LastName
```

Result:

LastName	FirstName	Address	City	State	Zip
Ackerman	Nicholas	5 Buckingham Dr	Dallas	TX	52347
Allen	Alfred	29 Water Street	New York	NY	12189
Ames	Pindar	23 Cornell Dr	New York	NY	45357
Andersen	Thomas	52 Betwood Street	Orlando	FL	89754

(There are more records in the result set than the ones shown in this image)
(201 row(s) returned)

9. Filter and Sort Records - WHERE and ORDER BY clauses

Select all customers except those in Boston and sort by last name

Discussion:

In this example, we use the * wildcard character to retrieve all columns in the customers table. For rows, we filter the result set by using the WHERE clause with the inequality predicate "<>" to select all customers except those in the city of Boston. Then, we sort ascending on lastname.

Code:

```
SELECT *
FROM Customers
WHERE city <> 'Boston'
ORDER BY lastname
```

Result:

CustomerID	FirstName	LastName	Address	City	State	Zip
93	Nicholas	Ackerman	5 Buckingham Dr	Dallas	TX	52347
141	Alfred	Allen	29 Water Street	New York	NY	12189
15	Pindar	Ames	23 Cornell Dr	New York	NY	45357
50	Thomas	Andersen	52 Betwood Street	Orlando	FL	89754

(There are more columns in the result set than the ones shown in this image)
(There are more records in the result set than the ones shown in this image)
(187 row(s) returned)

10. Group and filter records - WHERE, GROUP BY, HAVING and ORDER BY

Calculate the number of customers in all states except NY and show states with more than ten customers

Discussion:

Our business manager asked us to calculate the number of our customers in each state. She also asked us to exclude New York State from the results. From the remaining states, we need to exclude those with less than ten customers. Finally, states with the highest numbers of customers should appear first in the result set.

To comply with the above requirements, we need to use SELECT, WHERE, GROUP BY, HAVING, and ORDER BY in combination. Let us examine the purpose of each statement: First, we use the SELECT statement to select two fields from the customers table, the state field and the CustomerID field on which we apply the Count() function to calculate the number of occurrences of CustomerID in the table. Since CustomerID is the primary key of the table, we know that Count() will produce reliable results because there is no way to have null values in a primary key field.

Then, we use the WHERE clause with the inequality operator "<>" to exclude from the calculations customers in New York State. Practically, "<>" means retrieve everything else except 'NY'. Next, we use the GROUP BY clause to aggregate calculations by state. The database will calculate the number of customers and produce results by state since we group on that field.

The next point is a bit tricky if not understood well. The WHERE and HAVING clauses are both filtering statements. They do, however, have their specific roles in SQL statements, and they can be used individually or in combination. In this example, we exclude customers from NY state using WHERE, which will run before any groupings or calculations take effect by the GROUP BY clause. Next, the GROUP BY clause will produce groups of customers by state and count customers for the remaining records. After the groups of customers by state are generated and customer numbers are calculated by the count() function, the HAVING clause takes effect. It will exclude from the result any states with less than ten customers. Therefore, the HAVING clause will wait until the groupings and calculations are complete before it takes effect.

Finally, the ORDER BY clause takes effect, and it will sort results by the highest number of customers. What you need to remember is that when using the WHERE and HAVING clauses in combination, the WHERE clause always takes effect first, while the HAVING clause takes effect after the groups by the GROUP BY clause have been established. The ORDER BY clause will take effect last.

Code:

```
SELECT State, Count(CustomerID) As NumberOfCustomers
FROM Customers
WHERE State <> 'NY'
GROUP BY State
HAVING Count(CustomerID) >10
ORDER BY Count(CustomerID) DESC
```

Result:

State	NumberOfCustomers
CA	48
TX	25
FL	21
OH	14
MA	14
CO	13
AZ	13
DC	12

(8 row(s) returned)

DISCUSSION QUESTIONS

1. What is the primary purpose of the SELECT statement?
2. How do we select a subset of columns from a table?
3. What is the clause we use to select a subset of rows from a table?
4. What is the purpose of using column aliases in SELECT statements?
5. Can we insert text in SELECT statements? How can this help in business communications?
6. What is the purpose of the WHERE clause in the SELECT statement?
7. What is the purpose of the ORDER BY clause in the SELECT statement?
8. What is the purpose of using the GROUP BY clause?
9. Is HAVING a clause we can use with SELECT? What is its purpose?
10. What is the difference between the WHERE and HAVING clauses?

HANDS-ON EXERCISES

Case 1

For each of the questions in this case you need to create a new query in SQL view and name it as per the instructions in each question.

1. Create a query to select the fields ProductName, ContainerType, ProductWeight, IngredientType, QualityRating and all records from the Products table. Save the query as Select_Case1_Q1.

Result:

ProductName	ContainerType	ProductWeight	IngredientType	QualityRating
Almonds Hickory Smoked	Paper Bag	6 oz	GMO-Free	Excellent
Almonds Roasted and Salted	Plastic Bag	7 oz	Organic	Acceptable
Banana Chips	Flexible Pouch	14 oz	GMO-Free	Very Good
Berry Cherry	Plastic Bag	10 oz	GMO-Free	Top-Rated

(There are more records in the result set than the ones shown in this image)
(70 row(s) returned)

2. Create a query to select the same fields as in question 1 but only retrieve products for which the QualityRating is excellent. Save the query as Select_Case1_Q2.

Result:

ProductName	ContainerType	ProductWeight	IngredientType	QualityRating
Almonds Hickory Smoked	Paper Bag	6 oz	GMO-Free	Excellent
Cran Raisin Mix	Plastic Bag	8 oz	GMO-Free	Excellent
Raw Sunflower Seeds	Paper Bag	5 oz	All-Natural	Excellent
Roasted No-Salt Almonds	Plastic Bag	1 lb	Organic	Excellent

(There are more records in the result set than the ones shown in this image)
(14 row(s) returned)

3. Create a view that includes the fields ProductName, ProductPrice, UnitsInStock, and UnitsOnOrder to retrieve all products for which the UnitsOnOrder quantity is zero. Save the query as Select_Case1_Q3.

Result:

ProductName	ProductPrice	UnitsInStock	UnitsOnOrder
Almonds Roasted and Salted	22	32	0
Banana Chips	27	25	0
Berry Cherry	30	50	0
California Original Pistachios	29	35	0

(There are more records in the result set than the ones shown in this image)
(46 row(s) returned)

4. Create a query that includes the fields ProductName, ProductPrice, UnitsInStock, and UnitsOnOrder. The query should include all the records from the table. However, in the result set the field names should appear as: Product Name, Price, Units In Stock, and Units On Order. Save the query as Select_Case1_Q4.

Result:

Product Name	Price	Units In Stock	Units on Order
Almonds Hickory Smoked	35	40	5
Almonds Roasted and Salted	22	32	0
Banana Chips	27	25	0
Berry Cherry	30	50	0

(There are more records in the result set than the ones shown in this image)
(70 row(s) returned)

5. Create a query that includes the fields ProductName, ProductPrice, SKU, and ProductCost. Sort descending on the ProductPrice field. Save the query as Select_Case1_Q5.

Result:

ProductName	ProductPrice	SKU	ProductCost
Coffee biscuits	50	ASDT-3456	16.6
Pepper Cheese Box	50	PDKL-2389	16.6
Pizza croutons	49	ASDT-3456	16.26
Chocolate Chip Cookies	49	ADST 2345	16.26

(There are more records in the result set than the ones shown in this image)
(70 row(s) returned)

Case 2

For each of the questions in this case you need to create a new query in SQL view and name it as per the instructions in each question.

1. Create a query to select the fields LastName, FirstName, Address, City, State, and Zip from the Customers table. Include only customers from the state of Massachusetts. Save the query as Select_Case2_Q1.

Result:.

LastName	FirstName	Address	City	State	Zip
Cormack	Arnold	31 2nd Street	Boston	MA	22459
Currier	Carolyn	58 Holmes CT	Boston	MA	22459
Davis	Catherine	87 Coral Street	Boston	MA	22459
Geisler	Cristopher	93 Kate Street	Boston	MA	22459

(There are more records in the result set than the ones shown in this image)
(14 row(s) returned)

2. Create a query to select the same fields as in question 1 but only retrieve products for which the membership type is platinum. The MembershipType field should not appear in the result set. Save the query as Select_Case2_Q2.

Result:

LastName	FirstName	Address	City	State	Zip
Demers	George	23 New Scotland Ave	New York	NY	12189
Demizio	Michael	23 Grove Rd	New York	NY	12189
Demaria	Matthew	90 Park Ave	New York	NY	12110
Vanton	Kenneth	855 Hackett Blvd	Albany	NY	89890

(There are more records in the result set than the ones shown in this image)
(62 row(s) returned)

3. Create a query that includes the fields LastName, FirstName, City, State, and BonusPoints from the Customers table. Sort descending on the BonusPoints field so that customers with the most bonus points appear first. Save the query as Select_Case2_Q3.

Result:

LastName	FirstName	City	State	BonusPoints
Zartons	Lisa	Los Angeles	CA	4000
Basil	Julia	Los Angeles	CA	3998
Trassati	July	Los Angeles	CA	3989
Poppel	Robert	Chicago	OH	3984

(There are more records in the result set than the ones shown in this image)
(201 row(s) returned)

4. Create a query that includes the fields LastName, FirstName, CustomerSince, and MembershipType from the Customers table. The field names should appear as: Last Name, First Name, Date Became Customer, and Type of Membership. Save the query as Select_Case2_Q4.

Result:

Last Name	First Name	Date Became Customer	Type of Membership
Demarco	John	1/22/2021	Silver
Demania	Mary	7/17/2022	Gold
Demers	George	3/11/2022	Platinum
Demetriou	Phillip	10/12/2021	Gold

(There are more records in the result set than the ones shown in this image)
(201 row(s) returned)

5. Create a query that includes the fields LastName, FirstName, and concatenates the columns Address, City, State, and Zip into one field named CustomerAddress. In the CustomerAddress field the values should be separated by a blank space. Save the query as Select_Case2_Q5.

Result:

LastName	FirstName	CustomerAddress
Demarco	John	11 Lark Street New York NY 12189
Demania	Mary	12 Madison Ave New York NY 12189
Demers	George	23 New Scotland Ave New York NY 12189
Demetriou	Phillip	22 Academy Road New York NY 12189

(There are more records in the result set than the ones shown in this image)
(201 row(s) returned)

CHAPTER 3
SORTING DATA

The ORDER BY clause, with the ASC or DESC keywords, allows the sorting of records in ascending or descending order respectively. Sorting ascending means text is sorted from A to Z and numbers from 1 to 9. Sorting descending means Z to A and 9 to 1. When no ASC or DESC keyword is used after the ORDER BY clause, then ASC is assumed by default. The ORDER BY clause is much stronger than what is generally assumed and it allows for some cool tricks with the data.

11. Sorting ascending on one column

Create a list of customers sorting by last name in ascending order

Discussion:

This is a basic example of sorting our customers by last name in ascending order. Ascending order means we sort (A-Z) and (1-9). Consequently, customers whose last names start with an "A" will appear first in the result set. The keyword "ASC" is not required after the ORDER BY clause to sort records in ascending order. If we leave the keyword "ASC" out, the ORDER BY clause will sort ascending by default.

Code:

```
SELECT FirstName, LastName, Address, City, Zip, State
FROM Customers
ORDER BY LastName ASC
```

Result:

FirstName	LastName	Address	City	Zip	State
Nicholas	Ackerman	5 Buckingham Dr	Dallas	52347	TX
Alfred	Allen	29 Water Street	New York	12189	NY
Pindar	Ames	23 Cornell Dr	New York	45357	NY
Thomas	Andersen	52 Betwood Street	Orlando	89754	FL

```
(There are more records in the result set than the ones shown in this image)
(201 row(s) returned)
```

12. Sorting descending on one column

Create a list of customers sorting by last name in descending order

Discussion:

To sort records in descending order we must add the DESC keyword to our SQL statement.

Code:

```
SELECT FirstName, LastName, Address, City, Zip, State
FROM Customers
ORDER BY LastName DESC
```

Result:

FirstName	LastName	Address	City	Zip	State
Stephen	Zinter	110 Johnson Ave	Philadelphia	56789	PA
Lauren	Zentons	23 Crescent Dr	Los Angeles	94851	CA
Charles	Zensons	23 Tampa Ave	Los Angeles	94851	CA
Lisa	Zartons	34 Home Ave	Los Angeles	94851	CA

```
(There are more records in the result set than the ones shown in this image)
(201 row(s) returned)
```

13. Sorting on multiple columns

Create a customer list sorting by city and last name simultaneously

Discussion:

We can use multiple columns to sort records. In this example, we sort customers first by city and then, within each city, by last name. We have some customers in Albany and some in Boston. Sorting ascending on both the city and last name fields will create the following result: The records with the city of Albany will appear first in the result set, followed by the records with the city of Boston. Now, within the Albany records, customers will be sorted alphabetically and in ascending order. Within the city of Boston records, customers will again be sorted alphabetically and in ascending order.

Code:

```
SELECT City, LastName, FirstName
FROM Customers
ORDER BY City, LastName ASC
```

Result:

City	LastName	FirstName
Albany	Miller	Anthony
Albany	Riegert	Joanne
Albany	Trindan	Luis
Albany	Vanton	Kenneth
Boston	Cormack	Arnold
Boston	Currier	Carolyn
Boston	Davis	Catherine
Boston	Geisler	Cristopher

```
(There are more records in the result set than the ones shown in this image)
(201 row(s) returned)
```

14. Sort on multiple columns but with different sorting direction for each column

Create a customer list sorting by city ascending and customer name descending

Discussion:

We could sort on multiple columns forcing a different sorting direction for each column. In this example we sort ascending on the city and then for each city we sort descending on last name.

Code:

```
SELECT City, LastName, FirstName
FROM Customers
ORDER BY city ASC, LastName DESC
```

Result:

City	LastName	FirstName
Albany	Vanton	Kenneth
Albany	Trindan	Luis
Albany	Riegert	Joanne
Albany	Miller	Anthony
Boston	Strack	Joanne
Boston	Sterling	Fred
Boston	Powers	Gerald
Boston	Ming	Thomas

(There are more records in the result set than the ones shown in this image)
(201 row(s) returned)

15. Use the ORDER BY clause with blank values

Find customers who do not have a first name entered in the database

Discussion:

Sorting ascending on a column can quickly identify NULL or blank values. To work on this example, open the Customers table and delete the first name "**John**" from the first customer "**John Demarco**". Now, sort ascending on the first name field. As you can see, the customer without a first name shows first. After you run the code in this example, **retype in the table the first name "John" for Demarco**.

Code:

```
SELECT LastName, FirstName
FROM Customers
ORDER BY FirstName
```

Result:

LastName	FirstName
Demarco	
Kashisnky	Alfred
Tranton	Alfred
Allen	Alfred

(There are more records in the result set than the ones shown in this image)
(201 row(s) returned)

16. The ORDER BY clause with numbers

Create an inventory report listing products with the biggest quantities first

Discussion:

In this example, we list inventory products with the biggest quantities on hand at the top. When sorting numbers, the DESC keyword will cause the biggest ones to show first, while the ASC keyword will cause the smallest numbers to show first.

Code:

```
SELECT ProductName, UnitsInStock
FROM Products
ORDER BY UnitsInStock DESC
```

Result:

ProductName	UnitsInStock
Chocolate Chip Cookies	50
Artichokes in white sauce	50
Berry Cherry	50
Green Sauce	49

(There are more records in the result set than the ones shown in this image)
(70 row(s) returned)

17. The ORDER BY clause with dates

Create a list with the latest orders on top

Discussion:

The ORDER BY clause works with dates the same way it works with numbers. So, to list the newest dates first, we use the DESC keyword. To list the oldest dates first, we use the ASC keyword.

Code:

```
SELECT ProductName, ProductPrice, DateEnteredInventory
FROM Products
ORDER BY  DateEnteredInventory DESC
```

Result:

ProductName	ProductPrice	DateEnteredInventory
Raspberry brownie bar	22	12/28/2018
Coconut Chocolate Chip Cookies	25	10/19/2018
Chocolate Covered Apples	37	10/17/2018
Dried Cranberries	16	8/31/2018

(There are more records in the result set than the ones shown in this image)
(70 row(s) returned)

18. TIP: Combine the ORDER BY and TOP clauses to control the result set

List the five products with the biggest quantities on hand

Discussion:

The ORDER BY clause produces very meaningful results when used in combination with the TOP clause. In this instance, we want to list the five products in our inventory with the highest quantities on hand. Keep in mind that the TOP clause does not apply or relates to fields in the SELECT statement. It will apply to the field used in the ORDER BY clause.

Code:

```
SELECT TOP 5 UnitsInStock, ProductName
FROM Products
ORDER BY UnitsInStock DESC
```

Result:

UnitsInStock	ProductName
50	Chocolate Chip Cookies
50	Artichokes in white sauce
50	Berry Cherry
49	Green Sauce
49	Biscuits with Cream

(5 row(s) returned)

19. Combine the ORDER BY and TOP clauses with PERCENT

List the top ten percent of products in the inventory with the biggest quantities on hand

Discussion:

In this example, we use TOP with the PERCENT keyword to retrieve the 10% of the products with the most units in stock. We will get the ones with the most units in stock because we sort descending on the UnitsInStock field. Since we have seventy products in the products table, we would expect to see seven products in the result set but we get nine. This is because product 7 in the result set has 45 units in stock. Since however we have another two products with the same quantity of units in stock they will appear in the result set as well. This is a behavior inherent to the TOP clause.

Code:

```
SELECT TOP 10 PERCENT UnitsInStock, ProductName
FROM Products
ORDER BY UnitsInStock DESC
```

Result:

UnitsInStock	ProductName
50	Chocolate Chip Cookies
50	Artichokes in white sauce
50	Berry Cherry
49	Green Sauce
49	Biscuits with Cream
47	Chocolate Chip Brownie
45	Pepper Cheese Box
45	Lemon Biscuits
45	Dried Cranberries

(9 row(s) returned)

DISCUSSION QUESTIONS

1. What is the difference between sorting ascending and sorting descending?
2. Is the keyword "ASC" ascending optional or required in the ORDER BY clause?
3. Is the keyword "DESC" optional or required in the ORDER BY clause?
4. Can we use the ORDER BY clause to sort multiple fields? In what order are multiple fields sorted?
5. If we sort ascending on a field that contains null values, do those values appear at the top or the bottom of the sorted column?
6. If we sort descending on a number field, do big numbers appear at the top or the bottom of the sorted column?
7. We want to sort a date field so that the most recent dates appear first. Shall we use ASC or DESC?
8. You need to obtain the five most recent orders. Shall you use ORDER BY, TOP, and DESC or ORDER BY, TOP, and ASC on the date field?
9. You need to obtain the top five most expensive products. Shall you use ORDER BY, TOP, and DESC or ORDER BY, TOP, and ASC on the price field?
10. You need to find the five least productive salespeople. Shall you use ORDER BY, TOP, and DESC or ORDER BY, TOP, and ASC on the commission field?

HANDS-ON EXERCISES

Case 1

For each of the questions in this case you need to create a new query in SQL view and name it as per the instructions in each question.

1. Create a query that includes the fields ProductName, ProductPrice, UnitsInStock, UnitsOnOrder, and SKU from the Products table. Your supervisor wants the records sorted in a way so that products with no UnitsOnOrder show first in the result set. Save the query as Sorting_Case1_Q1.

Result:

ProductName	ProductPrice	UnitsInStock	UnitsOnOrder	SKU
Dark Chocolate Apricots	46	38	0	DKLS-4732
Cocoa and Hazelnut Biscuits	35	42	0	ASDT-3456
Cream and honey biscuits	22	22	0	ASDT-3456
Fried Jalapenos	15	32	0	EPDA-2345

```
(There are more records in the result set than the ones shown in this image)
(70 row(s) returned)
```

2. Create a query that includes the fields ProductName, ProductPrice, UnitsInStock, UnitsOnOrder, and SKU from the Products table. Your supervisor wants the records sorted in a way so that products with the most UnitsInStock show first in the result set. Save the query as Sorting_Case1_Q2.

Result:

ProductName	ProductPrice	UnitsInStock	UnitsOnOrder	SKU
Chocolate Chip Cookies	49	50	0	ADST 2345
Artichokes in white sauce	22	50	0	ADST 2345
Berry Cherry	30	50	0	PDK-2589
Green Sauce	35	49	0	EPDA-2345

(There are more records in the result set than the ones shown in this image)
(70 row(s) returned)

3. Create a query that includes the fields ProductName, ProductPrice, UnitsInStock, UnitsOnOrder, and SKU from the Products table. Your supervisor needs a list of the ten products with the highest number of units in stock. Save the query as Sorting_Case1_Q3.

Result:

ProductName	ProductPrice	UnitsInStock	UnitsOnOrder	SKU
Chocolate Chip Cookies	49	50	0	ADST 2345
Artichokes in white sauce	22	50	0	ADST 2345
Berry Cherry	30	50	0	PDK-2589
Green Sauce	35	49	0	EPDA-2345
Biscuits with Cream	27	49	0	ASDT-3456
Chocolate Chip Brownie	30	47	0	KTRT-4589
Pepper Cheese Box	50	45	0	PDKL-2389
Lemon Biscuits	48	45	0	ASDT-3456
Dried Cranberries	16	45	0	EPDA-2345
Water Crackers	24	44	0	PDKL-2389
Pizza croutons	49	44	0	ASDT-3456

(11 row(s) returned)

4. Create a query that includes the fields ProductName, ProductPrice, UnitsInStock, UnitsOnOrder, and SKU from the Products table. Your supervisor wants a list of the five products with the highest number of units on order. Save the query as Sorting_Case1_Q4.

Result:

ProductName	ProductPrice	UnitsInStock	UnitsOnOrder	SKU
Nacho Chips	25	24	25	PDKL-2389
Chunky Chocolate Cookies	15	33	20	KDRT-2345
Chocolate Chunk Cookies	48	15	20	ASDT-3456
Oatmeal Raisin Walnut Cookies	43	19	20	KDRT-2345
Apple Cinnamon Raisin Cookies	27	15	20	KTRT-4589

(5 row(s) returned)

5. Create a query that includes the fields ProductName, ProductPrice, UnitsInStock, UnitsOnOrder, and SKU from the Products table. Your supervisor wants a list of the ten products with the lowest unitsinstock number. Save the query as Sorting_Case1_Q5.

Result:

ProductName	ProductPrice	UnitsInStock	UnitsOnOrder	SKU
Raw Sunflower Seeds	25	12	15	PDKLS-2347
Fresh Cranberries	35	15	10	PDKLS-2347
Apple Cinnamon Raisin Cookies	27	15	20	KTRT-4589
Chocolate Chunk Cookies	48	15	20	ASDT-3456
Dried Light Red Tart Cherries	43	18	15	EPDA-2345
Oatmeal Raisin Walnut Cookies	43	19	20	KDRT-2345
Chocolate Almonds	25	21	0	DKLS-4732
Mushroom Sauce	21	22	10	ADST 2345
Choice Apricots	32	22	0	PDKLS-2347
Cream and honey biscuits	22	22	0	ASDT-3456
Roasted & Salted Cashews	30	22	15	PDKL-2389

(11 row(s) returned)

Case 2

For each of the questions in this case you need to create a new query in SQL view and name it as per the instructions in each question.

1. Create a query that includes the fields FirstName, LastName, City, State, and Zip from the Customers table. Your supervisor wants the records sorted simultaneously by State and then City, both in ascending order. Save the query as Sorting_Case2_Q1.

Result:

FirstName	LastName	City	State	Zip
Gerald	Moore	Phoenix	AZ	44895
Christine	Lanci	Phoenix	AZ	44895
Lloyd	Latta	Phoenix	AZ	44895
Angelo	Lareous	Phoenix	AZ	44895

(There are more records in the result set than the ones shown in this image)
(201 row(s) returned)

2. Create a query that includes the fields FirstName, LastName, City, State, and Zip from the Customers table. Your supervisor wants the records sorted simultaneously by State ascending and then City in descending order. Save the query as Sorting_Case2_Q2.

Result:

FirstName	LastName	City	State	Zip
Angelo	Lareous	Phoenix	AZ	44895
Gerald	Moore	Phoenix	AZ	44895
James	Mondo	Phoenix	AZ	44895
Thomas	McMaster	Phoenix	AZ	44895

(There are more records in the result set than the ones shown in this image)
(201 row(s) returned)

3. Create a query that includes the fields Orderid, OrderDate, ShippedDate, PackagingType, InvoiceAmount, and ShippingCost from the Orders table. Provide a list with the ten most recently shipped orders. Save the query as Sorting_Case2_Q3.

Result:

OrderID	OrderDate	ShippedDate	PackagingType	InvoiceAmount	ShippingCost
156	12/26/2022	12/31/2022	Box	248	21
245	12/25/2022	12/30/2022	Plastic	291	19
831	12/23/2022	12/28/2022	Bio-Plastic	215	18
561	12/21/2022	12/26/2022	Box	307	21
558	12/18/2022	12/23/2022	Shrink film	94	17
176	12/18/2022	12/23/2022	Shrink film	165	18
452	12/17/2022	12/22/2022	Plastic	31	23
967	12/16/2022	12/21/2022	Shrink film	96	19
118	12/16/2022	12/21/2022	Shrink film	187	21
486	12/14/2022	12/19/2022	Box	226	32
446	12/14/2022	12/19/2022	Paperboard	114	11
266	12/14/2022	12/19/2022	Foil	46	29

(12 row(s) returned)

4. Create a query that includes the fields OrderID, OrderDate, ShippedDate, PackagingType, InvoiceAmount, and ShippingCost from the Orders table. Provide a list with the ten orders with the most expensive shipping cost. Save the query as Sorting_Case2_Q4.

Result:

OrderID	OrderDate	ShippedDate	PackagingType	InvoiceAmount	ShippingCost
346	2/5/2021	2/10/2021	Box	342	32
281	2/7/2021	2/12/2021	Plastic	247	32
969	6/26/2021	7/1/2021	Box	92	32
695	7/19/2020	7/24/2020	Bio-Plastic	141	32

(There are more records in the result set than the ones shown in this image)
(57 row(s) returned)

5. Create a query that includes the fields FirstName, LastName, City, State, and Zip from the Customers table. The marketing people want a list of customers sorted by city ascending that includes customers from Boston Albany, Orlando, and Miami. The same query should also export the data to a new table named "tble_CustomerList_ch5. Save the query as Sorting_Case2_Q5.

Result:

"You are about to paste 39 row(s) into a new table"

CHAPTER 4
THE OR AND AND LOGICAL OPERATORS

There are four points you need to remember about the OR and AND operators: First, their task is to produce a subset of records from the total records in a table or query. Second, they have no effect on the columns we retrieve from that table or query; they affect the number of rows only. Third, they are always used with other operators such as LIKE, equality and inequality predicates, and wildcard characters. Fourth, the OR and AND operators can be used individually or in combination with varying results as we shall see in the following examples.

The OR operator is inclusive which means that records will be returned for every OR condition satisfied in our query. The AND operator is exclusive, and it will produce results only when all of the AND conditions are met.

20. Using OR on the same column

Create a quick report with customers in New York or Houston

Discussion:

Let us suppose we have a request to produce a list of all customers who reside in the city of New York or in the city of Houston. We can use the OR operator on the same column multiple times as in this example to retrieve customers from multiple cities. However, we cannot use the AND operator multiple times on the same column because we would ask the impossible: that is, having a customer who resides in many cities simultaneously.

Code:

```
SELECT *
FROM customers
WHERE city = 'New York' OR city = 'Houston'
```

Result:

CustomerID	FirstName	LastName	Address	City	State	Zip	Country
1	John	Demarco	11 Lark Street	New York	NY	12189	USA
2	Mary	Demania	12 Madison Ave	New York	NY	12189	USA
3	George	Demers	23 New Scotland Ave	New York	NY	12189	USA
4	Phillip	Demetriou	22 Academy Road	New York	NY	12189	USA

```
(There are more columns in the result set than the ones shown in this image)
(There are more records in the result set than the ones shown in this image)
(39 row(s) returned)
```

21. Use the IN operator to replace multiple OR operators

Produce a report of customers from four cities

Discussion:

The OR operator works fine with two cities as we have seen in the previous example. What if we need to use OR with five or six cities as criteria? We have two problems in this case: First, we need to write a long SQL statement using multiple OR operators. Second, if we have a big number of records in the table, the query will be slow to return results. In cases like this one, we can use the IN operator that produces much cleaner code which is also easier to modify and maintain as you can see below:

Code:

```
SELECT LastName, FirstName, City, State
FROM Customers
WHERE city IN ('Albany', 'Denver', 'Houston', 'Phoenix')
ORDER BY LastName ASC
```

Result:

LastName	FirstName	City	State
Bink	Jim	Houston	TX
Bittel	David	Houston	TX
Clark	Allen	Houston	TX
Clarson	Erin	Houston	TX

(There are more records in the result set than the ones shown in this image)
(42 row(s) returned)

22. Using OR on multiple columns

Create an inventory report listing product quantities for units in stock and units on order

Discussion:

In this example, we have a request to create an inventory report that lists products that have more than 40 units in stock and also products that have more than 10 units on order. Any product record that satisfies at least one of the conditions will appear in the result set.

Now, notice that for some records, the UnitsOnOrder is zero. We have asked for UnitsInStock > 40 or UnitsOnOrder > 10. These particular records satisfy only the first condition, and this is enough for them to appear in the result set. The outcome will be very different when we use the AND operator as we will see presently.

Code:

```
SELECT ProductName, UnitsInStock, UnitsOnOrder
FROM Products
WHERE UnitsInStock > 40 OR UnitsOnOrder > 10
```

Result:

ProductName	UnitsInStock	UnitsOnOrder
Berry Cherry	50	0
Raw Sunflower Seeds	12	15
Chocolate Covered Apples	42	0
Sesame Crackers	43	0

(There are more records in the result set than the ones shown in this image)
(31 row(s) returned)

23. Use UNION instead of OR to speed up results

Create an inventory report using UNION instead of OR operators

Discussion:

We can use the UNION statement instead of multiple OR operators to speed up the response time of the database engine. This is a trick and the difference in response time is significant. The SQL statement below with the UNION operation achieves the exact same results as the SQL code in the previous example. However, the response time using UNION is instant, while it takes quite a few seconds using the OR operators.

Response times deteriorate as the number of records or the number of OR operators increase. Consequently, if you have statements with multiple OR operators that you use often, you might consider replacing them with

UNION statements. The only difference is the order in which the retrieved records appear since in this case, the results of the first SELECT statement in the UNION operation will appear first. The results of the second SELECT will follow and so on. You can easily reorder the recordset using the ORDER BY clause with a UNION statement.

Code:

```
SELECT ProductName, UnitsInStock, UnitsOnOrder
FROM Products
WHERE UnitsInStock > 40
UNION
SELECT ProductName, UnitsInStock, UnitsOnOrder
FROM Products
WHERE UnitsOnOrder > 10
```

Result:

ProductName	UnitsInStock	UnitsOnOrder
All-Purpose Marinade	27	15
Apple Cinnamon Raisin Cookies	15	20
Artichokes in white sauce	50	0
Berry Cherry	50	0

(There are more records in the result set than the ones shown in this image)
(31 row(s) returned)

24. Using AND on multiple columns

Produce a report of customers from a specific state and a specific city

Discussion:

This time, we will produce a report of customers who reside in the state of NY and at the same time in the city of Albany. In this case, we need to use the AND operator to retrieve records which satisfy both criteria at the same time. Note that if we use only the city as a criterion it will be a problem since there are twenty-eight cities in the U.S. named Albany! If we do business worldwide, there are six additional cities named Albany. An experienced programmer will always use AND to list customers only for Albany in New York. As you can see from the result, we have only four customers that satisfy both criteria.

Code:

```
SELECT LastName, FirstName, City, State
FROM Customers
WHERE State = 'NY' AND City = 'Albany'
```

Result:

LastName	FirstName	City	State
Vanton	Kenneth	Albany	NY
Trindan	Luis	Albany	NY
Riegert	Joanne	Albany	NY
Miller	Anthony	Albany	NY

(There are more records in the result set than the ones shown in this image)
(4 row(s) returned)

25. Using OR and AND in combination

Produce a report of customers from one state and two cities

Discussion:

Our objective in this scenario is to produce a report that will list customers from the cities of Albany and New York in NY State. In this case, we need to use the AND operator twice and the OR operator once as it appears in the code below:

Code:

```
SELECT LastName, FirstName, City, State
FROM Customers
WHERE
State = 'NY' AND City = 'Albany'
OR
State = 'NY' AND City = 'New York'
ORDER BY LastName
```

Result:

LastName	FirstName	City	State
Allen	Alfred	New York	NY
Ames	Pindar	New York	NY
Anderson	Peter	New York	NY
Anthopolis	Ricky	New York	NY

(There are more records in the result set than the ones shown in this image)
(31 row(s) returned)

DISCUSSION QUESTIONS

1. What is the primary purpose of the OR and AND operators in a query?
2. Is the OR operator inclusive or exclusive? What is the implication of this?
3. Is the AND operator inclusive or exclusive? What is the implication of this?
4. When using the OR and AND operators, can we control what columns (fields) will appear in the result set?
5. Can we use the OR and AND operators alone or in conjunction with other operators and predicates?
6. Can we use the OR operator multiple times on the same column? What is the meaning of doing this?
7. Can we use the OR operator on multiple columns? How many conditions need to be true to obtain results?
8. What operator can we use to replace multiple OR operators?
9. Can we use the AND operator multiple times on the same column? Why it does not make sense to use the AND operator on the same column?
10. What will the result be if we use the AND operator on multiple columns? How many conditions need to be true to obtain results?

HANDS-ON EXERCISES

Case 1

For each of the questions in this case you need to create a new query in SQL view and name it as per the instructions in each question.

1. Create a query to select all customers from the states of New York and Massachusetts. The query should contain the fields FirstName, LastName, City, State, and Zip from the Customers table. Save the query as LogicalOperators_Case1_Q1.

Result:

FirstName	LastName	City	State	Zip
John	Demarco	New York	NY	12189
Mary	Demania	New York	NY	12189
George	Demers	New York	NY	12189
Phillip	Demetriou	New York	NY	12189

```
(There are more records in the result set than the ones shown in this image)
(45 row(s) returned)
```

2. Create a query to select all customers from the states of New York, Massachusetts, Ohio, Texas, and Colorado. The query should contain the fields FirstName, LastName, City, State, and Zip from the Customers table. Hint: Use the IN operator. Save the query as LogicalOperators_Case1_Q2.

Result:

FirstName	LastName	City	State	Zip
John	Demarco	New York	NY	12189
Mary	Demania	New York	NY	12189
George	Demers	New York	NY	12189
Phillip	Demetriou	New York	NY	12189

```
(There are more records in the result set than the ones shown in this image)
(97 row(s) returned)
```

3. Create a query to select all customers from the city of Boston and the State of California. The query should contain the fields FirstName, LastName, City, State, and Zip from the Customers table. Save the query as LogicalOperators_Case1_Q3.

Result:

FirstName	LastName	City	State	Zip
Joseph	Anderson	Los Angeles	CA	94851
Allen	Restad	Los Angeles	CA	94851
Charles	Zensons	Los Angeles	CA	94851
Erin	Erin	Los Angeles	CA	94851

(There are more records in the result set than the ones shown in this image)
(62 row(s) returned)

4. Create a query to select all customers from the city of Albany in the state of New York and the city of San Jose in the state of California. The query should contain the fields FirstName, LastName, City, State, and Zip from the Customers table. Name the query LogicalOperators_Case1_Q4.

Result:

FirstName	LastName	City	State	Zip
Kenneth	Vanton	Albany	NY	89890
Luis	Trindan	Albany	NY	45357
Roy	Cutillo	San Jose	CA	36945
Diane	Darek	San Jose	CA	36945

(There are more records in the result set than the ones shown in this image)
(12 row(s) returned)

5. Create a query to select all customers form the cities of San Jose, Phoenix, and Boston, for the states of California, Arizona, and Massachusetts respectively. The query should contain the fields FirstName, LastName, City, State, and Zip from the Customers table. Save the query as LogicalOperators_Case1_Q5.

Result:

FirstName	LastName	City	State	Zip
Roy	Cutillo	San Jose	CA	36945
Diane	Darek	San Jose	CA	36945
Julia	Datek	San Jose	CA	36945
Gerald	Edwards	San Jose	CA	36945

(There are more records in the result set than the ones shown in this image)
(35 row(s) returned)

Case 2

For each of the questions in this case you need to create a new query in SQL view and name it as per the instructions in each question.

1. Create a query to select all customers from the states of New York, Massachusetts, Arizona, and Texas. The query should contain the fields FirstName, LastName, City, State, Address, and Zip from the Customers table. Use the OR operator to achieve your result. Save the query as LogicalOperators_Case2_Q1.

Result:

FirstName	LastName	City	State	Address	Zip
John	Demarco	New York	NY	11 Lark Street	12189
Mary	Demania	New York	NY	12 Madison Ave	12189
George	Demers	New York	NY	23 New Scotland Ave	12189
Phillip	Demetriou	New York	NY	22 Academy Road	12189

```
(There are more records in the result set than the ones shown in this image)
(83 row(s) returned)
```

2. Create the same query as in step 1 but this time use the IN operator to achieve your result. Name the query LogicalOperators_Case2_Q2.

Result:

FirstName	LastName	City	State	Address	Zip
John	Demarco	New York	NY	11 Lark Street	12189
Mary	Demania	New York	NY	12 Madison Ave	12189
George	Demers	New York	NY	23 New Scotland Ave	12189
Phillip	Demetriou	New York	NY	22 Academy Road	12189

```
(There are more records in the result set than the ones shown in this image)
(83 row(s) returned)
```

3. Create the same query as in step 1 but this time use the UNION operator to achieve your result. Name the query LogicalOperators_Case2_Q3. Notice how the sort order changes.

Result:

FirstName	LastName	City	State	Address	Zip
Alfred	Allen	New York	NY	29 Water Street	12189
Allan	Cimo	New York	NY	24 Crestwood CT	45357
Allen	Clark	Houston	TX	8 Aspen Street	53289
Andrew	Demichele	New York	NY	14 Glandel Ave	12189

```
(There are more records in the result set than the ones shown in this image)
(83 row(s) returned)
```

4. Create a query to select all customers except those in the states of California, Arizona, and Massachusetts. The query should contain the fields FirstName, LastName, City, State, Address, and Zip from the Customers table. Save the query as LogicalOperators_Case2_Q4.

Result:

FirstName	LastName	City	State	Address	Zip
John	Demarco	New York	NY	11 Lark Street	12189
Mary	Demania	New York	NY	12 Madison Ave	12189
George	Demers	New York	NY	23 New Scotland Ave	12189
Phillip	Demetriou	New York	NY	22 Academy Road	12189

```
(There are more records in the result set than the ones shown in this image)
(126 row(s) returned)
```

5. Create a query to select all customers except those in area code 22459. The query should contain the fields FirstName, LastName, City, State, Address, and Zip from the Customers table. Save the query as LogicalOperators_Case2_Q5.

Result:

FirstName	LastName	City	State	Address	Zip
John	Demarco	New York	NY	11 Lark Street	12189
Mary	Demania	New York	NY	12 Madison Ave	12189
George	Demers	New York	NY	23 New Scotland Ave	12189
Phillip	Demetriou	New York	NY	22 Academy Road	12189

(There are more records in the result set than the ones shown in this image)
(187 row(s) returned)

CHAPTER 5
WILDCARD CHARACTERS

Wildcard characters like (*, ?, !, [], -, #) provide essential functionality and filtering power in databases. They are used in combination with operators such as (LIKE, OR, AND, BETWEEN, IN, etc.) and predicates like (<, >, <>, =, >=). They allow for the formulation of very sophisticated search criteria on text and number data.

Character	Description	Example
*	Matches any number of characters. You can use the asterisk (*) anywhere in a character string.	**wh*** finds what, white, and why, but not awhile or watch.
?	Matches any single alphabetic character.	**B?ll** finds ball, bell, and bill.
[ ]	Matches any single character within the brackets.	**B[ae]ll** finds ball and bell, but not bill.
!	Matches any character not in the brackets.	**b[!ae]ll** finds bill and bull, but not ball or bell.
-	Matches any one of a range of characters. You must specify the range in ascending order (A to Z, not Z to A).	**b[a-c]d** finds bad, bbd, and bcd.
#	Matches any single numeric character.	**1#3** finds 103, 113, and 123.

Figure 13: List of wildcard characters

Source: https://support.microsoft.com/en-us/office/access-wildcard-character-reference-af00c501-7972-40ee-8889-e18abaad12d1?ui=en-us&rs=en-us&ad=us

26. The * wildcard to look for any number of alphanumeric characters

Create a list of customers whose last name starts with D

Discussion:

The * is the wildest of the wildcard characters, and it will match any numeric or alphabetic character whether we put it in the beginning, middle, or end of a search condition. As we can see in this example, every customer whose last name starts with a D will appear in the result set. Notice in the code the * is positioned after the letter D. This means that entries such as Dem, D1a, d123, or Dzo will appear in the result set.

Code:

```
SELECT FirstName, LastName, Address, City, State, Zip
FROM customers
WHERE LastName Like 'D*'
```

Result:

FirstName	LastName	Address	City	State	Zip
John	Demarco	11 Lark Street	New York	NY	12189
Mary	Demania	12 Madison Ave	New York	NY	12189
George	Demers	23 New Scotland Ave	New York	NY	12189
Phillip	Demetriou	22 Academy Road	New York	NY	12189

(There are more records in the result set than the ones shown in this image)
(21 row(s) returned)

27. The ? wildcard character in combination with *

Create a customer list using ? and * to create intricate search patterns
Discussion:

The ? character matches any single character. Though not used as much as the *, it can still make the difference and enable us to get exactly the results we want. Usually, we use it in combination with other wildcard characters. For instance, let us say we want to find names starting with "Da", have one character after the "Da" pattern, the next letter is "e" followed by any number of characters—"Da?e*". This will give us results such as Darek, Datek, Dale, and Daleney.

Code:

```
SELECT FirstName, LastName, Address, City, State, Zip
FROM Customers
WHERE ((LastName) Like 'Da?e*')
```

Result:

FirstName	LastName	Address	City	State	Zip
Diane	Darek	9 North Bridge Dr	San Jose	CA	36945
Julia	Datek	3 Woodscape Dr	San Jose	CA	36945
Matthew	Darek	78 Unity Street	Denver	CO	21214
Jason	Datek	19 Paul Street	Denver	CO	21214

(4 row(s) returned)

28. Create multi-character search patterns with [ ]

Create a customer list using multi-character search patterns
Discussion:

Using the brackets [ ] wildcard expression, we can search for any characters included within the brackets. For example, C[ru]* will find Croney, Culey, but not Colonie. Note that we use the * in this example to allow any characters to be included after the brackets.

Code:

```
SELECT FirstName, LastName, Address, City, State, Zip
FROM Customers
WHERE ((LastName) Like 'C[ru]*')
```

Result:

FirstName	LastName	Address	City	State	Zip
Kenneth	Crondos	158 West Lawrence Ave	Houston	TX	53289
Pindar	Crooney	16 Warren Street	Houston	TX	53289
Joseph	Crandil	192 Tampa Ave	Houston	TX	53289
Mary	Crawford	21 Aegean Dr	Houston	TX	53289

```
(There are more records in the result set than the ones shown in this image)
(8 row(s) returned)
```

29. Use the ! and [ ] wildcard characters to create exclusion patterns

Create a customer list using specific characters as exclusion search patterns

Discussion:

Sometimes, we need to exclude a set of characters to form the search expression we need. For example, if we want to retrieve all customers except those whose names start with an A, B, C, D, or E, we can use the [!] wildcard character. Any customers whose names start with a letter [abcde] will be excluded from the recordset. Note that the returned recordset is sorted by last name, and the first customer record to appear has a last name value starting with "F".

Code:

```
SELECT FirstName, LastName, Address, City, State, Zip
FROM Customers
WHERE ((LastName) Like '[!abcde]*')
ORDER BY LastName
```

Result:

FirstName	LastName	Address	City	State	Zip
Sonya	Ford	5 Beach Ave	San Jose	CA	36945
Cristopher	Geisler	93 Kate Street	Boston	MA	22459
William	Gibson	17 Grove Street	San Jose	CA	36945
Kathy	Giordano	21 Garden Ave	San Diego	CA	33521

```
(There are more records in the result set than the ones shown in this image)
(130 row(s) returned)
```

30. Use the ! and [ ] and - wildcards to create exclusion ranges

Create a customer list using sets of characters as exclusion ranges

Discussion:

What if we continue from the previous example using ! and [], but instead of typing in all the characters one by one, we use ranges? For example, we might want to obtain a recordset of customers whose names do not start with a letter in the range A-P. We can do this by using the "[!a-p]*" exclusion pattern. As you can see from the result below, the customers who appear in the list have names starting with an "R", which is the one immediately following "P" that was included in our exclusion range.

Code:

```
SELECT FirstName, LastName, Address, City, State, Zip
FROM customers
WHERE ((LastName) Like '[!a-p]*')
ORDER BY LastName
```

Result:

FirstName	LastName	Address	City	State	Zip
Richard	Ramirez	48 Mereline Ave	Miami	FL	88987
Lisa	Read	12 Madison Ave	Washington	DC	11882
Allen	Restad	72 Providence Dr	Los Angeles	CA	94851
Joanne	Riegert	31 Arizona Ave	Albany	NY	12189

```
(There are more records in the result set than the ones shown in this image)
(59 row(s) returned)
```

31. The # wildcard to look for single numeric values

Create a customer list using # to create search patterns

Discussion:

If we want to look for numeric values, then we can use the # character to look for single digits. For example, to retrieve the zip codes starting with 12 followed by three digits we could write:

Code:

```
SELECT FirstName, LastName, Address, City, State, Zip
FROM Customers
WHERE Zip Like '12###'
```

Result:

FirstName	LastName	Address	City	State	Zip
John	Demarco	11 Lark Street	New York	NY	12189
Mary	Demania	12 Madison Ave	New York	NY	12189
George	Demers	23 New Scotland Ave	New York	NY	12189
Phillip	Demetriou	22 Academy Road	New York	NY	12189

```
(There are more records in the result set than the ones shown in this image)
(23 row(s) returned)
```

32. The [0-9] wildcard to look for single numeric values

Create a customer list using [0-9] to create search patterns

Discussion:

We can achieve the same result as with the previous example using the [0-9] expression which by the way will work in other databases as well.

Code:

```
SELECT FirstName, LastName, Address, City, State, Zip
FROM Customers
WHERE Zip Like '12[0-9][0-9][0-9]'
```

Result:

FirstName	LastName	Address	City	State	Zip
John	Demarco	11 Lark Street	New York	NY	12189
Mary	Demania	12 Madison Ave	New York	NY	12189
George	Demers	23 New Scotland Ave	New York	NY	12189
Phillip	Demetriou	22 Academy Road	New York	NY	12189

```
(There are more records in the result set than the ones shown in this image)
(23 row(s) returned)
```

33. Use the - and [ ] wildcards to create inclusion ranges

Create a customer list using sets of characters as inclusion ranges

Discussion:

We can use [] and - to create inclusion ranges such as retrieving customers whose names start with a letter between A and P.

Code:

```
SELECT FirstName, LastName, Address, City, State, Zip
FROM Customers
WHERE ((LastName) Like '[a-p]*')
ORDER BY LastName
```

Result:

FirstName	LastName	Address	City	State	Zip
Nicholas	Ackerman	5 Buckingham Dr	Dallas	TX	52347
Alfred	Allen	29 Water Street	New York	NY	12189
Pindar	Ames	23 Cornell Dr	New York	NY	45357
Thomas	Andersen	52 Betwood Street	Orlando	FL	89754

(There are more records in the result set than the ones shown in this image)
(142 row(s) returned)

DISCUSSION QUESTIONS

1. What is the role of the * wildcard character?
2. How is the ? wildcard character different from the * one?
3. What is the role of the ! wildcard character?
4. Can the * wildcard character find only letters, only numbers, or both?
5. What is the function of the [] wildcard character?
6. What is the difference between a range and a pattern?
7. What wildcard character can we use if we want to look for ranges?
8. What wildcard character can we use if we want to look for patterns?
9. How can we define exclusion ranges using wildcard characters?
10. How can we define inclusion ranges using wildcard characters?

HANDS-ON EXERCISES

Case 1

For each of the questions in this case you need to create a new query in SQL view and name it as per the instructions in each question.

1. Create a query that includes the fields ProductName, ProductPrice, ContainerType, IngredientType, and SKU from the Products table. The query should return all records having a product name that starts with "ch". Save the query as Wildcard_Characters_Case1_Q1.

Your result should look like:

ProductName	ProductPrice	ContainerType	IngredientType	SKU
Choice Apricots	32	Paper Bag	All-Natural	PDKLS-2347
Chocolate Covered Apples	37	Flexible Pouch	Organic	PDKLS-2347
Chocolate Raspberries	29	Paper Bag	GMO-Free	PDKLS-2347
Chocolate Fudge	41	Paper Bag	All-Natural	DKLS-4732

(There are more records in the result set than the ones shown in this image)
(16 row(s) returned)

2. Create a query that includes the fields ProductName, ProductPrice, ContainerType, IngredientType, and SKU from the Products table. The inventory department needs a list of all the products whose name starts with a "C", the second character is any character, the third character is a "C", followed by any characters after that. Save the query as Wildcard_Characters_Case1_Q2.

Your result should look like:

ProductName	ProductPrice	ContainerType	IngredientType	SKU
Coconut Flavour Cream Wafers	38	Flexible Pouch	Organic	ASDT-3456
Cocoa and Hazelnut Biscuits	35	Plastic Container	GMO-Free	ASDT-3456
Cocoa Biscuits	28	Flexible Pouch	All-Natural	ADSD 2345
Coconut Chocolate Chip Cookies	25	Paper Bag	GMO-Free	KTRT-4589

(4 row(s) returned)

3. Create a query that includes the fields ProductName, ProductPrice, ContainerType, IngredientType, and SKU from the Products table. This time, the inventory department needs a list of all the products whose SKU starts with "ASD", followed by any of the characters T,D,L, followed by any character or number. Save the query as Wildcard_Characters_Case1_Q3.

Your result should look like:

ProductName	ProductPrice	ContainerType	IngredientType	SKU
Chocolate Chunk Cookies	48	Flexible Pouch	Organic	ASDT-3456
Peanut Butter Creme Cookies	18	Paper Bag	Organic	ASDT-3456
Cinnamon Flavor Cookies	24	Paper Box	All-Natural	ASDT-3456
Coconut Flavour Cream Wafers	38	Flexible Pouch	Organic	ASDT-3456

(There are more records in the result set than the ones shown in this image)
(10 row(s) returned)

4. Create a query that includes the fields ProductName, ProductPrice, ContainerType, IngredientType, and SKU from the Products table. The inventory department needs a list of all the products whose ContainerType does not start with "pap". Save the query as Wildcard_Characters_Case1_Q4.

Your result should look like:

ProductName	ProductPrice	ContainerType	IngredientType	SKU
Almonds Roasted and Salted	22	Plastic Bag	Organic	PDKLSD-2344
Banana Chips	27	Flexible Pouch	GMO-Free	PDKLSD-2347
Berry Cherry	30	Plastic Bag	GMO-Free	PDK-2589
California Original Pistachios	29	Plastic Container	GMO-Free	PDK-2347

(There are more records in the result set than the ones shown in this image)
(41 row(s) returned)

5. Create a query that includes the fields ProductName, ProductPrice, ContainerType, IngredientType, and SKU from the Products table. Your manager needs to send to the inventory department a list of all the products whose IngredientType does not start with the letters A,B,C,D, E, F, G . Save the query as Wildcard_Characters_Case1_Q5.

Your result should look like:

ProductName	ProductPrice	ContainerType	IngredientType	SKU
Almonds Roasted and Salted	22	Plastic Bag	Organic	PDKLSD-2344
Fresh Cranberries	35	Paper Bag	Organic	PDKLS-2347
Chocolate Covered Apples	37	Flexible Pouch	Organic	PDKLS-2347
Chocolate Blueberries	24	Plastic Bag	Organic	DKLS-4732

(There are more records in the result set than the ones shown in this image)
(21 row(s) returned)

Case 2

For each of the questions in this case you need to create a new query in SQL view and name it as per the instructions in each question.

1. Create a query that includes the fields ProductName, ProductPrice, ContainerType, IngredientType, and SKU from the Products table. The query should return all products having a product name starting with the letters a through e. Save the query as Wildcard_Characters_Case2_Q1.

Your result should look like:

ProductName	ProductPrice	ContainerType	IngredientType	SKU
Almonds Hickory Smoked	35	Paper Bag	GMO-Free	PDKLS-2332
Almonds Roasted and Salted	22	Plastic Bag	Organic	PDKLSD-2344
Banana Chips	27	Flexible Pouch	GMO-Free	PDKLSD-2347
Berry Cherry	30	Plastic Bag	GMO-Free	PDK-2589

```
(There are more records in the result set than the ones shown in this image)
(45 row(s) returned)
```

2. Create a query that includes the fields ProductName, ProductPrice, ContainerType, IngredientType, and SKU from the Products table. The query should return all products with a container type starting with the letters p and f. Save the query as Wildcard_Characters_Case2_Q2.

Your result should look like:

ProductName	ProductPrice	ContainerType	IngredientType	SKU
Almonds Hickory Smoked	35	Paper Bag	GMO-Free	PDKLS-2332
Almonds Roasted and Salted	22	Plastic Bag	Organic	PDKLSD-2344
Banana Chips	27	Flexible Pouch	GMO-Free	PDKLSD-2347
California Original Pistachios	29	Plastic Container	GMO-Free	PDK-2347

```
(There are more records in the result set than the ones shown in this image)
(51 row(s) returned)
```

3. Create a query that includes the fields ProductName, ProductPrice, ContainerType, IngredientType, and SKU from the Products table. The query should return all products having an SKU starting with the letters PD, having any characters after PD, followed by a dash, and ending with exactly four digits. Save the query as Wildcard_Characters_Case2_Q3.

Your result should look like:

ProductName	ProductPrice	ContainerType	IngredientType	SKU
Almonds Hickory Smoked	35	Paper Bag	GMO-Free	PDKLS-2332
Almonds Roasted and Salted	22	Plastic Bag	Organic	PDKLSD-2344
Banana Chips	27	Flexible Pouch	GMO-Free	PDKLSD-2347
Berry Cherry	30	Plastic Bag	GMO-Free	PDK-2589

```
(There are more records in the result set than the ones shown in this image)
(23 row(s) returned)
```

4. Create a query that includes the fields ProductName, ProductPrice, ContainerType, IngredientType, and SKU from the Products table having an SKU starting with any letters between A and P, any characters after those letters, followed by a dash, and ending with exactly four digits. The first two digits should be any digits and the last two 89. Save the query as Wildcard_Characters_Case2_Q4.

Your result should look like:

ProductName	ProductPrice	ContainerType	IngredientType	SKU
Berry Cherry	30	Plastic Bag	GMO-Free	PDK-2589
Chocolate Coconut Bar	26	Plastic Bag	GMO-Free	PDKL-2389
Roasted & Salted Almonds	19	Paper Box	GMO-Free	PDKL-2389
Roasted & Salted Cashews	30	Paper Bag	Organic	PDKL-2389

```
(There are more records in the result set than the ones shown in this image)
(21 row(s) returned)
```

5. Create a query that includes the fields ProductName, ProductPrice, ContainerType, IngredientType, and SKU from the Products table. The query should return all products having an SKU starting with any number of characters, followed by a dash, and ending in 2345. Save the query as Wildcard_Characters_Case2_Q5.

Your result should look like:

ProductName	ProductPrice	ContainerType	IngredientType	SKU
Oatmeal Raisin Walnut Cookies	43	Plastic Container	Organic	KDRT-2345
Chunky Chocolate Cookies	15	Flexible Pouch	All-Natural	KDRT-2345
Fudge Nut Brownie Cookies	44	Flexible Pouch	All-Natural	KDRT-2345
Dried Light Red Tart Cherries	43	Paper Bag	Organic	EPDA-2345

```
(There are more records in the result set than the ones shown in this image)
(13 row(s) returned)
```

CHAPTER 6
SEARCH PATTERNS with the LIKE OPERATOR

We use the LIKE operator to create search expressions and patterns on text data. It works but it is not recommended with number and date data types. For numbers and dates our first choice for search expressions should be the equality and inequality predicates.

We need to remember four points when using the LIKE operator. First, to supply its flexibility and functionality, it consumes resources, so it should not be the first choice to resort to for our search expressions. Second, we should really know how to use it to get the results we intent to, since it might not always return the expected results. Third, the LIKE operator is always used within the WHERE clause of the SQL statement. Fourth, the LIKE operator must be used in combination with wildcard characters such as (*, ?, !, [], -) to produce results.

34. The LIKE operator with the * wildcard character for simple search patterns

Create a list of products with a product name starting with a P

Discussion:

In this example, we use a simple search pattern to retrieve product names that start with the character P and have any alphanumeric characters after P.

.

Code:

```
SELECT ProductName, ContainerType, ProductWeight, ProductPrice, SKU
FROM Products
WHERE ProductName like 'P*'
```

Result:

ProductName	ContainerType	ProductWeight	ProductPrice	SKU
Pepper Cheese Box	Paper Box	6 oz	50	PDKL-2389
Peanut Butter Creme Cookies	Paper Bag	1 lb	18	ASDT-3456
Pizza croutons	Paper Bag	6 oz	49	ASDT-3456

(3 row(s) returned)

35. The LIKE operator with [ ] and * to create multi-character search ranges

Find products whose prices start with a number between 1 and 3

Discussion:

This time, we create a product report listing products whose price starts with numbers between 1 and 3. To obtain the report, we use the LIKE operator in combination with the [] and * wildcard characters. The [] wildcard will retrieve all product prices starting with 1, 2, and 3. Then, the * will allow for the retrieval of any number of characters after 1, 2, and 3. So, price numbers comprised of any number of digits will appear in the result set. Finally, notice in the result set that there are no product prices starting with 4 or any number above that.

Code:

```
SELECT ProductName, ContainerType, ProductWeight, ProductPrice, SKU
FROM Products
WHERE ProductPrice LIKE '[1-3]*'
```

Result:

ProductName	ContainerType	ProductWeight	ProductPrice	SKU
Almonds Hickory Smoked	Paper Bag	6 oz	35	PDKLS-2332
Almonds Roasted and Salted	Plastic Bag	7 oz	22	PDKLSD-2344
Banana Chips	Flexible Pouch	14 oz	27	PDKLSD-2347
Berry Cherry	Plastic Bag	10 oz	30	PDK-2589

```
(There are more records in the result set than the ones shown in this image)
(55 row(s) returned)
```

36. The LIKE operator with [ ] and ? to create precise-character search ranges

Find products whose cost value starts with any number between 7 and 9 and have three digits only

Discussion:

In this example, the [] (brackets) wildcard will retrieve all products with cost numbers starting with 7, 8, and 9. Then, the ??? characters will allow for the retrieval of cost values with three characters only.

Code:

```
SELECT ProductName, ContainerType, ProductWeight, ProductPrice, ProductCost, SKU
FROM Products
WHERE ProductCost LIKE '[7-8]???'
```

Result:

ProductName	ContainerType	ProductWeight	ProductPrice	ProductCost	SKU
Banana Chips	Flexible Pouch	14 oz	27	8.96	PDKLSD-2347
Chocolate Blueberries	Plastic Bag	5 oz	24	7.96	DKLS-4732
Chocolate Coconut Bar	Plastic Bag	8 oz	26	8.63	PDKL-2389
Water Crackers	Paper Box	1 lb	24	7.96	PDKL-2389

```
(There are more records in the result set than the ones shown in this image)
(10 row(s) returned)
```

37. The LIKE operator with date fields

Create a report of orders for the month of April for all years

Discussion:

We look for orders in the month of April irrespective of the day or year they were placed. Notice how we use the * for days and years, while we fix the month at 4 (April). In your own working environment, dates might have a different sequence of month-date-year but this is not an issue since you can place the * at the appropriate place in the search condition.

Code:

```
SELECT OrderID, OrderDate, PackagingType, PackageWeight, QuotationAmount
FROM Orders
WHERE OrderDate Like '4/*/*'
```

Result:

OrderID	OrderDate	PackagingType	PackageWeight	QuotationAmount
8	4/6/2021	Plastic	25.4	126
9	4/19/2021	Box	36	255
31	4/14/2021	Metal	25.4	156
42	4/19/2021	Cardboard	31.3	72

(There are more records in the result set than the ones shown in this image)
(82 row(s) returned)

38. The LIKE operator with number fields

Create a report of customer orders with a quotation amount of exactly $230

Discussion:

In this example, we retrieve customer orders with a quotation amount at exactly $230. When we use LIKE with numbers, we do not enclose the numbers in quotes.

Code:

```
SELECT OrderID, OrderDate, PackagingType, PackageWeight, QuotationAmount
FROM Orders
WHERE QuotationAmount Like 230
```

Result:

OrderID	OrderDate	PackagingType	PackageWeight	QuotationAmount
26	5/29/2020	Box	33.3	230
40	6/1/2021	Plastic	22.3	230
111	9/23/2022	Box	7.4	230
214	12/12/2022	Bio-Plastic	31.6	230

(There are more records in the result set than the ones shown in this image)
(8 row(s) returned)

Although we can use LIKE to search for numbers, it is a much better practice to use equality and inequality predicates such as (<, >, <>, =, >=). The above example could have been written with the equality predicate "=", and it would have produced the same results in a more reliable and efficient way.

Code:

```
SELECT OrderID, OrderDate, PackagingType, PackageWeight, InvoiceAmount
FROM Orders
WHERE QuotationAmount = 230
```

39. Compare LIKE, BETWEEN, and "<=" "=>" for number ranges

Create a report of customer orders with an invoice amount between $200 and $400

Discussion:

In this scenario, we prepare a report listing customer orders with invoice amounts between $200 and $400. To achieve this goal, we have three alternatives: We can use the LIKE operator, the BETWEEN operator, or the "<=" "=>" predicates. Which one is the best solution? Let us see. In the first case, we use the LIKE operator with the [ ] wildcard for ranges and the "?" character to establish the number of characters to be returned at 3. In other words, we are looking for numbers such as 234, 345, or 385. If we have used * after the [], we will also get numbers such as 26, 30, and 35, which is not what we want.

The result set includes records starting with invoice amounts at $200 and going all the way up to $393. Attention here, the LIKE operator is not able to include invoice amounts that are exactly $400. It can go as far up as $399 if it exists. Consequently, if we have any amounts at exactly $400, they will not be included.

Code:

```
SELECT OrderID, OrderDate, PackagingType, PackageWeight, InvoiceAmount
FROM Orders
WHERE InvoiceAmount LIKE '[2-3]??'
ORDER BY InvoiceAmount
```

Result:

OrderID	OrderDate	PackagingType	PackageWeight	InvoiceAmount
444	7/21/2022	Box	32.8	200
808	9/24/2022	Paperboard	22.3	200
636	5/18/2020	Paperboard	5.4	200
491	4/7/2020	Metal	8.1	200

```
(There are more records in the result set than the ones shown in this image)
(446 row(s) returned)
```

Discussion:

Now we will use the BETWEEN operator to achieve the same task. The BETWEEN operator is inclusive, that is boundaries will be included in the result set. For ranges of invoice amounts between $200 and $400, it will include the amounts of exactly $200 and exactly $400 if they are available. Notice that now we have two more records in the result set.

Code:

```
SELECT OrderID, OrderDate, PackagingType, PackageWeight, InvoiceAmount
FROM Orders
WHERE InvoiceAmount BETWEEN 200 AND 400
ORDER BY InvoiceAmount
```

Result:

OrderID	OrderDate	PackagingType	PackageWeight	InvoiceAmount
444	7/21/2022	Box	32.8	200
808	9/24/2022	Paperboard	22.3	200
636	5/18/2020	Paperboard	5.4	200
491	4/7/2020	Metal	8.1	200

```
(There are more records in the result set than the ones shown in this image)
(448 row(s) returned)
```

Discussion:

In this case, we are using the "<=" "=>" predicates to achieve the same goal of finding orders between $200 and $400. When it comes to numbers, the "<=" "=>" predicates are the most flexible and trusted to work with. In addition, predicates will produce consistent results, while operators have issues with result accuracy and performance.

Code:

```
SELECT OrderID, OrderDate, PackagingType, PackageWeight, InvoiceAmount
FROM Orders
WHERE  InvoiceAmount >= 200 AND InvoiceAmount <=  400
ORDER BY InvoiceAmount
```

Result:

OrderID	OrderDate	PackagingType	PackageWeight	InvoiceAmount
444	7/21/2022	Box	32.8	200
808	9/24/2022	Paperboard	22.3	200
636	5/18/2020	Paperboard	5.4	200
491	4/7/2020	Metal	8.1	200

(There are more records in the result set than the ones shown in this image)
(448 row(s) returned)

Conclusion: Do not use LIKE with numbers. We can reliably use BETWEEN or equality and inequality predicates and preferably we use the latter.

Find customer orders with invoice amounts different than $200
Discussion:
We can use the negation keyword "NOT" to completely change the result set of an operation using LIKE. In this example, we are looking for invoice amounts different than $200. Though we can use LIKE to achieve this, we will be better off using the inequality predicates "!=" or "<>". All three pieces of code will produce the same result but prefer to use the "<>" predicate instead because it is more reliable than LIKE and ANSI compliant.

Code1:

```
SELECT OrderID, OrderDate, PackagingType, PackageWeight, InvoiceAmount
FROM Orders
WHERE InvoiceAmount NOT Like 200
```

Code2:

```
SELECT OrderID, OrderDate, PackagingType, PackageWeight, InvoiceAmount
FROM Orders
WHERE InvoiceAmount <> 200
```

Result:

OrderID	OrderDate	PackagingType	PackageWeight	InvoiceAmount
1	11/11/2020	Box	39.5	31
2	7/30/2020	Plastic	21.7	214
3	7/4/2020	Bio-Plastic	22.7	235
4	12/19/2021	Cardboard	12.7	46

(There are more records in the result set than the ones shown in this image)
(994 row(s) returned)

40. LIKE with the ltrim() function to eliminate blank spaces in the beginning of the field

Filter customer names correctly by eliminating blank spaces

Discussion:

We have a request from our manager to list customers with the first name Mary so that she can send them a card for their name day. We know how to use the LIKE operator, so we write a statement like the one below and we get two records. We provide the report to our manager, and two weeks later, she comes back and says we missed three customers. What happened? Well, for three Marys, there were spaces in front of their first names and the LIKE operator did not pick them up. When it comes to LIKE, the statement (LIKE ' Mary') is different from (LIKE 'Mary'). Consequently, if there are any spaces, the two LIKE statements above will produce different results. What can we do about it? We can use the ltrim() function to trim any spaces in front of the customer's first name and obtain the results we want:

Code:

```
SELECT Firstname, LastName, City, State, Zip
FROM tbls_Customers
WHERE firstname LIKE 'Mary'
```

Result:

Firstname	LastName	City	State	Zip
Mary	Williams	Dallas	TX	52347
Mary	Crawford	Houston	TX	53289

(2 row(s) returned)

Discussion:

The ltrim() function will eliminate any spaces before a string in a field, and this will allow the LIKE operator to function properly. Notice this time, the database returned five records instead of two.

Code:

```
SELECT Firstname, LastName, City, State, Zip
FROM tbls_Customers
WHERE ltrim(firstname) LIKE 'Mary'
```

Result:

Firstname	LastName	City	State	Zip
Mary	Demania	New York	NY	12189
Mary	Simmons	Los Angeles	CA	94851
Mary	Williams	Dallas	TX	52347
Mary	Crawford	Houston	TX	53289
Mary	Stewart	Washington	DC	11882

(5 row(s) returned)

41. LIKE to identify blank spaces in the beginning of the field value

Check for the presence of blank spaces in the beginning of the name field

Discussion:

In this example, we are looking for spaces in the beginning of the field value. To achieve this, we use the left function to isolate and retrieve the first character of the FirstName field and then we test if this character is a blank space or not. If it is, the record will appear in the result set. Notice that the left function has two arguments: the first is the field name on which we use it and the second defines the number of characters to be retrieved from this field name. Notice also, that LIKE is followed by two single quotes which enclose one blank space. We can change the second argument of the LEFT() function and include more spaces within the single quotes to identify FisrtNames with two or more specific spaces in the beginning of the field. For example, we can look for exactly two blank values (spaces) using as Left(FisrtName, 2) LIKE ' '. However, the code Left(FisrtName,1) LIKE ' ' will identify all the FirstName field values with any number of spaces in the beginning of the field. Notice in the result set, the third record contains five blank characters (spaces) in the beginning of the field, and it is still displayed in the result.

Code:

```
SELECT Firstname, LastName, City, State, Zip
FROM tbls_Customers
WHERE Left(FirstName,1) LIKE ' '
```

Result:

Firstname	LastName	City	State	Zip
Mary	Demania	New York	NY	12189
Mary	Simmons	Los Angeles	CA	94851
Mary	Stewart	Washington	DC	11882

(3 row(s) returned)

42. LIKE to test for blank spaces within the field values

Check for the presence of blank spaces in a field

Discussion:

The same supervisor comes back and says she needs a report of customers from certain cities. This time, we are wise enough to know that to get the right results, we need to check for spaces first. Then, however, we reason that some city names do contain spaces. For example, New York contains a space and Los Angeles contains a space. In addition, we realize that the ltrim() and rtrim() functions are good for leading and trailing spaces only. What if there is a space right in the middle of the city name, however? We can look for spaces using the LIKE operator with the * wildcard character. In this example, we are looking for two spaces in any part of the field value. To achieve this, we use the * wildcard three times. We can test for one space using the * twice ('* *').

Code:

```
SELECT Firstname, LastName, City, State, Zip
FROM tbls_Customers
WHERE city LIKE '* * *'
```

Result:

Firstname	LastName	City	State	Zip
Phillip	Demetriou	New Yor k	NY	12189
Joseph	Anderson	Los Angel s	CA	94851

(2 row(s) returned)

43. LIKE to test a field for the presence of numbers

Check for the presence of numbers in a city field

Discussion:

Now, what if someone entered some city names and did not pay attention, and as he was typing, he mingled some numbers with the name of the city? For example, he might have entered "New 9York". How can we check a field for the presence of numbers within text strings? The answer is by using the LIKE operator, the [ ] wildcard character for ranges, and the * wildcard character as in the code below. Notice we use the [ ] to check for any number between 0 and 9. In addition, we use the * twice to look for the presence of a number at any part of the field, including the end and the beginning of its value. We actually caught two records with numbers mistyped in them.

Code:

```
SELECT Firstname, LastName, City, State, Zip
FROM tbls_Customers
WHERE city LIKE '*[0-9]*'
```

Result:

Firstname	LastName	City	State	Zip
Michael	Demizio	New York9	NY	12189
Nicholas	Demaico	9New York	NY	12110
Sonya	Stanford	Los 8Angeles	CA	94851
Christine	Catler	Philadelphia5	PA	56789

(4 row(s) returned)

44. TIP: Create an index on a field when used often with the LIKE operator

Create an index on the city field

Discussion:

In the previous example in which we used LIKE to look for numbers within the city field values, it took the database engine two long seconds to process the query (in my system). That is an extremely long time considering that the table contains only two hundred records. If the table contained hundreds of thousands of records, this query might be slow to produce output. We can create an index on the city field using the code below to accelerate this filtering operation. This SQL statement will create a non-unique index because we want to be able to store two cities with the same name in the "city" field. After you create the index, and you run the previous example again, you will see that the query is executed in zero seconds.

Code:

```
CREATE INDEX indCity ON tbls_Customers (city)
```

Result:

Access does not provide output but the index has been created in the table

DISCUSSION QUESTIONS

1. What is the purpose of the LIKE operator?
2. On what kind of data types can we use the LIKE operator?
3. What is the most appropriate data type to use with LIKE?
4. Can we use the LIKE operator by itself or do we need to combine it with special characters?
5. What is the tradeoff for the LIKE operator's flexibility?
6. How can we use the LIKE operator to test for the presence of spaces?
7. If we use LIKE repeatedly on a field, what can we do to accelerate the query results?
8. What wildcard character can we use with LIKE to search for patterns?
9. What wildcard character can we use with LIKE to search for ranges?
10. How can we use the LIKE operator to test field values for the presence of numbers?

HANDS-ON EXERCISES

Case 1

For each of the questions in this case you need to create a new query in SQL view and name it as per the instructions in each question.

1. Create a query that includes the fields ProductName, ContainerType, Qualityrating, SKU, ProductPrice, UnitsInStock from the tbls_Products table. Your manager wants to see all products whose name starts with the letter C. Save the query as LIKE_Case1_Q1.

Your result should look like:

ProductName	ContainerType	Qualityrating	SKU	ProductPrice	UnitsInStock
California Original Pistachios	Plastic Container	Acceptable	PDK-2347	29	35
Choice Apricots	Paper Bag	Very Good	PDKLS-2347	32	22
Cran Raisin Mix	Plastic Bag	Excellent	PDKLS-2347	31	24
Cappuccino Almonds	Plastic Container	Very Good	PDKLS-2347	35	32

```
(There are more records in the result set than the ones shown in this image)
(29 row(s) returned)
```

2. Create a query that includes the fields ProductName, ContainerType, Qualityrating, SKU, ProductPrice, UnitsInStock from the tbls_Products table. Your supervisor wants to see all products whose price is between $15 and a $30. Boundary values should be included in the result set. You can use any operator you want so that you are certain the result is correct. Sort results by ProductPrice ascending. Save the query as LIKE_Case1_Q2.

Your result should look like:

ProductName	ContainerType	Qualityrating	SKU	ProductPrice	UnitsInStock
Chunky Chocolate Cookies	Flexible Pouch	Very Good	KDRT-2345	15	33
Fried Jalapenos	Plastic Bag	Very Good	EPDA-2345	15	32
Dried Cranberries	Plastic Container	Excellent	EPDA-2345	16	45
Dried Tart Cherries	Paper Box	Need to Improve	EPDA-2345	16	30

```
(There are more records in the result set than the ones shown in this image)
(39 row(s) returned)
```

3. Create a new query that includes the fields ProductName, ContainerType, QualityRating, SKU, ProductPrice, and UnitsInStock from the tbls_Products table. Retrieve all the records that contain blank spaces in the beginning of the ProductName field. Save the query as LIKE_Case1_Q3.

Your result should look like:

ProductName	ContainerType	Qualityrating	SKU	ProductPrice	UnitsInStock
Roasted & Salted Almonds	Paper Box	Need to Improve	PDKL-2389	19	35
Roasted & Salted Cashews	Paper Bag	Acceptable	PDKL-2389	30	22
Roasted No-Salt Almonds	Plastic Bag	Excellent	PDKL-2389	39	38

(3 row(s) returned)

4. Create a query that includes the fields ProductName, ContainerType, Qualityrating, SKU, ProductPrice, UnitsInStock from the tbls_Products table and lists all the products which have one blank space anywhere in the SKU field. Save the query as LIKE_Case1_Q4.

Your result should look like:

ProductName	ContainerType	Qualityrating	SKU	ProductPrice	UnitsInStock
Dark Chocolate Apricots	Plastic Container	Very Good	DKLS-473 2	46	38
Sesame Crackers	Paper Box	Need to Improve	D KLS-4732	39	43
Crispy Pears	Paper Box	Top-Rated	D KLS-4732	33	31
Chocolate Coconut Bar	Plastic Bag	Top-Rated	PDK L-2389	26	37

(There are more records in the result set than the ones shown in this image)
(11 row(s) returned)

5. Create a query that includes the fields ProductName, ContainerType, Qualityrating, SKU, ProductPrice, UnitsInStock from the tbls_Products table. The result set should list all products with prices starting with 1, 4, and 5. Order by ProductPrice ascending. Name the query as LIKE_Case1_Q5.

Your result should look like:

ProductName	ContainerType	Qualityrating	SKU	ProductPrice	UnitsInStock
Chunky Chocolate Cookies	Flexible Pouch	Very Good	KDRT-2345	15	33
Fried Jalapenos	Plastic Bag	Very Good	EPDA-2345	15	32
Dried Cranberries	Plastic Container	Excellent	EPDA-2345	16	45
Dried Tart Cherries	Paper Box	Need to Improve	EPDA-2345	16	30

(There are more records in the result set than the ones shown in this image)
(23 row(s) returned)

Case 2

For each of the questions in this case you need to create a new query in SQL view and name it as per the instructions in each question.

1. Create a query that includes the fields OrderID, OrderDate, PackagingType, PackageWeight, InvoiceAmount, and FulfillmentCost from the Orders table. List all orders in which the PackagingType starts with the letters c and m. Name the query LIKE_Case2_Q1.

Your result should look like:

OrderID	OrderDate	PackagingType	PackageWeight	InvoiceAmount	FulfillmentCost
4	12/19/2021	Cardboard	12.7	46	6
14	9/10/2021	Metal	5.7	279	28
24	3/12/2022	Metal	25.3	371	18
25	9/11/2022	Cardboard	32.7	350	21

```
(There are more records in the result set than the ones shown in this image)
(263 row(s) returned)
```

2. Create a query that includes the fields OrderID, OrderDate, PackagingType, PackageWeight, InvoiceAmount, and FulfillmentCost from the Orders table. Retrieve all orders placed in November 2022. Name the query LIKE_Case2_Q2.

Your result should look like:

OrderID	OrderDate	PackagingType	PackageWeight	InvoiceAmount	FulfillmentCost
5	11/19/2022	Box	12.2	258	26
20	11/13/2022	Plastic	39.9	15	2
39	11/11/2022	Bio-Plastic	39	115	2
110	11/21/2022	Plastic	7.7	168	18

```
(There are more records in the result set than the ones shown in this image)
(25 row(s) returned)
```

3. Create a query that includes the fields OrderID, OrderDate, PackagingType, PackageWeight, InvoiceAmount, and FulfillmentCost from the Orders table. Retrieve all orders with an invoice amount between $100 and a $200. Boundary values should be included in the result set. Sort results by InvoiceAmount so that higher values appear first. Name the query LIKE_Case2_Q3.

Your result should look like:

OrderID	OrderDate	PackagingType	PackageWeight	InvoiceAmount	FulfillmentCost
745	6/13/2020	Metal	26.6	300	28
700	10/7/2022	Foil	27.8	299	14
249	7/17/2022	Cardboard	8.3	299	30
345	1/7/2021	Plastic	13	299	30

```
(There are more records in the result set than the ones shown in this image)
(698 row(s) returned)
```

4. Create a query that includes the fields OrderID, OrderDate, PackagingType, PackageWeight, InvoiceAmount, and FulfillmentCost from the Orders table. Retrieve the orders which in the PackagingType field have one blank space anywhere in the field. Name the query LIKE_Case2_Q4.

Your result should look like:

OrderID	OrderDate	PackagingType	PackageWeight	InvoiceAmount	FulfillmentCost
10	12/13/2020	Shrink film	26.1	31	4
19	9/28/2020	Shrink film	21.5	420	18
28	10/30/2020	Shrink film	17.4	192	10
30	6/2/2022	Shrink film	26	275	28

```
(There are more records in the result set than the ones shown in this image)
(103 row(s) returned)
```

5. Create a query that includes the fields OrderID, OrderDate, PackagingType, PackageWeight, InvoiceAmount, and FulfillmentCost from the Orders table. The result set should list all orders with a package weight that does

not start with numbers between 1 and 6. Order by PackageWeight ascending. Name the query LIKE_Case2_Q5.

Your result should look like:

OrderID	OrderDate	PackagingType	PackageWeight	InvoiceAmount	FulfillmentCost
22	11/29/2020	Paperboard	7	333	34
511	10/14/2022	Bio-Plastic	7	282	17
967	12/16/2022	Shrink film	7	96	24
375	9/4/2021	Metal	7.1	314	32

```
(There are more records in the result set than the ones shown in this image)
(81 row(s) returned)
```

CHAPTER 7
ABSOLUTE SEARCHES with EQUALITY AND INEQUALITY PREDICATES

We use equality and inequality predicates to create precise and unambiguous search expressions. They are more flexible than using LIKE, and their results are solid and unquestionable. They are used in the WHERE clause of a SQL statement to construct a search condition without the need of any wildcard characters. For instance, the statement (WHERE lastname = 'Smith') is valid. They should be given preference over operators such as LIKE, BETWEEN, and TOP.

The equality and inequality predicates in MS Access 365 are the following:

Meaning	Operator
Equal to	= =
Not equal to	<>
Less than	<
Less than or equal to	<=
Greater than	>
Greater than or equal to	>=

45. The equality predicate "=" for absolute searches in text data

Find a specific customer record searching on last name

Discussion:

In this example, we use the equality predicate to look for a specific customer last name, which is for a known value. That is, we know in advance the last name of the customer we are looking for. This is different when we conduct approximate searches using the LIKE operator where we might know part of the customer's last name, but we are not certain for the rest of it. The point to remember is that whenever we can, we should give preference to the equality predicate over the LIKE operator because it will retrieve exactly what we need, faster, and with less overhead for the database.

Code:

```
SELECT FirstName, LastName, City, State, Zip
FROM Customers
WHERE lastname = 'Delaney'
```

Result:

FirstName	LastName	City	State	Zip
Jason	Delaney	New York	NY	89890
Dolores	Delaney	Philadelphia	PA	56789

(2 row(s) returned)

46. The equality predicate "=" for absolute searches in number data

Find a specific customer record searching on CustomerID

Discussion:

The equality predicate should be preferred in scenarios involving numbers and especially primary keys. For example, let us assume we need to use an UPDATE statement to edit the record of a customer. We should unequivocally identify the customer using the equality predicate on the primary key of the table so that we are certain we are updating the right customer. The same logic is valid with DELETE statements where we should use the equality predicate to identify the correct customer for deletion. In this example, we retrieve a customer order searching on the OrderID, which is the primary key of the Orders table.

Code:

```
SELECT OrderID, OrderDate, PackagingType, PackageWeight,  InvoiceAmount
FROM Orders
WHERE OrderID = 972
```

Result:

OrderID	OrderDate	PackagingType	PackageWeight	InvoiceAmount
972	8/24/2022	Plastic	15	192

(1 row(s) returned)

47. The ">" inequality predicate with date data

Retrieve orders placed after a certain date

Discussion:

The ">" inequality predicate means "greater than", and we can use it with numbers and dates. In this example, we look for orders placed after June 2022. We also sort ascending on OrderDate so that older orders appear first.

Code:

```
SELECT OrderID, OrderDate, PackagingType, PackageWeight,  InvoiceAmount
FROM Orders
WHERE OrderDate > #6/30/2022#
ORDER BY OrderDate
```

Result:

OrderID	OrderDate	PackagingType	PackageWeight	InvoiceAmount
201	7/1/2022	Box	20.6	394
905	7/1/2022	Paperboard	39.5	149
712	7/4/2022	Metal	28.1	178
103	7/4/2022	Bio-Plastic	21.2	201

(There are more records in the result set than the ones shown in this image)
(151 row(s) returned)

48. The ">=" inequality predicate with date data

Retrieve orders placed after a certain date including the date specified

Discussion:

The ">=" inequality predicate means "greater than or equal to", and we can use it with numbers and dates. In this example, we want to find orders placed after July 2022 including the last day of July. We sort ascending on orderdate so that older orders appear first.

Code:

```
SELECT OrderID, OrderDate, PackagingType, PackageWeight, InvoiceAmount
FROM Orders
WHERE OrderDate >= #7/31/2022#
ORDER BY OrderDate
```

Result:

OrderID	OrderDate	PackagingType	PackageWeight	InvoiceAmount
605	7/31/2022	Paperboard	28.9	222
513	8/3/2022	Shrink film	11	151
197	8/3/2022	Bio-Plastic	30.5	424
327	8/4/2022	Bio-Plastic	23.1	169

(There are more records in the result set than the ones shown in this image)
(130 row(s) returned)

49. The "<" inequality predicate with number data

Find orders for which the package weight is less than 28.8

Discussion:

The "<" inequality predicate means "less than", and in this example we use it to find package weights less than 28.80. Notice we do not use quotes or other symbols to enclose numerical data in criteria expressions. We simply type in the number. The first number appearing in the result set is 28.7 because we specifically asked for "less than 28.8".

Code:

```
SELECT OrderID, OrderDate, PackagingType, PackageWeight, InvoiceAmount
FROM Orders
WHERE PackageWeight < 28.8
ORDER BY PackageWeight DESC
```

Result:

OrderID	OrderDate	PackagingType	PackageWeight	InvoiceAmount
433	8/19/2020	Cardboard	28.7	463
227	11/6/2020	Bio-Plastic	28.7	318
79	6/7/2022	Shrink film	28.6	146
963	5/10/2020	Foil	28.6	15

(There are more records in the result set than the ones shown in this image)
(669 row(s) returned)

50. The "<>" inequality predicate with number data

Find orders for which the invoice amount is not equal to $200

Discussion:

The "<>" inequality predicate means "not equal to". In this example, we list orders with invoice amounts different from 200. Notice we do not use quotes or other symbols to enclose numerical data as criteria.

Code:

```
SELECT OrderID, OrderDate, PackagingType, PackageWeight, InvoiceAmount
FROM Orders
WHERE InvoiceAmount <> 200
ORDER BY InvoiceAmount DESC
```

Result:

OrderID	OrderDate	PackagingType	PackageWeight	InvoiceAmount
944	9/18/2020	Plastic	34.9	601
354	4/28/2022	Bio-Plastic	15.5	599
326	6/15/2021	Plastic	13.7	587
867	1/17/2022	Shrink film	18.4	585

(There are more records in the result set than the ones shown in this image)
(994 row(s) returned)

51. The ">" predicate with number and date data concurrently

Find orders placed after a certain date and with an invoice amount less than $150

Discussion:

In this example, we are looking for orders placed after July 2022 and with an invoice amount less than 150.

Code:

```
SELECT OrderID, OrderDate, PackagingType, PackageWeight, InvoiceAmount
FROM Orders
WHERE OrderDate > #7/31/2022#
AND InvoiceAmount < 150
ORDER BY InvoiceAmount DESC
```

Result:

OrderID	OrderDate	PackagingType	PackageWeight	InvoiceAmount
131	11/29/2022	Foil	31.9	146
758	12/13/2022	Shrink film	30.9	143
185	10/11/2022	Cardboard	16.9	142
603	9/22/2022	Box	8.4	142

(There are more records in the result set than the ones shown in this image)
(46 row(s) returned)

DISCUSSION QUESTIONS

1. What is the difference between absolute and approximate searches?
2. What SQL operator do we use to conduct approximate data searches?
3. What is the rationale behind absolute data searches?
4. Why inequality and equality predicates are the first choice for number searches?
5. Do we have to use wildcard characters with equality and inequality predicates?
6. On what data types can we use equality and inequality predicates?
7. Why is it a very good idea to use the equality predicate "=" in delete and update statements?
8. What is the difference between the "=>" and ">" inequality predicates?
9. How does the BETWEEN operator compare with the "=>" and ">" inequality predicates?
10. Why do we prefer equality and inequality predicates over operators such as BETWEEN and LIKE which can achieve the same results?

HANDS-ON EXERCISES

Case 1

For each of the questions in this case you need to create a new query in SQL view and name it as per the instructions in each question.

1. The Accounting department is looking for orders with a processing cost less than $2. Create a new query that includes the fields OrderID, OrderDate, BoxType, PackageWeight, MaterialCost, and ProcessingCost from the Orders table and satisfies the accounting department request. Save the query as EqualityInequalityPredicates_Case1_Q1.

Your result should look like:

OrderID	OrderDate	BoxType	PackageWeight	MaterialCost	ProcessingCost
1	11/11/2020	Cube	39.5	10	1.53
10	12/13/2020	Multi-Height	26.1	10	1.53
20	11/13/2022	Side Loading	39.9	5	0.76
21	10/7/2022	Cube	16.7	13	1.91

```
(There are more records in the result set than the ones shown in this image)
(110 row(s) returned)
```

2. The accounting people are calling for help because a customer has complained about the number of invoices she received to pay. They need to know what is happening with the orders of customer with customer ID 199. Create a new query that includes the fields OrderID, OrderDate, BoxType, PackageWeight, MaterialCost, and ProcessingCost from the Orders table. Save the query as EqualityInequalityPredicates_Case1_Q2.

Your result should look like:

OrderID	OrderDate	BoxType	PackageWeight	MaterialCost	ProcessingCost
113	6/14/2020	Long	35	63	9.09
668	10/26/2022	Tall	36.2	45	4.25
719	1/7/2020	Multi-Height	34.2	24	6.88
743	2/8/2022	Cube	39.2	80	9.47

(There are more records in the result set than the ones shown in this image)
(9 row(s) returned)

3. The inventory people want to plan for package movement and need to know the number of packages with a package weight above 35 pounds. Create a new query that includes the fields OrderID, OrderDate, BoxType, PackageWeight, MaterialCost, and ProcessingCost from the Orders table that satisfies the inventory department request. Save the query as EqualityInequalityPredicates_Case1_Q3.

Your result should look like:

OrderID	OrderDate	BoxType	PackageWeight	MaterialCost	ProcessingCost
1	11/11/2020	Cube	39.5	10	1.53
9	4/19/2021	Side Loading	36	75	10.83
20	11/13/2022	Side Loading	39.9	5	0.76
34	3/17/2020	Tall	36.6	89	12.87

(There are more records in the result set than the ones shown in this image)
(146 row(s) returned)

4. A few weeks later the inventory department complains heavily to your supervisor. Apparently, many orders were left out from the report you gave them. Create a new query that includes the fields OrderID, OrderDate, BoxType, PackageWeight, MaterialCost, and ProcessingCost from the Orders table which includes the products that have a package weight of exactly 35 pounds. Save the query as EqualityInequalityPredicates_Case1_Q4.

Your result should look like:

OrderID	OrderDate	BoxType	PackageWeight	MaterialCost	ProcessingCost
113	6/14/2020	Long	35	63	9.09
466	11/12/2021	Tall	35	4	0.59
548	6/11/2021	Cube	35	58	8.41

(3 row(s) returned)

5. Finally, for order processing purposes, the Orders department asks for a report of orders with a material cost between $30 and $40, boundaries included. Create a new query that includes the fields OrderID, OrderDate, BoxType, PackageWeight, MaterialCost, and ProcessingCost from the Orders table and satisfies the Order department request. Use equality and inequality predicates only for this case question. Save the query as EqualityInequalityPredicates_Case1_Q5.

Your result should look like:

OrderID	OrderDate	BoxType	PackageWeight	MaterialCost	ProcessingCost
8	4/6/2021	Cube	25.4	37	5.35
12	12/29/2020	Telescopic	28.9	37	5.35
28	10/30/2020	Side Loading	17.4	31	4.59
29	12/4/2022	Cube	17.5	37	5.35

(There are more records in the result set than the ones shown in this image.
148 row(s) returned)

Case 2

For each of the questions in this case you need to create a new query in SQL view and name it as per the instructions in each question.

1. The sales department needs a report of orders placed in the month of April 2022. Create a query that includes the fields OrderID, OrderDate, ShippedDate, BoxType, PackageWeight, and MaterialCost from the Orders table and satisfies the above criteria. You must use equality and inequality predicates in the WHERE clause. Sort results by OrderDate so that the latest orders show first. Save the query as EqualityInequalityPredicates_Case2_Q1.

Your result should look like:

OrderID	OrderDate	ShippedDate	BoxType	PackageWeight	MaterialCost
85	4/30/2022	5/5/2022	Tall	37.3	24
354	4/28/2022	5/3/2022	Side Loading	15.5	99
381	4/28/2022	5/3/2022	Long	26.8	59
181	4/27/2022	5/2/2022	Multi-Height	14.1	50

(There are more records in the result set than the ones shown in this image)
(30 row(s) returned)

2. The marketing department needs to understand the seasonality effects on sales. For this reason, they asked for a list of orders for the months of March and April for the years 2020, 2021, 2022. Create a query that includes the fields OrderID, OrderDate, ShippedDate, BoxType, PackageWeight, and MaterialCost from the Orders table. You must use equality and inequality predicates in the WHERE clause. Order results so that the latest order dates appear first. Save the query as EqualityInequalityPredicates_Case2_Q2.

Your result should look like:

OrderID	OrderDate	ShippedDate	BoxType	PackageWeight	MaterialCost
85	4/30/2022	5/5/2022	Tall	37.3	24
354	4/28/2022	5/3/2022	Side Loading	15.5	99
381	4/28/2022	5/3/2022	Long	26.8	59
181	4/27/2022	5/2/2022	Multi-Height	14.1	50

(There are more records in the result set than the ones shown in this image)
(150 row(s) returned)

3. Accounting is asking for a report that lists the orders with a material cost between $30 and $40, boundaries included. Create a query that includes the fields OrderID, OrderDate, ShippedDate, BoxType, PackageWeight, and MaterialCost from the Orders table. You must use equality and inequality predicates in the WHERE clause. Sort results by material cost so that lower amounts appear first. Save the query as EqualityInequalityPredicates_Case2_Q3.

Your result should look like:

OrderID	OrderDate	ShippedDate	BoxType	PackageWeight	MaterialCost
359	5/30/2022	6/4/2022	Side Loading	29	30
118	12/16/2022	12/21/2022	Telescopic	27.1	30
652	11/7/2021	11/12/2021	Long	23.1	30
151	3/2/2020	3/7/2020	Side Loading	24.3	30

(There are more records in the result set than the ones shown in this image)
(148 row(s) returned)

4. Your supervisor is asking for a report that includes the fields OrderID, OrderDate, ShippedDate, BoxType, PackageWeight, and MaterialCost from the Orders table. It should list all orders except those with a package weight equal to 30 or equal to 35 or equal to 40. You must use equality and inequality predicates in the WHERE clause. Sort results by package weight so that larger amounts appear first. Save the query as EqualityInequalityPredicates_Case2_Q4.

Your result should look like:

OrderID	OrderDate	ShippedDate	BoxType	PackageWeight	MaterialCost
1	11/11/2020	11/16/2020	Cube	39.5	10
2	7/30/2020	8/4/2020	Long	21.7	74
3	7/4/2020	7/9/2020	Long	22.7	81
4	12/19/2021	12/24/2021	Tall	12.7	16

(There are more records in the result set than the ones shown in this image)
(994 row(s) returned)

5. The inventory people need a report that lists all orders with a box type of telescopic, side loading, and cube. Create a new query that includes the fields OrderID, OrderDate, ShippedDate, BoxType, PackageWeight, and MaterialCost from the Orders table and satisfies the above criteria. You must use equality and inequality predicates in the WHERE clause. Save the query as EqualityInequalityPredicates_Case2_Q5.

Your result should look like:

OrderID	OrderDate	ShippedDate	BoxType	PackageWeight	MaterialCost
1	11/11/2020	11/16/2020	Cube	39.5	10
8	4/6/2021	4/11/2021	Cube	25.4	37
11	6/7/2020	6/12/2020	Telescopic	24.3	101
12	12/29/2020	1/3/2021	Telescopic	28.9	37

(There are more records in the result set than the ones shown in this image)
(319 row(s) returned)

CHAPTER 8
FILTERING BOUNDARIES WITH THE BETWEEN OPERATOR

The BETWEEN ... AND operator filters data. It retrieves records that exist between two dates or numbers that act as boundaries. Boundary values will be included in the recordset. That is, if we use BETWEEN with two date values, the records containing those date values will be included in the result set.

52. BETWEEN to retrieve records within two numeric boundaries

Find orders with invoice amounts between $150 and $180

Discussion:

In this example, we are looking for orders with invoice amounts between $150 and $180. The BETWEEN operator is inclusive, so orders with invoice amounts of exactly 150 and exactly 180 will be included in the result set. We sort descending so that larger invoice amounts appear first.

Code:

```
SELECT OrderID, OrderDate, ShippedDate, InvoiceAmount, PackageWeight, MaterialCost
FROM Orders
WHERE InvoiceAmount BETWEEN 150 AND 180
ORDER BY InvoiceAmount DESC
```

Result:

OrderID	OrderDate	ShippedDate	InvoiceAmount	PackageWeight	MaterialCost
682	3/4/2021	3/9/2021	180	29.5	45
297	3/24/2021	3/29/2021	179	33.1	62
892	3/24/2021	3/29/2021	178	22.5	10
541	1/26/2022	1/31/2022	178	5.5	61

(There are more records in the result set than the ones shown in this image)
(108 row(s) returned)

53. BETWEEN to retrieve records within two date boundaries

Find orders shipped within a date range

Discussion:

In this example, we retrieve orders that were shipped between 5/15/2022 and 6/15/2022. The BETWEEN operator is inclusive, and it will include orders shipped on 5/15/2022 and 6/15/2022 as it is shown in the result set.

Code:

```
SELECT OrderID, OrderDate, ShippedDate, InvoiceAmount, PackageWeight, MaterialCost
FROM Orders
WHERE ShippedDate BETWEEN #2022-05-15# AND #2022-06-15#
ORDER BY ShippedDate DESC
```

Result:

OrderID	OrderDate	ShippedDate	InvoiceAmount	PackageWeight	MaterialCost
342	6/10/2022	6/15/2022	31	6.1	10
755	6/10/2022	6/15/2022	150	38.3	35
781	6/10/2022	6/15/2022	278	16.6	44
79	6/7/2022	6/12/2022	146	28.6	16

(There are more records in the result set than the ones shown in this image)
(35 row(s) returned)

54. BETWEEN with functions to customize boundary values

Use the year() function to retrieve orders placed within a year range

Discussion:

We use the year() function to extract the year out of the OrderDate field so that we can use year values as the lower and upper boundaries. All orders from 2021 and 2022 will be included in the result set.

Code:

```
SELECT OrderID, OrderDate, ShippedDate, InvoiceAmount, PackageWeight, MaterialCost
FROM Orders
WHERE year(orderdate) BETWEEN 2021 AND 2022
ORDER BY orderdate DESC
```

Result:

OrderID	OrderDate	ShippedDate	InvoiceAmount	PackageWeight	MaterialCost
777	12/29/2022	1/3/2020	196	27	16
573	12/29/2022	1/3/2020	328	29.1	61
943	12/27/2022	1/1/2020	341	38.8	59
260	12/27/2022	1/1/2020	8	31.7	3

(There are more records in the result set than the ones shown in this image)
(653 row(s) returned)

55. NOT BETWEEN to retrieve records outside two numeric boundaries

Find Orders with package weights outside a price range

Discussion:

In this instance, we are looking for products with prices outside the $10 to $40 range, so we are asking the database to give us all products whose prices do not fall between $10 and $40. In practical terms, when we use the BETWEEN operator with NOT, we are usually looking for extreme values or outliers. The products with prices of exactly $10 or $40 will not be included in the result set.

Code:

```
SELECT OrderID, OrderDate, ShippedDate, InvoiceAmount, PackageWeight, MaterialCost
FROM Orders
WHERE PackageWeight NOT BETWEEN 10 AND 30
ORDER BY PackageWeight ASC
```

Result:

OrderID	OrderDate	ShippedDate	InvoiceAmount	PackageWeight	MaterialCost
188	5/9/2020	5/14/2020	97	5	33
958	8/20/2021	8/25/2021	181	5	20
752	2/10/2021	2/15/2021	46	5.1	16
271	5/2/2022	5/7/2022	142	5.1	31

```
(There are more records in the result set than the ones shown in this image)
(441 row(s) returned)
```

56. Comparison of BETWEEN and "<=" or "=>"

Find Orders with material cost between 30 and 40

Discussion:

In this paradigm, we show that using the BETWEEN operator is the same as using the two inequality predicates "<=" and "=>". Both SQL statements below will produce the same result. However, we should give preference to equality and inequality predicates since they produce faster results with less overhead for the database engine.

Code:

```
SELECT OrderID, OrderDate, ShippedDate, InvoiceAmount, PackageWeight, MaterialCost
FROM Orders
WHERE MaterialCost BETWEEN 30 AND 40
ORDER BY MaterialCost ASC
```

Or

Code:

```
SELECT OrderID, OrderDate, ShippedDate, InvoiceAmount, PackageWeight, MaterialCost
FROM Orders
WHERE MaterialCost >=30 AND MaterialCost <=40
ORDER BY MaterialCost ASC
```

Result:

OrderID	OrderDate	ShippedDate	InvoiceAmount	PackageWeight	MaterialCost
359	5/30/2022	6/4/2022	237	29	30
118	12/16/2022	12/21/2022	187	27.1	30
652	11/7/2021	11/12/2021	237	23.1	30
151	3/2/2020	3/7/2020	237	24.3	30

```
(There are more records in the result set than the ones shown in this image)
(148 row(s) returned)
```

DISCUSSION QUESTIONS

1. What is the primary goal of the BETWEEN operator?
2. What equality/inequality predicates can we use to simulate the function of the BETWEEN operator?
3. Are boundary values included in the result set when we use the BETWEEN operator?
4. Can we use the BETWEEN operator with wildcard characters or predicates for more intricate searches?
5. With what data types do we primarily use the BETWEEN operator?
6. How can we use the BETWEEN operator with functions to augment its functionality?
7. Can we use the BETWEEN operator with dates?
8. Why would someone prefer to use equality and inequality predicates instead of the BETWEEN operator?
9. What do we need to do if we do not want to include the boundaries of a range in our searches?
10. The BETWEEN operator allows us to get the range within two numbers. What keyword can we use to retrieve the respective outside range?

HANDS-ON EXERCISES

Case 1

For each of the questions in this case you need to create a new query in SQL view and name it as per the instructions in each question.

1. The marketing department needs a list of orders with an invoice amount between $100 and $200. Create a new query that includes the fields OrderID, OrderDate, PackageWeight, MaterialCost, and InvoiceAmount from the Orders table satisfying the marketing request. Order results by InvoiceAmount so that bigger amounts show first. Save the query as Between_Case1_Q1.

Your result should look like:

OrderID	OrderDate	PackageWeight	MaterialCost	InvoiceAmount
636	5/18/2020	5.4	35	200
370	2/6/2022	36.9	69	200
808	9/24/2022	22.3	52	200
491	4/7/2020	8.1	69	200

```
(There are more records in the result set than the ones shown in this image)
(397 row(s) returned)
```

2. The inventory people need a list of orders placed in May and June 2022 to compare it against their shipments for accuracy. Create a new query that includes the fields OrderID, OrderDate, PackageWeight, MaterialCost, and InvoiceAmount from the Orders table satisfying the inventory department's request. Order results by OrderDate so that the latest orders show first. Save the query as Between_Case1_Q2.

Your result should look like:

OrderID	OrderDate	PackageWeight	MaterialCost	InvoiceAmount
733	6/29/2022	38.7	59	171
36	6/29/2022	15	37	257
644	6/26/2022	32.1	55	259
426	6/25/2022	18	14	41

```
(There are more records in the result set than the ones shown in this image)
(67 row(s) returned)
```

3. The management asked for a report that includes all orders in the months of September 2021 and September 2022. They need this data for a historical assessment of sales. Create a new query that includes the fields

OrderID, OrderDate, PackageWeight, MaterialCost, and InvoiceAmount from the Orders table. You must only use the BETWEEN operator in the WHERE clause. Save the query as Between_Case1_Q3.

Your result should look like:

OrderID	OrderDate	PackageWeight	MaterialCost	InvoiceAmount
14	9/10/2021	5.7	96	279
25	9/11/2022	32.7	69	350
65	9/10/2021	23.5	48	140
68	9/3/2022	7.8	101	293

```
(There are more records in the result set than the ones shown in this image)
(59 row(s) returned)
```

4. The management is asking for a list of orders within 2022 but outside the period between June 2022 and August 2022 for reviewing performance outside the summer months. Create a new query that includes the fields OrderID, OrderDate, PackageWeight, MaterialCost, and InvoiceAmount from the Orders table and satisfies the managerial request. Sort the result set by OrderDate so that the oldest orders appear first. Save the query as Between_Case1_Q4.

Your result should look like:

OrderID	OrderDate	PackageWeight	MaterialCost	InvoiceAmount
573	12/29/2022	29.1	61	328
777	12/29/2022	27	16	196
260	12/27/2022	31.7	3	8
943	12/27/2022	38.8	59	341

```
(There are more records in the result set than the ones shown in this image)
(235 row(s) returned)
```

5. The salespeople need a list of orders with invoice amounts between $200 and $300 and with order dates in the month of September for all the years we have data in the database. Create a new query that includes the fields OrderID, OrderDate, PackageWeight, MaterialCost, and InvoiceAmount from the Orders table and satisfies the salespeople request. Order the results by invoice amounts so that smaller amounts appear first. Save the query as Between_Case1_Q5.

Your result should look like:

OrderID	OrderDate	PackageWeight	MaterialCost	InvoiceAmount
808	9/24/2022	22.3	52	200
912	9/16/2020	28.3	69	201
650	9/24/2022	21.7	70	204
751	9/24/2021	32.2	71	206

```
(There are more records in the result set than the ones shown in this image)
(20 row(s) returned)
```

Case 2

For each of the questions in this case you need to create a new query in SQL view and name it as per the instructions in each question.

1. The management of the company needs to review shipped orders within the year 2022 but outside of the months January through March. Create a new query that includes the fields OrderID, ShippedDate, QuotationAmount, ProcessingCost, and DailyInventoryCost from the Orders table and satisfies the above criteria. Order the results by ShippedDate so that the latest shipments show first. Save the query as Between_Case2_Q1.

Your result should look like:

OrderID	ShippedDate	QuotationAmount	ProcessingCost	DailyInventoryCost
156	12/31/2022	256	2.38	0.95
245	12/30/2022	342	14.53	5.81
831	12/28/2022	226	15.89	1.29
561	12/26/2022	361	15.34	6.13

```
(There are more records in the result set than the ones shown in this image)
(246 row(s) returned)
```

2. The marketing people need a list of orders shipped within the period June 2022 to December 2022 which also have quotation amounts between $200 and $300. Create a new query that includes the fields OrderID, ShippedDate, QuotationAmount, ProcessingCost, and DailyInventoryCost from the Orders table and satisfies the above criteria. Sort results by QuotationAmount so that bigger amounts show on top. Save the query as Between_Case2_Q2.

Your result should look like:

OrderID	ShippedDate	QuotationAmount	ProcessingCost	DailyInventoryCost
74	8/15/2022	292	1.78	0.71
644	7/1/2022	287	8.75	3.17
66	8/19/2022	286	1.53	0.61
435	7/26/2022	286	1.53	0.61

```
(There are more records in the result set than the ones shown in this image)
(53 row(s) returned)
```

3. The inventory people need a report of orders shipped within the month of June for all the years we have data and with a processing cost outside the range of 2 to 4. They had a breakdown with their trucks, and they need to compare their shipment slips with your report data to see if they missed any shipments. Create a new query that includes the fields OrderID, ShippedDate, QuotationAmount, ProcessingCost, and DailyInventoryCost from the Orders table and satisfies the above criteria. Save the query as Between_Case2_Q3.

Your result should look like:

OrderID	ShippedDate	QuotationAmount	ProcessingCost	DailyInventoryCost
79	6/12/2022	154	2.29	0.91
362	6/25/2022	228	3.31	1.32
416	6/5/2021	76	3.23	1.29
426	6/30/2022	48	2.04	0.81

```
(There are more records in the result set than the ones shown in this image)
(15 row(s) returned)
```

4. The accounting department asks for a report of orders with quotation amounts between $0 and $50 shipped in the year 2022. You must use the year() function to define the year as 2022. There have been discrepancies with the billing of small orders which need to be checked. Create a new query that includes the fields OrderID, ShippedDate, QuotationAmount, ProcessingCost, and DailyInventoryCost from the Orders table and satisfies the above criteria. Sort results so that smaller quotation amounts appear first. Save the query as Between_Case2_Q4.

Your result should look like:

OrderID	ShippedDate	QuotationAmount	ProcessingCost	DailyInventoryCost
20	11/18/2022	18	0.76	0.3
363	9/22/2022	19	0.8	0.32
737	8/18/2022	24	9.47	0.4
940	10/31/2022	33	2.67	0.56

```
(There are more records in the result set than the ones shown in this image)
(12 row(s) returned)
```

5. The senior management of the company needs a report that lists the orders shipped in July, September, and November 2022. It has been reported to them that orders shipped in those months experienced higher processing cycles. Consequently, they want to check those months, especially for orders with daily inventory costs between 5 and 10. Create a new query that includes the fields OrderID, ShippedDate, QuotationAmount, ProcessingCost, and DailyInventoryCost from the Orders table and satisfies the above criteria. Sort the results so that bigger daily inventory costs show first. Save the query as Between_Case2_Q5. **Hint**: Pay attention to enclose all three date intervals in parenthesis when using AND with the DailyInventoryCost, otherwise your code will not produce the desired results.

Your result should look like:

OrderID	ShippedDate	QuotationAmount	ProcessingCost	DailyInventoryCost
325	9/7/2022	588	24.99	9.99
687	11/2/2022	519	1.14	8.82
836	11/23/2022	502	1.53	8.53
968	7/30/2022	494	2.29	8.39

```
(There are more records in the result set than the ones shown in this image)
(14 row(s) returned)
```

CHAPTER 9
DYNAMIC FILTERS WITH THE IN OPERATOR

The IN operator is used to create search conditions for filtering records and it is always used in the WHERE clause of the SQL statement. It has two major uses: First, it takes the place of multiple OR operators. We create much cleaner search expressions with IN instead of using multiple OR operators. Second, we use IN to create subqueries, that is, dynamic search conditions. For example, we can look for customers in the Customers table using criteria from the Orders table. The IN operator is indispensable when used with subqueries as it will be shown briefly in this chapter and in detail in the chapter dedicated to subqueries. Using IN with subqueries allows the database professional to obtain results that would have been very difficult or impossible to obtain otherwise. Finally, the IN operator can be used with text, number, and date data. The IN operator should be well understood and at the top of the toolbox of a database user or developer.

57. Filter data with IN using multiple text values as criteria

Create a report of customers from multiple cities

Discussion:

We want to list all customers from the cities of New York, Boston, Chicago, Los Angeles, and Dallas. We could use the OR operator to produce this report:

Code:

```
SELECT FirstName, LastName, City, State, CustomerSince, BonusPoints
FROM Customers
WHERE city = 'New York'
OR city = 'Boston'
OR city = 'Chicago'
OR city = 'Los Angeles'
OR city = 'Dallas'
```

Using multiple OR operators to obtain a solution is tedious in both time and effort. Then, as soon as we provide the report to the supervisor, she comes back and says: "This is excellent; can I please have another report with our customers in the rest of the cities in the country?" To produce the second report, we will need to create a multitude of OR statements with the remaining cities. The IN operator solves these problems quickly and efficiently.

Code:

```
SELECT FirstName, LastName, City, State, CustomerSince, BonusPoints
FROM Customers
WHERE city in ('New York', 'Boston', 'Chicago', 'Los Angeles', 'Dallas')
```

Result:

FirstName	LastName	City	State	CustomerSince	BonusPoints
John	Demarco	New York	NY	1/22/2021	543
Mary	Demania	New York	NY	7/17/2022	2977
George	Demers	New York	NY	3/11/2022	3875
Phillip	Demetriou	New York	NY	10/12/2021	1337

```
(There are more records in the result set than the ones shown in this image)
(99 row(s) returned)
```

58. Filter data with NOT IN excluding multiple text criteria

Create a report of customers excluding several cities

Discussion:

This time, our supervisor reverses the request and asks for a report of customers from all cities not included in our previous report—every city except New York, Boston, Chicago, Los Angeles, and Dallas. Since we have the code using the IN operator from the previous example, the only thing we need to do is put the keyword "NOT" in front of the IN operator!

Code:

```
SELECT FirstName, LastName, City, State, CustomerSince, BonusPoints
FROM Customers
WHERE city NOT IN ('New York', 'Boston', 'Chicago', 'Los Angeles', 'Dallas')
```

Result:

FirstName	LastName	City	State	CustomerSince	BonusPoints
Kenneth	Vanton	Albany	NY	4/6/2021	3290
Luis	Trindan	Albany	NY	5/3/2020	1871
Linda	Cendernic	Philadelphia	PA	9/25/2021	1125
Kelly	Costa	Philadelphia	PA	8/17/2021	3812

```
(There are more records in the result set than the ones shown in this image)
(102 row(s) returned)
```

59. Filter data with IN using multiple numbers as criteria

Create a report of products based on their prices

Discussion:

In this scenario, we need to produce a report that lists products from our product catalog with the following prices: 15, 19, 22, 23, and 42. Since the numbers are not sequential, we cannot use the BETWEEN operator to get our results. We can, however, use the IN operator to produce the report as fast. When we employ IN with numbers, we do not use quotes.

Code:

```
SELECT ProductName, IngredientType, ProductWeight, ProductPrice
FROM Products
WHERE ProductPrice in (15, 19, 22, 23, 42)
```

Result:

ProductName	IngredientType	ProductWeight	ProductPrice
Almonds Roasted and Salted	Organic	7 oz	22
Chunky Pretzels	All-Natural	14 oz	22
Roasted & Salted Almonds	GMO-Free	1.5 lb	19
Cream and honey biscuits	GMO-Free	11 oz	22

```
(There are more records in the result set than the ones shown in this image)
(11 row(s) returned)
```

60. Filter data with IN using multiple dates as criteria

Create a report of products based on prices

Discussion:

We have a request from the sales department to have a look at the orders in the first day of the three summer months of 2022. They are missing an order and they want to know what happened and communicate with the customer. Pay attention that the dates used as criteria are actual date values and not ranges. We cannot use date ranges with the IN operator.

Code:

```
SELECT OrderID, OrderDate, ShippedDate, InvoiceAmount
FROM Orders
WHERE
OrderDate IN (#6/1/2022#, #7/1/2022#, #8/1/2022#)
```

Result:

OrderID	OrderDate	ShippedDate	InvoiceAmount
170	6/1/2022	6/6/2022	107
201	7/1/2022	7/6/2022	394
905	7/1/2022	7/6/2022	149
959	6/1/2022	6/6/2022	157

```
(4 row(s) returned)
```

61. Use IN to search for the same value in multiple fields

Search for the same text value in multiple fields

Discussion:

Let us assume we have inherited an un-normalized database and we need to search for the same value in multiple fields. For instance, the previous database administrator might have used four "SupplierName" fields in the products table to keep track of available suppliers for the same product. This is unacceptable under database normalization rules and our first step should be to normalize our database which means creating a separate supplier table. However, if we must do the search now, the IN operator can solve our problem if we use it upside down!

For instance, we normally use the IN operator such as: **Field IN (value1, value2, value3).** To search an un-normalized database, we do **value IN (field1, field2, field3).** We can search in multiple unrelated fields. For instance, we can search for the value "Davis" in the Firstname, Lastname, and Address fields in the customer table to find a customer whose first name is Davis, or last name is Davis, or we have an address with the name Davis! As you can see, we have two records returned with the name "Davis" in the Lastname and Address fields. This result is not correct unfortunately as we shall see in the next example.

Code:

```
SELECT FirstName, LastName, Address, City, State
FROM Customers
WHERE 'Davis' IN (Firstname, Lastname, Address)
```

Result:

FirstName	LastName	Address	City	State
Roy	Sars	Davis	Los Angeles	CA
Catherine	Davis	87 Coral Street	Boston	MA

(2 row(s) returned)

62. Pay attention to the different filtering functionality of IN vs LIKE

LIKE can be used with wildcard characters and IN is working with exact values only

Discussion:

In the previous example, we have retrieved two records when we used IN to search for the value "Davis" in the FirstName, LastName, and Address fields. However, there is one more "Davis" entry in the Address field that IN did not pick up. LIKE will retrieve it as you can see in the code below. Using LIKE with multiple OR operators produces all entries for "Davis" in the three fields. IN is a very strong and very useful operator, and the purpose of this example is to show how to use it, what to expect, and how to think about data retrieval.

Code:

```
SELECT FirstName, LastName, Address, City, State
FROM Customers
WHERE LastName LIKE '*Davis*' OR Firstname LIKE '*Davis*' OR Address LIKE '*Davis*'
```

Result:

FirstName	LastName	Address	City	State
Roy	Sars	Davis	Los Angeles	CA
Matthew	Baker	89 Davis Ave	Dallas	TX
Catherine	Davis	87 Coral Street	Boston	MA

(3 row(s) returned)

63. Filter the records in a table using criteria from a different table

Filter the Customers table using criteria from the Orders table

Discussion

The IN operator shows its real power when used with criteria generated dynamically. Instead of typing in the values for the IN operator, we use subqueries to create value lists automatically. In this example, we are looking for a list of customers who have orders with an invoice amount above 400. The problem with this request is that we want to retrieve records from the Customers table using criteria from the Orders table. We have two solutions in this case, one that will take forever to implement, and the other that will take a couple of minutes:

Forever Solution: Create a query on the Orders table retrieving the CustomerIDs (Foreign Keys) for which the invoice amount is above 400. Then, create a new query on the Customers table entering manually those CustomerIDs in a filtering expression with LIKE, equality predicates, IN (preferred) etc. It will take a lot of time to create and even more time to maintain such a query.

Two-minute Solution: Create a subquery. The subquery in this case will generate a list of CustomerIDs from the Orders table for which the InvoiceAmount is above 400. Then, this dynamic list of CustomerIDs will be used as filtering criteria by the IN operator on the Customers table. This way, we dynamically create a list of values for the IN operator. That is, if more orders with InvoiceAmounts above 400 are entered in the Orders table, this code does not need any updates, it will still work.

Code:

```
SELECT FirstName, LastName, Address, City, MembershipType
FROM Customers
WHERE CustomerID
IN (SELECT CustomerID FROM Orders WHERE InvoiceAmount > 400)
```

Result:

FirstName	LastName	Address	City	MembershipType
Mary	Demania	12 Madison Ave	New York	Gold
George	Demers	23 New Scotland Ave	New York	Platinum
Kenneth	Vanton	855 Hackett Blvd	Albany	Platinum
Joseph	Anderson	34 Cortland Ave	Los Angeles	Platinum

```
(There are more records in the result set than the ones shown in this image)
(51 row(s) returned)
```

Wait, we are not done yet. There is a question for you: Why the above code produces 51 records and the one below 56?

Code:

```
SELECT CustomerID FROM Orders WHERE InvoiceAmount > 400
```

Result:

CustomerID
196
85
177
25

```
(There are more records in the result set than the ones shown in this image)
(56 row(s) returned)
```

Answer:

Some customers have more than one order in the Orders table but they will appear only once in the main query that retrieves customers from the Customers table.

64. Use IN with GROUP BY and HAVING to use grouped data as criteria in subqueries

Generate a report of orders for which all included products have a discount of zero

Discussion

In this example, we want to produce a list of orders for which all the included products have a discount of zero. That is, if four products are included in an order, the discount rate for all four of them should be zero. To obtain this result, we will use the IN operator to look in the JoinOrdersProducts table for OrderIDs of orders with zero total discounts.

We will obtain the result we want by using the IN operator, a subquery, the GROUP BY clause, the HAVING clause, and the sum() function. In the subquery, the GROUP BY clause will run first to produce a list of unique OrderIDs since we group by OrderID. Then, the HAVING clause will filter out any OrderIDs with a discount different than zero. Next, the SELECT statement in the subquery will generate the list of OrderIDs for which the total discount is equal to zero. Finally, the WHERE clause in the main query will use the OrderIDs generated from the subquery as criteria to filter orders from the Orders table.

Code:

```
SELECT Orderid, Orderdate, ShippedDate, InvoiceAmount
FROM Orders
WHERE Orderid
IN (SELECT Orderid FROM JoinOrdersProducts GROUP BY OrderID HAVING sum(Discount) =0)
```

Result:

Orderid	Orderdate	ShippedDate	InvoiceAmount
30	6/2/2022	6/7/2022	275
124	1/30/2020	2/4/2020	122
273	3/26/2020	3/31/2020	126
356	3/3/2020	3/8/2020	32

(There are more records in the result set than the ones shown in this image)
(10 row(s) returned)

65. Filter data with IN using date ranges in subqueries

Find customers who have not placed any orders in the second half of 2022

Discussion

In this scenario we look for customers who have not placed any orders in the second half of 2022. The management needs this information to initiate promotions for inactive customers. We will use the NOT IN operator, the BETWEEN operator, and a subquery for this task. Remember that the purpose of a subquery is always the same—to generate a list of values to be used by the IN operator. Here, the subquery will generate a list of CustomerIDs from the Orders table, which will be used by the main query to filter records in the Customers table.

Code:

```
SELECT FirstName, LastName, City, MemberShipType
FROM Customers
WHERE CustomerID NOT IN
(Select CustomerID FROM Orders WHERE
OrderDate BETWEEN #6/1/2022# AND #12/31/2022#)
```

Result:

FirstName	LastName	City	MemberShipType
Andrew	Demichele	New York	Silver
Paul	Demarist	New York	Gold
Matthew	Demaria	New York	Platinum
Pindar	Ames	New York	Platinum

(There are more records in the result set than the ones shown in this image)
(82 row(s) returned)

66. Filter data with IN using date functions in subqueries

Find customers who have not placed any orders in the year 2022

Discussion

Continuing from the previous example, we now want to retrieve customers who have not placed any orders in the year 2022. Of course, we do not track years separately in the Orders table, but we can easily extract the year out of the OrderDate field using the year() function. Then, we can use it in the subquery as shown below. Only fifty customers have not placed any orders in the year 2022. This type of query is excellent to keep track of customer retention rates in business.

Code:

```
SELECT FirstName, LastName, City, MemberShipType
FROM Customers
WHERE CustomerID NOT IN
(Select CustomerID FROM Orders WHERE year(orderdate) = 2022)
```

Result:

FirstName	LastName	City	MemberShipType
Matthew	Demaria	New York	Platinum
Pindar	Ames	New York	Platinum
Erin	Erin	Los Angeles	Platinum
Roy	Sars	Los Angeles	Silver

(There are more records in the result set than the ones shown in this image)
(50 row(s) returned)

DISCUSSION QUESTIONS

1. What are the primary roles of the IN operator?
2. Why is it a good idea to use IN instead of multiple OR operators?
3. What is a subquery?
4. What are the data types with which we can use the IN operator?
5. What is the purpose of the NOT IN operator?
6. Can we use the IN operator with dates?
7. Can we use date ranges with the IN operator?
8. How can we provide dynamic lists for the IN operator?
9. How can we filter data in one table using criteria from another table?
10. Can we use the GROUP BY and HAVING clauses with the IN operator in a subquery?

HANDS-ON EXERCISES

Case 1

For each of the questions in this case create a new query in SQL view and name it as per the instructions in each question.

1. Create a list of customers in the States of New York, California, and Florida. Create a new query that includes the fields FirstName, LastName, City, State, CustomerSince, and MembershipType from the Customers table satisfying this request. Save the query as IN_Case1_Q1.

Your result should look like:

FirstName	LastName	City	State	CustomerSince	MembershipType
John	Demarco	New York	NY	1/22/2021	Silver
Mary	Demania	New York	NY	7/17/2022	Gold
George	Demers	New York	NY	3/11/2022	Platinum
Phillip	Demetriou	New York	NY	10/12/2021	Gold

```
(There are more records in the result set than the ones shown in this image)
(100 row(s) returned)
```

2. Your supervisor needs a report of customers who do not reside in the States of Ohio and Texas. Create a new query that includes the fields FirstName, LastName, City, State, CustomerSince, and MembershipType from the Customers table satisfying your supervisor's request. Save the query as IN_Case1_Q2.

Your result should look like:

FirstName	LastName	City	State	CustomerSince	MembershipType
John	Demarco	New York	NY	1/22/2021	Silver
Mary	Demania	New York	NY	7/17/2022	Gold
George	Demers	New York	NY	3/11/2022	Platinum
Phillip	Demetriou	New York	NY	10/12/2021	Gold

```
(There are more records in the result set than the ones shown in this image)
(162 row(s) returned)
```

3. The salespeople need a list of customers with orders which have a quotation amount above $300. Create a new query that includes the fields FirstName, LastName, City, State, CustomerSince, MembershipType from the Customers table satisfying this request. Save the query as IN_Case1_Q3.

Your result should look like:

FirstName	LastName	City	State	CustomerSince	MembershipType
Mary	Demania	New York	NY	7/17/2022	Gold
George	Demers	New York	NY	3/11/2022	Platinum
Phillip	Demetriou	New York	NY	10/12/2021	Gold
Robert	Demaggio	New York	NY	5/6/2021	Gold

```
(There are more records in the result set than the ones shown in this image)
(147 row(s) returned)
```

4. The sales department is asking for a list of customers who have placed orders between January 1, 2021, and June 30, 2021. Create a new query that includes the fields FirstName, LastName, City, State, CustomerSince, MembershipType from the Customers table and satisfies this request. Save the query as IN_Case1_Q4.

Your result should look like:

FirstName	LastName	City	State	CustomerSince	MembershipType
John	Demarco	New York	NY	1/22/2021	Silver
Mary	Demania	New York	NY	7/17/2022	Gold
Nicholas	Demaico	New York	NY	11/18/2021	Gold
Paul	Demarist	New York	NY	10/24/2020	Gold

```
(There are more records in the result set than the ones shown in this image)
(117 row(s) returned)
```

5. The salespeople are asking for a list of customers who have not placed any orders between July 1, 2022, and December 31, 2022. Create a new query that includes the fields FirstName, LastName, City, State, CustomerSince, MembershipType from the Customers table and satisfies this request. Save the query as IN_Case1_Q5.

Your result should look like:

FirstName	LastName	City	State	CustomerSince	MembershipType
Mary	Demania	New York	NY	7/17/2022	Gold
Andrew	Demichele	New York	NY	9/27/2020	Silver
Robert	Demaggio	New York	NY	5/6/2021	Gold
Paul	Demarist	New York	NY	10/24/2020	Gold

```
(There are more records in the result set than the ones shown in this image)
(97 row(s) returned)
```

Case 2

For each of the questions in this case create a new query in SQL view and name it as per the instructions in each question.

1. Your supervisor is asking for a list of sales representatives who reside in the zip codes 22459 and 12189. Create a new query that includes the SalesRepID, FirstName, LastName, City, Zip, Salary, Bonus, and DateOfHire fields from the SalesReps table and satisfies the supervisor's request. Save the query as IN_Case2_Q1.

Your result should look like:

SalesRepID	FirstName	LastName	City	Zip	Salary	Bonus	DateOfHire
1	John	Anderson	Boston	22459	108000	10000	1/1/2001
2	Mary	Teall	Boston	22459	110000	20000	6/12/2021
3	George	Spicer	Boston	22459	89000	15000	5/15/2004
4	Phillip	Zensons	New York	12189	125000	10000	6/10/2021

(There are more records in the result set than the ones shown in this image)
(8 row(s) returned)

2. HR needs a list of sales reps who have been hired on 'June 12, 2021, or May 12, 2021. Create a new query that includes the fields SalesRepID, FirstName, LastName, City, Zip, Salary, Bonus, and DateOfHire from the SalesReps table and satisfies this request. You must use IN to create your query. Save the query as IN_Case2_Q2.

Your result should look like:

SalesRepID	FirstName	LastName	City	Zip	Salary	Bonus	DateOfHire
2	Mary	Teall	Boston	22459	110000	20000	6/12/2021
7	Jason	Vanderback	New York	12189	102000	20000	5/12/2021

(2 row(s) returned)

3. The HR department is asking for a report of sales representatives who do not have any orders in the last 15 days of December 2022, that is in the holiday period (17 December to 31 December). HR feels these employees are not getting the help and training they need to be successful in their jobs. Create a new query that includes the fields SalesRepID, FirstName, LastName, City, Zip, Salary, Bonus, and DateOfHire from the SalesReps table satisfying the HR request. Save the query as IN_Case2_Q3.

Your result should look like:

SalesRepID	FirstName	LastName	City	Zip	Salary	Bonus	DateOfHire
1	John	Anderson	Boston	22459	108000	10000	1/1/2001
4	Phillip	Zensons	New York	12189	125000	10000	6/10/2021
7	Jason	Vanderback	New York	12189	102000	20000	5/12/2021
10	Gerald	Williams	Dallas	52347	120000	15000	1/11/2012

(4 row(s) returned)

4. Your supervisor is asking you to look for sales reps with orders which have in invoice amounts above $500. Create a new query that includes the fields SalesRepID, FirstName, LastName, City, Zip, Salary, Bonus, and DateOfHire from the SalesReps table satisfying your supervisor's request. Save the query as IN_Case2_Q4.

Your result should look like:

SalesRepID	FirstName	LastName	City	Zip	Salary	Bonus	DateOfHire
3	George	Spicer	Boston	22459	89000	15000	5/15/2004
4	Phillip	Zensons	New York	12189	125000	10000	6/10/2021
6	Kenneth	Delaney	New York	12189	98000	15000	5/10/2020
9	Jim	Baker	Dallas	52347	115000	15000	1/10/2018
10	Gerald	Williams	Dallas	52347	120000	15000	1/11/2012

(5 row(s) returned)

5. The marketing department is asking for a list of sales reps who processed orders paid with cash on delivery. Create a new query that includes the fields SalesRepID, FirstName, LastName, City, Zip, Salary, Bonus, and DateOfHire from the SalesReps table satisfying the marketing department's request. Save the query as IN_Case2_Q5.

Your result should look like:

SalesRepID	FirstName	LastName	City	Zip	Salary	Bonus	DateOfHire
1	John	Anderson	Boston	22459	108000	10000	1/1/2001
2	Mary	Teall	Boston	22459	110000	20000	6/12/2021
3	George	Spicer	Boston	22459	89000	15000	5/15/2004
4	Phillip	Zensons	New York	12189	125000	10000	6/10/2021

```
(There are more records in the result set than the ones shown in this image)
(10 row(s) returned)
```

CHAPTER 10
RETRIEVING UNIQUE RECORDS - THE DISTINCT PREDICATE

The DISTINCT predicate is used to eliminate duplicate rows from the results of a SELECT statement. It belongs to a set of four predicates (ALL, TOP, DISTINCT, DISTINCTROW) which we use to manipulate the number of records returned from a SQL statement. All four of them are used right after the SELECT keyword, and all of them are optional. If we do not use a predicate with the SELECT statement, [ALL] is assumed by default.

```
SELECT [ALL] [TOP] [DISTINCT] [DISTINCTROW] field1, field2, ... fieldn
FROM table
```

From the four predicates above, we will focus on DISTINCT in this chapter and TOP in the next one, since they are the ones used the most in practice. The column on which we use DISTINCT will return only its unique values. When we apply DISTINCT on multiple columns, the database will return the unique combinations of their values. Let us see how this works through examples.

67. A SELECT statement without the DISTINCT predicate

Retrieve cities in which we have customers

Discussion:

Using a classic SQL statement to retrieve the "city" from the Customers table will return multiple instances of the same city since it is logical to have multiple customers in the same city. For example, in the result set, New York appears as many times as the number of customers we have in this city. There are 201 records returned with multiple instances of various cities.

Code:

```
SELECT city
FROM customers
```

Result:

city
New York
New York
New York
New York

(There are more records in the result set than the ones shown in this image)
(201 row(s) returned)

68. A SELECT statement with the DISTINCT predicate

Retrieve unique cities in which we have customers

Discussion:

Sometimes, however, we need to select only unique names of the cities where we have customers. That is, we would like New York to appear only once, Boston only once, Los Angeles only once, and every other city name only once. This is the case where we use the DISTINCT predicate. In the result below, the value of each city is unique.

Code:

```
SELECT DISTINCT city
FROM customers
```

Result:

city
Albany
Boston
Chicago
Dallas

```
(There are more records in the result set than the ones shown in this image)
(15 row(s) returned)
```

69. Use DISTINCT on multiple columns to retrieve unique combinations of values

Retrieve unique combinations of cities and states

Discussion:

In this example, the DISTINCT predicate will return unique combinations of cities and states. Notice in the result set, that although some states appear multiple times, the combinations of cities and states are always unique. The same is true for the city field. If we had a city with the same name in multiple states, it would appear multiple times in the result set as soon as the city-state combinations were unique.

Code:

```
SELECT DISTINCT city, state FROM Customers
```

Result:

city	state
Albany	NY
Boston	MA
Chicago	OH
Dallas	TX

```
(There are more records in the result set than the ones shown in this image)
(15 row(s) returned)
```

70. Understanding the effect of DISTINCT on multiple columns

Finding unique customer names in various states

Discussion:

This is an additional example to understand what to expect when we use DISTINCT on multiple columns.

Code Case 1:

If we run a simple SELECT statement, we will get five customers with a first name John. Actually, these are all the Johns we have in our Customers table.

```
SELECT FirstName, State
FROM Customers
WHERE FirstName = 'John'
```

Result:

FirstName	State
John	NY
John	TX
John	TX
John	TX
John	CO

(5 row(s) returned)

If we include the DISTINCT predicate such as:

Code Case 2: (notice that the SQL code is case insensitive)

```
SELECT DISTINCT firstname, state
FROM customers
WHERE firstname = 'John'
```

We will get only three customers with a first name John. This is because we told the database to return unique combinations of first names and states. In the previous result set, we have three Johns in Texas. Since we have used DISTINCT on both the firstname and state, only one of the three will appear. The problem with DISTINCT and filtering criteria on multiple columns is that we cannot exactly control which ones will appear in the result set, and we might get results that we have not intended. So, pay extra attention when using DISTINCT and filtering statements on multiple columns.

Result:

firstname	state
John	CO
John	NY
John	TX

(3 row(s) returned)

71. Calculating the number of occurrences of unique values using GROUP BY

Retrieve unique city values and calculate their occurences

Discussion:

Although thematically it does not belong here, our next logical thought is probably: Okay, I know how to retrieve unique values of cities, states, job titles, and other fields. However, what is the total number I have from each? To answer this question, we use the GROUP BY clause, which we will explore in detail in its own chapter. Here, we calculate the number of instances of each city in the Customers table.

Code:

```
SELECT City, Count(City) AS NumberOfCities
FROM Customers
GROUP BY City
```

Result:

City	NumberOfCities
Albany	4
Boston	14
Chicago	14
Dallas	13

(There are more records in the result set than the ones shown in this image)
(15 row(s) returned)

DISCUSSION QUESTIONS

1. What is the primary role of the DISTINCT predicate?
2. What other predicates similar to DISTINCT can be used to manipulate the number of rows retrieved?
3. Is DISTINCT a required predicate or an optional one?
4. Can we use the DISTINCT predicate on multiple columns?
5. What is the default predicate used if we do not use DISTINCT in the SQL statement?
6. If we use DISTINCT on one column, what kind of values do we retrieve from that column?
7. If we use DISTINCT on multiple columns, what kind of values do we retrieve from those columns?
8. Where in the SELECT statement do we place the DISTINCT predicate?
9. From the four possible predicates of the SELECT statement which two are the most useful?
10. What do we need to pay attention to when we use DISTINCT with other filtering keywords such as equality and inequality predicates?

HANDS-ON EXERCISES

Case 1

For each of the questions in this case create a new query in SQL view and name it as per the instructions in each question.

1. Your supervisor is asking for a list of unique states in which we have customers. Create a new query that satisfies your supervisor's request. Order results by State ascending. Save the query as Distinct_Case1_Q1.

Your result should look like:

State
AZ
CA
CO
DC

```
(There are more records in the result set than the ones shown in this image)
(10 row(s) returned)
```

2. The marketing department is asking for a name day list so that they can send greeting cards to customers. They are asking you to give them a list of unique first names of customers. Create a new query that satisfies the marketing request. Order results by FirstName ascending. Save the query as Distinct_Case1_Q2.

Your result should look like:

FirstName
Alfred
Allan
Allen
Andrew

```
(There are more records in the result set than the ones shown in this image)
(70 row(s) returned)
```

3. The inventory people need a list of different SKUs we have in the Products table. Create a new query that satisfies the inventory department request. Order results by SKU ascending. Save the query as Distinct_Case1_Q3.

Your result should look like:

SKU
ADSE 2345
ADST 2345
ADSD 2345
ADSL 2345

(There are more records in the result set than the ones shown in this image)
(17 row(s) returned)

4. The inventory people came back, and they are now asking for a list that will display the unique SKUs as well as the number of products associated with each SKU. Create a query that satisfies this request and order results by SKU ascending. Save the query as Distinct_Case1_Q4.

Your result should look like:

SKU	CountNumber
ADSE 2345	1
ADST 2345	1
ADSD 2345	1
ADSL 2345	1

(There are more records in the result set than the ones shown in this image)
(17 row(s) returned)

5. The marketing people are back asking for a list of unique first names of customers and their respective numbers so that they know how many customers they have for each name day occasion. Create a query that satisfies this request and order results by FirstName ascending. Save the query as Distinct_Case1_Q5.

Your result should look like:

FirstName	CountNumber
Alfred	3
Allan	2
Allen	3
Andrew	2

(There are more records in the result set than the ones shown in this image)
(70 row(s) returned)

Case 2

For each of the questions in this case create a new query in SQL view and name it as per the instructions in each question.

1. The salespeople need a list of unique membership types from the Customers table. Create a new query that satisfies the sales department request. Order results by membership type ascending. Save the query as Distinct_Case2_Q1.

Your result should look like:

MembershipType
Gold
Platinum
Silver

(3 row(s) returned)

2. The salespeople are now asking for a list of unique combinations of product container type and product weight. Create a new query that satisfies the sales department request. Order results by ContainerType ascending. Save the query as Distinct_Case2_Q2.

Your result should look like:

ContainerType	ProductWeight
Flexible Pouch	10 oz
Flexible Pouch	11 oz
Flexible Pouch	14 oz
Flexible Pouch	2 lb

```
(There are more records in the result set than the ones shown in this image)
(40 row(s) returned)
```

3. The salespeople are asking for a list that will display the unique cities in which we have sales representatives and calculate the number of those salesreps in each city. Create a query on the SalesReps table that satisfies this request and order results by city ascending. Save the query as Distinct_Case2_Q3.

Your result should look like:

City	CountNumber
Boston	3
Dallas	2
New York	5

```
(3 row(s) returned)
```

4. The manager of salespeople is asking for a list of unique discount levels from the JoinOrdersProducts table. He wants to have an idea of the various discount percentages sales reps offer to the customers to close the sale. Create a new query that satisfies the sales department request. Order results by discount level descending. Save the query as Distinct_Case2_Q4.

Your result should look like:

Discount
0.2
0.15
0

```
(3 row(s) returned)
```

5. The sales manager is also asking for a report that will display the unique discount percentages and the number of associated products for those unique discount percentages. Use the JoinOrdersProducts table. Create a query that satisfies this request and order results by discount level ascending. Save the query as Distinct_Case2_Q5.

Your result should look like:

Discount	ProductNumber
0	140
0.15	1621
0.2	650

```
(3 row(s) returned)
```

CHAPTER 11
RETRIEVING TOP OR BOTTOM SETS OF DATA

The TOP predicate is used to select a specified number or percentage of records from a table or query. It belongs to a set of four predicates (ALL, TOP, DISTINCT, DISTINCTROW) used to manipulate the number of records returned from a SQL statement. All four of them are used right after the SELECT keyword, and all of them are optional. If we do not use a predicate with the SELECT statement, [ALL] is assumed by default.

```
SELECT  [ALL] [TOP] [DISTINCT] [DISTINCTROW] field1, field2, ... fieldn
FROM table
```

The TOP predicate used alone is not very useful since it does not return records in any special order; it simply returns the first n or n% of the records as they are stored in the table. However, when the TOP predicate is combined with ORDER BY, GROUP BY, and WHERE clauses, it shows its real potential and practicality.

72. Retrieve the first n records from a table

Retrieve the first 5 records from the products table

Discussion:

In this example, the TOP predicate will return the first five records from the Products table in the order these records are stored in the table. This process is useless for our business needs since it does not provide any special information. This example is provided to demonstrate how TOP works by itself.

Code:

```
SELECT TOP 5 Productname, ProductPrice, ProductWeight, Unitsinstock, DateEnteredInventory
FROM Products
```

Result:

ProductName	ProductPrice	ProductWeight	Unitsinstock	DateEnteredInventory
Almonds Hickory Smoked	35	6 oz	40	5/4/2015
Almonds Roasted and Salted	22	7 oz	32	5/4/2011
Banana Chips	27	14 oz	25	12/9/2010
Berry Cherry	30	10 oz	50	6/27/2017
California Original Pistachios	29	2 lb	35	1/19/2014

(5 row(s) returned)

73. Retrieve the top n largest amounts

Retrieve the five products with the most units in stock

Discussion:

In this example, we select the five products with the highest levels of inventory. The TOP predicate in combination with the ORDER BY clause provides very practical results. We use the DESC keyword with the ORDER BY clause so that highest quantities appear first.

Code:

```
SELECT TOP 5 ProductName, ProductPrice, ProductWeight, Unitsinstock, DateEnteredInventory
FROM Products
ORDER BY UnitsInStock DESC
```

Result:

Productname	ProductPrice	ProductWeight	Unitsinstock	DateEnteredInventory
Chocolate Chip Cookies	49	8 oz	50	5/1/2018
Artichokes in white sauce	22	2 lb	50	7/12/2018
Berry Cherry	30	10 oz	50	6/27/2017
Green Sauce	35	8 oz	49	10/14/2010
Biscuits with Cream	27	2 lb	49	9/25/2017

(5 row(s) returned)

74. What to pay attention to with TOP results

Top will not always return the number of records specified

Discussion:

Let us try to retrieve the six products with the highest units on order. We use the code below and instead of getting six records we get twelve! Why is this? As you can see from the result set, the UnitsOnOrder for record six is 15 and it needs to be included in the result set. However, since there are six more records with a UnitsOnOrder number equal to 15, Access will display them in the result set as well. This TOP behavior differs in various database engines. Some of them would display only six records no matter how many identical numbers for units on order we have. This example is presented so that you are aware of this behavior in Access and check the TOP results in your analytics reports.

Code:

```
SELECT TOP 6 ProductName, ProductPrice, ProductWeight, UnitsOnOrder
FROM Products
ORDER BY UnitsOnOrder DESC
```

Result:

ProductName	ProductPrice	ProductWeight	UnitsOnOrder
Nacho Chips	25	14 oz	25
Chunky Chocolate Cookies	15	8 oz	20
Chocolate Chunk Cookies	48	2 lb	20
Oatmeal Raisin Walnut Cookies	43	2 lb	20

(There are more records in the result set than the ones shown in this image)
(12 row(s) returned)

75. Retrieve the top N% of highest numbers

Retrieve 10% of the products with the highest prices

Discussion:

This time, management asked for the top 10% of the most expensive products in the inventory. To answer, we will use the TOP predicate, the ORDER BY clause, and the word "10 PERCENT" (not 10%). Note that seven records have been returned because the total number of records in the Products table is seventy.

Code:

```
SELECT TOP 10 PERCENT ProductName, ProductPrice, ProductWeight, Unitsinstock,
DateEnteredInventory
FROM Products
ORDER BY ProductPrice DESC
```

Result:

ProductName	ProductPrice	ProductWeight	Unitsinstock	DateEnteredInventory
Coffee biscuits	50	7 oz	24	1/31/2016
Pepper Cheese Box	50	6 oz	45	3/28/2016
Pizza croutons	49	6 oz	44	7/30/2012
Chocolate Chip Cookies	49	8 oz	50	5/1/2018

```
(There are more records in the result set than the ones shown in this image)
(7 row(s) returned)
```

76. Retrieve the N latest dates - TOP with ORDER BY and dates

Retrieve the 5 most recent products that entered our inventory

Discussion:

In this example, we are looking for the five most recent products that entered our inventory. We use the DESC keyword and ORDER BY to obtain this result.

Code:

```
SELECT TOP 5 ProductName, ProductPrice, ProductWeight, Unitsinstock, DateEnteredInventory
FROM Products
ORDER BY DateEnteredInventory DESC
```

Result:

ProductName	ProductPrice	ProductWeight	Unitsinstock	DateEnteredInventory
Raspberry brownie bar	22	11 oz	23	12/28/2018
Coconut Chocolate Chip Cookies	25	7 oz	28	10/19/2018
Chocolate Covered Apples	37	9 oz	42	10/17/2018
Dried Cranberries	16	11 oz	45	8/31/2018
Artichokes in white sauce	22	2 lb	50	7/12/2018

```
(5 row(s) returned)
```

77. The TOP predicate with calculated fields and the GROUP BY clause

Retrieve the 5 largest orders from customers

Discussion:

Our manager asked for a report of the five orders with the highest amounts. We do not have order totals in the Orders table but we do have the quantity and price of each product sold in each order in the JoinOrdersProducts table. That is, if an order contained five products, we do have the price sold and the quantity sold for each product in the JoinOrdersProducts table. Therefore, we first calculate the order subtotals (multiply the quantity of each product with the price it was sold) for all the products contained in one order and do a GROUP BY on the OrderID followed by an ORDER BY DESC to get the largest orders. Then, we use the TOP predicate to retrieve only the five largest orders.

Code:

```
SELECT TOP 5 OrderID, Sum(unitprice*quantity) AS OrderAmount
FROM JoinOrdersProducts
GROUP BY OrderID
ORDER BY Sum(unitprice*quantity) DESC
```

Result:

OrderID	OrderAmount
354	576
944	574
609	530
308	512
404	510

(5 row(s) returned)

DISCUSSION QUESTIONS

1. What is the primary role of the TOP predicate?
2. What is the difference between TOP and TOP PERCENT?
3. What other predicates like TOP can be used to manipulate the number of rows retrieved?
4. Is TOP a required predicate or an optional one?
5. What is the default predicate if we do not specify one in the SQL statement?
6. What result shall we get when we use TOP by itself in the SQL statement?
7. What other SQL keywords can we use with TOP to retrieve useful results?
8. Where in the SELECT statement do we place the TOP predicate?
9. What do we need to pay attention to when using TOP?
10. What are some data types with which we can use TOP?

HANDS-ON EXERCISES

Case 1

For each of the questions in this case create a new query in SQL view and name it as per the instructions in each question.

1. The inventory people ask for a list of the five products with the highest quantities per unit. Create a new query that includes the ProductName, ProductPrice, QuantityPerUnit, ProductCost, and DateEnteredInventory fields from the Products table and satisfies the inventory department request. Save the query as TOP_Case1_Q1.

Your result should look like:

ProductName	ProductPrice	QuantityPerUnit	ProductCost	DateEnteredInventory
Coconut Chocolate Chip Cookies	25	35	8.3	10/19/2018
Chocolate Covered Apples	37	35	12.28	10/17/2018
Dark Chocolate Apricots	46	35	15.27	5/7/2010
Dried Blackberry	26	35	8.63	1/6/2018

(There are more records in the result set than the ones shown in this image)
(7 row(s) returned)

2. The inventory people are asking for a list that will display the top 15% of products with the highest product prices. Create a query that includes the ProductName, ProductPrice, QuantityPerUnit, ProductCost, and DateEnteredInventory fields from the Products table that satisfies the inventory people request. Save the query as TOP_Case1_Q2.

Your result should look like:

ProductName	ProductPrice	QuantityPerUnit	ProductCost	DateEnteredInventory
Coffee biscuits	50	30	16.6	1/31/2016
Pepper Cheese Box	50	22	16.6	3/28/2016
Pizza croutons	49	20	16.26	7/30/2012
Chocolate Chip Cookies	49	25	16.26	5/1/2018

(There are more records in the result set than the ones shown in this image)
(11 row(s) returned)

3. The marketing department is asking for a list of the five products that first entered inventory. Create a query that includes the ProductName, ProductPrice, QuantityPerUnit, ProductCost, and DateEnteredInventory fields

from the Products table that satisfies this request and save it as TOP_Case1_Q3.

Your result should look like:

ProductName	ProductPrice	QuantityPerUnit	ProductCost	DateEnteredInventory
Crispy Pears	33	20	10.95	1/24/2010
Chili Salsa	45	32	14.94	2/25/2010
Chocolate Almonds	25	25	8.3	4/5/2010
Chocolate Fudge	41	28	13.61	4/18/2010
Dark Chocolate Apricots	46	35	15.27	5/7/2010

(5 row(s) returned)

4. The sales department is looking for a list of the first five products in the Products table according to their physical sequence in the table. Create a query that includes the ProductName, ProductPrice, QuantityPerUnit, ProductCost, and DateEnteredInventory fields that satisfies this request. Save it as TOP_Case1_Q4.

Your result should look like:

ProductName	ProductPrice	QuantityPerUnit	ProductCost	DateEnteredInventory
Almonds Hickory Smoked	35	12	11.62	5/4/2015
Almonds Roasted and Salted	22	12	7.3	5/4/2011
Banana Chips	27	12	8.96	12/9/2010
Berry Cherry	30	15	9.96	6/27/2017
California Original Pistachios	29	15	9.62	1/19/2014

(5 row(s) returned)

5. The marketing department is asking for a list of the five products with the highest product cost. Create a query that includes the ProductName, ProductPrice, QuantityPerUnit, ProductCost, and DateEnteredInventory fields from the products table that satisfies this request. Save it as TOP_Case1_Q5.

Your result should look like:

ProductName	ProductPrice	QuantityPerUnit	ProductCost	DateEnteredInventory
Coffee biscuits	50	30	16.6	1/31/2016
Pepper Cheese Box	50	22	16.6	3/28/2016
Pizza croutons	49	20	16.26	7/30/2012
Chocolate Chip Cookies	49	25	16.26	5/1/2018
Fruit Dip	49	30	16.26	4/27/2014

(5 row(s) returned)

Case 2

For each of the questions in this case create a new query in SQL view and name it as per the instructions in each question.

1. The HR department is looking for a list of the four most senior employees in the organization. Create a query that includes the FirstName, LastName, Salary, Bonus, DateOfHire, and DateOfBirth fields from the SalesReps table and satisfies this request. Save the query as TOP_Case2_Q1.

Your result should look like:

FirstName	LastName	Salary	Bonus	DateOfHire	DateOfBirth
John	Anderson	108000	10000	1/1/2001	4/15/1980
George	Spicer	89000	15000	5/15/2004	4/4/1983
Gerald	Williams	120000	15000	1/11/2012	4/1/1992
Michael	Bernstein	95000	10000	5/25/2015	1/1/1985

(4 row(s) returned)

2. The sales department is looking for the four youngest employees in the organization. Create a query that includes the FirstName, LastName, Salary, Bonus, DateOfHire, and DateOfBirth fields from the Salesreps table and satisfies this request. Save it as TOP_Case2_Q2.

Your result should look like:

FirstName	LastName	Salary	Bonus	DateOfHire	DateOfBirth
Andrew	Simmons	95000	15000	5/11/2020	10/18/2001
Kenneth	Delaney	98000	15000	5/10/2020	5/25/2000
Mary	Teall	110000	20000	6/12/2021	2/6/2000
Phillip	Zensons	125000	10000	6/10/2021	4/3/1998

(4 row(s) returned)

3. The marketing department has asked for a list of the five largest orders from our customers. Create a query that includes the OrderID, and a calculated field named OrderAmount from the JoinOrdersProducts table and satisfies this request. Do not take into consideration discounts. Save the query as TOP_Case2_Q3.

Your result should look like:

OrderID	OrderAmount
1	30
2	210
3	231
4	45
5	253

(5 row(s) returned)

4. The marketing department is now asking for a report of the five largest orders for a particular product: California Original Pistachios. Create a query that includes the OrderID, and a calculated field named OrderAmount from the JoinOrdersProducts table and satisfies this request. Do not take into consideration discounts. Order results by OrderAmount descending. Save the query as TOP_Case2_Q4.

Your result should look like:

OrderID	OrderAmount
904	90
223	75
238	75
248	75
346	75
932	75

(6 row(s) returned)

5. The HR department is preparing for the employee of the year event and has asked for a list of the three SalesRepIDs with the most orders. Create a query that includes the SalesRepID field, and a calculated field named CountOfOrders using the count() function that satisfies this request. Use the Orders table. Save the

query as TOP_Case2_Q5.

Your result should look like:

SalesRepID	CountOfOrders
5	124
7	123
3	112

(3 row(s) returned)

CHAPTER 12
MOVING AND APPENDING DATA

Using SQL, we can copy, paste, append, and move data around fast, using simple code. Data migration is a fundamental skill for the SQL professional. A scenario where we are given a large data set on which we will use SQL to derive analytics, is a purely theoretical one. In practice, we will need to move data from multiple data sources such as tables and queries from other relational databases, NoSQL databases, data warehouses, data lakes, XML files, text files, and other formats so that we can construct the appropriate dataset to serve as the basis for our business intelligence goals. On some occasions, we will have to move all the data, sometimes only a subset of it, and in some cases only the source table structures. Let us explore some examples of accomplishing these tasks.

78. SELECT with INSERT INTO to append records to an existing table

Append records from the customer table to a historical table

Discussion:

Our goal in this example is to copy records from the Customers table and append them to another table in which we keep historical customer data. This scenario applies in situations where for instandfe we no longer do business with those customers, but we do not want to delete them from the database. At the same time, we do not want these old customer records to clutter our operational Customers table, slow it down, or interfere with our calculations. We can do this using the INSERT INTO statement and its syntax appears below:

```
INSERT INTO TargetTable (field1, field2, field3...)
SELECT (field1, field2, field3...)
FROM SourceTable
```

In this example, we copy records from the Customers table and add them to the Customer2 table. Since Customer2 does not exist, we create it with the CREATE statement below.

Code:

```
CREATE TABLE Customers31 (
[CustomerID] Counter Primary key,
[LastName] text(50),
[FirstName] text(50),
[Address] text(100),
[City] text(50))
```

Result:

```
Access does not provide any feedback but the table has been created successfully.
```

Code:

```
INSERT INTO Customers31 (FirstName, LastName, Address, City)
SELECT FirstName, LastName, Address, City
FROM Customers
```

Result:

```
You are about to append 201 row(s)
```

79. SELECT with INSERT INTO to append specific records into a table

Append selected customer records to a historical table

Discussion:

On some occasions, we might want to copy only a subset of records from one table into another table. We can achieve this by using the INSERT TO statement and the WHERE clause in combination. In this example, we append customer records from NY only.

Code:

```
INSERT INTO Customers31 (FirstName, LastName, Address, City)
SELECT FirstName, LastName, Address, City
FROM Customers
WHERE State = 'NY'
```

Result:

```
You are about to append 31 row(s)
```

80. SELECT INTO to create a backup or temporary table

Create a backup copy of the products table

Discussion:

The SELECT INTO statement accomplishes two tasks simultaneously. First, it creates a new table, and second, it populates this table with records from another table. We can use the SELECT INTO statement to create backup copies of tables, or we can create temporary tables and work on their data leaving the original tables untouched. For instance, we might want to manipulate data in the products table, but we would like to first see the results of the edits before we apply them in the operational products table. In this example, we create a backup copy of the products table, and we name it Products_Backup.

Code:

```
SELECT *
INTO Products_Backup
FROM Products
```

Result:

```
You are about to paste 70 row(s) into a new table.
```

81. SELECT INTO to create a backup table with a subset of data from the original table

Create a temporary table that contains a subset of data from the products table

Discussion:

We can use the SELECT INTO statement and the WHERE clause in combination to create a new table that will contain a subset of data from the original table. Using the SELECT INTO statement in combination with the WHERE clause, we can transfer any fields and records we wish. In this example, we create a new table named "Products_Subset" which will contain three fields and records from suppliers with supplier ID 1, 2, 3, and 4 only.

Code:

```
SELECT ProductName, UnitsInStock, UnitsOnOrder
INTO Products_Subset
FROM Products
WHERE SupplierID IN (1,2,3,4)
```

Result:

```
You are about to paste 32 row(s) into a new table.
```

82. SELECT INTO to create a new table with a subset of data from three joined tables

Create a new table that contains data from three joined tables

Discussion:

In this example, we create a new table that contains fields from the Customers, Orders, and JoinOrdersProducts tables. In addition, we filter the number of records it will contain by using the WHERE clause for customers in NY only. Why do we need to create a new table since we can easily retrieve the same records using a view? Such an action serves multiple purposes. First, we might want to give access to this data to other people and not worry if they edit or change it. If we provide them with a query, they could affect the data in the underlying tables. Another scenario might be that we would like to hide the complexities of the joins to the people working with this data. It is much easier to work with one table than with two inner joins from three tables. Finally, we might be in a business scenario in which this table is the data source for XML or PHP or ASP.Net or other server-side pages on our website, and we generate this table every week. Those pages will return results much faster working out of a table data source instead of multiple joins and WHERE clauses.

Code:

```
SELECT Customers.LastName, Customers.FirstName, Orders.OrderDate,
JoinOrdersProducts.UnitPrice, JoinOrdersProducts.Quantity
INTO TempCustomersOrders
FROM (Customers INNER JOIN Orders ON Customers.CustomerID = Orders.CustomerID) INNER
JOIN JoinOrdersProducts ON Orders.OrderID = JoinOrdersProducts.OrderID
WHERE Customers.State='NY'
```

Result:

```
You are about to paste 375 row(s) into a new table.
```

83. SELECT INTO to create a new table with the structure of an existing table but without any data

Discussion:

Using the code below, we will create a new table named "Products1" which will be identical to the Products table but without its data. Field names and corresponding data types transfer wonderfully but remember to define the primary key and any indexes in your new table as these properties do not transfer using SELECT INTO. However, the identity property of the primary key will transfer as is from the source table. That is, if in the Products table the identity property (auto-increasing values) is set to "Yes", it will transfer to the Products1 table as "Yes". If it is set to "No", it will transfer as "No" to the Products1 table. We must set the identity property of the destination Products1 PK to "No" so that we can transfer PK values from the Products table. Of course, we are in no way obligated to transfer primary key values from the source Products table as we can always transfer a subset of its fields. The business operation will dictate our choices of transferring PK values.

Code:

```
SELECT * INTO Products1
FROM Products
WHERE 1=2
```

Result:

```
You are about to paste 0 row(s) into a new table.
```

84. SELECT INTO to create a new table with part of the structure of an existing table

Discussion:

As a continuation from the previous example, we can transfer part of the structure of an existing table to a new one as in the code below. Remember, no data will be moved to the new table.

Code:

```
SELECT ProductID, ProductName, QuantityPerUnit, ProductPrice INTO Products2
FROM Products
WHERE 1=2
```

Result:

```
You are about to paste 0 row(s) into a new table.
```

DISCUSSION QUESTIONS

1. Why data migration is so important for business intelligence?
2. What is the role of the INSERT INTO statement?
3. What is the role of the SELECT INTO statement?
4. What is the difference between INSERT INTO and SELECT INTO?
5. What statement shall we use to append data to an existing table?
6. What statement shall we use to create a backup copy of a table?
7. What statement can we use to create a copy of the structure of an existing table?
8. What clause do we use to limit the number of records we move using INSERT INTO?
9. Can we use the WHERE clause with the SELECT INTO statement?
10. What keyword do we use to create and populate a new table using a single SELECT statement??

HANDS-ON EXERCISES

Case 1

For each of the questions in this case you need to create a new query in SQL view and name it as per the instructions in each question.

1. Create a copy of the Customers table and name it Customers32. Save the query as MovingRecords_Case1_Q1.

Result:

```
You are about to paste 201 row(s) into a new table.
```

2. Create a copy of the Customers table that includes only the FirstName, LastName, Address, City, State and Zip fields. Name this table Customers33. Save the query as MovingRecords_Case1_Q2.

Result:

```
You are about to paste 201 row(s) into a new table.
```

3. Create a copy of the Customers table that includes only the FirstName, LastName, Address, City, State and Zip fields. It must also include only customers from the state of Massachusetts. Name this table Customers34. Save the query as MovingRecords_Case1_Q3.

Result:

```
You are about to paste 14 row(s) into a new table.
```

4. Create a new table with the same design as the Customers table but without moving any data into it. Name this table Customers35. Then, open it in design view and assign the CustomerID as the PK field of the table and set its identity property to "No". Save the query as MovingRecords_Case1_Q4.

Result:

```
You are about to paste 0 row(s) into a new table.
```

5. Insert into Customers35, customers from the Customers table who have a silver membership type. Save the query as MovingRecords_Case1_Q5.

Result:
```
You are about to append 73 row(s).
```

Case 2

For each of the questions in this case you need to create a new query in SQL view and name it as per the instructions in each question.

1. Create a copy of the Products table. Name this copy Products32. Save the query as MovingRecords_Case2_Q1.

Result:
```
You are about to paste 70 row(s) into a new table.
```

2. Create a copy of the products table. However, only include the ProductName, QuantityPerUnit, ProductPrice, and UnitsInStock fields. Also, the copied table should include products only from suppliers with SupplierID 5,6,7,8, and 9. Name the new table Products33. Save the query as MovingRecords_Case2_Q2.

Result:
```
You are about to paste 34 row(s) into a new table.
```

3. Create a new table with the same structure as the Products table but without moving any data into this new table. Name this table Products34. Then, assign the ProductID as the PK of the table and set the identity property for the ProductID PK to "No". Check chapter 31 for more details on the identity property. Save the query as MovingRecords_Case2_Q3.

Result:
```
You are about to paste 0 row(s) into a new table.
```

4. Now, insert into the Products34 table only those products from the Products table whose price is more than $25. Save the query as MovingRecords_Case2_Q4.

Result:
```
You are about to append 45 row(s).
```

5. Create a query to select the fields ProductName, ContainerType, IngredientType, and ProductPrice from the Products34 table. Include products with ProductPrice above $48. Sort descending on ProductPrice. Save the query as MovingRecords_Case2_Q5.

Result:

ProductName	ContainerType	IngredientType	ProductPrice
Coffee biscuits	Flexible Pouch	All-Natural	50
Pepper Cheese Box	Paper Box	All-Natural	50
Fruit Dip	Flexible Pouch	Organic	49
Chocolate Chip Cookies	Flexible Pouch	GMO-Free	49
Pizza croutons	Paper Bag	Organic	49

```
(5 row(s) returned)
```

CHAPTER 13
COMBINING DATASETS - THE UNION OPERATOR

The primary goal of the UNION operator is to combine records from multiple data sets. In this respect, we can merge records from two or more SQL statements, from a SQL statement and a table, or from two or more tables. In contrast to popular belief, we can combine fields with different data types, sizes, or field names. The number of fields, however, does need to be the same. The UNION operator will return no duplicate records, while the UNION ALL operator will return all records from the combined data sets.

The UNION operator is not just a dull SQL statement that we use to combine records from multiple sources. We will see in this chapter that we can use it with clauses like WHERE, ORDER BY, and GROUP BY, operators like IN, NOT IN, and BETWEEN, and even subqueries for powerful results. Understanding the UNION operator will enable you to perform operations and achieve results that other database users cannot even imagine is possible.

In this chapter, we will work with two customer tables under the assumption that we have two distribution centers with one as our main center and the other as a regional center. For the most part, customers order from one of the two distribution centers. However, just to complicate our scenario a bit, we do have customers who can order from both. Consequently, we need to pay attention how customer records are merged to exclude duplicates.

We will use two tables: The tbls_customers_un1 table with 201 records and the tbls_customers_un2 table with 20 records. Fifteen of the customers in the tbls_customers_un2 table are included in the tbls_customers_un1 table as well, while five are unique customers.

85. Combine records from similar fields

Combine unique customer records from two tables

Discussion:

In this example, we use UNION to combine customer records from the two distribution centers. Notice that the number of customers returned is 206. This is because we combined 201 customers from the first table and 20 from the second. Since 15 customers are identical in both tables, and we use the UNION operator, we will get 206 unique customers. If we have used the UNION ALL operator, we would get 221 records.

Code:

```
SELECT LastName, FirstName, City, State, Zip
FROM tbls_Customers_un1
UNION
SELECT LastName, FirstName, City, State, Zip
FROM tbls_Customers_un2
```

Result:

LastName	FirstName	City	State	Zip
Ackerman	Nicholas	Dallas	TX	52347
Allen	Alfred	New York	NY	12189
Ames	Pindar	New York	NY	45357
Andersen	Thomas	Orlando	FL	89754

```
(There are more records in the result set than the ones shown in this image)
(206 row(s) returned)
```

86. Combine records from different fields

Combine customer and supplier records from two different tables

Discussion:

In this example, we combine data from the Customers and Supplier tables. Notice the different field names. In addition, check the resulting number of records. We get all the customers from the customers table (201) and all the suppliers (10) from the suppliers table for a total of 211 records.

Code:

```
SELECT LastName, FirstName, City, State, Zip
FROM Customers
UNION
SELECT CompanyName, ContactName, City, State, Zip
FROM Suppliers
```

Result:

LastName	FirstName	City	State	Zip
Ackerman	Nicholas	Dallas	TX	52347
Allen	Alfred	New York	NY	12189
American Foods	John Marrey	Boston	MA	22459
American Imports	Maria Hopkins	Boston	MA	22459

```
(There are more records in the result set than the ones shown in this image)
(211 row(s) returned)
```

87. Combine records from a table and a SQL statement

Combine customer records from a table and a SQL statement

Discussion:

In this example, we will combine the records from the customers table with some of the records in the tbls_customers_un2 table. Essentially, we merge a table and a SQL statement. Notice the absence of a SELECT statement for the customers table and the use of the WHERE clause in the code below:

Code:

```
TABLE [customers]
UNION
SELECT *
FROM tbls_customers_un2
WHERE state='TX'
```

Result:

CustomerID	FirstName	LastName	Address	City	State	Zip	Country	DateOfBirth
1	John	Demarco	11 Lark Street	New York	NY	12189	USA	1/22/2005
2	Mary	Demania	12 Madison Ave	New York	NY	12189	USA	7/17/2004
3	George	Demers	23 New Scotland Ave	New York	NY	12189	USA	3/11/2005
4	Phillip	Demetriou	22 Academy Road	New York	NY	12189	USA	10/12/2003

```
(There are more records in the result set than the ones shown in this image)
(There are more columns in the result set than the ones shown in this image)
(203 row(s) returned)
```

88. Combine records from multiple tables

Combine records from two customer tables and a supplier table

Discussion:

We can use UNION to merge records from two or more data sources. In this example, we merge data from three tables. Notice that while the first two SELECT statements contain identical fields, the third one uses different ones. Also, we must pay attention to our numbers. The first table (tbls_customers_un1) contains 201 records, the second (tbls_customers_un2) 20, and the third (suppliers) 10. We have a total of 231 records, but our result set contains only 216. This is correct since fifteen customers in tbls_customers_un1 and tbls_customers_un2 are identical. Consequently, the result is 231-15 = 216 records.

Code:

```
SELECT LastName, FirstName, City, State, Zip
FROM tbls_customers_un1
UNION
SELECT LastName, FirstName, City, State, Zip
FROM tbls_customers_un2
UNION
SELECT CompanyName, ContactName, City, State, Zip
FROM suppliers
```

Result:

LastName	FirstName	City	State	Zip
Ackerman	Nicholas	Dallas	TX	52347
Allen	Alfred	New York	NY	12189
American Foods	John Marrey	Boston	MA	22459
American Imports	Maria Hopkins	Boston	MA	22459

```
(There are more records in the result set than the ones shown in this image)
(216 row(s) returned)
```

89. The UNION ALL operator

Combine records from two tables and allow duplicates to appear

Discussion:

The UNION operator will exclude duplicate records. If we want duplicate records to appear, we will use the UNION ALL operator. Have a look at the number of records returned. In this case, it should be 201 from tbls_customers_un1 plus 20 from tbls_customers_un2 for a total of 221, and this is exactly what we get.

Code:

```
SELECT LastName, FirstName, city, state, zip
FROM tbls_customers_un1
UNION ALL
SELECT LastName, FirstName, city, state, zip
FROM tbls_customers_un2
```

Result:

LastName	FirstName	city	state	zip
Demarco	John	New York	NY	12189
Demania	Mary	New York	NY	12189
Demers	George	New York	NY	12189
Demetriou	Phillip	New York	NY	12189

(There are more records in the result set than the ones shown in this image)
(221 row(s) returned)

90. Sorting records correctly when using UNION

Sort customer records correctly when using UNION

Discussion:

The ORDER BY clause is used at the end of the SQL statement when using UNION, not after every individual SQL statement.

Code:

```
SELECT LastName, FirstName, City, State, Zip
FROM tbls_Customers_un1
UNION
SELECT LastName, FirstName, City, State, Zip
FROM tbls_Customers_un2
ORDER BY LastName
```

Result:

LastName	FirstName	City	State	Zip
Ackerman	Nicholas	Dallas	TX	52347
Allen	Alfred	New York	NY	12189
Ames	Pindar	New York	NY	45357
Andersen	Thomas	Orlando	FL	89754

(There are more records in the result set than the ones shown in this image)
(206 row(s) returned)

91. Filtering records with UNION operations

Create customer lists using the WHERE clause

Discussion:

In this example, we use the WHERE clause in each SELECT statement. We can use the WHERE clause in some or all SQL statements or tables to get exactly what we need from the individual data sets. Here, we want to get customers from New York in the first table and customers from Texas in the second.

Code:

```
SELECT LastName, FirstName, City, State, Zip
FROM tbls_Customers_un1
WHERE state = 'NY'
UNION
SELECT LastName, FirstName, City, State, Zip
FROM tbls_Customers_un2
WHERE State ='TX'
ORDER BY State
```

Result:

LastName	FirstName	City	State	Zip
Allen	Alfred	New York	NY	12189
Ames	Pindar	New York	NY	45357
Anderson	Peter	New York	NY	12189
Anthopolis	Ricky	New York	NY	12189

(There are more records in the result set than the ones shown in this image)
(33 row(s) returned)

92. Using UNION with IN and NOT IN

Create customer lists with filtering criteria using IN and NOT IN

Discussion:

We can perform detailed filtering using the IN and NOT IN operators within each individual SELECT statement in UNION operations. Notice we can apply criteria with different operators on different fields. We might have used the WHERE clause with the AND operator in the first SELECT and the IN operator in the second. In addition, we could have applied some criteria on the city field in the first SELECT and some criteria on the state field in the second.

Code:

```
SELECT LastName, FirstName, City, State, Zip
FROM customers
WHERE City IN('New York', 'Los Angeles')
UNION
SELECT LastName, FirstName, City, State, Zip
FROM tbls_Customers_un2
WHERE City IN('Dallas', 'Miami', 'Orlando', 'Ontario')
ORDER BY LastName
```

Result:

LastName	FirstName	City	State	Zip
Allen	Alfred	New York	NY	12189
Ames	Pindar	New York	NY	45357
Anderson	Joseph	Los Angeles	CA	94851
Anderson	Peter	New York	NY	12189

(There are more records in the result set than the ones shown in this image)
(59 row(s) returned)

93. Add a totals row at the end of the combined data sets

Display total customer numbers dynamically

Discussion:

Here, we display all records from the tbls_customers_un1 table and we add a total row at the end of the recordset. Notice in the second SQL statement we use quotes instead of fields to satisfy the UNION requirement of having the same number of fields in both statements. In addition, notice that we start the name of the first field of the second SQL statement with a "z", which has no other purpose but to force the total row to appear last in the recordset since z is the last letter in the alphabet. Finally, for our trick to succeed, we need to use the ORDER BY clause on the first field of the first SQL statement.

Code:

```
SELECT LastName, FirstName, City, State, Zip, CustomerID
FROM tbls_Customers_un1
UNION
SELECT
'zTotal customer count', '', '', '', '', Count(CustomerID)
FROM tbls_Customers_un1
ORDER BY LastName ASC
```

Result:

LastName	FirstName	City	State	Zip	CustomerID
Ackerman	Nicholas	Dallas	TX	52347	93
Allen	Alfred	New York	NY	12189	141
Ames	Pindar	New York	NY	45357	15
Andersen	Thomas	Orlando	FL	89754	50

(There are more records in the result set than the ones shown in this image)
(202 row(s) returned)

94. Using UNION with SELECT INTO

Combine customer data from multiple tables and save the combined dataset dynamically in a different table

Discussion:

This is a useful way to get data from multiple tables and queries and save it in a different table. We can use SELECT INTO to pull this off, but we must pay attention! The first of the following two SQL statements may naturally come to mind, but it will not work. We need to use a subquery like we do in the second SQL statement. Pay attention to the number of records. It has to be 206 (201 from the first table and 5 from the second) since we are asking for unique records to be moved. If we want to move everything, we can use UNION ALL.

Code: (Will not work)

```
SELECT LastName, FirstName, City, State, Zip INTO Temp_Union_Table
FROM Customers
UNION
SELECT LastName, FirstName, City, State, Zip
FROM tbls_Customers_un2
```

Code: (Will work)

```
SELECT LastName, FirstName, City, State, Zip INTO Temp_Union_Table
FROM
(SELECT LastName, FirstName, City, State, Zip
FROM customers
UNION
SELECT LastName, FirstName, City, State, Zip
FROM tbls_customers_un2
)
```

Result:

(You are about to paste 20 row(s) into a new table)

95. Using UNION with INSERT INTO

Combine records from multiple data sources, filter them, and append them into an existing table

Discussion:

If we want to combine data from multiple tables and queries and append it to an existing table, we can use INSERT INTO. The table "temp_tbl_Union_InsertInto" used in this example needs to exist before we run the SQL statement. Notice in the CREATE TABLE statement below the usage of the Counter specification so that the values of the primary key auto increase.

Code1:

```
CREATE TABLE temp_tbl_Union_InsertInto (
[CustomerID] Counter Primary key,
[LastName] text(50),
[FirstName] text(50),
[City] text(50),
[State] text(2),
[Zip] text(15)
)
```

Notice in the code below how we use the WHERE clause to filter the records we want to transfer.

Code2:

```
INSERT INTO temp_tbl_Union_InsertInto (lastname, firstname, city, state, zip)
SELECT lastname, firstname, city, state, zip
FROM
(SELECT lastname, firstname, city, state, zip
FROM customers
WHERE state = 'NY'
UNION
SELECT lastname, firstname, city, state, zip
FROM tbls_customers_un2
WHERE state = 'NY'
)
```

Result:

(You are about to append 34 row(s))

96. Using UNION with GROUP BY within each SELECT statement

Combine customer data from all distribution centers, count the totals, and show in the view the center they came from

Discussion:

The business goal in this example is to calculate the number of customers for the "Main" and "Regional" centers in each state. Practically, we would like to know how many customers buy from the main centers and how many from the regional ones. We use a number of tricks and functions to arrive at the results we need. First, notice we use a GROUP BY clause in both SQL statements in the query. Second, we use the count() function to get the number of customers by state. Third, we create a field of our own ("Main" and "Regional") in the beginning of each of the two SQL statements to display customer numbers according to distribution center. Finally, we use the ORDER BY clause to present results by state for easy comparison of numbers. Some states appear only once because they have just one distribution center.

Code:

```
SELECT 'Main' As DisCenter, state, count(CustomerID) AS Customers
FROM customers
GROUP BY State
UNION
SELECT 'Regional' As Center, state, Count(CustomerID) AS Customers
FROM tbls_customers_un2
GROUP BY State
ORDER BY STATE
```

Result:

DisCenter	state	Customers
Main	AZ	13
Main	CA	48
Main	CO	13
Main	DC	12
Main	FL	21

(There are more records in the result set than the ones shown in this image)
(12 row(s) returned)

97. Using UNION with GROUP BY outside each SELECT statement

Combine customer data from all distribution centers, count the totals, and group results by state

Discussion:

In this example, the GROUP BY clause produces combined results from each state regardless of distribution center. Unlike what we did in the previous example, we first combine the data and then we use the GROUP BY clause. Notice the use of the subquery with the UNION operator that enables us to GROUP results from the two data sets.

Code:

```
SELECT state, count(customerid) as Customers
FROM

(SELECT state, CustomerID
FROM customers
UNION
SELECT state, CustomerID
FROM tbls_customers_un
)

GROUP BY state
ORDER BY STATE
```

Result:

DisCenter	state	Customers
Main	AZ	13
Main	CA	48
Main	CO	13
Main	DC	12
Main	FL	21

(There are more records in the result set than the ones shown in this image)
(12 row(s) returned)

98. Using UNION with two subqueries to filter records for aggregations

Compare customer numbers from two distribution centers

Discussion:

In this example, we compare customer numbers from the "main" and "regional" distribution centers but only for states where both distribution centers exist. As "main" center we consider customers from the table "tbls_customers_un1" and as a regional center we consider customers from the "tbls_customers_un2" table.
To achieve the desired comparison, we use a subquery in the first SELECT statement which will search for matching states in the table in the second SELECT statement.

Code:

```
SELECT 'Main' As DisCenter, state, count(CustomerID) AS Customers
FROM tbls_customers_un1
WHERE State in (SELECT state from tbls_customers_un2)
GROUP BY state
UNION
SELECT 'Regional' As Center, state, Count(CustomerID) AS Customers
FROM tbls_customers_un2
GROUP BY state
ORDER BY STATE
```

Result:

DisCenter	state	Customers
Main	NY	31
Regional	NY	18
Main	TX	25
Regional	TX	2

(4 row(s) returned)

99. Trick for knowing which table the row came from when using UNION

Discussion:

In certain occasions with UNION operators, it is useful to know the source table or query for each record in the result set. In this example, we combine data from the suppliers and customers table, but we want to know who the customers are and who the suppliers. To achieve this, we add a text entry in each of the SQL statements.

Code:

```
SELECT LastName, FirstName, City, State, Zip, 'customer' AS TypeOfContact
FROM Customers
UNION
SELECT CompanyName, ContactName, City, State, Zip, 'supplier'
FROM Suppliers
```

Result:

LastName	FirstName	City	State	Zip	TypeOfContact
Ackerman	Nicholas	Dallas	TX	52347	customer
Allen	Alfred	New York	NY	12189	customer
American Foods	John Marrey	Boston	MA	22459	supplier
American Imports	Maria Hopkins	Boston	MA	22459	supplier

(There are more records in the result set than the ones shown in this image)
(211 row(s) returned)

DISCUSSION QUESTIONS

1. What is the basic goal of the UNION operator?
2. Can we combine the results of a table and a query using the UNION operator?
3. When using the UNION operator to combine two or more tables, do we need to have the same number of fields?
4. When using the UNION operator to combine two or more tables, do we need to have the same data types and sizes of fields in both tables?
5. Which operator returns duplicate values? UNION or UNION ALL?
6. Can we use the ORDER BY clause with UNION and multiple SQL statements? Where should we place it in the SQL statement?
7. Can we use the WHERE clause with UNION and multiple SQL statements? Where should we place it in the SQL statement? How many WHERE clauses can we use within a UNION statement?
8. Can we use different criteria for each of the WHERE clauses used in the SQL statements combined with the UNION operator?
9. What trick can we use to indicate the source table of each record in the result of the UNION statement?
10. What difference it will make if we use the GROUP BY clause within each SQL statement with the UNION operator or if we use the GROUP BY clause outside all SQL statements with a UNION operator?

HANDS-ON EXERCISES

Case 1

For each of the questions in this case create a new query in SQL view and name it as per the instructions in each question.

1. The salespeople are asking for a new product catalog that will combine records from the Products and tbls_products_union tables. They also want the new catalog to contain only the ProductName field. Create a new query that satisfies the salespeople request and save it as Union_Case1_Q1. Why do you think the resulting recordset contains 76 records?

Your result should look like:

ProductName
All-Purpose Marinade
Almonds Hickory Smoked
Almonds Roasted and Salted
Apple Cinnamon Raisin Cookies

```
(There are more records in the result set than the ones shown in this image)
(76 row(s) returned)
```

2. The salespeople are back asking for a new report that will again combine the Products and tbls_products_union tables. They want the new report to contain the ProductName, SupplierID, and ProductPrice fields. Create a new query that satisfies the salespeople request and save it as Union_Case1_Q2. Why do you think the resulting recordset contains 80 records?

Your result should look like:

ProductName	SupplierID	ProductPrice
All-Purpose Marinade	9	29
Almonds Hickory Smoked	1	35
Almonds Roasted and Salted	1	22
Apple Cinnamon Raisin Cookies	7	27

(There are more records in the result set than the ones shown in this image)
(80 row(s) returned)

3. After your explanation from question 2, the salespeople are explicitly asking for a new report that will combine ALL the products in the Products table with ALL the products in the tbls_products_union table. They want the new report to contain the ProductName, SupplierID, and ProductPrice fields. Create a new query that satisfies the salespeople request and save it as Union_Case1_Q3. Why do you think the resulting recordset still contains 80 records? What is the explanation here?

Your result should look like:

ProductName	SupplierID	ProductPrice
Almonds Hickory Smoked	1	35
Almonds Roasted and Salted	1	22
Banana Chips	1	27
Berry Cherry	1	30

(There are more records in the result set than the ones shown in this image)
(80 row(s) returned)

4. The salespeople are happy with your ability to provide them with these pieces of information. Now, they are asking for a report that will combine the products from suppliers 1, 2, and 3 from the Products table and suppliers 2, 5, and 10 from the tbls_products_union table. They want the new report to contain the ProductName, SupplierID, and ProductPrice fields. They also need the report to be sorted by ProductName ascending. Create a new query that satisfies the salespeople request and save it as Union_Case1_Q4.

Your result should look like:

ProductName	SupplierID	ProductPrice
Almonds Hickory Smoked	1	35
Almonds Roasted and Salted	1	22
Banana Chips	1	27
Berry Cherry	1	30

(There are more records in the result set than the ones shown in this image)
(27 row(s) returned)

5. The salespeople now need a report that will combine the products from suppliers 1 through 5 from the Products table and suppliers 1 through 5 from the tbls_Products_union table. They want the new report to contain the ProductName, SupplierID, and ProductPrice fields. They also need the report to be sorted by ProductName ascending. Create a new query that satisfies the salespeople request and save it as Union_Case1_Q5.

Your result should look like:

ProductName	SupplierID	ProductPrice
Almonds Hickory Smoked	1	35
Almonds Roasted and Salted	1	22
Banana Chips	1	27
Banana Glazed Chips	1	30

```
(There are more records in the result set than the ones shown in this image)
(44 row(s) returned)
```

Case 2

For each of the questions in this case create a new query in SQL view and name it as per the instructions in each question.

1. The marketing people are asking for a list of contact information from Customers, Suppliers, and SalesReps so they can send out an end of the year thank you note. Create a new query that includes the fields lastname, firstname, city, state, zip from the Customers and SalesReps tables and the fields companyname, contactname, city, state, zip from the Suppliers table. Save the query as Union_Case2_Q1.

Your result should look like:

lastname	firstname	city	state	zip
Ackerman	Nicholas	Dallas	TX	52347
Allen	Alfred	New York	NY	12189
American Foods	John Marrey	Boston	MA	22459
American Imports	Maria Hopkins	Boston	MA	22459

```
(There are more records in the result set than the ones shown in this image)
(221 row(s) returned)
```

2. The marketing people are back asking you to create a new table that contains all the records from question 1. Design a new query which creates a new table, named tbls_greeting_cards, with all the records from the Customers, Suppliers, and SalesReps tables and the fields specified in question 1. Save the query as Union_Case2_Q2.

Your result should look like:

```
(You are about to paste 221 row(s) into a new table)
```

3. The inventory department asks for a report that will list the number of products by stock keeping unit (SKU) in the tbls_products_local and tbls_products_regional tables. They want the report to show if the units exist in the local or regional warehouse. Create a new query that satisfies the inventory people request and save it as Union_Case2_Q3.

Your result should look like:

Location	Sku	NumberOfProducts
Local	ADSE 2345	1
Local	ADST 2345	1
Local	ASDT-3456	1
Local	ADSD 2345	1

```
(There are more records in the result set than the ones shown in this image)
(20 row(s) returned)
```

4. The inventory people liked the report you created for them in question 3. Now, they want the same report of product units by sku without however differentiating between local and regional warehouses. Create a new query that satisfies the inventory people request and save it as Union_Case2_Q4.

Your result should look like:

Sku	NumberOfProducts
ADSE 2345	1
ADST 2345	1
ASDT-3456	1
ADSD 2345	1

```
(There are more records in the result set than the ones shown in this image)
(20 row(s) returned)
```

5. The director of inventory is super happy with the reports you have provided. They have a final request. They need a report identical to the one in question 4 with the following additions: First, they need to include only products with ProductPrices between $20 and $35. Second, they want to include products with a total count by SKU of more than 1. Create a new query that satisfies the inventory people request and save it as Union_Case2_Q5.

Your result should look like:

Sku	NumberOfProducts
ADST 2345	2
ASDT-3456	3
DKLS-4732	4
EPDA-2345	4

```
(There are more records in the result set than the ones shown in this image)
(9 row(s) returned)
```

CHAPTER 14
PERFORMING CALCULATIONS

Using SQL, we can perform calculations using arithmetic operators such as (+, *, -, /, ^, Mod). For instance, we can multiply a numeric field by a certain number or percentage, or we can multiply two numeric fields themselves. Or we can multiply two fields and divide the result by another field. We can also create calculated fields conditionally using the iif() and switch() functions. In addition, we often combine calculated fields with aggregate functions to generate insightful analytics. We can also use calculated fields with UPDATE statements to change the values of hundreds or thousands of records instantly. There are multiple essential applications of calculations in databases and we will present various examples in this chapter.

Operator	Meaning
+	Add two numbers or numeric fields
*	Multiply two numbers or numeric fields
-	Subtract one number or field from another number or field
/	Divide one number or field by another number or field
\	Division by rounding the numbers and converting them to integers
Mod	Divide two numbers or fields and return the remainder
^	Raise a number or field to the power of an exponent

When creating calculations remember that it is not a good practice to create calculated fields in tables, they belong in queries. The third normal form rule of normalization says that all entity attributes should depend on the key. That is, all table fields need to be related to the entity they describe. For example, all customer attributes (fields) need to be connected to the Customer table and describe the Customer by associating the Customer with a first name, a last name, a phone number etc. The values of a calculated field used in a table change on a continuous basis, use resources to recalculate, and take up space unnecessarily. The most appropriate place for a calculated field is within a view/query. The rule of thumb is, if we can derive a field from a calculation of two or more fields in the table, then that field belongs to a view.

100. Add a number to a numeric field

Create a product catalog with updated prices on the fly

Discussion:

Here, the business goal is to create a new product catalog on the fly that will appear on the corporate website for two hours only. Specifically, management asked to add $2 to the price of each product in the catalog. To respond, we create a query with a calculated field that will add $2 to the price of each product without changing the prices of the products in the table.

Code:

```
SELECT ProductName, ProductPrice, ProductPrice + 2 AS CurrentProductPrice
FROM Products
```

Result:

ProductName	ProductPrice	CurrentProductPrice
Almonds Hickory Smoked	35	37
Almonds Roasted and Salted	22	24
Banana Chips	27	29
Berry Cherry	30	32

```
(There are more records in the result set than the ones shown in this image)
(70 row(s) returned)
```

101. Increase numeric values by a percentage

Update product prices by 20%

Discussion:

This time, due to increased replenishment costs, our manager is asking us to add a 20% markup to the price of every product in the catalog.

Code:

```
SELECT ProductName, ProductPrice, ProductPrice * (1.2) as CurrentProductPrice
FROM Products
```

Result:

ProductName	ProductPrice	CurrentProductPrice
Almonds Hickory Smoked	35	42
Almonds Roasted and Salted	22	26.4
Banana Chips	27	32.4
Berry Cherry	30	36

```
(There are more records in the result set than the ones shown in this image)
(70 row(s) returned)
```

102. Subtract a percentage from a numeric column

Provide customers with a 20% discount on every product

Discussion:

The management has decided to aggressively sell this month, and they have initiated a promotional campaign with a price discount of 20% for every product in the product catalog.

Code:

```
SELECT ProductName, ProductPrice, ProductPrice * (1-0.2) as PromotionalPrice
FROM Products
```

Result:

ProductName	ProductPrice	PromotionalPrice
Almonds Hickory Smoked	35	28
Almonds Roasted and Salted	22	17.6
Banana Chips	27	21.6
Berry Cherry	30	24

```
(There are more records in the result set than the ones shown in this image)
(70 row(s) returned)
```

103. Add two numeric fields

Calculate product inventory quantities

Discussion:

The management is asking for a report of product inventory quantities. Specifically, they want to know the number of units we currently have in the warehouse and the number of units we have on order. To answer this request, we create a new column named TotalUnits, which is simply the sum of the units we have in stock plus the ones we have on order and have not arrived yet.

Code:

```
SELECT ProductName, UnitsInstock, UnitsOnOrder, (UnitsInStock + UnitsOnOrder) AS TotalUnits
FROM products
```

Result:

ProductName	UnitsInstock	UnitsOnOrder	TotalUnits
Almonds Hickory Smoked	40	5	45
Almonds Roasted and Salted	32	0	32`
Banana Chips	25	0	25
Berry Cherry	50	0	50

(There are more records in the result set than the ones shown in this image)
(70 row(s) returned)

104. Multiply two numeric columns and group their result

Calculate total order amounts

Discussion:

In this example, we want to calculate the total order amount for each order we have in the database. Each order might contain multiple products with different quantities for each product. We first need to multiply product prices with the corresponding product quantities in each order and then sum the results. Then, we group by OrderID to obtain the total for every order. A sample data set on which to make these calculations appears below. The order with OrderID = 1, contains three different products with prices of 15, 12, and 18 and quantities of 2, 3, and 5 respectively. We first multiply the product price with the quantity for each product, get the subtotals, and sum up the results for each order.

JoinOrdersProducts			
OrderID	ProductID	ProductPrice	Quantity
1	1	15	2
1	2	12	3
1	3	18	5
2	1	15	2
2	3	18	8

Code:

```
SELECT OrderID, Sum(UnitPrice*Quantity) AS OrderSubtotal
FROM JoinOrdersProducts
GROUP BY OrderID
```

Result:

OrderID	OrderSubtotal
1	30
2	210
3	231
4	45

(There are more records in the result set than the ones shown in this image)
(919 row(s) returned)

105. Display currency symbols in calculated fields

Discussion:

We can display currency symbols in a calculated field using the format function with the syntax

FORMAT(<value>, <format_string>)

where value is the calculated field and for format string, we use the # character to designate any digit, and the 0 character to display a zero if a numeric value does not exist after the decimal placeholder.

Code:

```
SELECT ProductName, ProductPrice, format((ProductPrice * (1+0.2)),'$#,#.00') AS
DiscountedProductPrice
FROM products
```

Result:

ProductName	ProductPrice	DiscountedProductPrice
Almonds Hickory Smoked	35	$42.00
Almonds Roasted and Salted	22	$26.40
Banana Chips	27	$32.40
Berry Cherry	30	$36.00

(There are more records in the result set than the ones shown in this image)
(70 row(s) returned)

106. Conditional calculations with the iif() function

Determine employee bonus eligibility

Discussion:

In this example, we are looking for sales representatives who are eligible for a bonus. If the bonus amount assigned to them is less than 10% of their salary, then they are eligible for a bonus. Otherwise, they are not eligible.

Code:

```
SELECT LastName, FirstName, IIf(Bonus < Salary*0.1,'Bonus','No Bonus') AS BonusEligibility
FROM SalesReps
```

Result:

LastName	FirstName	BonusEligibility
Anderson	John	Bonus
Teall	Mary	No Bonus
Spicer	George	No Bonus
Zensons	Phillip	Bonus

```
(There are more records in the result set than the ones shown in this image)
(10 row(s) returned)
```

107. Multiple condtitional calculations with the switch() function

Provide customers with different discounts based on the product supplier

Discussion:

In some cases, we might want to offer different discount rates for each supplier. Let us suppose we want to provide a 20% discount for products from SupplierID=1, 15% for those from SupplierID=2, 18% for those from SupplierID=3, and 25% for those from SupplierID=4. Finally, we want to provide a 10% discount for all the remaining suppliers. The switch function comes to the rescue here, providing the flexibility to obtain the results we need.

Code:

```
SELECT ProductName,
SWITCH(
SupplierID = 1,          ProductPrice*(1-0.2),
SupplierID = 2,          ProductPrice*(1-0.15),
SupplierID = 3,          ProductPrice*(1-0.18),
SupplierID = 4,          ProductPrice*(1-0.25),
TRUE,                    ProductPrice*(1-0.1)
)
AS DiscountedProductPrice
FROM Products
```

Result:

ProductName	DiscountedProductPrice
Almonds Hickory Smoked	28
Almonds Roasted and Salted	17.6
Banana Chips	21.6
Berry Cherry	24

```
(There are more records in the result set than the ones shown in this image)
(70 row(s) returned)
```

108. Store results of calculated fields in an archive/backup table on the fly

Storing total order amounts in a separate table

Discussion:

Sometimes, we need to store the results of our calculations in a backup, archive, or temporary table. Storing results of calculated fields in production tables is not a good idea as we have already discussed but sometimes, we need a temporary table. In this example, we transfer the OrderID and OrderTotal fields in a new table named ArchivedOrders. Of course, the OrderTotal field is calculated from three different fields in the JoinOrdersProducts table.

Code:

```
SELECT OrderID, SUM((unitprice*Quantity)*(1-Discount)) AS OrderTotal
INTO ArchivedOrders
FROM JoinOrdersProducts
GROUP BY OrderID
```

Result:

```
You are about to paste 919 row(s) into a new table.
```

DISCUSSION QUESTIONS

1. What are two goals of calculated fields?
2. Is it a good idea to store calculated fields in tables?
3. Why knowledge of the usage of calculated fields affects the design of the database?
4. What is the purpose of arithmetic operators?
5. How many arithmetic operators do we have?
6. What is the best object (table, view) in which to use calculated fields?
7. How can we create calculated fields conditionally?
8. What is the difference between the iif() and switch() functions?
9. Why does it make perfect sense to use calculated fields with UPDATE statements?
10. Can we use calculated fields with the WHERE and HAVING clauses? What is the difference?

HANDS-ON EXERCISES

Case 1

For each of the questions in this case create a new query in SQL view and name it as per the instructions in each question.

1. The salespeople embark on a sales effort, and they want all product prices decreased by 20%. The new product catalog will be valid only for two days on the corporate web site and then, the prices will go back to normal. Name the new calculated field "NewPrice". Create a new query that includes the ProductName, ProductPrice, QuantityPerUnit, UnitsOnOrder, and NewPrice fields from the Products table and satisfies the salespeople request. Save the query as Calculations_Case1_Q1.

Your result should look like:

ProductName	ProductPrice	QuantityPerUnit	UnitsOnOrder	NewPrice
Almonds Hickory Smoked	35	12	5	28
Almonds Roasted and Salted	22	12	0	17.6
Banana Chips	27	12	0	21.6
Berry Cherry	30	15	0	24

```
(There are more records in the result set than the ones shown in this image)
(70 row(s) returned)
```

2. The accounts payable unit is conducting an internal audit and they are looking for product prices by quantity per unit. Divide the ProductPrice by QuantityPerUnit to arrive at item prices so that accounts payable can better assess supplier offers. Name the new calculated field "PricePerItem". Create a new query that includes the ProductName, ProductPrice, QuantityPerUnit, UnitsOnOrder, and PricePerItem fields from the Products table and satisfies the accounts payable request. Save the query as Calculations_Case1_Q2.

Your result should look like:

ProductName	ProductPrice	QuantityPerUnit	UnitsOnOrder	PricePerItem
Almonds Hickory Smoked	35	12	5	2.9166666666666666666667
Almonds Roasted and Salted	22	12	0	1.8333333333333333333333
Banana Chips	27	12	0	2.25
Berry Cherry	30	15	0	2

```
(There are more records in the result set than the ones shown in this image)
(70 row(s) returned)
```

3. The marketing people need to print a new product catalog that contains updated prices, decreased by 15%, for the following suppliers: American Foods, LLC, Berkley Bakery Co., Nature's Food, Inc., and Old York Foods, Inc. Create a new query that includes the fields ProductName, ProductPrice, QuantityPerUnit, and UnitsOnOrder from the Products table and satisfies the marketing request. Hint: First find the SupplierID from the suppliers table and then use the switch() function. The new report should contain all the products in the Products table. In addition, the order of the fields in the result set should follow their order in the select statement as in the image below. Save the query as Calculations_Case1_Q3. Sort results by ProductName ascending.

Your result should look like:

ProductName	NewProductPrice	QuantityPerUnit	UnitsOnOrder
All-Purpose Marinade	24.65	24	15
Almonds Hickory Smoked	35	12	5
Almonds Roasted and Salted	22	12	0
Apple Cinnamon Raisin Cookies	27	30	20

(There are more records in the result set than the ones shown in this image)
(70 row(s) returned)

4. At Accounts Payable they need to verify the payments we need to extend to suppliers, and they are asking for a report that includes all open requisitions. Create a new field by multiplying UnitsOnOrder by ProductPrice to calculate how much we must pay. Name the new field "OutstandingPayments". Create a new query that includes the ProductName, ProductPrice, QuantityPerUnit, UnitsOnOrder, and OutstandingPayments fields from the Products table and satisfies the accounts payable request. Sort results by OutstandingPayments descending. Save the query as Calculations_Case1_Q4.

Your result should look like:

ProductName	ProductPrice	QuantityPerUnit	UnitsOnOrder	OutstandingPayments
Chocolate Chunk Cookies	48	34	20	960
Oatmeal Raisin Walnut Cookies	43	30	20	860
Fruit Dip	49	30	15	735
Dried Light Red Tart Cherries	43	26	15	645

(There are more records in the result set than the ones shown in this image)
(70 row(s) returned)

5. The sales department is asking for a report that lists the total inventory value by ingredient type. Create a calculated field named "InventoryTotalByIngredientType" that adds the fields UnitsOnOrder and UnitsInStock and sum the results by IngredientType. Save the new query as Calculations_Case1_Q5.

Your result should look like:

IngredientType	InventoryTotalByIngredientType
All-Natural	837
GMO-Free	961
Organic	817

(There are more records in the result set than the ones shown in this image)
(70 row(s) returned)

Case 2

For each of the questions in this case create a new query in SQL view and name it as per the instructions in each question.

1. The inventory people need a report from the Products table that shows the difference between the quantities of units in stock plus the quantities of units on order minus the reorder level. Any negative amounts indicate that we need to order new quantities for those products. Name the new calculated field UnitStatus. Create a new query that includes the ProductName, ProductPrice, UnitsInStock, UnitsOnOrder, ReorderLevel, and UnitStatus fields from the Products table that satisfies the inventory people request. Sort results by UnitStatus ascending. Save the query as Calculations_Case2_Q1.

Your result should look like:

ProductName	ProductPrice	UnitsInStock	UnitsOnOrder	ReorderLevel	UnitStatus
All-Purpose Marinade	29	27	15	40	2
Almonds Hickory Smoked	35	40	5	45	0
Almonds Roasted and Salted	22	32	0	20	12
Apple Cinnamon Raisin Cookies	27	15	20	30	5

```
(There are more records in the result set than the ones shown in this image)
(70 row(s) returned)
```

2. The salespeople need a new product catalog they will use on the website for a day only. In this catalog, product prices for all organic products will be reduced by 20% and GMO-free by 25%. Name the new calculated field "NewProductPrice". Create a new query that includes the ProductName, IngredientType, ProdutPrice, and NewProductPrice fields from the Products table that satisfies the salespeople request. Sort results by ProductName ascending. Save the query as Calculations_Case2_Q2.

Your result should look like:

ProductName	IngredientType	ProductPrice	NewProductPrice
All-Purpose Marinade	Organic	29	23.2
Almonds Hickory Smoked	GMO-Free	35	26.25
Almonds Roasted and Salted	Organic	22	17.6
Apple Cinnamon Raisin Cookies	All-Natural	27	27

```
(There are more records in the result set than the ones shown in this image)
(70 row(s) returned)
```

3. The marketing department is asking for a report that will list the total order amount by OrderID. They want the discount given for each product in each order to be taken into consideration in the calculations. Use the OrderID field and create a new calculated field named OrderTotal from the JoinOrdersProducts table and group orders by OrderID. Save the query as Calculations_Case2_Q3.

Your result should look like:

OrderID	OrderTotal
1	24
2	184.5
3	190.05
4	38.25

```
(There are more records in the result set than the ones shown in this image)
(919 row(s) returned)
```

4. The sales director thinks that the field representatives go over the limit in providing discounts in order to get the sale. So, he wants a report that will ignore the salespeople discount offers if they are more than 15% and replace them with a discount of exactly 15%. Create a new query that includes the OrderID, ProductID, UnitPrice, and Discount from the JoinOrdersProducts table and meets the director's request. Name the new query as Calculations_Case2_Q4. Hint: Use the iif() function.

Your result should look like:

OrderID	ProductID	UnitPrice	Discount	AdjustedDiscount
1	61	15	0.2	0.15
2	23	15	0.15	0.15
2	24	15	0.2	0.15
2	32	15	0	0

(There are more records in the result set than the ones shown in this image)
(2411 row(s) returned)

5. The marketing director wants to initiate a new campaign of generous discounts to customers. She just received a memo that the following suppliers have now discounted their products with the percentages shown: Home of Snacks, 25%, Mediterranean Foods, LLC, 20%, Nature's Food, Inc., 30%, and Old York Foods, Inc., 30%. The marketing manager wants to pass 80% of the wholesale discount received to her customers. For all other products, prices will remain the same. Create a new query that contains the ProductName field, and a calculated field named ProductPrice from the Products table and satisfies the marketing director's request. Name the query Calculations_Case2_Q5. Hint: First identify the SupplierID from the suppliers table and then use it in the Products table to build the switch() function.

Your result should look like:

ProductName	NewProductPrice
Almonds Hickory Smoked	28
Almonds Roasted and Salted	17.6
Banana Chips	21.6
Berry Cherry	24

(There are more records in the result set than the ones shown in this image)
(70 row(s) returned)

CHAPTER 15
CONCATENATING DATA

Concatenating columns means displaying the contents of two or more fields in one. Concatenation happens on the fly through a query and it is extremely useful in analytics tasks. For example, if we want to calculate the sales amount by customer, we need to concatenate the customer first and last names since there might be customers with the same last name. If we feel that there might be customers with the same first and last names, then we can add the prefix, suffix, or any other field in the concatenation to make sure that the correct amounts are associated with the corresponding customers. That is, we must make sure that two different customers with identical first and last names do not appear as one in the grouped results.

Concatenation in databases can achieve much more than displaying the contents of two or more columns together. We can create mailing labels, write letters with the correct punctuation, combine field data with plain text, perform conditional concatenations based on the values of any field, and use string and other functions for truly powerful results. To concatenate fields, we use the "+" or "&" characters with "+" being the most common one.

109. Concatenate multiple columns without any spaces

Put all customer address information in one field

Discussion:

In this example, we create mailing labels for letters to our suppliers. For such tasks, most people will use a word processor to write the letter and then connect to the address data which is in a spreadsheet or database. Often, they will go through multiple steps and an intricate process to link the word processor with the back-end data. We can achieve this task using only a SQL query. Why do it in the database? Later on, we might need to create mailing labels only for a subset of our suppliers and, in the database, we can modify our view and enter any criteria expressions we need.

Code:

```
SELECT (Address+City+State+Zip) AS FullAddress
FROM Customers
```

Result:

FullAddress
11 Lark StreetNew YorkNY12189
12 Madison AveNew YorkNY12189
23 New Scotland AveNew YorkNY12189
22 Academy RoadNew YorkNY12189

(There are more records in the result set than the ones shown in this image)
(201 row(s) returned)

As you can see, the four fields are concatenated into one, but the data is cramped in a continuous string of characters. We need to add spaces between the field values to easily read them and print the results in a way that will make sense to USPS.

110. Concatenate multiple columns with spaces between their values

Put all customer address information in one field with spaces between values

Discussion:

In this example, we add spaces between the concatenated columns. We use single quotes with a space between them to achieve this output. If we need to add two spaces between the fields, then we add two spaces between the single quotes.

Code:

```
SELECT (Address &' '& City &' '& State &' '& Zip) AS FullAddress
FROM Customers
```

Result:

FullAddress
11 Lark Street New York NY 12189
12 Madison Ave New York NY 12189
23 New Scotland Ave New York NY 12189
22 Academy Road New York NY 12189

(There are more records in the result set than the ones shown in this image)
(201 row(s) returned)

111. Use concatenated fields to achieve the correct analytics

Calculating the number of orders by customer

Discussion:

In this example the goal is very simple, to calculate the number of orders by customer last name. Initially, we use the technically correct but conceptually wrong code below and we get 171 records. The issue is that we have multiple customers with the same last name and they are grouped together!

Code:

```
SELECT LastName, SUM(OrderID) AS NumberOfOrders
FROM Qry_Invoices
GROUP BY LastName
```

Result:

LastName	NumberOfOrders
Ackerman	1571
Ames	10162
Andersen	8952
Anderson	28475

(There are more records in the result set than the ones shown in this image)
(171 row(s) returned)

We change the code to the one below to group customers by last and first names together in one concatenated field. We see that the number of records returned went up to 190.

Code:

```
SELECT LastName +' '+ FirstName As [Customer Name], SUM(OrderID) AS NumberOfOrders
FROM Qry_Invoices
GROUP BY LastName +' '+ FirstName
```

Result:

Customer Name	NumberOfOrders
Ackerman Nicholas	1571
Ames Pindar	10162
Andersen Thomas	8952
Anderson Joseph	7131

(There are more records in the result set than the ones shown in this image)
(190 row(s) returned)

We are still very suspicious and we ask what if we have customers with identical first and last names? We again change the code to the one below to group customers by CustomerID, last name, and first name. We reason that the CustomerID is the PK of the table and it has to be unique. We see that the number of records returned is again 190 and since the CustomerID is unique our result should be correct.

Code:

```
SELECT CustomerID &' '& LastName &' '& FirstName As [Customer Name], SUM(OrderID) AS
NumberOfOrders
FROM Qry_Invoices
GROUP BY CustomerID &' '& LastName &' '& FirstName
```

Result:

Customer Name	NumberOfOrders
1 Demarco John	10205
10 Demaria Matthew	1707
100 Crooney Pindar	10776
101 Crandil Joseph	4413

(There are more records in the result set than the ones shown in this image)
(190 row(s) returned)

We are still very cautious, we go to the customers table, and select to return all records. We see that 201 unique customers are in the customers table! Now we must think. The combination of CustomerID, plus lastname, plus first name is definitely unique. However, why did we get 190 customers in the previous query instead of the 201 unique that are in the customers table?

Code:

```
SELECT CustomerID, FirstName, LastName
FROM Customers
```

Result:

CustomerID	FirstName	LastName
1	John	Demarco
2	Mary	Demania
3	George	Demers
4	Phillip	Demetriou

(There are more records in the result set than the ones shown in this image)
(201 row(s) returned)

The fact that might happen is that those eleven missing customers do not have any orders and consequently the query that groups customers by the number of orders, leaves them out. We need to write code to verify our thinking. This code that includes a subquery does not belong thematically in this chapter but it definitely belongs in our logical thinking process.

We are looking for customers without orders and we verify our thinking since the code below returns eleven records! Eleven customers in the database do not have a single order throughout the years; only their names appear in the customers table and it is up to the company policy to keep them or delete them from the system.

Code:

```
SELECT CustomerID, FirstName, LastName, Address, City, State
FROM Customers
WHERE CustomerID NOT IN
(SELECT CustomerID
FROM Orders)
```

Result:

CustomerID	FirstName	LastName	Address	City	State
19	Erin	Erin	28 Karrie Terrace	Los Angeles	CA
37	Allan	Cimo	24 Crestwood CT	New York	NY
40	Kelly	Costa	45 Sixth Ave	Philadelphia	PA
66	Arnold	Webster	53 Southern Blvd	Miami	FL

(There are more records in the result set than the ones shown in this image)
(11 row(s) returned)

112. Concatenating columns with plain text

Writing custom letters in databases

Discussion:

In this example, we combine plain text with field data to write a letter using the database. In the sample letter below notice how punctuation marks are enclosed in single quotes. In addition, the SELECT statement is practically comprised of one field, named "CustomerLetter".

Code:

```
SELECT 'Dear' + ' '+ (LastName + ' ' + FirstName) +'.' + ' '+ 'It is our pleasure to announce that we reviewed your resume, and we have set up an interview time for you. Can you please verify that your address is' + ' ' + (Address +' '+ City +' '+ State +' '+ Zip) + ' ' + 'to send you corporate policy details and directions?' AS CustomerLetter
FROM Customers
```

Result:

CustomerLetter
Dear Demarco John. It is our pleasure to announce that we reviewed your resume, and we have set up an interview time for you. Can you please verify that your address is 11 Lark Street New York NY 12189 to send you corporate policy details and directions?
Dear Demania Mary. It is our pleasure to announce that we reviewed your resume, and we have set up an interview time for you. Can you please verify that your address is 12 Madison Ave New York NY 12189 to send you corporate policy details and directions?
Dear Demers George. It is our pleasure to announce that we reviewed your resume, and we have set up an interview time for you. Can you please verify that your address is 23 New Scotland Ave New York NY 12189 to send you corporate policy details and directions?
Dear Demetriou Phillip. It is our pleasure to announce that we reviewed your resume, and we have set up an interview time for you. Can you please verify that your address is 22 Academy Road New York NY 12189 to send you corporate policy details and directions?

(There are more records in the result set than the ones shown in this image)
(201 row(s) returned)

113. Use the left() string function to concatenate a single character from a field

Displaying only the first letter from the customers' first names with the left() function.

Discussion:

Let us assume we want to write a letter, but instead of using the complete first name of the customer, we only want the first letter to appear. To achieve this, we use string (text) functions. In this example, we use the left() function to extract the first character from the first name field. The text functions chapter in this book contains a plethora of examples on string manipulation.

Code:

```
SELECT 'Dear' + ' '+ (LastName + ' ' + left(FirstName, 1)) +'.' + ' '+ 'Please complete the enclosed forms so that we can ship your order to your state.' AS CustomerLetter
FROM Customers
```

Result:

CustomerLetter
Dear Demarco J. Please complete the enclosed forms so that we can ship your order to your state.
Dear Demania M. Please complete the enclosed forms so that we can ship your order to your state.
Dear Demers G. Please complete the enclosed forms so that we can ship your order to your state.
Dear Demetriou P. Please complete the enclosed forms so that we can ship your order to your state.

```
(There are more records in the result set than the ones shown in this image)
(201 row(s) returned)
```

114. Conditional concatenation with the iif() function

Concatenating supplier fields using state as a condition

Discussion:

Sometimes, we might not want to apply the same concatenation rules for all the records in the view. For example, we might want to create a letter for suppliers in NY and a different letter for everyone else, all in the same query. We can do this using conditional functions like the iif() one. Using the iif(condition, true, false) function below, we tell the database to concatenate the companyname, contacttitle, and contactname fields if the state is NY. If it is not, the database will concatenate only the contacttitle and contactname fields. This way, we can create two different sets of letters within the same view.

Code:

```
SELECT IIf(([State]='NY'),[Companyname]+' '+[ContactTitle]+' '+[Contactname], [ContactTitle]+' '+[Contactname]) AS MailTo
FROM Suppliers
```

Result:

MailTo
Sales Manager Pedro Adkins
Purchasing Manager John Marrey
Sales Manager Maria Hopkins
America's Greatest Snacks Sales Manager Andrew Daves

```
(There are more records in the result set than the ones shown in this image)
(10 row(s) returned)
```

115. Powerful conditional concatenation with the switch() function

Concatenating supplier columns different for each city

Discussion:

Now that we know how conditional concatenation works, we want to create separate letters for suppliers based on the city they reside. Practically, we need to use multiple conditions since in the suppliers table there are three cities: Boston, New York, and Dallas. Our task is to create a different letter for suppliers from each city using the same query.

Code:

```
SELECT
SWITCH (
City = 'Boston',   'Dear' +' '+ [ContactName]+',' +' '+ 'for our current sale we offer a 10% discount in' +' '+ [City],
City = 'Dallas',   'Dear' +' '+ [ContactName]+',' +' '+ 'for our current sale we offer a 25% discount in' +' '+ [City],
City = 'New York',  'Dear' +' '+ [ContactName]+',' +' '+ 'for our current sale we offer a 30% discount in' +' '+ [City],
)
AS SupplierLetter
FROM Suppliers
```

Result:

SupplierLetter
Dear Pedro Adkins, for our current sale we offer a 10% discount in Boston
Dear John Marrey, for our current sale we offer a 10% discount in Boston
Dear Maria Hopkins, for our current sale we offer a 10% discount in Boston
Dear Andrew Daves, for our current sale we offer a 30% discount in New York

```
(There are more records in the result set than the ones shown in this image)
(10 row(s) returned)
```

116. Conditional concatenation with the switch(), left(), and instr() functions

Concatenate supplier fields conditionally for each city

Discussion:

In the previous example, we saw how to use the switch() function to create a different letter for suppliers based on the city where they reside. However, we used the full name of the supplier since the ContactName field in the suppliers table contains both the first and last names of the supplier. This time, we would like to send a more personal letter using only the first name. This means that we need to extract the first name from the ContactName field. First, we use the instr() function to find the position of the space between the first and last name strings in the ContactName field. Then, we use the left function to extract the firstname characters from the beginning of the field up to the position of the space that we have identified using instr(). The whole SQL statement is shown below. As you can see in the result set, only the first names of the suppliers appear now.

Code:

```
SELECT
SWITCH(
[City]= 'Boston',        'Dear' +' '+ left(ContactName, InStr(1, ContactName," ")-1)
 +',' +' '+ 'for our current sale we offer a 25% discount in' +' '+ [City] ,

[City] ='Dallas',        'Dear' +' '+ left(ContactName, InStr(1, ContactName," ")-1) +',' +' '+ 'for our
current sale we offer a 10% discount in' +' '+ [City] ,

[City] ='New York',      'Dear' +' '+ left(ContactName, InStr(1, ContactName," ")-1) +',' +' '+ 'for our
current sale we offer a 20% discount in' +' '+ [City] ,
)
AS SupplierLetter
FROM suppliers
```

Result:

SupplierLetter
Dear Pedro, for our current sale we offer a 25% discount in Boston
Dear John, for our current sale we offer a 25% discount in Boston
Dear Maria, for our current sale we offer a 25% discount in Boston
Dear Andrew, for our current sale we offer a 20% discount in New York

(There are more records in the result set than the ones shown in this image)
(10 row(s) returned)

DISCUSSION QUESTIONS

1. What is the goal of field concatenation?
2. How many fields can we concatenate? Two, three, or more?
3. What is the most common character for field concatenation in databases?
4. Is there any arithmetic involved in field concatenation?
5. In what database object is it a good idea to use concatenated fields?
6. Can we concatenate plain text with field data?
7. Could you name a few practical examples of field concatenation?
8. Why is it useful to use string functions to concatenate fields?
9. What do we need to pay attention to when we use commas, periods, and other characters with concatenated fields?
10. How many functions are available for conditional concatenation and what is the difference between them?

HANDS-ON EXERCISES

Case 1

For each of the questions in this case create a new query in SQL view and name it as per the instructions in each question.

1. The sales department is initiating a cross-selling campaign and is asking for mailing labels to be send out to customers. Create a new query that concatenates the FirstName, LastName, Address, City, State, and Zip fields from the customer table. Sort results by LastName ascending without including the LastName in the result set. Save the query as Concatenations_Case1_Q1.

Your result should look like:

MailingLabel
Nicholas Ackerman 5 Buckingham Dr Dallas TX 52347
Alfred Allen 29 Water Street New York NY 12189
Pindar Ames 23 Cornell Dr New York NY 45357
Thomas Andersen 52 Betwood Street Orlando FL 89754

(There are more records in the result set than the ones shown in this image)
(201 row(s) returned)

2. The sales department is asking again for mailing labels. This time they want only the first letter of the customer FirstName to appear in the label followed by a period. Create a new query that concatenates the FirstName, LastName, Address, City, State, and Zip fields from the customer table. Sort results by lastname ascending without including the lastname in the result set. Save the query as Concatenations_Case1_Q2.

Your result should look like:

MailingLabel
N. Ackerman 5 Buckingham Dr Dallas TX 52347
A. Allen 29 Water Street New York NY 12189
P. Ames 23 Cornell Dr New York NY 45357
T. Andersen 52 Betwood Street Orlando FL 89754

(There are more records in the result set than the ones shown in this image)
(201 row(s) returned)

3. The HR department needs mailing labels to send out letters containing employee W-2s. Create a new query that concatenates the FirstName, LastName, Title, Address, City, State, and Zip fields from the SalesReps table. Add to the beginning of this concatenated field the words: "Dear valued customer" (without the quotation marks). Sort results by LastName ascending without including the LastName in the result set. Save the query as Concatenations_Case1_Q3.

Your result should look like:

MailingLabel
Dear valued customer Anderson John Sales Reppresentative 32 Colonial Street Boston MA 22459
Dear valued customer Baker Jim Account Manager 5 Ormond Street Dallas TX 52347
Dear valued customer Bernstein Michael Sales Reppresentative 21 Garden Ave New York NY 12189
Dear valued customer Delaney Kenneth Assistant Manager 89 Edenburg Ave New York NY 12189

(There are more records in the result set than the ones shown in this image)
(10 row(s) returned)

4. The marketing people want to send a mail card to customers announcing the availability of a new product line. The letter should be worded: Dear FirstName, space LastName. Our company has just received a new line of products. If interested, please return this card and we will send you our new catalog at the following address (Address space City space State space Zip). Create a new query that satisfies the request of the marketing people and sort results by LastName ascending without including LastName in the result set. Save the query as Concatenations_Case1_Q4.

Your result should look like:

Letter
Dear Nicholas, Ackerman. Our company has just received a new line of products. If interested, please return this card and we will send you our new catalog at the following address: 5 Buckingham Dr Dallas TX 52347
Dear Alfred, Allen. Our company has just received a new line of products. If interested, please return this card and we will send you our new catalog at the following address: 29 Water Street New York NY 12189
Dear Pindar, Ames. Our company has just received a new line of products. If interested, please return this card and we will send you our new catalog at the following address: 23 Cornell Dr New York NY 45357
Dear Thomas, Andersen. Our company has just received a new line of products. If interested, please return this card and we will send you our new catalog at the following address: 52 Betwood Street Orlando FL 89754

(There are more records in the result set than the ones shown in this image)
(201 row(s) returned)

5. The salespeople from the Boston office want to send a thank you letter to customers. For the customers in the city of Boston they want the mailing label to include the FirstName, Address, City, State, and Zip fields. For everyone else they want the label to include the FirstName, LastName, Address, City, State, and Zip fields. Create a new query that satisfies the marketing request. Sort results by LastName ascending without including the LastName in the result set. Save the query as Concatenations_Case1_Q5.

Your result should look like:

MailingLabel
Nicholas Ackerman 5 Buckingham Dr Dallas TX 52347
Alfred Allen 29 Water Street New York NY 12189
Pindar Ames 23 Cornell Dr New York NY 45357
Thomas Andersen 52 Betwood Street Orlando FL 89754

(There are more records in the result set than the ones shown in this image)
(201 row(s) returned)

Case 2

For each of the questions in this case create a new query in SQL view and name it as per the instructions in each question.

1. The HR department needs mailing labels for a letter to the employees of the organization. Create a new query that concatenates the Title, FirstName, LastName, Address, City, State, and Zip fields from the SalesReps table. Sort results by LastName ascending. Save the query as Concatenations_Case2_Q1.

Your result should look like:

MailingLabel
Sales Reppresentative John Anderson 32 Colonial Street Boston MA 22459
Account Manager Jim Baker 5 Ormond Street Dallas TX 52347
Sales Reppresentative Michael Bernstein 21 Garden Ave New York NY 12189
Assistant Manager Kenneth Delaney 89 Edenburg Ave New York NY 12189

(There are more records in the result set than the ones shown in this image)
(10 row(s) returned)

2. The director of inventory wants to send out a letter to suppliers asking for a reduction of their prices by 5%. The letter should be worded: "Dear [ContactName], due to the recent downturn in the market we would like to ask for a 5% discount for the products we buy from you. Please let us know if this is a possibility." Create a new query that satisfies the request of the inventory director, sort results by ContactName ascending without including ContactName in the result set. Save the query as Concatenations_Case2_Q2.

Your result should look like:

SupplierLetter
Dear Andrew Daves, due to the recent downturn in the market we would like to ask for a 5% discount for the products we buy from you. Please let us know within the week if this is a possibility.
Dear Frank Baker, due to the recent downturn in the market we would like to ask for a 5% discount for the products we buy from you. Please let us know within the week if this is a possibility.
Dear George Casey, due to the recent downturn in the market we would like to ask for a 5% discount for the products we buy from you. Please let us know within the week if this is a possibility.
Dear John Marrey, due to the recent downturn in the market we would like to ask for a 5% discount for the products we buy from you. Please let us know within the week if this is a possibility.

(There are more records in the result set than the ones shown in this image)
(10 row(s) returned)

3. The president of the company wants to send out a letter of appreciation to employees hired before 12/31/2012 to invite them to a special evening dinner. The letter should be written: "Dear [FirstName], you are now working with us for more than ten years and the company highly appreciates your work and loyalty. You are invited to our family dinner this Friday night at 6:30 PM. Create a new query that satisfies the request of the president, sort results by LastName ascending without including LastName in the result set. Save the query as Concatenations_Case2_Q3.

Your result should look like:

EmployeeLetter
Dear John, you are now working with us for more than ten years and the company highly appreciates your work and loyalty. You are invited to our family dinner this Friday night at 6:30 PM.
Dear George, you are now working with us for more than ten years and the company highly appreciates your work and loyalty. You are invited to our family dinner this Friday night at 6:30 PM.
Dear Gerald, you are now working with us for more than ten years and the company highly appreciates your work and loyalty. You are invited to our family dinner this Friday night at 6:30 PM.

```
(3 row(s) returned)
```

4. The sales director needs to send a letter to sales reps with information about upcoming events so that they can perform better in their sales quests. For each state the instructions are different, but you need to create one SQL statement that contains all three letters. Specifically:

   a. For NY: Dear [FirstName], Our major competitor cut prices by 15%. Cut our own prices by up to 20% but not more.
   b. For MA: Dear [FirstName], Start introducing our new product immediately before any of our competitors enters the market with their own updated products.
   c. For TX: Dear [FirstName], We were able to get significant discounts from our suppliers and as such try to increase market share by reducing our current prices by 20% for the next two months.

Create a new query that satisfies the request of the sales director, sort results by LastName ascending without including LastName in the result set. Save the query as Concatenations_Case2_Q4.

Your result should look like:

SalesRepLetter
Dear John, Start introducing our new product immediately before any of our competitors enters the market with their own updated products.
Dear Jim, We were able to get significant discounts from our suppliers and as such try to increase market share by reducing our current prices by 20% for the next two months
Dear Michael, Our major competitor cut prices by 15%. Cut our own prices by up to 20% but not more.
Dear Kenneth, Our major competitor cut prices by 15%. Cut our own prices by up to 20% but not more.

```
(There are more records in the result set than the ones shown in this image)
(10 row(s) returned)
```

5. The marketing director wants to send a letter to customers announcing new discounts for next month. The letter should be written: Dear [FirstName], space [LastName]. For the next 30 days only, take the opportunity to obtain our product at the generous discount rate of [

   a. 15% for the customers in NY state
   b. 20% for the customer in Texas,
   c. 25% for customers in Florida
   d. 20% for California

Create a new query that satisfies the request of the marketing director and sort results by LastName ascending without including LastName in the result set. Limit the results of the query to contain only customers from the states of NY, TX, FL, and CA. Save the query as Concatenations_Case2_Q5.

Your result should look like:

CustomerDiscountLetter
Dear Nicholas Ackerman. For the next 30 days only, take the opportunity to obtain our product at the generous discount rate of 20%.
Dear Alfred Allen. For the next 30 days only, take the opportunity to obtain our product at the generous discount rate of 15%.
Dear Pindar Ames. For the next 30 days only, take the opportunity to obtain our product at the generous discount rate of 15%.
Dear Thomas Andersen. For the next 30 days only, take the opportunity to obtain our product at the generous discount rate of 25%.

```
(There are more records in the result set than the ones shown in this image)
(125 row(s) returned)
```

CHAPTER 16
GROUPING DATA

The GROUP BY clause is a cloudy keyword for beginners and due to its intricacies, users and developers alike do not have a clear understanding of how it is used. In this chapter, we have two goals: First, to understand in detail when and how the GROUP BY clause is used, and second, to understand what results to expect. The fundamental goal of the GROUP BY clause is to summarize data. The general syntax of the GROUP BY clause appears below and we will explore the role of each option in detail in the examples. Notice that in the statement below the WHERE, HAVING, and ORDER BY clauses are optional. However, we need to use an aggregate function (sum, avg, min, max, etc.) in conjunction with the GROUP BY clause.

SELECT fields, aggregate function (field or calculated field)
FROM table
WHERE criteria (optional)
GROUP BY field(s)
HAVING criteria (optional)
ORDER BY field – (optional)

Before we start, let us have a look at the table tbls_customersgr below which is especially prepared for this chapter. It is a simple table with only twelve records about customers and their orders. The goal is to run the GROUP BY examples on this table and give you the ability to do the calculations manually so that you know exactly how every result is obtained. First, notice that there are four customers in total. Second, the customer, Mr. Mahoney, ordered twice: orders 57 and 502. Third, the rest of the three customers have only one order. Fourth, Mr. Riegert has one order with one product only, but he ordered two units of it. Fifth, orders 57, 494, 502, and 509 contain multiple products. Sixth, dark chocolate is a product included in two orders (in 57 and 509). At this point, we are ready to go through our examples.

PK	LastName	OrderID	OrderDate	ProductName	UnitPrice	Quantity
1	Riegert	1	11/6/2021	Dried Red Tart Cherries Gift Box - 6 oz	15	2
2	Mahoney	57	5/29/2022	Dark Chocolate Apricots in 20 oz. Bag	28	5
3	Mahoney	57	5/29/2022	Mushrooms Sauce	5	2
4	Mahoney	57	5/29/2022	Chocolate Chip Brownie	15	1
5	Martin	494	9/30/2022	Traditional Swedish Cookies, 5.25 oz	5	5
6	Martin	494	9/30/2022	Cream and honey biscuits	32	3
7	Mahoney	502	8/3/2022	Sesame Crackers in 20 oz. Pack	15	3
8	Mahoney	502	8/3/2022	Roasted No-Salt Almonds	15	1
9	Spicer	509	9/17/2021	Dark Chocolate Apricots in 20 oz. Bag	28	3
10	Spicer	509	9/17/2021	Corn Chips Bag	15	2
11	Spicer	509	9/17/2021	Oatmeal Raisin Walnut Cookies	8	3
12	Spicer	509	9/17/2021	All-Purpose Marinade II	15	2

tbls_customersgr

117. The GROUP BY clause on one column and one aggregated field

Calculate the total product units ordered by customer

Discussion:

In this scenario, the objective is to calculate the total units of products ordered by each customer. There are only two fields used in the SQL code below. LastName is the field on which we apply the GROUP BY clause, and TotalUnits is the aggregated field that results from applying the sum() function on the Quantity column.

Code:

```
SELECT LastName, SUM(quantity) AS TotalUnits
FROM tbls_Customersgr
GROUP BY LastName
```

Result:

LastName	TotalUnits
Mahoney	12
Martin	8
Riegert	2
Spicer	10

(4 row(s) returned)

118. The GROUP BY clause on one column and one aggregated-calculated field

Retrieve the total order amount by customer

Discussion:

In this scenario, we have a request to calculate the total order amount by customer in order to create a list with our best customers. There are two fields used in the SQL code. LastName is the field on which we apply the GROUP BY clause. TotalUnits is the aggregated field. However, this time, the aggregation occurs on the result of the multiplication of two columns. It is necessary to multiply the unitprice by the quantity columns to retrieve the total for each product in each order and then, sum the results by customer LastName. Pay attention when grouping on last name since multiple customers might have the same last name and your results will be incorrect. In this case, we group by last name because we know each customer last name corresponds to a unique customer.

Code:

```
SELECT LastName, SUM(unitprice*quantity) AS OrderTotal
FROM tbls_Customersgr
GROUP BY LastName
```

Result:

LastName	OrderTotal
Mahoney	225
Martin	121
Riegert	30
Spicer	168

(4 row(s) returned)

We see some interesting results here. First, since we grouped by customer last name, the result set produced four records, which is the exact number of unique customers we have in the tbls_customersgr table. Let us check the results to verify that the calculations are correct. We will use Mahoney as an example.

LastName	Unit Price	Quantity	UnitPrice* Quantity
Mahoney	15	1	15
Mahoney	15	3	45
Mahoney	15	1	15
Mahoney	5	2	10
Mahoney	28	5	140
		SUM()	**225**

First, the database multiplies the price of each product ordered * its quantity ordered for all products in all orders for the particular customer and then, it will SUM() the results. Doing the calculations manually, we arrived at 225 for Mr. Mahoney, which is the same number the database produced for this customer.

119. The GROUP BY clause on one column and two aggregated fields

Find total and average order amounts by customer

Discussion:

In this scenario, the goal is to produce a report that will show the total and average order amounts grouped by customer. There are three fields used in the SQL code: LastName, OrderTotal, and AvgOrder. The lastname is the field used with the GROUP BY clause. The fields OrderTotal and AvgOrder are the two aggregated fields.

Code:

```
SELECT LastName, SUM(UnitPrice*Quantity) AS OrderTotal, AVG(Unitprice*Quantity) AS
AvgOrder
FROM tbls_Customersgr
GROUP BY LastName
```

Result:

LastName	OrderTotal	AvgOrder
Mahoney	225	45
Martin	121	60.5
Riegert	30	30
Spicer	168	42

(4 row(s) returned)

120. The GROUP BY clause on one column, one aggregated field, and WHERE

Find total order amounts for a subset of customers

Discussion:

Sometimes, we want to exclude certain records from our aggregate calculations. In these cases, we can use the WHERE clause to exclude records we are not interested in working with. Using WHERE, we exclude records before the GROUP BY clause takes effect. Therefore, if we have a source dataset and use WHERE, the GROUP BY clause takes effect on the remaining records only.

In this example, we look for order totals by customer, but we want to exclude the orders from our customer Spicer. Mr. Spicer has only one order with orderid = 509. We use three fields in this SQL statement: Lastname, OrderTotal, and OrderID. LastName is the GROUP BY field, OrderTotal the aggregated field, and OrderID the filtering field. The order from Mr. Spicer will be filtered before the GROUP BY clause takes effect.

Code:

```
SELECT LastName, SUM(unitprice*quantity) AS OrderTotal
FROM tbls_customersgr
WHERE OrderID <> 509
GROUP BY LastName
```

Result:

LastName	OrderTotal
Mahoney	225
Martin	121
Riegert	30

(3 row(s) returned)

121. The GROUP BY clause on one column, one aggregated field, and HAVING

Find customer orders with total order amount exceeding $100

Discussion:

In this example, we want to exclude from the result set the customers whose order totals are less than $100. However, we do not know beforehand who these customers are. We need to run the GROUP BY clause, calculate the totals, and then exclude those below $100. This is exactly the case where HAVING is used, that is after the GROUP BY calculations have taken place. We use the HAVING clause only in conjunction with the GROUP BY clause. Looking at the result set, we can see that only three customers appear. The customer named Riegert does not appear because his order total is only 30.

Code:

```
SELECT LastName, SUM(UnitPrice*Quantity) AS OrderTotal
FROM tbls_customersgr
GROUP BY LastName
HAVING SUM(UnitPrice*Quantity) > 100
```

Result:

LastName	OrderTotal
Mahoney	225
Martin	121
Spicer	168

(3 row(s) returned)

122. The GROUP BY clause on one column, one aggregated field, WHERE and HAVING

Calculate order totals above $100 excluding a subset of products

Discussion:

In this example, pay attention to the combined use of WHERE and HAVING, which are both filtering statements. We want to calculate customer order totals, but we want to exclude from the result set customers whose order totals are less than $100. In addition, we want to exclude from the calculations the product "Chocolate Chip Brownie".

When it comes to filtering records in GROUP BY statements, we need to think if we need to use WHERE or HAVING, or a combination of the two. The way of thinking should be: Use the WHERE clause to exclude records that you do not want to be included in the aggregate calculations, and use HAVING to exclude values after the aggregations by GROUP BY take place. In this case, we use WHERE to exclude the product "Chocolate Chip

Brownie" from aggregations, and we use GROUP BY to create the aggregations on whatever records remain. After the aggregations are made, the HAVING clause takes effect to exclude order totals less than $100. The bottom line is that in the SQL statement below, the WHERE clause will run first, then the GROUP BY, and finally the HAVING clause.

Code:

```
SELECT LastName, SUM(unitprice*quantity) AS OrderTotal
FROM tbls_customersgr
WHERE productname <> 'Chocolate Chip Brownie'
GROUP BY LastName
HAVING SUM(unitprice*quantity)>100
```

Result:

LastName	OrderTotal
Mahoney	210
Martin	121
Spicer	168

(3 row(s) returned)

123. The GROUP BY clause with WHERE, HAVING, and ORDER BY

Sorting customer order totals

Discussion:

In this example, we introduce the ORDER BY clause. When the ORDER BY clause is used with GROUP BY, it will take effect after the database completes the calculations from the GROUP BY clause. In addition, we exclude from the calculations the order with orderid=509.

Code:

```
SELECT LastName, SUM(UnitPrice*Quantity) AS OrderTotal
FROM tbls_Customersgr
WHERE orderid <> 509
GROUP BY LastName
HAVING SUM(UnitPrice*Quantity)>100
ORDER BY LastName DESC
```

Result:

LastName	OrderTotal
Martin	121
Mahoney	225

(2 row(s) returned)

124. The GROUP BY clause with NULL VALUES

Calculate average customer order amounts with and without null values

Discussion:

For the purposes of this example, open the table tbls_customersgr and delete the value of 28 for the unitprice of Dark Chocolate Apricots for OrderID = 57. The idea is to demonstrate what happens when null values exist in data used for calculations in GROUP BY clauses. Using 3 records in this table, you can check the results manually and learn so that when you deal with 500,000 records, you know exactly what to do.

tbls_Customersgr					
LastName	OrderID	OrderDate	ProductName	UnitPrice	Quantity
Mahoney	57	2022/5/29	Dark Chocolate Apricots in 20 oz. Bag		5
Mahoney	57	2022/5/29	Mushrooms Sauce	5	2
Mahoney	57	2022/5/29	Chocolate Chip Brownie	15	1

Let us run two pieces of code:

Code:

```
SELECT OrderID, Avg(UnitPrice*Quantity) AS AverageOrderAmount
FROM tbls_Customersgr
GROUP BY OrderID
```

Result with null values:

OrderID	AverageOrderAmount
1	30
57	12.5
494	60.5
502	30
509	42

(5 row(s) returned)

Now replace the unit price for Dark Chocolate Apricots at $28 and run the SQL statement again:

Code:

```
SELECT OrderID, Avg(UnitPrice*Quantity) AS AverageOrderAmount
FROM tbls_Customersgr
GROUP BY OrderID
```

Result without null values:

OrderID	AverageOrderAmount
1	30
57	55
494	60.5
502	30
509	42

(5 row(s) returned)

As you can see from the first result set, all the calculations look right except for orderid = 57. In this case, the database gave us an average of 12.5 with null values and an average of 55 without null values. In other words, it takes into consideration only the two products in that order and leaves out the third—the one with the missing UnitPrice. I simply want you to know that when missing data exists, aggregate functions will ignore the missing values. Some might argue that this is correct because if we do not have data for an item, it should not be included in the calculations. Others might say that when missing data exists, they should be taken into consideration. It takes a few seconds to check for nulls (see the chapter on null values), and you will not have to worry about how aggregate functions will handle your data.

125. The GROUP BY clause on multiple columns

Find order totals grouped by customer and order number at the same time

Discussion:

Sometimes, we want to have a more detailed view of our data. For example, we might want to retrieve order totals by customer and OrderID at the same time. We can easily achieve this with GROUP BY. Since we grouped first by last name and then by OrderID, orders will be totaled by lastname first, followed by OrderID. We can reverse the order of grouping or add more grouping fields according to the level of the detail we would like to see.

Code:

```
SELECT LastName, OrderID, SUM([UnitPrice]*[Quantity]) AS OrderTotal
FROM tbls_Customersgr
GROUP BY LastName, OrderID
```

Result:

LastName	OrderID	OrderTotal
Mahoney	57	165
Mahoney	502	60
Martin	494	121
Riegert	1	30
Spicer	509	168

(5 row(s) returned)

DISCUSSION QUESTIONS

1. What is the basic goal of the GROUP BY clause in relational databases?
2. Are aggregate functions optional or required with the GROUP BY clause?
3. Can we use multiple aggregate fields with the GROUP BY clause?
4. Can we summarize values in multiple fields with the GROUP BY clause?
5. What do we need to pay attention to when we have null values in the fields on which we use aggregate functions?
6. How exactly does the WHERE clause work with GROUP BY?
7. What is the purpose of the HAVING clause in GROUP BY statements?
8. Are the HAVING and WHERE clauses mandatory or optional with GROUP BY?
9. Can we use the HAVING clause without the GROUP BY clause?
10. Which one takes precedence? The WHERE clause or the HAVING clause?

HANDS-ON EXERCISES

Case 1

For each of the questions in this case create a new query in SQL view and name it as per the instructions in each question.

1. The inventory people are asking for a report that will display the total shipping cost by shipping company (hint: group by ShipperID) for all orders in the Orders table. Create a new query that satisfies the inventory people request. Save the query as GroupBy_Case1_Q1.

Your result should look like:

ShipperID	TotalShipping
1	9661
2	7609
3	4354

(3 row(s) returned)

2. The marketing people need a report that will provide the number of orders placed by each customer (hint: group by CustomerID) in the Orders table. Create a new query that satisfies the marketing people request. Save the query as GroupBy_Case1_Q2.

Your result should look like:

CustomerID	NumberOfOrders
1	7
2	4
3	6
4	9

(There are more records in the result set than the ones shown in this image)
(190 row(s) returned)

3. The marketing people are asking for a report that will provide the number of customers by zip code. Use the Customers table to create a new query that satisfies the marketing people request. Save the query as GroupBy_Case1_Q3.

Your result should look like:

Zip	NumberOfCustomers
11882	12
12110	4
12189	19
21214	13

```
(There are more records in the result set than the ones shown in this image)
(17 row(s) returned)
```

4. The salespeople are asking for a report that will provide the average, minimum, and maximum shipping cost of orders by customer from the Orders table (Hint: group by CustomerID). Create a new query that satisfies the salespeople request. Save the query as GroupBy_Case1_Q4.

Your result should look like:

CustomerID	MinShippingCost	AvgShippingCost	MaxShippingCost
1	11	19.8571428571429	30
2	13	20.25	26
3	13	22.5	30
4	15	22.3333333333333	32

```
(There are more records in the result set than the ones shown in this image)
(190 row(s) returned)
```

5. The salespeople now want the same report as in question four, excluding however any customers with an average shipping cost of more than 20. Create a new query that satisfies the salespeople request. Save the query as GroupBy_Case1_Q5.

Your result should look like:

CustomerID	MinShippingCost	AvgShippingCost	MaxShippingCost
1	11	19.8571428571429	30
5	12	19.25	25
7	12	19	26
10	15	17.6666666666667	22

```
(There are more records in the result set than the ones shown in this image)
(60 row(s) returned)
```

Case 2

For each of the questions in this case create a new query in SQL view and name it as per the instructions in each question.

1. The sales department is asking for a report that will provide the total product quantity sold by productID for all order items in the table JoinOrdersProducts. Create a new query that satisfies the salespeople request. Sort results by TotalProductUnitsSold descending. Save the query as GroupBy_Case2_Q1.

Your result should look like:

ProductID	TotalProductUnitsSold
38	164
33	159
35	150
53	149

```
(There are more records in the result set than the ones shown in this image)
(70 row(s) returned)
```

2. The marketing people are asking for a report listing the most successful products in terms of overall sales. Specifically, they are asking for a report that will provide the total order amount by productID for all order items in the table JoinOrdersProducts. Do not take into consideration any product discounts given to customers. Sort results by TotalOrderAmount DESC. Create a new query that satisfies the marketing people request. Save the query as GroupBy_Case2_Q2.

Your result should look like:

ProductID	TotalOrderAmount
31	4640
39	4448
17	4088
37	3744

```
(There are more records in the result set than the ones shown in this image)
(70 row(s) returned)
```

3. Accounts payable is asking for a report that will provide the min, average, and max shipping cost by ShipperID for all orders in the Orders table. Create a new query that satisfies the accounts payable request. Save the query as GroupBy_Case2_Q3.

Your result should look like:

ShipperID	MinShippingCost	AvgShippingCost	MaxShippingCost
1	11	22.1582568807339	32
2	11	20.6766304347826	32
3	11	22.2142857142857	32

```
(3 row(s) returned)
```

4. The marketing people are asking for a report that will provide the total order amount by productID for all order items in the table JoinOrdersProducts. However, this time they want the products with ProductIDs 1,14,15, and 28 to be excluded from the results. They also want to see total order amounts above $2000. Do not take into consideration any product discounts given to customers. Create a new query that satisfies the marketing people request. Save the query as GroupBy_Case2_Q4.

Your result should look like:

ProductID	TotalOrderAmount
2	2175
4	2340
11	2025
12	3668

```
(There are more records in the result set than the ones shown in this image)
(23 row(s) returned)
```

5. The marketing people need one additional report that will provide the total order amount for each product within each order in the JoinOrdersProducts table. This time you need the results aggregated by OrderID first

and then by ProductID within each order. Do not include any sorting in your query and do not take into consideration any discounts extended to customers. Save the query as GroupBy_Case2_Q5.

Your result should look like:

OrderID	ProductID	TotalOrderAmount
1	61	30
2	23	60
2	24	15
2	32	45

(There are more records in the result set than the ones shown in this image)
(2411 row(s) returned)

CHAPTER 17
AGGREGATING DATA

Aggregate functions like sum(), avg(), count(), count(*), max(), and min() summarize data into useful pieces of information. Aggregate functions process many values from a table column to produce a summary value, like a summation, an average, or a maximum value. Aggregate functions are often used with calculated fields which are themselves the result of the multiplication, summation, or division of two or more fields.

With aggregate functions, you need to pay attention to null values in your data. In this chapter, we will clarify the effect of null values on aggregate calculations. However, with null values, we should only have one goal in mind: To eliminate null values from the columns on which we do aggregations. In other words, we need to develop a habit to examine our data for nulls before we even use aggregate functions. Of course, experienced developers do not allow null values in their tables, and they use default values and constraints to avoid them altogether.

Aggregate functions are extremely useful when combined with the GROUP BY clause. We have examined GROUP BY in a previous chapter and we are now ready to go deeper, using it with aggregate functions to demonstrate the usefulness of the analytics obtained. For the purposes of this chapter, we have created a special table called tbls_customersag with only 20 records so that we can check the results against this small dataset by making calculations manually. You might want to have a close look at this table before you start this chapter.

126. The count() function

Count the number of orders

Discussion:

The count() function calculates the number of records in a dataset. It will produce correct results provided it is used on a field that does not contain null values. In practice, the count() function is usually applied on the primary key of the table since it is the one field that is certain not to contain nulls. In this example, we use it on the OrderID field, which is not the primary key, but I use it to show you the different results produced by count() in the subsequent examples. In this example, the count() function returns 20 for the number of records in the table and we can be certain that the OrderID field does not contain any null values since the number returned from the count() function is equal to the number of records in the table.

Code:

```
SELECT count(OrderID) as NumberofOrders
FROM tbls_Customersag
```

Result:

NumberofOrders
20

(1 row(s) returned)

127. The count() and count(*) functions in comparison

Count the number of records in a table using count(*)

Discussion:

In this scenario, the objective is to understand the differences between Count(), Count(*), and Count DISTINCT so that we can take full advantage of them in our data tasks. For this purpose, let us delete temporarily the name of the customer Davis from the table tbls_customersag. Now we still have 20 records in the table but with the last name of a customer missing.

tbls_Customersag					
CustID	LastName	OrderID	ProductID	UnitPrice	Quantity
1		4	55	15	3
2	Sterling	60	56	12	5
3	Sterling	60	21	15	4

In the example below, we use the count() function first. As you can see from the result set, the number returned is 19. This is because we used count() on the lastname field in which a value is missing. Consequently, while the table contains 20 records, we received only 19. You do not need to worry about these intricacies if you follow a simple piece of advice: Any time you work with aggregate functions, calculated fields, or GROUP BY, check your records for null values, and make the necessary edits and replacements. Then, you do not need to worry about the intricacies of how aggregate functions or calculated fields behave with missing data.

Code:

```
SELECT count(LastName) as NumberofCustomers
FROM tbls_Customersag
```

Result:

NumberofCustomers
19

```
(1 row(s) returned)
```

Now, let us use the count(*) function. As you can see from the result set, the count(*) function returned the correct result of 20 records in the table.

Code:

```
SELECT count(*) as NumberofCustomers
FROM tbls_Customersag
```

Result:

NumberofCustomers
20

```
(1 row(s) returned)
```

Now, let's use count(*) with DISTINCT. As you can see from the result set, the number of unique customers returned is 9. We know already, however, that we have 8 unique customers in the table. What happened? This time, the count(*) function returned 9 because it counted the "blank" customer as an additional unique customer.

Code:

```
SELECT Count(*) AS NumberofCustomers
FROM
(SELECT DISTINCT LastName FROM tbls_Customersag)
```

Result:

NumberofCustomers
9

(1 row(s) returned)

Now, open the tbls_Customersag table and reinsert the value "Davis" for CustID = 1.

128. The count() function with the GROUP BY clause

Count the number of orders by customer

Discussion:

The business goal is to calculate the number of orders by customer. We can answer this using the count() function with the GROUP BY clause. From the result set, we obtain two pieces of information. First, we know we have 9 unique customers in a dataset of 20 records. Second, we have a count of the number of orders by each customer.

Code:

```
SELECT LastName, count(OrderID) as NumberofOrders
FROM tbls_Customersag
GROUP BY LastName
```

Result:

LastName	NumberofOrders
Currier	1
Davis	1
Johnson	4
Madsen	2

(There are more records in the result set than the ones shown in this image)
(9 row(s) returned)

129. The AVG() function

Calculate the average order amount by customer

In this example we calculate the number of orders and the average order amount by customer. Some customers might have many orders but with minimal order amounts.

Code:

```
SELECT LastName, count(OrderID) as NumberofOrders, AVG(UnitPrice*Quantity)
AS AvgOrderAmount
FROM tbls_Customersag
GROUP BY LastName
```

Result:

LastName	NumberofOrders	AvgOrderAmount
Currier	1	30
Davis	1	45
Johnson	4	18.75
Madsen	2	52.5

(There are more records in the result set than the ones shown in this image)
(9 row(s) returned)

130. The avg() function with the WHERE clause

Calculate the number of orders and average order amounts for specific customers

Discussion:

Using WHERE will cause the database engine to first eliminate the records as per the WHERE clause and then perform any calculations on the remaining ones. In this example, we exclude two customers using the NOT IN operator.

Code:

```
SELECT LastName, count(orderid) as NumberofOrders, AVG(unitprice*quantity)
AS AvgOrderAmount
FROM tbls_customersag
WHERE lastname NOT IN ('Johnson', 'Madsen')
GROUP BY lastname
```

Result:

LastName	NumberofOrders	AvgOrderAmount
Currier	1	30
Davis	1	45
McGrath	1	10
Miller	2	25

(There are more records in the result set than the ones shown in this image)
(7 row(s) returned)

131. The sum() function

Calculate the number of orders, average, and total order amounts by customer

Discussion:

Here, we continue from the previous example and add the sum() function to calculate the total order amount by customer. We are still excluding two customers from the calculations using the NOT IN operator in the WHERE clause.

Code:

```
SELECT LastName, count(orderid) as Num, avg(unitprice*quantity)
AS Avg, sum(unitprice*quantity) AS Total
FROM tbls_customersag
WHERE LastName NOT IN ('Johnson', 'Madsen')
GROUP BY LastName
```

Result:

LastName	Num	Avg	Total
Currier	1	30	30
Davis	1	45	45
McGrath	1	10	10
Miller	2	25	50
Ming	2	60	120

(There are more records in the result set than the ones shown in this image)
(7 row(s) returned)

132. The min() function

Calculate the minimum order amount by customer

Discussion:

In this example, we add the computation of the minimum order amount by customer.

Code:

```
SELECT LastName, count(orderid) as Num, min(unitprice*quantity) AS Min, avg(unitprice*quantity)
AS Avg, sum(unitprice*quantity) AS Total
FROM tbls_customersag
WHERE lastname NOT IN ('Johnson', 'Madsen')
GROUP BY lastname
```

Result:

LastName	Num	Min	Avg	Total
Currier	1	30	30	30
Davis	1	45	45	45
McGrath	1	10	10	10
Miller	2	20	25	50

```
(There are more records in the result set than the ones shown in this image)
(7 row(s) returned)
```

133. The max() function

Calculate the maximum value of customer orders

Discussion:

The max() function will calculate the value of the biggest order for each customer, and it will report just that in the result set.

Code:

```
SELECT LastName, count(orderid) as Num, min(unitprice*quantity) AS Min, avg(unitprice*quantity)
AS Avg, max(unitprice*quantity) AS Max, sum(unitprice*quantity) AS Total
FROM tbls_customersag
WHERE lastname NOT IN ('Johnson', 'Madsen')
GROUP BY lastname
```

Result:

LastName	Num	Min	Avg	Max	Total
Currier	1	30	30	30	30
Davis	1	45	45	45	45
McGrath	1	10	10	10	10
Miller	2	20	25	30	50

```
(There are more records in the result set than the ones shown in this image)
(7 row(s) returned)
```

134. The Standard Deviation and Variance functions

Calculate the standard deviation and variance of customer order amounts

Discussion:

Using SQL, we can do much more than the usual arithmetic calculations. Actually, we can even perform some statistical analysis. In this example, we are looking for the standard deviation and variance of order amounts for each customer. We use the cint() conversion function to avoid multiple decimals for the standard deviation column. In the result set, Currier and McGrath have only one order and, as it is logical, no variance and standard deviation can be calculated. From a business point of view, customers Davis, Sterling, and Powers are prone to making orders that vary a lot in size.

Code:

```
SELECT lastname, count(orderid) as Num, min(unitprice*quantity) AS Min, avg(unitprice*quantity)
AS Avg, max(unitprice*quantity) AS Max, sum(unitprice*quantity) AS Total, convert(decimal(5,2),
stdev(unitprice*quantity)) As stdev, var(unitprice*quantity) as var
 FROM tbls_customersag
WHERE lastname NOT IN ('Johnson', 'Madsen')
GROUP BY lastname
```

Result:

lastname	Num	Min	Avg	Max	Total	stdev	var
Currier	1	30	30	30	30		
Davis	1	45	45	45	45		
McGrath	1	10	10	10	10		
Miller	2	20	25	30	50	7	50

(There are more records in the result set than the ones shown in this image)
(7 row(s) returned)

135. Aggregate functions with GROUP BY and HAVING

Calculate order amounts and filter records based on results of aggregate functions

Discussion:

This time, our manager wants a report that shows the number of orders, minimum, average, maximum, and total order amounts calculated by customer. In addition, he wants products with ProductID 13, 56, and 30 to not participate in the calculations. He also wants us to exclude from the result set any customers with total order amounts of less than $100 and any customers with average order amounts of less than $40. Finally, he wants us to exclude from the calculations any customers with a standard deviation in their order amounts of 20 and above, but the standard deviation calculation should not appear in the result set.

The above sounds complicated, and it is complicated to a degree. Still, it is not difficult to achieve. I would like you to learn to follow a process when it comes to complicated SQL statements. This process involves the incremental building of the SQL statement instead of trying to think about everything at once. Essentially, we will build the solution one step at a time.

Our first step in any complicated problem involving SQL is to try to identify the fields. In this example, we need seven fields to do our job, and this step is straightforward. The SELECT statement with the seven fields appears below. We include the type conversion function cint() to restrict the number of decimals for the standard deviation field.

```
SELECT lastname, count(orderid) as Num, min(unitprice*quantity) AS Min, avg(unitprice*quantity)
AS Avg, max(unitprice*quantity) AS Max, sum(unitprice*quantity) AS Total,
cint(stdev(unitprice*quantity)) As stdev
FROM tbls_customersag
GROUP BY lastname
```

Our next step is to exclude products with productID 13, 56, and 30. For this task, we make use of the WHERE clause with the NOT IN operator as it appears below:

```
SELECT lastname, count(orderid) as Num, min(unitprice*quantity) AS Min, avg(unitprice*quantity)
AS Avg, max(unitprice*quantity) AS Max, sum(unitprice*quantity) AS Total,
cint(stdev(unitprice*quantity)) As stdev
FROM tbls_customersag
WHERE productID NOT IN (13,56,30)
GROUP BY lastname
```

The next step is to exclude from the result set any customers with total order amounts of less than $100 and any customers with average order amounts of less than $40. For cases like this one, we make use of the HAVING clause, which is the filtering clause you can use to filter records after aggregate calculations have been performed. The code will now look like this:

```
SELECT lastname, count(orderid) as Num, min(unitprice*quantity) AS Min, avg(unitprice*quantity)
AS Avg, max(unitprice*quantity) AS Max, sum(unitprice*quantity) AS Total,
cint(stdev(unitprice*quantity)) As stdev
FROM tbls_customersag
WHERE productID NOT IN (13,56,30)
GROUP BY lastname
HAVING sum(unitprice*quantity) > 100 AND avg(unitprice*quantity) > 40
```

The final step in building the SQL statement is to exclude from the calculations any customers with a standard deviation in their order amounts of 20 and above but without including the standard deviation calculation in the result set. In the SQL code below, we took out the expression cint(stdev(unitprice*quantity)) from the SELECT statement and put it in the HAVING clause. This way, the filtering happens, but the standard deviation calculations do not appear in the result set.

Code:

```
SELECT LastName, count(orderid) as Num, min(unitprice*quantity) AS Min, avg(unitprice*quantity)
AS Avg, max(unitprice*quantity) AS Max, sum(unitprice*quantity) AS Total FROM tbls_customersag
WHERE productID NOT IN (13,56,30)
GROUP BY LastName
HAVING sum(unitprice*quantity) > 100 AND avg(unitprice*quantity) > 40 AND
cint(stdev(unitprice*quantity)) < 20
```

After all of the filtering, only one customer out of nine satisfied all of the criteria.

Result:

LastName	Num	Min	Avg	Max	Total
Ming	2	60	60	60	120

(1 row(s) returned)

DISCUSSION QUESTIONS

1. What is the main purpose of aggregate functions?
2. Name four aggregate functions and their corresponding roles.
3. Can we use aggregate functions with calculated fields?
4. What is the clause that enhances the usefulness of aggregate functions?
5. Why do we need to pay attention to null values when using aggregate functions?
6. How can we avoid null values by design?
7. What is the difference between the Count() and Count(*) aggregate functions?
8. If we want to filter the results of an aggregated column, which filtering keyword do we use?
9. What other clauses can we use with aggregate functions to improve their usefulness?
10. Can you name two aggregate functions that are used in statistics?

HANDS-ON EXERCISES

Case 1

For each of the questions in this case create a new query in SQL view and name it as per the instructions in each question.

1. The salespeople are asking for the total number of customers in the customer table. Create a new query that satisfies the salespeople request. Save the query as Aggregations_Case1_Q1.

Your result should look like:

NumberofCustomers
201

```
(1 row(s) returned)
```

2. The salespeople are now asking for a report that will display the number of customers by city. Create a new query that satisfies the salespeople request and sort results by the number of customers in descending order. Save the query as Aggregations_Case1_Q2.

Your result should look like:

City	NumberofCustomers
Los Angeles	31
New York	27
Chicago	14
Boston	14

```
(There are more records in the result set than the ones shown in this image)
(15 row(s) returned)
```

3. Create a query that will display the number of customers by city excluding customers from NY State. Sort results by number of customers descending. Save the query as Aggregations_Case1_Q3.

Your result should look like:

City	NumberofCustomers
Los Angeles	31
Chicago	14
Boston	14
Phoenix	13

(There are more records in the result set than the ones shown in this image)
(13 row(s) returned)

4. Create a report that will display the number of customers by city excluding customers from NY State. Also, excludes any cities with less than 10 customers. Create a new query that satisfies these criteria and sort results by number of customers descending. Save the query as Aggregations_Case1_Q4.

Your result should look like:

City	NumberofCustomers
Los Angeles	31
Chicago	14
Boston	14
Phoenix	13
Denver	13

(There are more records in the result set than the ones shown in this image)
(10 row(s) returned)

5. Create a query that will display the number of customers by zip code excluding customers from NY State. In addition, exclude any zip codes with less than 10 customers. Sort results by number of customers ascending. Save the query as Aggregations_Case1_Q5.

Your result should look like:

Zip	NumberofCustomers
56789	10
88987	12
53289	12
11882	12

(There are more records in the result set than the ones shown in this image)
(10 row(s) returned)

Case 2

For each of the questions in this case create a new query in SQL view and name it as per the instructions in each question.

1. The sales department is asking for a report that will display the total number of products by SupplierID from the Products table. Create a new query that satisfies the salespeople request. Save the query as Aggregations_Case2_Q1.

Your result should look like:

SupplierId	NumberofProducts
1	10
2	9
3	7
4	6

```
(There are more records in the result set than the ones shown in this image)
(10 row(s) returned)
```

2. The marketing department is asking for a report that will provide the minimum, average, maximum, and total product units sold. Create a new query that satisfies the marketing people request. Use the cint() function where appropriate so that you do not get multiple decimals. Save the query as Aggregations_Case2_Q2. Hint: Use the JoinOrdersProducts table.

Your result should look like:

MinSold	AverageSold	MaxSold	TotalUnitsSold
1	3	6	8429

```
(1 row(s) returned)
```

3. The marketing department is asking for a report that will provide the minimum, average, maximum, and total product units sold grouped by ProductID. Sort results by ProductID ascending. Create a new query that satisfies the marketing people request and save it as Aggregations_Case2_Q3. Hint: Use the JoinOrdersProducts table. Use the cint() function where appropriate so that you do not get multiple decimals.

Your result should look like:

ProductID	MinSold	AverageSold	MaxSold	TotalUnitsSold
1	1	3	6	97
2	1	4	6	145
3	1	4	6	132
4	1	3	6	117

```
(There are more records in the result set than the ones shown in this image)
(70 row(s) returned)
```

4. The marketing department is asking for a report that will provide the minimum, average, maximum, and total product units sold grouped by ProductID. The result should only include products with unit prices above 20. Sort results by ProductID ascending. Create a new query that satisfies the marketing people request and save it as Aggregations_Case2_Q4. Hint: Use the JoinOrdersProducts table. Use the cint() function where appropriate so that you do not get multiple decimals.

Your result should look like:

ProductID	MinSold	AverageSold	MaxSold	TotalUnitsSold
12	1	4	6	131
17	1	4	6	146
19	1	4	6	112
22	1	4	6	120

```
(There are more records in the result set than the ones shown in this image)
(14 row(s) returned)
```

5. The marketing department is asking for a report that will provide the minimum, average, maximum, and total product units sold grouped by ProductID. The result should only include products with unit prices above 20 and total units sold equal or greater than 100. Sort results by ProductID ascending. Create a new query that satisfies the marketing people request and save it as Aggregations_Case2_Q5. Hint: Use the JoinOrdersProducts table. Use the cint() function where appropriate so that you do not get multiple decimals.

Your result should look like:

ProductID	MinSold	AverageSold	MaxSold	TotalUnitsSold
12	1	4	6	131
17	1	4	6	146
19	1	4	6	112
22	1	4	6	120

```
(There are more records in the result set than the ones shown in this image)
(13 row(s) returned)
```

CHAPTER 18
CROSSTABBING DATA

Crosstab queries have a reputation of being complicated and intricate objects but we can work efficiently with them once we recognize their basic structure. In essence, to create a crosstab query, we use three fields only. One field will generate the columns, the second will generate the columns, and the third will generate the values. The value field is the actual field on which the calculations occur using aggregate functions like sum(), avg(), count(), count(*), max(), and min(). Let us assume we want to calculate order totals by state and year, that is, we would like to know how much we sold in every state in every year. The basic design of our query will look like:

	Year
State	**Value**

When we run the query, since we have multiple states and years in our data, our result set will look like this:

	Year1	Year2	Year3
State1	Value	Value	Value
State2	Value	Value	Value
State3	Value	Value	Value

The state row field will expand automatically to include data for as many states as we have in our database. The year field will expand to include as many columns as the number of years we have in our data. The value field will present the sum of order amounts for all of the combinations of years and states.

The above diagram represents the basic structure of a crosstab query. However, we have a couple of bonuses at this point. Once we understand how crosstab queries work, we also understand how pivot tables work in Excel, how pivot charts summarize their data, how OLAP cubes work, how data visualization software like Tableau works, and we have an advantage over someone who creates pivot tables and charts without full knowledge of data summaries under the hood. In the following examples, we start with basic crosstab queries and incrementally add techniques that will make our crosstab queries powerful tools for our work.

Working with crosstab queries usually involves the joining of multiple tables. We might need a field from the customers table, a field from the orders table, and a field from the products table. Since joins are not the focus of this chapter, I would like to spare you the intricacies of joining tables and focus on the actual crosstab queries themselves. That is why the examples in this chapter are based on a query purposely made for this chapter. Its name is "Qry_Crosstab_Base" from which we will take all of the fields we need to work with. Of course, we also provide a chapter in this book to explain joins in detail so that you can professionally work with joined tables.

136. A crosstab query with three fields - example 1

Find total sales by state and year

Discussion:

As you can see from the SQL code, we use three fields to create this very informative crosstab query. The first is the state field, which we use for row headings, and the second is the OrderDate field which we use for column headings. For the OrderDate field there is a catch: We use the year() function to extract the year out of the order dates we have in the database. The third field is the value field, which we name OrderTotal. This is a calculated field that sums the (unitprice * the quantity) of each product for each of our customer orders.

When you look at the SQL code, you will notice the use of a new statement called TRANSFORM. The TRANSFORM statement relates to the value field in a crosstab query, and it always precedes the SQL statement. Additionally, it is always followed by the aggregate function used for the value field, which in this case is sum(Quantity * UnitPrice). Below is the SQL code for the crosstab query explaining it step by step:

TRANSFORM Sum([unitprice]*[quantity]) AS Ordertotal
The TRANSFORM statement is used for the value field in a crosstab query.

SELECT State FROM Qry_Crosstab_Base
The SELECT statement is used for the row-heading field of the crosstab query.

GROUP BY State
The GROUP BY clause follows next, and it is applied on the same field used in the SELECT statement. Since we used State for the SELECT statement, we use State for the GROUP BY clause as well.

PIVOT Year([OrderDate])
The PIVOT statement is the last one used in a crosstab query, and it is applied on the column-heading field.

Below is the general structure of a crosstab query in SQL code.

```
TRANSFORM ValueField
SELECT ColumnField
FROM DataSource
GROUP BY ColumnField
PIVOT RowField
```

Code:

```
TRANSFORM sum(unitprice*quantity) AS Ordertotal
SELECT CustomerState
FROM Qry_Crosstab_Base
GROUP BY CustomerState
PIVOT Year(OrderDate)
```

Looking at the results below, we can quickly understand and compare sales volumes by state and year. For example, the highest sales revenues come from California but they have dropped in 2022. In Ohio, we need to have a look at what is happening because sales are dropping continuously year by year. This is the power of crosstab queries; we get summarized results in seconds. If you notice an amount without an associated year, it means right away that we have an order or orders without date values in the OrderDate field which means we have null values in our data. As we have said multiple times before, null values always interfere with calculations and they need to be dealt with.

Result:

CustomerState	2020	2021	2022
AZ	2386	3460	2849
CA	13364	14919	12216
CO	3326	1937	1961
DC	3351	3102	3020
FL	4736	3413	4439

```
(10 row(s) returned)
(There are more records in the result set than the ones shown in this image)
```

137. A crosstab query with three fields—example 2

Find total sales by city and year

Discussion:

Our business manager is very happy with the comprehensive sales report we provided by state and year. Now that she knows what the database can do, she asks for an additional report that will show sales volumes by city and year. In about three seconds we replace the state field with the city field in our query, and our new crosstab query is ready!

Code:

```
TRANSFORM Sum([unitprice]*[quantity]) AS Ordertotal
SELECT CustomerCity
FROM Qry_Crosstab_Base
GROUP BY CustomerCity
PIVOT Year([OrderDate])
```

Result:

CustomerCity	2020	2021	2022
Albany	1214	1356	1199
Boston	2020	859	1999
Chicago	4924	3076	2353
Dallas	4174	3292	2691
Denver	3326	1937	1961

```
(15 row(s) returned)
(There are more records in the result set than the ones shown in this image)
```

138. The issue of uniqueness of values in crosstab queries

Find total sales by customer and year

Discussion:

Now, our supervisor asks for additional detail. Specifically, he wants a sales report by customer and year. Again, in a few seconds, we replace the city field from the previous example with the customer lastname and presumably, we are done!

Unfortunately, this is not the case this time! Our problem is that multiple customers might have the same last name. Since we are grouping on the last name field, all of the customers with the same lastname will be grouped together! This is a very common problem in crosstab queries and when using the GROUP BY clause. Consequently, I would like you to develop a process to think thoroughly about the uniqueness of values when using the GROUP BY clause. For instance, you should think about the possibility of having the same last name in your data for multiple customers. The same is true for city fields since the same city name might refer to multiple distinct cities, as is the case with Portland, Oregon and Portland, Maine. In the next example, we will solve this problem using concatenated fields.

Also, notice that in the result set that there are some blank values. For example, there are blank values for the customer Ames in 2020 and 2022. These blanks mean that Ames has not placed any orders in those years.

Code:

```
TRANSFORM sum([unitprice]*[quantity]) AS Ordertotal
SELECT CustomerLastName
FROM Qry_Crosstab_Base
GROUP BY CustomerLastName
PIVOT year([OrderDate])
```

Result:

CustomerLastName	2020	2021	2022
Ackerman	32	207	120
Ames		871	
Andersen		393	350
Anderson	924	1434	965
Anthopolis	240	48	220
Aversa			469
Baker	482	617	255
Balfur	313	75	100
Barra	105	475	294
Basil	15	204	440

(171 row(s) returned)
(There are more records in the result set than the ones shown in this image)

139. Crosstab queries with concatenated fields

Find total sales by customer and year displaying full customer names

Discussion:

In the previous example, the results of the crosstab query were questionable because multiple customers might have the same last name. In this example, we need to make sure to summarize sales volumes by unique customers. The knowledge acquired from the concatenated fields chapter comes in handy here. In this example, we will GROUP BY a field that is made from the concatenation of the last and first name fields of the customers to obtain more accurate results.

I know what you are thinking: What if there are customers with the same last and first names? This is a possibility, after all. We have three ways to solve this problem depending on its nature. First, if two customer records pertain to the same customer, it means we have duplicated records in the data set. Read the chapter on duplicate and orphaned records to explore a range of specific solutions.

Second, if the two customer records pertain to two different customers, we can add middle names, zip codes, or PK values to the concatenated expression to obtain unique results.

Third, to avoid this problem in its conception, we can add to the customer table a unique multiple-field index on the last and first name fields so that values of customers with the same last and first names are not accepted at all in the table. See the chapter on indexes for the exact syntax of multi-field unique indexes.

Let us create an additional problem for us: Open the Customers table and delete the first name for the customer "John Demarco" with CustomerID=1. Then run the code below. When you look at the result set, you will notice that the first record is blank! When this is the case, go immediately to your record set, and check the values of the fields you use in the concatenated expression for blanks.

Code:

```
TRANSFORM Sum([unitprice]*[quantity]) AS Ordertotal
SELECT (CustomerLastname+' '+CustomerFirstName) AS Customer
FROM Qry_Crosstab_Base
GROUP BY (CustomerLastname+' '+CustomerFirstName)
PIVOT Year([OrderDate])
```

Result:

Customer	2020	2021	2022
	226	45	333
Ackerman Nicholas	32	207	120
Ames Pindar		871	
Andersen Thomas		393	350
Anderson Joseph	575	477	110

```
(190 row(s) returned)
(There are more records in the result set than the ones shown in this image)
```

Now, enter the first name "John" for Demarco in the Customers table, run the query again, and you will notice that the blank record disappears from the result set.

Result:

Customer	2020	2021	2022
Ackerman Nicholas	32	207	120
Ames Pindar		871	
Andersen Thomas		393	350
Anderson Joseph	575	477	110
Anderson Paul	72	513	371

```
(190 row(s) returned)
(There are more records in the result set than the ones shown in this image)
```

140. Display column totals in crosstab queries

Calculate order totals by state and year and provide grand totals for the year columns

Discussion:

There are two types of grand totals in crosstab queries: column totals and row totals. In this example, we obtain column totals for the total order amounts for all states for each year. To achieve this task let us run this crosstab query first.

Code:

```
TRANSFORM sum(unitprice*quantity) AS Ordertotal
SELECT CustomerState
FROM Qry_Crosstab_Base
GROUP BY CustomerState
PIVOT Year(OrderDate)
```

Result:

CustomerState	2020	2021	2022
AZ	2386	3460	2849
CA	13364	14919	12216
CO	3326	1937	1961
DC	3351	3102	3020
FL	4736	3413	4439

```
(10 row(s) returned)
(There are more records in the result set than the ones shown in this image)
```

Then, we use the Σ command on the ribbon. We can find it at the "Home" tab in the "Records" group. By clicking on Σ, an additional row will become available at the bottom of the crosstab query where we can select the grand totals we want such as sum, count, average, and others. In this case we used sum.

CustomerState	2020	2021	2022
AZ	2386	3460	2849
CA	13364	14919	12216
CO	3326	1937	1961
DC	3351	3102	3020
FL	4736	3413	4439
MA	2020	859	1999
NY	6089	7188	8584
OH	4924	3076	2353
PA	1781	1738	1525
TX	9187	5310	5284
Total	**51164**	**45002**	**44230**

```
(10 row(s) returned)
```

141. Display row totals in crosstab queries

Calculate order totals by state and year and provide grand totals for the state rows

Discussion

In this example, we calculate row grand totals for the state rows in the crosstab query. To accomplish this task, we add the expression Sum([unitprice]*[quantity]) AS GrandTotal in the SELECT line of the SQL statement as it appears below. The grand totals appear in the second column of the result set.

Code:

```
TRANSFORM Sum(unitprice*quantity) AS Ordertotal
SELECT CustomerState, Sum(unitprice*quantity) AS GrandTotal
FROM Qry_Crosstab_Base
GROUP BY CustomerState
PIVOT Year(OrderDate)
```

Result:

CustomerState	GrandTotal	2020	2021	2022
AZ	8695	2386	3460	2849
CA	40499	13364	14919	12216
CO	7224	3326	1937	1961
DC	9473	3351	3102	3020
FL	12588	4736	3413	4439
MA	4878	2020	859	1999
NY	21861	6089	7188	8584
OH	10353	4924	3076	2353
PA	5044	1781	1738	1525
TX	19781	9187	5310	5284

(10 row(s) returned)

142. Filtering rows in crosstab queries

Calculate total sales by product and year for specific products

Discussion:

All the crosstab queries we have examined to this point produce summaries from every record in the underlying database table. Experience shows, however, that in the vast majority of cases, we will make calculations on a subset of data. We can use the WHERE clause to filter the data we want to cross tabulate. The WHERE clause always affects the number of records returned from a query whether this query is a simple SELECT or a crosstab one. In this example, the goal is to provide sales volumes by product and year, excluding some products from the calculations. Specifically, the products 'Chocolate Chip Cookies' and 'Chocolate Fudge' should be excluded from the calculations. We use the WHERE clause with the NOT IN operator to get the results we need.

Code:

```
TRANSFORM Sum(unitprice*quantity) AS Ordertotal
SELECT ProductName
FROM Qry_Crosstab_Base
WHERE Productname NOT IN ('Chocolate Chip Cookies','Chocolate Fudge ')
GROUP BY ProductName
PIVOT Year(OrderDate)
```

Result:

ProductName	2020	2021	2022
All-Purpose Marinade	560	560	392
Almonds, Hickory Smoked	180	675	600
Almonds, Roasted and Salted	975	540	660
Apple Cinnamon Raisin Cookies	540	696	552
Artichokes in white sauce	810	735	420

```
(68 row(s) returned)
(There are more records in the result set than the ones shown in this image)
```

143. Limit the number of columns in crosstab queries

Find total sales by product and year for specific years

Discussion:

Let us assume that our dataset contains sales data for the last ten years and we do not want to include all of them in our crosstab results. We might want to see only the last two or three years. In this scenario, we are looking to control the number of columns appearing in the crosstab results. To achieve this task, we can use the IN operator in the PIVOT statement. In this example, we only want to see sales volumes for the years 2021 and 2022.

Code:

```
TRANSFORM Sum(unitprice*quantity) AS Ordertotal
SELECT ProductName
FROM Qry_Crosstab_Base
GROUP BY ProductName
PIVOT Year(OrderDate) IN (2021,2022)
```

Result:

ProductName	2021	2022
All-Purpose Marinade	560	392
Almonds, Hickory Smoked	675	600
Almonds, Roasted and Salted	540	660
Apple Cinnamon Raisin Cookies	696	552
Artichokes in white sauce	735	420

```
(70 row(s) returned)
(There are more records in the result set than the ones shown in this image)
```

144. Filter crosstab queries using any field as filtering criteria

Calculate total sales by product and year in AZ, CA, and OH

Discussion:

In the previous two examples of filtering crosstab queries, we used the WHERE clause on the productname field to limit the number of rows and the PIVOT IN on the Orderdate field to limit the number of columns. Both of these fields are part of the crosstab query. The productname field is used for rows, and the orderdate field for columns. However, we can use any field to filter records in a crosstab query without this field being an integral part of the crosstab query. We can simply designate it as a field in the WHERE clause as in the SQL code below. The state field, used as a "WHERE" field in this example, will not appear in the result set.

Code:

```
TRANSFORM Sum(unitprice*quantity) AS Ordertotal
SELECT ProductName
FROM Qry_Crosstab_Base
WHERE CustomerState IN ('AZ','CA','OH')
GROUP BY ProductName
PIVOT Year(OrderDate)
```

Result:

ProductName	2020	2021	2022
All-Purpose Marinade	70	238	182
Almonds, Hickory Smoked	45	495	360
Almonds, Roasted and Salted	615	315	225
Apple Cinnamon Raisin Cookies	108	276	180
Artichokes in white sauce	495	465	60

```
(70 row(s) returned)
(There are more records in the result set than the ones shown in this image)
```

145. Using parameters with crosstab queries

Find sales by customer and year using state as a parameter

Discussion:

Now, we have a new situation. Corporate managers are ecstatic about our ability to produce such useful results with crosstab queries. However, they call on us constantly to design the queries they need, and we spend a lot of time defining simple criteria. To solve this problem, we can use parameters with crosstab queries. The items to notice in the SQL code below are the PARAMETER statement in the first line and the WHERE clause. Notice that the WHERE clause is waiting for a value from the PARAMETERS statement.

Code:

```
PARAMETERS [Enter CustomerState:] Text ( 255 );
TRANSFORM Sum([unitprice]*[quantity]) AS Ordertotal
SELECT (CustomerLastname+' '+CustomerFirstName) AS Customer
FROM Qry_Crosstab_Base
WHERE Qry_Crosstab_Base.CustomerState=[Enter CustomerState:]
GROUP BY (CustomerLastname+' '+CustomerFirstName)
PIVOT Year(OrderDate)
```

Result:

The result produced in this example is for the state of NY.

Customer	2020	2021	2022
Ames Pindar		871	
Anderson Peter	277	444	484
Anthopolis Ricky	240	48	220
Aversa Scott			469
Carr Edward	541		301

```
(29 row(s) returned)
(There are more records in the result set than the ones shown in this image)
```

146. Conditional processing of crosstab queries using the iif() function

Calculate discounted sales volumes depending on revenue volumes

Discussion:

Our business assignment in the first example of this chapter was to give our manager a report of sales totals by state and year. We were able to do that successfully and in no time. Now, however, our task is a little bit more complicated. Management wants to know the resulting sales volumes if they gave a 10% discount to customers in states with total sales of more than $10,000. In addition, they want to know the sales volumes if they gave a discount of 5% to customers in states with total sales of less than $10,000. And they want to see all results in one report.

The key here is to use the iif() function with the crosstab query. The expression for the value field in the crosstab query is the expression shown below. We ask the database to apply a 10% discount if total sales are higher than $10,000 or to apply a 5% discount if total sales are less than $10,000.

Code:

```
TRANSFORM Sum(iif([unitprice]*[quantity]>10000, ([unitprice]*[quantity])*(0.9),
([unitprice]*[quantity])*(0.95))) AS Ordertotal
SELECT CustomerState
FROM Qry_Crosstab_Base
GROUP BY CustomerState
PIVOT Year(OrderDate)
```

Result:

CustomerState	2020	2021	2022
AZ	2266.7	3287	2706.55
CA	12695.8	14173.05	11605.2
CO	3159.7	1840.15	1862.95
DC	3183.45	2946.9	2869
FL	4499.2	3242.35	4217.05

```
(10 row(s) returned)
(There are more records in the result set than the ones shown in this image)
```

147. Format output in crosstab queries

Find total sales by product and year and show results as currency

Discussion:

There might be some instances in which we would like to format the results of the value field of a crosstab query as currency so that the dollar sign appears in front of the numbers. This can be accomplished by using the format() function right in the TRANSFORM statement as it appears below.

Code:

```
TRANSFORM Format(Sum(unitprice*quantity), 'Currency') AS Ordertotal
SELECT ProductName
FROM Qry_Crosstab_Base
GROUP BY ProductName
PIVOT Year(OrderDate)
```

Result:

ProductName	2020	2021	2022
All-Purpose Marinade	$560.00	$560.00	$392.00
Almonds, Hickory Smoked	$180.00	$675.00	$600.00
Almonds, Roasted and Salted	$975.00	$540.00	$660.00
Apple Cinnamon Raisin Cookies	$540.00	$696.00	$552.00
Artichokes in white sauce	$810.00	$735.00	$420.00

```
(70 row(s) returned)
(There are more records in the result set than the ones shown in this image)
```

148. Replace blank values with zeros in crosstab queries

Find total customer orders by customer and year

Discussion:

In the cross-tabbed results below, the many blanks in the grid are immediately noticeable and do not appear very professional. Using the nz() function, we can replace the blank values with zeros. The code below will generate a crosstab query with multiple blank values.

Code:

```
TRANSFORM Sum(unitprice*quantity) AS Ordertotal
SELECT (CustomerLastname + ' ' + CustomerFirstName) AS Customer
FROM Qry_Crosstab_Base
WHERE ((CustomerState) In ('AZ','CO','MD'))
GROUP BY (CustomerLastname + ' ' + CustomerFirstName)
PIVOT Year(OrderDate)
```

Result:

Customer	2020	2021	2022
Cutillo Paul	377	120	
Darek Matthew	1172	286	
Datek Jason	145		286
Edwards Jim		216	75
Lanci Christine			378

```
(24 row(s) returned)
(There are more records in the result set than the ones shown in this image)
```

Using the nz() function we replace these blank values with zeros. Notice how we use three functions in the TRANSFORM line to obtain the results we need.

Code:

```
TRANSFORM Ccur(Nz(Sum(unitprice*quantity))) AS Ordertotal
SELECT (CustomerLastname + ' ' + CustomerFirstName) AS Customer
FROM Qry_Crosstab_Base
WHERE ((CustomerState) In ('AZ','CO','MD'))
GROUP BY (CustomerLastname + ' ' + CustomerFirstName)
PIVOT Year([OrderDate])
```

Result:

Customer	2020	2021	2022
Cutillo Paul	$377.00	$120.00	$0.00
Darek Matthew	$1,172.00	$286.00	$0.00
Datek Jason	$145.00	$0.00	$286.00
Edwards Jim	$0.00	$216.00	$75.00
Lanci Christine	$0.00	$0.00	$378.00

```
(24 row(s) returned)
(There are more records in the result set than the ones shown in this image)
```

149. Conditional crosstab queries with the switch() function

Calculate sales totals for "expensive" and "inexpensive" products

Discussion:

This time, management wants to know the contribution to the total sales volume of products selling above $25 per unit and the contribution of products selling below $25 per unit. Depending on the results we give them, they will change their sales priorities to focus more on products that will generate the most sales for the company. In addition, they would like to have the results by year so that they can also distinguish any trends in sales volumes. We can use the switch function right in the PIVOT statement to create product categories exactly the way management has asked.

Code:

```
TRANSFORM Sum(unitprice*quantity) AS Ordertotal
SELECT Year(OrderDate) As Year
FROM Qry_Crosstab_Base
GROUP BY Year(OrderDate)
PIVOT
SWITCH(
unitprice >= 25 ,        'ExpensiveProducts',
unitprice < 25,          'InexpensiveProducts'
)
```

Result:

Year	ExpensiveProducts	InexpensiveProducts
2020	15256	35908
2021	11844	33158
2022	12344	31886

(3 row(s) returned)

DISCUSSION QUESTIONS

1. How many fields do we need for a basic crosstab query?
2. What is the purpose of the TRANSFORM statement in crosstab queries?
3. What is the purpose of the PIVOT statement in crosstab queries?
4. What is the purpose of the GROUP BY clause in cross tab queries?
5. Why do we need to pay attention to the uniqueness of values in the GROUP BY field?
6. What is the meaning of blank values in the results of crosstab queries? Is this a database issue or a business fact?
7. How do we calculate totals for columns and rows in crosstab queries?
8. How do we limit the number of rows in crosstab queries?
9. How do we limit the number of columns in crosstab queries?
10. Why do we use the nz() function in crosstab queries?

HANDS-ON EXERCISES

Case 1

For each of the questions in this case create a new query in SQL view and name it as per the instructions in each question.

1. The management of the company needs a report that will provide the total number of orders by city and year. Create a new query that satisfies the managerial request and name it Crosstabbing_Case1_Q1. Hint: use the Qry_Crosstab_Base and pay attention to use the CustomerCity field because there is also a "city" field from the suppliers table.

Your result should look like:

CustomerCity	2020	2021	2022
Albany	22	23	20
Boston	37	23	37
Chicago	88	53	46
Dallas	71	55	45
Denver	60	35	33

```
(15 row(s) returned)
(There are more records in the result set than the ones shown in this image)
```

2. The management of the company is now asking for a report that will provide the total number of orders by state and year. Create a new query that satisfies the managerial request and name it Crosstabbing_Case1_Q2. Hint: use the Qry_Crosstab_Base and pay attention to use the CustomerState field because there is also a "state" field from the suppliers table.

Your result should look like:

CustomerState	2020	2021	2022
AZ	40	56	41
CA	226	263	202
CO	60	35	33
DC	55	57	53
FL	71	64	81

```
(10 row(s) returned)
(There are more records in the result set than the ones shown in this image)
```

3. The management is really very happy with all the useful information. They now want the report you created in question 2 to exclude the states of California and New York. Create a new query that satisfies the managerial request and name it Crosstabbing_Case1_Q3. Hint: use the Qry_Crosstab_Base and pay attention to use the CustomerState field because there is also a "state" field from the suppliers table.

Your result should look like:

CustomerState	2020	2021	2022
AZ	40	56	41
CO	60	35	33
DC	55	57	53
FL	71	64	81
MA	37	23	37

```
(8 row(s) returned)
(There are more records in the result set than the ones shown in this image)
```

4. The management now wants a report like the one you created in question 3 but to exclude the year 2020. Create a new query that satisfies the managerial request and name it Crosstabbing_Case1_Q4.

Your result should look like:

CustomerState	2021	2022
AZ	56	41
CO	35	33
DC	57	53
FL	64	81
MA	23	37

```
(8 row(s) returned)
(There are more records in the result set than the ones shown in this image)
```

5. Finally, the management requests a report like the one you created in question 4 but which calculates the total shipping cost by state instead of the total number of orders. All the other criteria they want to remain the same. Create a new query that satisfies the managerial request and name it Crosstabbing_Case1_Q5.

Your result should look like:

CustomerState	2021	2022
AZ	1301	845
CO	723	628
DC	1213	1093
FL	1307	1905
MA	535	707

```
(8 row(s) returned)
(There are more records in the result set than the ones shown in this image)
```

Case 2

For each of the questions in this case create a new query in SQL view and name it as per the instructions in each question.

1. The marketing department is asking for a report that will provide the total order amount by customer state and year. Create a new query that satisfies the marketing people request. Do not forget to deduct the given discounts from the calculations. Hint: use the Qry_Crosstab_Base and pay attention to use the CustomerState field because there is also a "state" field from the suppliers table. Save the query as Crosstabbing_Case2_Q1.

Your result should look like:

CustomerState	2020	2021	2022
AZ	2032.35	2922.5	2380.5
CA	11322.55	12586.85	10422.05
CO	2807.45	1649.1	1662.7
DC	2856.75	2579.45	2581.9
FL	4021.85	2885.35	3744.05

```
(10 row(s) returned)
(There are more records in the result set than the ones shown in this image)
```

2. The salespeople are asking for a report that will provide the total order amount by customer name and year. To avoid any potential issues with duplicates they are asking you to provide the report by concatenating the customer first name with the customer last name. Create a new query that satisfies the salespeople request. Use the Qry_Crosstab_Base. Save the query as Crosstabbing_Case2_Q2.

Your result should look like:

CustomerName	2020	2021	2022
Ackerman Nicholas	27.2	173.7	99
Ames Pindar		744.75	
Andersen Thomas		343.55	291.5
Anderson Joseph	495.75	407.7	93.5
Anderson Paul	58.4	431.55	319.85

```
(190 row(s) returned)
(There are more records in the result set than the ones shown in this image)
```

3. The salespeople are happy with the very useful report you created for them in question 2. They are now asking you for the same report but limiting the customers to those in the states of Florida and California only. Create a new query that satisfies the salespeople request. Use the Qry_Crosstab_Base. Save the query as Crosstabbing_Case2_Q3.

Your result should look like:

CustomerName	2020	2021	2022
Andersen Thomas		343.55	291.5
Anderson Joseph	495.75	407.7	93.5
Balfur Carolyn	286.25	60	85
Basil Julia	12	169.2	386.6
Batto Gerald	275.45	345.9	23.8

```
(64 row(s) returned)
(There are more records in the result set than the ones shown in this image)
```

4. The salespeople are now asking if it is possible to add customer grand totals. Create a new query that satisfies the latest salespeople request. Use the Qry_Crosstab_Base . Save the query as Crosstabbing_Case2_Q4.

Your result should look like:

CustomerName	GrantTotal	2020	2021	2022
Andersen Thomas	635.05		343.55	291.5
Anderson Joseph	996.95	495.75	407.7	93.5
Balfur Carolyn	431.25	286.25	60	85
Basil Julia	567.8	12	169.2	386.6
Batto Gerald	645.15	275.45	345.9	23.8

(64 row(s) returned)
(There are more records in the result set than the ones shown in this image)

5. At this point the management asks for a report showing the contribution of products to sales based on their sales price. Specifically, the management wants to see what is the total revenue from products within the 10-20 price range, including the boundaries (that is those with the price of 10 and those with the price of 20), from products with prices between 21 and 30 including boundaries, and 31 to 40 including boundaries. Total contributions need to be reported by year. In addition, your report should leave out any products with prices less than 10 or more than 40. Create a new query that satisfies the management request and save it as Crosstabbing_Case2_Q5. Use the Qry_Crosstab_Base as the basis for your report and do not take into consideration any discounts in the JoinOrdersProducts table.

Your result should look like:

Year	10-20	21-30	31-40
2020	31702	11594	6016
2021	28786	9832	4256
2022	26894	9298	6016

(3 row(s) returned)

CHAPTER 19
PARAMETERIZING QUERY OUTPUT

The primary goal of a parameter query is to provide flexibility and time savings for the corporate analytics reports. Instead of hard coding criteria values in the query code, it allows users to supply the values they want to work with. For example, instead of hard coding the values "NY", "Dallas", and "9/15/2022" in the query, the parameter query allows users to enter any state, city, and order date they want and get the corresponding results. For business, it means that the analytics professionals do not need to take the time to create multiple queries but instead they can set one or more parameters for users to obtain the reports they need.

Parameter queries in their simplest form will include one or two parameterized fields but they can become more complex with wildcard characters, operators, equality and inequality predicates, and even functions. We will go through examples of all the above in this chapter so that you can make full use of the power and flexibility of parameter queries.

150. Creating a query with one parameter field

Retrieve order information using state as a parameter

Discussion:

The simplest form of a parameter query is one with a single parameter field. The parameter field always appears in the WHERE clause of the query and its parameter prompt is enclosed in brackets. In this example, the parameter field is "state", and its prompt will appear as [Enter State:]. The colon at the end of the prompt is optional, and you can omit it if you want. In this specific example, we used the equality predicate "=" in the expression ((State)=[Enter State:]). This is because the parameter in this query is waiting for complete state values like "NY", "AZ", "FL", or "CA". However, you are not restricted to equality or inequality predicates such as (=, <>, <, <=, >, =>). Later, you will learn how you can enter only part of the value you are looking for, in which case you can use an operator such as LIKE. You could also use the BETWEEN operator or even wildcard characters and functions as you will see in this chapter.

Code:

```
SELECT OrderID, OrderDate, City, State
FROM Qry_Parameters_Base
WHERE State=[Enter State:]
```

Parameter Prompt:

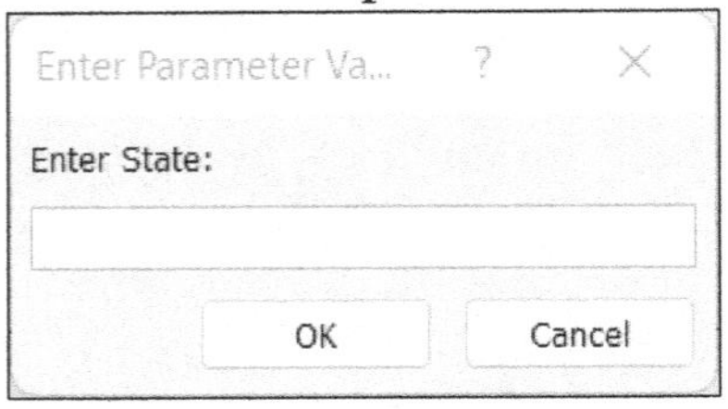

Result:

OrderID	OrderDate	City	State
43	5/6/2020	New York	NY
115	1/27/2022	New York	NY
264	2/9/2022	New York	NY
642	3/16/2020	New York	NY

```
(141 row(s) returned)
(There are more records in the result set than the ones shown in this image)
```

151. Creating a query with two parameter fields

Retrieve order information using state and city as parameters

Discussion:

We can also create multi-field parameter queries. In this example, we use the state and city as parameter fields using the AND operator. This means that we force our users to select a state first and then, a city within that state. In this example, we select "NY" and then "New York". Of course, we can use the OR operator so that our users can select any state and city they want.

Code:

```
SELECT OrderID, OrderDate, City, State
FROM Qry_Parameters_Base
WHERE State=[Enter State:] AND City=[Enter City:]
```

Result:

OrderID	OrderDate	City	State
43	5/6/2020	New York	NY
115	1/27/2022	New York	NY
264	2/9/2022	New York	NY
642	3/16/2020	New York	NY

```
(141 row(s) returned)
(There are more records in the result set than the ones shown in this image)
```

152. Create a query with three parameter fields, one of them an expression

Retrieve order information using state, city, and ordertotal as parameters

Discussion:

In this example, we use three parameters for the State, City, and TotalOrder fields. Notice the third parameter ">[Enter Amount Bigger Than:]" for the TotalOrder field. Here, we use the ">" greater than inequality predicate to retrieve orders from "NY" state and "New York" city, which are bigger than $200. Equality and inequality predicates allow amazing flexibility in parameter queries.

Code:

```
SELECT OrderID, OrderDate, City, State
FROM Qry_Parameters_Base
WHERE State = [Enter State:] AND City= [Enter City:] AND OrderTotal > [Enter Amount
Bigger Than:]
```

Result:

OrderID	OrderDate	City	State
341	4/24/2022	New York	NY
411	8/29/2021	New York	NY
429	3/28/2021	New York	NY
447	4/21/2022	New York	NY

(30 row(s) returned)
(There are more records in the result set than the ones shown in this image)

153. Define the sequence of the parameter prompts

Retrieve order information using orderdate, state, and ordertotal as parameters

Discussion:

If we enter multiple parameters in the query design grid, Access will present them to the users from left to right according to the lineup of the columns in the grid. Some sources suggest entering parameters in the "Parameters" sheet in the "Show/Hide" group of the "design" tab to force order. It is really not necessary to type our parameters a second time. In our SQL statement, we just type our parameters in the order we would like them to appear. However, always think about the logic behind the parameter lineup. In this example with the AND operator, the order will not make a difference in the result set since all three parameter values will apply concurrently on the fields for which they are specified. However, there might be cases in which we want a certain date range to be specified first and then, use operators to search for data within that range using operators different from AND.

In this example, the parameters are: NY, 1/1/2022, and $200.

Code:

```
SELECT OrderID, OrderDate, City, State
FROM Qry_Parameters_Base
WHERE State=[Enter State:] AND orderdate>[Enter Date Later Than:] AND ordertotal>[Enter
Amount Bigger Than:]
```

Result:

OrderID	OrderDate	City	State
341	4/24/2022	New York	NY
447	4/21/2022	New York	NY
354	4/28/2022	New York	NY
401	7/7/2022	New York	NY

(13 row(s) returned)
(There are more records in the result set than the ones shown in this image)

154. Retrieve records providing only part of the parameter value

Find customers by supplying only part of the name

Discussion:

We want to give our users the ability to search orders by customer name without remembering the exact last name of the customer. In this example, we use the * wildcard character and lastname as the parameter field. Of course, we can use our creativity and employ any wildcard character we want with any kind of equality or inequality predicates to achieve amazing results. In this example, we will look for all customer names starting with "Ba*". As you might expect, the same customer will come up multiple times since each customer might have multiple orders. That is why the name Balfur appears multiple times.

Code:

```
SELECT LastName, FirstName, City, State
FROM Qry_Parameters_Base
WHERE LastName LIKE [Enter last name:] + "*"
```

Result:

LastName	FirstName	City	State
Balfur	Carolyn	Miami	FL
Balfur	Carolyn	Miami	FL
Balfur	Carolyn	Miami	FL
Balfur	Carolyn	Miami	FL

(28 row(s) returned)
(There are more records in the result set than the ones shown in this image)

155. Using numeric ranges in parameter queries

Find sales volume ranges from customer orders

Discussion:

In this example, we enable managers to retrieve order records using any order total boundaries they want. For instance, they might want to retrieve orders with total order amounts between $200 and $300. To achieve this, we use the "<" and ">" inequality predicates because we do not want the lower and upper limits of our boundaries ($200, $300) to appear in the result set. If we have used BETWEEN, which is inclusive, the boundaries would have been included in the result set. The same would happen if we have used the "<=" and "=>" inequality predicates.

Code:

```
SELECT OrderID, OrderDate, City, State, OrderTotal
FROM Qry_Parameters_Base
WHERE OrderTotal>[Enter Min Order Amount:] AND OrderTotal<[Enter Maximum Order
Amount:]
```

Result:

OrderID	OrderDate	City	State	OrderTotal
508	10/21/2021	Orlando	FL	211
96	3/6/2020	Washington	DC	202
227	11/6/2020	Washington	DC	279
102	10/26/2020	San Diego	CA	249

(159 row(s) returned)
(There are more records in the result set than the ones shown in this image)

156. Using date ranges in parameter queries

Find total order amounts between specific dates

Discussion:

This time, our goal is to retrieve order records between specific order dates. We might want to retrieve sales volumes only for a period of five days, ten days, a few months, or years. In this example, we are looking for orders between 1/1/2022 and 1/15/2022.

Code:

```
SELECT OrderID, OrderDate, City, State, OrderTotal
FROM Qry_Parameters_Base
WHERE OrderDate>[Enter Min Date:] AND OrderDate<[Enter Max Date:]
```

Result:

OrderID	OrderDate	City	State	OrderTotal
351	1/14/2022	Orlando	FL	108

(1 row(s) returned)

157. Using functions in parameter queries

Find orders for a specific month for any range of years

Discussion:

Now, we have a very peculiar request from our company. Management wants to do some decision-making, and they have asked us for a way to run multiple scenarios such as: What were the sales volumes in the months of May for the last two years? Or for the month of June in the last three years? Or for any month for any range of years? They want to be able to perform these scenarios at will. To achieve this goal, we use the month() function to extract the month out of the OrderDate field, the year() function to extract the years out of the OrderDate field, and the BETWEEN operator!

In this example, we used May (enter 5 in the prompt) for the month and 2021 to 2022 for the year range.

Code:

```
SELECT OrderID, OrderDate, City, State, OrderTotal
FROM Qry_Parameters_Base
WHERE Month(OrderDate)=[Enter Month Number:] AND Year(OrderDate) BETWEEN [
Enter Min Year:] And [Enter Max Year:]
```

Result:

OrderID	OrderDate	City	State	OrderTotal
378	5/4/2022	Washington	DC	156
271	5/2/2022	Chicago	OH	105
841	5/22/2021	New York	NY	156
398	5/22/2021	Los Angeles	CA	162

(47 row(s) returned)
(There are more records in the result set than the ones shown in this image)

158. Calculations and functions in parameter queries

Find fulfillment cycle times for customer orders for specific periods

Discussion:

Management now wants to see fulfillment cycle times for customer orders for internal efficiency indicators. Practically, they are looking to retrieve the amount of time it takes to ship an order from the time it is received. To achieve this, we first use the day() function twice to construct a calculated field (lagTimesInDays) to measure the difference between ShippedDate and OrderDate in days. Second, we use two parameters on the OrderDate field so that managers can enter the time period they desire.

In this example, we measure the lag time in days for the period between 1/1/2022 and 1/30/2022. As you see from the result set, it takes us five days to ship an order from the time we received it.

Code:

```
SELECT OrderID, (day(ShippedDate) - day(OrderDate)) AS LagTimeInDays, OrderTotal
FROM Qry_Parameters_Base
WHERE OrderDate>[Enter Min Date:] AND OrderDate<[Enter Max Date:]
```

Result:

OrderID	LagTimeInDays	OrderTotal
351	5	108
360	5	245
115	-26	79
693	5	75

(19 row(s) returned)
(There are more records in the result set than the ones shown in this image)

DISCUSSION QUESTIONS

1. What is the primary goal of parameter queries?
2. Why do parameter queries save time?
3. Can we use multiple parameters in a parameter query?
4. Are parameters restricted to certain data types?
5. Can we use wildcard characters in parameters?
6. Can we use operators in parameters?
7. Can we use functions to construct parameters in parameter queries?
8. Can we define the order of the parameter prompts? Why is this useful?
9. How can we use numeric ranges as parameters in parameter queries?
10. How can we use date ranges in parameter queries?

HANDS-ON EXERCISES

Case 1

For each of the questions in this case create a new query in SQL view and name it as per the instructions in each question.

1. The inventory people are asking for a list of customers they can dynamically generate by entering any state they need. Create a new query that includes the fields FirstName, LastName, City, State, and Zip from the customers table and satisfies the inventory people request. Use "NY" as the parameter. Order the results by state and then city ascending. Save the query as Parameters_Case1_Q1.

Your result should look like:

FirstName	LastName	City	State	Zip
Anthony	Miller	Albany	NY	12189
Joanne	Riegert	Albany	NY	12189
Kenneth	Vanton	Albany	NY	89890
Luis	Trindan	Albany	NY	45357

```
(31 row(s) returned)
(There are more records in the result set than the ones shown in this image)
```

2. The inventory people are asking again for a list of customers which they can dynamically generate by entering any state and city they need. Create a new query that includes the fields FirstName, LastName, City, State, and Zip from the customer table and satisfies the inventory people request. Use "NY" and "Albany" as parameters. Order the results by lastname ascending. Save the query as Parameters_Case1_Q2.

Your result should look like:

FirstName	LastName	City	State	Zip
Anthony	Miller	Albany	NY	12189
Joanne	Riegert	Albany	NY	12189
Luis	Trindan	Albany	NY	45357
Kenneth	Vanton	Albany	NY	89890

```
(4 row(s) returned)
```

3. The inventory people are now asking for a list of customers which they can dynamically generate by entering any state, city, and zip they need. Create a new query that includes the fields FirstName, LastName, State, City, Zip, and MembershipType from the Customers table and satisfies the inventory people request. Use "NY", "Albany", and "12189" as parameters for this example. Sort the results by LastName ascending. Save the query as Parameters_Case1_Q3.

Your result should look like:

FirstName	LastName	State	City	Zip	MembershipType
Joanne	Riegert	NY	Albany	12189	Platinum
Anthony	Miller	NY	Albany	12189	Gold

(2 row(s) returned)

4. The salespeople are asking for a list of orders which they can dynamically generate by entering any orderdate period they want. Create a new query that includes the fields OrderID, CustomerID, OrderDate, ShippedDate, and InvoiceAmount from the orders table and satisfies the salespeople request. Sort the results by orderdate so that the latest dates appear first in the result set. Use "1/1/2022" and "1/31/2022" as parameters. Save the query as Parameters_Case1_Q4.

Your result should look like:

OrderID	CustomerID	OrderDate	ShippedDate	InvoiceAmount
121	140	1/29/2022	2/3/2022	210
324	47	1/29/2022	2/3/2022	219
115	5	1/27/2022	2/1/2022	187
154	132	1/27/2022	2/1/2022	161

(21 row(s) returned)
(There are more records in the result set than the ones shown in this image)

5. The salespeople are now asking for a list of orders which they can dynamically generate by entering any InvoiceAmount range they need. Create a new query that includes the OrderID, CustomerID, OrderDate, ShippedDate, and InvoiceAmount fields from the orders table and satisfies the salespeople request. Use "130" and "180" as boundaries. The boundary values should not be included in the result set. Order results by InvoiceAmount so that higher amounts appear first. Save the query as Parameters_Case1_Q5.

Your result should look like:

OrderID	CustomerID	OrderDate	ShippedDate	InvoiceAmount
297	31	3/24/2021	3/29/2021	179
456	94	7/25/2020	7/30/2020	178
59	184	11/25/2021	11/30/2021	178
427	85	9/25/2021	9/30/2021	178

(191 row(s) returned)
(There are more records in the result set than the ones shown in this image)

Case 2

For each of the questions in this case create a new query in SQL view and name it as per the instructions in each question.

1. The marketing people are asking for a list of orders which they can dynamically generate by entering any specific order date they need. Create a new query that includes the fields OrderID, CustomerID, OrderDate, ShippedDate, and InvoiceAmount from the Orders table and satisfies the marketing people

request. Use "5/30/2022" as the parameter. Order results by OrderDate so that the latest orders appear first. Save the query as Parameters_Case2_Q1.

Your result should look like:

OrderID	CustomerID	OrderDate	ShippedDate	InvoiceAmount
971	54	5/30/2022	6/4/2022	31
359	88	5/30/2022	6/4/2022	237

(2 row(s) returned)

2. The marketing people are sking for a list of orders which they can dynamically generate by entering the year and the month. Create a new query that includes the fields OrderID, CustomerID, OrderDate, ShippedDate, and InvoiceAmount from the Orders table and satisfies the marketing people request. Hint: (When you run the query, enter months in number format like 4 for April, 5 for May). Use "5" for May and "2022" as the parameters. Order results by OrderDate so that the latest orders appear first. Save the query as Parameters_Case2_Q2.

Your result should look like:

OrderID	CustomerID	OrderDate	ShippedDate	InvoiceAmount
875	13	5/31/2022	6/5/2022	252
971	54	5/30/2022	6/4/2022	31
359	88	5/30/2022	6/4/2022	237
48	96	5/29/2022	6/3/2022	136

(35 row(s) returned)
(There are more records in the result set than the ones shown in this image)

3. The inventory people are asking for a list of products which they can dynamically generate by entering minimum and maximum UnitsInStock quantities. Create a new query that includes the ProductID, ProductName, ProductPrice, and UnitsInStock fields from the products table and satisfies the inventory people request. Use 20 and 50 as parameters. Boundary values (20, 50) should be included in the result set. Sort results by UnitsInStock so that biggest quantities appear first. Save the query as Parameters_Case2_Q3.

Your result should look like:

ProductID	ProductName	ProductPrice	UnitsInStock
4	Berry Cherry	30	50
46	Artichokes in white sauce	22	50
47	Chocolate Chip Cookies	49	50
69	Green Sauce	35	49

(64 row(s) returned)
(There are more records in the result set than the ones shown in this image)

4. The marketing people are asking for a list of customers which they can dynamically generate by entering any customer last name they need. However, they also want the query to provide results even if they do not remember the full last name of the customer and they enter part of it. Create a new query that includes the fields FirstName, LastName, State, City, and Zip from the Customers table and satisfies the marketing people request. Use "Da" as the parameter. Sort results by LastName ascending. Save the query as Parameters_Case2_Q4.

Your result should look like:

FirstName	LastName	State	City	Zip
Janet	Dalton	NY	New York	12189
Matthew	Darek	CO	Denver	21214
Diane	Darek	CA	San Jose	36945
Jason	Datek	CO	Denver	21214

(6 row(s) returned)
(There are more records in the result set than the ones shown in this image)

5. The inventory people ask for a report in which they will be able to see the units of inventory by supplier. Create a calculated field, UnitsOfInventory, which will be the sum of the units in stock, and the units on order. The inventory people want to select the supplierID dynamically and get the UnitsOfInventory associated with that supplier. Create a new query that includes the SupplierID, ProductID, UnitsOfInventory, and ReorderLevel field from the Products table and satisfies the inventory people request. Use "1" for the SupplierID parameter value. Sort results by UnitsOfInventory so that biggest quantities appear first. In addition, include in the query only UnitsOfInventory quantities that are higher than zero. Save the query as Parameters_Case2_Q5.

Your result should look like:

SupplierID	ProductID	UnitsOfInventory	ReorderLevel
1	4	50	30
1	1	45	45
1	5	35	30
1	2	32	20

(10 row(s) returned)
(There are more records in the result set than the ones shown in this image)

CHAPTER 20
CONDITIONAL DATA MANIPULATION

The iif(), switch(), and partition() functions are the most useful and practical functions for conditional data manipulation in Access. Keep in mind that CASE does not work in Access, so do not bother wasting your time looking for it.

What exactly do we mean by conditional data manipulation? Let us assume we have a customer database we use for promotional campaigns. We might decide we want to provide different discount levels for customers in the Northeast, Midwest, West, Southeast, and Southwest states. Since we do not have region information in our database, we need to create multiple SELECT queries for these categories and apply the appropriate discount for each region. Using conditional data processing, on the other hand, will enable us to do our job in just one query.

You might be thinking at this point that it does not bother you to create four queries to do your job. What matters in the end is getting the job done. I totally agree. However, what will happen after a couple of years at work is that you will end up with several hundred queries. In the end, you will not remember what was what, and you will be afraid to delete even one of them since you no longer know what it was used for. During the last 20 years, I have seen this happen countless times with departmental databases.

To encourage you to use conditional processing, let me give you another example. Let's say we have a database in which we store our products, along with the corresponding suppliers. Every now and then, our suppliers send us updated prices, and we need to update our own product catalog as well. We have only 20 suppliers and 200 products in our database, and we need to update our prices every few weeks.

Of course, thinking logically, suppliers will provide us with different price updates. Some of them will increase their prices by 3%, some by 5%, some by 3.5%, some by 4%, ending up with four clusters in this example. Still, we will have to create four update queries and include the specific calculated fields for the updates and specific criteria so that the appropriate supplier products are updated and with the correct percentages.

Furthermore, every time we have price updates, we will need to modify our current update queries, create new ones, modify their criteria, and calculate new prices for the updates. We will end up with an unmanageable number of queries even for this simple scenario. Using conditions, on the other hand, we can do the job very effectively using just a single query!

A final point on conditional statements: Those who understand conditional statements will produce much better database designs and entity relationship diagrams since they know in advance what needs to be stored and what can be produced automatically by the database.

159. Using the iif() and switch() functions with one condition

Produce a product catalog with special discounts for one product

Discussion:

The inventory department says that we have a large quantity of Chocolate Fudge which needs to go out into the market fast. We need to produce a new product catalog for this week and send it to our customers. All of the product prices in this catalog should remain the same except for Chocolate Fudge, which will be reduced by 50%.

Solution 1: using the iif() function

We will provide a solution using an iif() conditional function. The translation of the iif() function in this example says: For the product with ProductID = 14, reduce the price by 50%, and for the rest of the products in the catalog, leave the price as is in the table. Notice in the result set that the price of Chocolate Fudge is now $20.50 in the query but it will remains $41 in the products table.

Code:

```
SELECT ProductID, ProductName, QuantityPerUnit, ProductPrice, iif(ProductID = 14,
ProductPrice * 0.5, ProductPrice) AS NewProductPrice
FROM Products
```

Solution 2: using the switch() function

There is no need to use the switch function in this case since there is only one condition. We will use this example to see how the switch() function works. There is no doubt that the switch() function is much cleaner than the iif() function. This becomes more evident as the number of conditions goes up.

Code:

```
SELECT ProductID, ProductName, QuantityPerUnit, ProductPrice,
SWITCH(
ProductID = 14,      ProductPrice *0.5,
ProductID <>14,      ProductPrice
)
AS NewProductPrice
FROM Products
```

Result:

ProductID	ProductName	QuantityPerUnit	ProductPrice	NewProductPrice
1	Almonds Hickory Smoked	12	35	35.00
2	Almonds Roasted and Salted	12	22	22.00
3	Banana Chips	12	27	27.00
4	Berry Cherry	15	30	30.00

```
(70 row(s) returned)
(There are more records in the result set than the ones shown in this image)
```

160. Using the iif() and switch() functions with two conditions but multiple criteria

Provide custom discounts for customers in NY, TX, and CA

Discussion:

The management wants to offer a 20% discount in large states such as NY, TX, and CA and 10% to everyone else around the country. They want a list of customers and their corresponding discount rates for review.

Solution 1: using the iif() function

Using the iif() function becomes a bit more complicated this time and requires two OR operators. The iif() function translates to: If the customer is in NY, CA, or TX, provide a discount of 20%. Otherwise, provide a discount of 10%.

Code:

```
SELECT State, LastName, FirstName, OrderTotal,
iif(State = 'NY' Or State = 'CA' Or State = 'TX', '20%', '10%')
AS Discount
FROM Qry_Conditions
Order BY LastName
```

Solution 2: using the switch() function

The use of the switch function with two conditions and multiple criteria is again more legible than using the iif() function and, therefore, easily editable if we need to update our criteria later on.

Code:

```
SELECT State, LastName, FirstName, OrderTotal,
SWITCH(
[State]= 'NY' Or [State]= 'CA' Or [State] = 'TX',        '20%',
[State] <> 'NY' Or 'CA' Or 'TX',                          '10%'
)
AS Discount
FROM Qry_Conditions
Order BY LastName
```

Result:

State	LastName	FirstName	OrderTotal	Discount
TX	Ackerman	Nicholas	359	20%
NY	Ames	Pindar	871	20%
FL	Andersen	Thomas	743	10%
NY	Anderson	Peter	1205	20%

(190 row(s) returned)
(There are more records in the result set than the ones shown in this image)

161. Working with multiple conditions and criteria

Calculate discount amounts based on customer sales volumes

Discussion:

Our sales manager wants to provide order discounts to customers based on their historical sales volume with the company. Thus, if a customer has a certain historical sales volume, the next time she orders, she will get a predetermined discount rate regardless of her new order amount.

If the total historical order amount for a customer is less than $200, that customer will receive no discounts. If it is between $200 and $300, the customer will get a 5% discount. If it is between $300 and $500, the customer will get a 10% discount. For anything above that, our manager will offer a generous

25% discount. Our job is to create a report that will list our customers and their corresponding discount rates.

Solution 1: using nested iif() functions

Our first option is to use a series of nested iif() functions as shown below—four iif() functions, one inside the other to accomplish our goal. However, the use of nested iif() functions is a convoluted process. In addition, if we need to change the business logic behind our statement by adding additional categories, our task will be a complicated preposition. The problem originates from the fact that the iif() function takes only two arguments. For more outcomes we need to nest, which results in complicated statements.

Code:

```
SELECT LastName, FirstName, OrderTotal, iif(OrderTotal < 200, 0, iif(OrderTotal >= 200 AND
OrderTotal < 300,'5%', iif(OrderTotal >= 300 AND OrderTotal < 500,'10%', iif(OrderTotal >
500,'25%')))) AS Discount
FROM Qry_Conditions
```

Solution 2: using the switch() function

The first observation is that the switch() function is very clean and the logic becomes immediately apparent to us and everyone else who will need to edit the SQL statement.

Code:

```
SELECT LastName, FirstName, OrderTotal,
SWITCH(
OrderTotal < 200,                              '0' ,
OrderTotal >= 200 and OrderTotal < 300,        '5%' ,
OrderTotal > 300 and OrderTotal <= 500,        '10%' ,
OrderTotal > 500 ,                             '25%'
)
AS Discount
FROM Qry_Conditions
```

Result:

LastName	FirstName	OrderTotal	Discount
Kashisnky	Alfred	556	25%
Tranton	Alfred	931	25%
Hudson	Allan	1119	25%

```
(190 row(s) returned)
(There are more records in the result set than the ones shown in this image)
```

162. An effective trick with the switch() function

Calculate customer discounts based on location

Discussion:

This time, the task is to provide discounts for customers in five specific states. At the same time, a general discount percentage should be extended to all customers in states not included in the criteria of the function. We can achieve this task by using the TRUE keyword as part of the last expression in a switch() function. This last expression will evaluate true for every state not included in the specific state list, and we will extend the 10% discount to all the customers in states different from NY, AZ, CO, FL, and MA.

Code:

```
SELECT State, LastName, FirstName, OrderTotal,
SWITCH(
[State]= 'NY',  '20%',
[State] ='AZ',  '15%',
[State] ='CO',  '12%',
[State] ='FL',  '18%',
[State] ='MA',  '18%',
TRUE,           '10%',
)
AS Discount FROM Qry_Conditions
Order by LastName
```

Result:

State	LastName	FirstName	OrderTotal	Discount
TX	Ackerman	Nicholas	359	10%
NY	Ames	Pindar	871	20%
FL	Andersen	Thomas	743	18%
NY	Anderson	Peter	1205	20%

(190 row(s) returned)
(There are more records in the result set than the ones shown in this image)

163. Using switch() with WHERE and IN

Calculate order totals based on customer sales volumes

Discussion:

We offer discounts to our customers with order totals between $200 and $500 and we extend these discounts to customers in AZ, CO, TX, and FL only. After the switch function, we use the WHERE clause with the IN operator to define the exact records on which our calculations will apply.

Code:

```
SELECT OrderID, LastName, FirstName, State,
SWITCH(
OrderTotal >= 200 and ordertotal < 300,    OrderTotal *(1-0.1) ,
OrderTotal > 300 and ordertotal <= 500,    OrderTotal *(1-0.15) ,
OrderTotal > 500 ,                         OrderTotal*(1-0.2),
TRUE,                                      OrderTotal
)
as DiscountedOrders
FROM Qry_Conditions
WHERE State IN ('AZ', 'CO', 'TX', 'FL')
ORDER BY OrderTotal DESC
```

Result:

OrderID	LastName	FirstName	State	DiscountedOrders
944	Corelli	John	TX	459.2
308	Darek	Matthew	CO	409.6
404	Crandil	Joseph	TX	408
932	Weinberger	Fred	FL	386.75

(301 row(s) returned)
(There are more records in the result set than the ones shown in this image)

164. Using switch() with calculated fields

Produce product categories based on product prices

Discussion:

This time, the management needs a list that specifies each product as "economical", "moderate", and "expensive" based on its price. Although we carry no such field in the database, we can absolutely create this list using the switch() function with calculated fields. In essence, we calculate the price times its quantity per unit to get the total price for the product, and then we assign categories based on price. For instance, if the price falls between $500 and $1000, we designate these products as "moderately" priced.

Code:

```
SELECT ProductName, UnitsInStock, UnitsOnOrder,
SWITCH(
ProductPrice * QuantityPerUnit < 500,      'Economical',
ProductPrice * QuantityPerUnit >= 500 AND ProductPrice * QuantityPerUnit <1000,
'Moderate',
ProductPrice * QuantityPerUnit >= 1000, 'Expensive',
)
as PricingCategory
FROM Products
ORDER BY  ProductPrice * QuantityPerUnit DESC
```

Result:

ProductName	UnitsInStock	UnitsOnOrder	PricingCategory
Chocolate Chunk Cookies	15	20	Expensive
Dark Chocolate Apricots	38	0	Expensive
Buttermilk Muffins	31	0	Expensive
Coffee biscuits	24	0	Expensive

(70 row(s) returned)
(There are more records in the result set than the ones shown in this image)

165. Using switch() with aggregate functions

Calculate employee commissions and bonuses based on their sales volume

Discussion:

In this example we have multiple tasks. First, we calculate employee commissions as a percentage of their sales. Second, we calculate employee bonuses Third, we sum up the commission and bonus amounts. Fourth, we present the results as currency.

Do not be intimidated by the long SQL statement. It is long but not as tough as it looks. In two minutes, you will have a total grasp of it. First, notice we use only three fields in this SQL statement: LastName,

OrderDate, and CommissionAndBonus. We use the LastName field as is. For the OrderDate field, we use the function year() to extract the year part of the date. The CommissionAndBonus field will be the result of the switch function calculations.

Next, notice that we use three functions, sum(), Ccur(), and switch(), one after the other. We use the sum() function to obtain the total order amounts sold by our salesperson. Since we do not have a field for order totals in the database (correctly, since we can calculate them), we need to multiply the quantity of each product sold by its price in every order and sum() the results. Then, we use the Ccur() function to convert the data type of the CommissionAndBonus field to appear as currency. Finally, we use the switch function to assign commissions and bonuses according to sales volumes.

Next, we have a FROM statement but do not pay attention to the joins since Access will create the joins automatically when we paste this code in a query and look at its design. In the final part of the SQL statement, we group by employee and year since we need to have commissions and bonuses shown by employee. We filter the year by using the HAVING clause as we examined in our "GROUP BY" chapter. In the end, the whole query is reduced to three fields: LastName and year by which we group by and the CommissionandBonus field on which we apply the sum() aggregate function.

Code:

```
SELECT LastName,  Year([OrderDate]) AS [Year],

SUM(CCur(SWITCH(
([UnitPrice] * [Quantity]) < 5000,          ([UnitPrice] * [Quantity]) * (0.1) + 500 ,
([UnitPrice] * [Quantity]) >= 5000 and  ([UnitPrice] * [Quantity]) <10000,
([UnitPrice] * [Quantity]) * (0.15) + 1000,
([UnitPrice] * [Quantity]) >= 10000 and  ([UnitPrice] * [Quantity]) <15000,
([UnitPrice] * [Quantity]) * (0.2) + 3000,
([UnitPrice] * [Quantity]) >= 15000 ,       ([UnitPrice] * [Quantity]) * (0.25) + 5000,
)))
as CommissionAndBonus

FROM SalesReps INNER JOIN (Orders INNER JOIN JoinOrdersProducts ON Orders.OrderID
= JoinOrdersProducts.OrderID) ON SalesReps.SalesRepID = Orders.SalesRepID

GROUP BY LastName, Year([OrderDate])
HAVING Year([OrderDate])=2022
ORDER BY Sum([UnitPrice]*[Quantity]) DESC
```

Result:

LastName	Year	CommissionAndBonus
Zensons	2022	$47,092.40
Spicer	2022	$46,563.40
Anderson	2022	$39,988.80
Baker	2022	$44,976.60

(10 row(s) returned)
(There are more records in the result set than the ones shown in this image)

166. Using partition() for data visualization

Create intervals on sales volumes and count orders included

Discussion:

What if we encounter a request for a visualization of the distribution of our orders? That is to create bins as they are called in analytics. For example, we would want to know how many orders fall between 0 and $50, how many between $50 and $100, how many between $100 and $150, etc. We can provide an answer using the partition() function.

The partition() function has the syntax:

Partition(field, beginning number, ending number, interval)

For instance, if we want to categorize orders in $50 increments starting at $0 and ending at $500, we can write: Partition(ordertotal, 0, 500, 50).

In this example, we use two fields: "Range" and "Count". Both of these fields are calculated fields. The contents of the Range field are produced by the partition function, and the contents of the Count field are produced by counting the number of orders in each partition according to their order total amount. We can change the parameters of the partition function at will to produce any intervals we want.

In this example, we defined the boundaries between $0 and $500 with intervals of $50. This does not mean that the partition function will stop at $500. It will stop producing intervals at $500, and from $501 and above, it will put all remaining orders in the same bin. We will still know how many orders we have above $501.

Code:

```
SELECT DISTINCTROW Partition([OrderTotal],0, 500, 50) AS Range,
Count(OrderTotal) AS Count
FROM Qry_Conditions
GROUP BY Partition([OrderTotal],0, 500, 50)
```

Result:

Range	Count
0: 49	138
50: 99	188
100:149	194
150:199	144
200:249	94
250:299	70
300:349	49
350:399	17
400:449	16
450:499	4
501:	5

(10 row(s) returned)

167. Using switch() with update statements

Update multiple product prices from multiple suppliers conditionally

Discussion:

Now, this is an occasion where a switch() function will show its true and unique power. When we combine it with update statements, we can produce highly effective updates that otherwise would have required multiple update queries to obtain.

In this example, we want to update 70 products from ten suppliers, and for each supplier, we apply different update percentages. Those percentages start from 2% all the way up to 11%, as you can see from the SQL code below. By combining the switch() function with the UPDATE statement, we can do it in one single query. We can save this query and use it every time we need to update our prices.

Code:

```
UPDATE tbls_Products_upd
SET ProductPrice =
SWITCH (
SupplierID=1,     ProductPrice*(1.1) ,
SupplierID =2,    ProductPrice*(1.08),
SupplierID =3,    ProductPrice *(1.07) ,
SupplierID =4,    ProductPrice *(1.05) ,
SupplierID =5,    ProductPrice *(1.03) ,
SupplierID =6,    ProductPrice *(1.02) ,
SupplierID =7,    ProductPrice *(1.03) ,
SupplierID =8,    ProductPrice *(1.07) ,
SupplierID =9,    ProductPrice *(1.11) ,
SupplierID =10,   ProductPrice *(1.08) ,
)
```

Result:

```
You are about to update 70 row(s)
```

168. Using switch() with crosstab queries

Create a crosstab query that calculates order totals for "big" and "small" cities

Discussion:

In this example, we will calculate sales volumes by year and at the same time categorize results by small and big cities. We want to see sales volumes for big cities like New York and Los Angeles and sales volumes for the rest of the smaller cities. We combine the power of the switch function with the flexibility of crosstab queries. Instead of pivoting by the city field as we did in the crosstabbing chapter, we use the switch function right in the PIVOT statement to create the city categories we need!

Code:

```
TRANSFORM Sum([UnitPrice]*[Quantity]) AS Ordertotal
SELECT Year([OrderDate]) As Year
FROM Qry_Crosstab_Base
GROUP BY Year([OrderDate])
PIVOT
SWITCH(
[CustomerCity]= 'New York' Or [CustomerCity]= 'Los Angeles' ,        'BigCities',
[CustomerCity] <> 'New York' Or 'Los Angeles',              'SmallCities'
)
```

Result:

Year	BigCities	SmallCities
2020	13445	37719
2021	15950	29052
2022	13110	31120

```
(10 row(s) returned)
```

DISCUSSION QUESTIONS

1. What are the goals of conditional data manipulation?
2. Which are the basic three functions for conditional data manipulation?
3. Why do we prefer to use the switch() function?
4. Why the understanding of conditional statements leads to better database design?
5. How many conditions can we process with the iif() function?
6. How many conditions can we process with the switch() function?
7. What is the purpose of nested iif() functions?
8. What is the purpose of the "TRUE" keyword in the switch() function?
9. Can we use calculated fields within the switch() function?
10. How is the partition function different from the iif() and switch() functions?

HANDS-ON EXERCISES

Case 1

For each of the questions in this case create a new query in SQL view and name it as per the instructions in each question.

1. The marketing department initiates a new campaign to offer customers discount coupons. The customers in NY and CA will receive 20% discounts while the customers in the rest of the country 25%. Create a query that will contain the fields FirstName, LastName, Address, City, State, and Zip fields from the Customers table. In addition, include a field that will show the actual discount the customers will get. Name the new field CouponDiscount. You must use the iif() function to get your result. Save the query as Conditions_Case1_Q1.

Your result should look like:

FirstName	LastName	Address	City	State	Zip	CouponDiscount
John	Demarco	11 Lark Street	New York	NY	12189	20%
Mary	Demania	12 Madison Ave	New York	NY	12189	20%
George	Demers	23 New Scotland Ave	New York	NY	12189	20%
Phillip	Demetriou	22 Academy Road	New York	NY	12189	20%

```
(201 row(s) returned)
(There are more records in the result set than the ones shown in this image)
```

2. Create the same outcome as in number 1 but using the switch function this time. Save the query as Conditions_Case1_Q2.

Your result should look like:

FirstName	LastName	Address	City	State	Zip	CouponDiscount
John	Demarco	11 Lark Street	New York	NY	12189	20%
Mary	Demania	12 Madison Ave	New York	NY	12189	20%
George	Demers	23 New Scotland Ave	New York	NY	12189	20%
Phillip	Demetriou	22 Academy Road	New York	NY	12189	20%

```
(201 row(s) returned)
(There are more records in the result set than the ones shown in this image)
```

3. The management plans to extend a bonus to employees based on seniority. Employees with 5 years or less with the company will receive $2500, between five and ten years $5,000, and more than 10 years $7500. Create a new query that includes the FirstName, LastName, Title, DateofHire, and one additional field to show the associated bonus. HINT: use the datediff() function in the following way datediff("yyyy", [dateofhire], date()) to calculate the difference in years between today's date and the date the employee was hired. Save the query as Conditions_Case1_Q3.

Your result should look like:
(It might be slightly different depending on when you run this example)

FirstName	LastName	Title	DateofHire	Bonus
John	Anderson	Sales Reppresentative	1/1/2001	7500
Mary	Teall	Sales Director	6/12/2021	2500
George	Spicer	Account Manager	5/15/2004	7500
Phillip	Zensons	Sales Reppresentative	6/10/2021	2500

```
(10 row(s) returned)
(There are more records in the result set than the ones shown in this image)
```

4. The marketing department is asking for a report that will display the number of customers in "big" and "small" cities. "Big" cities are considered to be the cities of New York, Los Angeles, and Houston. Every other city is considered to be a "small" city. The results need to be crosstabbed by state. In addition, results should be limited to the states of NY, CA, and TX only. Create a new query that satisfies the marketing people request and save it as Conditions_Case1_Q4.

Your result should look like:

State	BigCities	SmallCities
CA	31	17
NY	27	4
TX	12	13

```
(3 row(s) returned)
```

5. The inventory director needs a report that will list the number of products within specific price ranges. Specifically, he needs the number of products in the price ranges of 0-10, 10-20, 20-30, 30-40, and 40-50. You must use the partition() function to produce your results. Create a new query that satisfies the inventory director's request and save it as Conditions_Case1_Q5.

Your result should look like:

Range	Count
10:19	8
20:29	28
30:39	19
40:49	13
50:50	2

(5 row(s) returned)

Case 2

For each of the questions in this case create a new query in SQL view and name it as per the instructions in each question.

1. For the next couple of days the products Almonds Hickory Smoked, Almonds Roasted and Salted, and Banana Chips, are on sale with a generous discount of 20%. The salespeople are asking for a new product catalog to reflect these discounts which will be valid only for two days. Create a new query that includes the fields ProductID, ProductName, ProductPrice, and a calculated field, named NewProductPrice, from the products table and satisfies the salespeople request. Order the results by ProductID ascending. You must use a logical iif() function. Hint: use the IN operator within the iif() function. Save the query as Conditions_Case2_Q1.

Your result should look like:

ProductID	ProductName	ProductPrice	NewProductPrice
1	Almonds Hickory Smoked	35	28
2	Almonds Roasted and Salted	22	17.6
3	Banana Chips	27	21.6
4	Berry Cherry	30	30

(70 row(s) returned)
(There are more records in the result set than the ones shown in this image)

2. Achieve the same result as in question one using the switch() function. Save the query as Conditions_Case2_Q2.

Your result should look like:

ProductID	ProductName	ProductPrice	NewProductPrice
1	Almonds Hickory Smoked	35	28
2	Almonds Roasted and Salted	22	17.6
3	Banana Chips	27	21.6
4	Berry Cherry	30	30

(70 row(s) returned)
(There are more records in the result set than the ones shown in this image)

3. The marketing people are initiating a new campaign to get rid of high inventory items. Create a new product catalog with the following discounts: 20% discount for products with units in stock below 20, 25% discount for products with units in stock greater than or equal to 20 and less than 30, 30% discount for products with units in stock greater than or equal to 30 and less than 40, and 35% discount for products with units in stock greater than or equal to 40. Create a new query that includes the fields ProductName, UnitsInStock, ProductPrice, and a calculated field, named NewPrice, from the products table that satisfies the marketing people request. Order results by ProductName ascending. Save the query as Conditions_Case2_Q3.

Your result should look like:

ProductName	UnitsInStock	ProductPrice	NewPrice
All-Purpose Marinade	27	29	21.75
Almonds Hickory Smoked	40	35	22.75
Almonds Roasted and Salted	32	22	15.4
Apple Cinnamon Raisin Cookies	15	27	21.6

(70 row(s) returned)
(There are more records in the result set than the ones shown in this image)

4. The marketing people are amazingly happy from your report in question three. However, someone from replenishment pointed out that the report in question three though amazing does not solve the problem with highly inventoried items. They propose to add to the units in stock the units on order so that we know what we actually have in inventory even though the units on order are not physically in yet. Consequently, recreate the query in question three taking into consideration the sum of units in stock and units on order to provide the corresponding discounts. The new query should include the fields ProductName, UnitsInStock, UnitsOnOrder, ProductPrice, and a calculated field, named NewPrice, from the Products table and satisfies the replenishing people request. Save the query as Conditions_Case2_Q4.

Your result should look like:

ProductName	UnitsInStock	UnitsOnOrder	ProductPrice	NewPrice
All-Purpose Marinade	27	15	29	18.85
Almonds Hickory Smoked	40	5	35	22.75
Almonds Roasted and Salted	32	0	22	15.4
Apple Cinnamon Raisin Cookies	15	20	27	18.9

(70 row(s) returned)
(There are more records in the result set than the ones shown in this image)

5. The management is asking for a report identical to that in question 4. However, this time they want to also see the discount extended (for example 20%, 25%, 30%) for each product instead of the new price. Create a new query that satisfies the management's request and save it as Conditions_Case2_Q5.

Your result should look like:

ProductName	UnitsInStock	UnitsOnOrder	ProductPrice	DiscountExtended
All-Purpose Marinade	27	15	29	35%
Almonds Hickory Smoked	40	5	35	35%
Almonds Roasted and Salted	32	0	22	30%
Apple Cinnamon Raisin Cookies	15	20	27	30%

(70 row(s) returned)
(There are more records in the result set than the ones shown in this image)

CHAPTER 21 DUPLICATE, RELATED, and UNRELATED DATA

This chapter focuses on four specific learning goals: The identification of duplicate, orphaned, related, and unrelated records. Orphaned and duplicate records will affect your database integrity, while related and unrelated records will affect your business decisions.

Orphaned records occur when there are no primary key values for existing foreign key values in a one-to-many relationship. For example, in a relationship between customers and orders, you might have orders without corresponding customers. This scenario can occur if referential integrity for this relationship is not set (see the table relationships chapter). This will allow a user to delete a customer without any warning that there are existing orders for this customer. Alternatively, it might allow a user to enter an order without first entering a customer.

We need to have referential integrity on to avoid the occurrence of orphaned records. Yet, what happens when we already have orphaned records in the database? There are two solutions with orphaned records. The first is to delete orphaned records from the database which means we must first find them. In this chapter, there will be plenty of examples to locate orphaned records. The second scenario might occur if we need to keep orphaned records such as past orders in the database. In this case, we need to enter their corresponding customer information. In any case, we must be able to identify and manipulate orphaned records.

A second common occurrence in business databases is duplicate records. In this chapter, you will learn several techniques to isolate and deal with duplicate records, which are not synonymous to identical records. Two customer records might be duplicates if they have the same name but different address information. So, you will learn how to find duplicate records based on the values of one, two, or multiple fields.

A third case involves unrelated records. For example, we might have customers in the database who have not placed any orders for quite some time. These customers have no related orders in the Orders table for a specific period. This is a business and not a database problem. However, we need to act, and we have two choices for inactive customers. The first is to use a marketing campaign to entice them to start buying again. If this is not feasible, we might want to delete them from the database or move them to a historical Customer table. To delete or move these records, we need to be able to first find them.

The fourth scenario is that of related records. For example, we might want to know how many customers placed orders over a period of a year, month, or quarter. In other words, we want to know how many customers have related order entries in the orders table. In this chapter, you will learn how to quickly identify such customers to increase the effectiveness of your business operations.

So that we can check our numbers, we will use the table named tbls_orders, which contains a number of orphaned and duplicate records. Specifically, the records with OrderID = 8, 45, 254, 820, 993 are duplicate records. In addition, there are two records with null OrderIDs, which I put in to make our work a bit more complicated.

SECTION 1 – DUPLICATE RECORDS

169. Detect duplicate records based on the values of one field

Find duplicate customer orders based on the value of the OrderID

Discussion:

In this example, we are looking for records in the tbls_orders table that have the same value for the OrderID field. We use the count(*) function to calculate the number of duplicate records for each OrderID value. Remember, this example will give us duplicate field values in various records and not necessarily duplicate records. Though the OrderID values are the same, the rest of the fields in the returned records might have different values. Still, it is very useful to know how to search for duplicate values in one field. As you can see from the result set, two records have null values for the OrderID. In addition, there are two instances of duplicate records for OrderIDs with values 8, 45, 254, and 820. Finally, the OrderID with value 993 appears in three records in the table.

Code:

```
SELECT OrderID, Count(*) AS NumberofDuplicates
FROM tbls_orders
GROUP BY OrderID
HAVING count(*)>1
ORDER BY OrderID
```

Result:

OrderID	NumberofDuplicates
	2
8	2
45	2
254	2
820	2
993	3

(6 row(s) returned)

170. Detect duplicate records based on the values of two fields

Find duplicate customer orders based on the values of OrderID and CustomerID

Discussion:

In this example, we are looking for duplicate records based on the values of OrderID and CustomerID. If the values of the OrderID and CustomerID are the same for at least two records, they will appear in the result set as duplicates. The count(*) function will calculate the number of records with identical OrderID and CustomerID values. We can replace the two fields used in this example with any fields on which we would like to look for duplicate values. Keep in mind that while two records might have matching values for two fields, this does not necessarily mean that they are duplicate records. This code will allow us to locate potential duplicate records based on the values of two fields. We need to examine the individual records to verify that they are indeed duplicates.

Code:

```
SELECT OrderID, CustomerID, Count(*) AS NumberofDuplicates
FROM tbls_orders
GROUP BY OrderID, CustomerID
HAVING count(*)>1
```

Result:

OrderID	CustomerID	NumberofDuplicates
8	71	2
45	93	2
254	198	2
820	46	2
993	99	3

(5 row(s) returned)

171. Detect duplicate records based on the values of multiple fields

Find duplicate customer orders based on the values of multiple fields

Discussion:

In this example, we are looking for duplicate records based on the values of eight fields. That is, if the values of eight fields of at least two records are identical, those records will appear as duplicates. Of course, with eight identical values, two records will most probably be duplicate entries. Notice that there are two identical records for OrderIDs with values 8, 45, 254, and 820, while there are three identical records for OrderID = 993.

Code:

```
SELECT Count(*) AS NumberofDuplicates, OrderID, CustomerID, SalesRepID, OrderDate,
RequiredDate, ShippedDate, ShippingCost
FROM tbls_orders
GROUP BY OrderID, CustomerID, SalesRepID, OrderDate, RequiredDate, ShippedDate,
ShippingCost
HAVING count(*)>1
```

Result:

NumberofDuplicates	OrderID	CustomerID	SalesRepID	OrderDate	RequiredDate	ShippedDate	ShippingCost
2	8	71	3	4/1/2022	4/16/2022	4/6/2022	36
2	45	93	1	10/23/2020	11/7/2020	10/28/2020	46
2	254	198	3	7/15/2020	7/30/2020	7/20/2020	36
2	820	46	8	9/4/2022	9/19/2022	9/9/2022	39
3	993	99	10	10/14/2020	10/29/2020	10/19/2020	49

(5 row(s) returned)

172. Display all duplicate records in a table

Find and display all duplicate records in the Orders table

Discussion:

In the previous examples, we were able to identify duplicate records in the table but display only one instance from each in the result set. There are cases, however, in which we will want to display all instances from all duplicate records. We can achieve this using a subquery. In this example, we will display all instances of all duplicate records based on the values of the OrderID field, or put it another way, based on the values of one field.

Code:

```
SELECT *
FROM tbls_orders WHERE OrderID IN(
SELECT OrderID
FROM tbls_Orders
GROUP BY OrderID
HAVING count(*)>1)
ORDER BY OrderID
```

Result:

OrderID	CustomerID	SalesRepID	ShipperID	OrderDate	RequiredDate	ShippedDate	ShippingCost
8	71	3	1	4/1/2022	4/16/2022	4/6/2022	36
8	71	3	1	4/1/2022	4/16/2022	4/6/2022	36
45	93	1	3	10/23/2020	11/7/2020	10/28/2020	46
45	93	1	3	10/23/2020	11/7/2020	10/28/2020	46
254	198	3	2	7/15/2020	7/30/2020	7/20/2020	36
254	198	3	2	7/15/2020	7/30/2020	7/20/2020	36
820	46	8	1	9/4/2022	9/19/2022	9/9/2022	39
820	46	8	1	9/4/2022	9/19/2022	9/9/2022	39
993	99	10	2	10/14/2020	10/29/2020	10/19/2020	49
993	99	10	2	10/14/2020	10/29/2020	10/19/2020	49
993	99	10	2	10/14/2020	10/29/2020	10/19/2020	49

(11 row(s) returned)

SECTION 2 – ORPHANED RECORDS

173. What are orphaned records and how to deal with them

In the figure below, there are five orders in the Orders table with OrderIDs from 1 to 5. For the first four orders, there are corresponding customers in the Customers table. For order with OrderID=5, there does not exist a corresponding customer in the database. This is an order that belongs to no one. The record in the Orders table with OrderID=5 is called an orphaned record.

CUSTOMERS	
CustID	**Name**
1	John
2	Mary
3	George
4	Stacy

ORDERS		
OrderID	**CustID**	**OrderDate**
1	2	9/10/2021
2	2	10/10/2021
3	1	11/10/2023
4	3	11/11/2023
5	7	11/15/2023

A reason for this might be that when the database was created and relationships established, referential integrity was not set. The immediate consequence is that a user of the database deleted the customer with CustomerID=7 either by mistake or on purpose. Although the customer record has been deleted, his or her orders are still in the database, useless and compromising data integrity. Another reason might be that a user received an order from a new customer. The correct process would have been to check if the customer existed and then enter the order. If referential integrity is off a representative can enter an order without an existing customer. To avoid orphaned records, referential integrity should be set for a relationship between two tables.

174. Identify orphaned records using a subquery

Find orders for which there are no customers using a subquery

Discussion:

Let us assume that we want to set on referential integrity for the relationship between Customers and Orders. If Access does not allow us to do this, our first action should be to look for orphaned records in the Orders table or in the table in the many side of the relationship. We can use the code below to do just that. As you can see from the result set, there are three orders (OrderID= 1500, 1501, and 1502) that came up as orphaned records. This means that the customers with CustomerID values of 250, 251, and 252 do not exist in the Customers table.

Code:

```
SELECT OrderID, SalesRepID, ShipperID, OrderDate
FROM tbls_orders
WHERE CustomerID
NOT IN (SELECT CustomerID from Customers)
```

Result:

OrderID	SalesRepID	ShipperID	OrderDate
1500	11	2	1/20/2020
1501	12	2	11/18/2020
1502	14	3	2/5/2021

(3 row(s) returned)

175. Find orphaned records using a join

Find orders for which there are no customers using a join

Discussion:

We can use a LEFT join between Customers and tbls_orders to identify orphaned records in the tbls_orders table. This is faster than a subquery and as you can see, the result set is identical.

Code:

```
SELECT OrderID, SalesRepID, ShipperID, OrderDate
FROM tbls_Orders
LEFT JOIN Customers ON tbls_Orders.CustomerID = Customers.CustomerID
WHERE Customers.CustomerID Is Null
```

Result:

OrderID	SalesRepID	ShipperID	OrderDate
1500	11	2	1/20/2020
1501	12	2	11/18/2020
1502	14	3	2/5/2021

(3 row(s) returned)

176. Delete orphaned records

Delete orders for which there are no customers

Discussion:

We can use a subquery to identify and delete orphaned records in one step. In the code below, we use the DELETE statement to delete orders in the tbls_orders table for which there are no customers in the customers table. The subquery will isolate CustomerID values in the tbls_Orders1 table for which there are no corresponding CustomerID values in the Customers table. Notice that the CustomerID is the primary key in the Customers table and the foreign key in the tbls_Orders1 table. In this example we will first create the tbls_orders1 table which is an exact copy of the tbls_orders table.

Code1:
```
SELECT *
INTO tbls_orders1
FROM tbls_orders
```

Result:
```
(You are about to paste 1008 row(s) into a new table)
```

Code2:
```
DELETE
FROM tbls_orders1
WHERE CustomerID
NOT IN (SELECT CustomerID FROM Customers)
```

Result:
```
(You are about to delete 3 row(s) from the specified table)
```

177. Delete orphaned records using a join

Delete orders for which there are no customers using a join

Discussion:

We can use a LEFT join to identify and delete orphaned records in a table. Notice the WHERE clause in the code below which looks for CustomerID values in the LEFT JOIN with a null value, i.e., CustomerID or foreign key values in the tbls_orders2 table for which there are no primary key values in the Customers table. Joins work faster than subqueries especially on indexed fields, and while they are more complicated, their use might well be justified in cases with many records. However, this does not mean that a join will always be faster than a subquery. In this example we first create the tbls_Orders2 table, an exact copy of the tbls_Orders table.

Code1:
```
SELECT *
INTO tbls_Orders2
FROM tbls_Orders
```

Result:
```
(You are about to paste 1008 row(s) into a new table)
```

Code2:
```
DELETE tbls_Orders2.*
FROM tbls_Orders2
LEFT JOIN Customers ON tbls_Orders2.CustomerID = Customers.CustomerID
WHERE (Customers.CustomerID Is Null)
```

Result:
```
(You are about to delete 3 row(s) from the specified table)
```

SECTION 3 – UNRELATED RECORDS

The knowledge to identify unrelated records is fundamental in data analytics. It allows us to reply to questions such as: How many students have not taken classes this semester? What sales reps did not have sales last week? How many customers have not placed any orders? Practically, we are looking for customers who have no orders over a period knowing that there is a one-to-many relationship between Customers and Orders. Keep in mind that finding customers without orders is not a problematic situation when it comes to database integrity; it is simply a business fact. However, finding orders without customers represents a database integrity problem, and we call these orphaned records.

178. Identify unrelated records using a subquery

Find customers for whom there are no orders

Discussion:

In this example, we use a subquery with the NOT IN operator to find customers who have not placed any orders. Technically, we are looking for records in the Customers table that have no related records in the tbls_Orders table. In other words, we are looking for CustomerID values (1, 2, 3 etc.) in the Customers table, which do not exist in the Orders table. Put it in another way, we are looking for primary key values (CustomerID) in the Customers table with no corresponding foreign key values (CustomerIDs) in the tbls_Orders table.

Code:

```
SELECT CustomerID, FirstName, LastName, Address, City, State
FROM Customers
WHERE CustomerID
NOT IN (SELECT CustomerID from tbls_orders)
```

Result:

CustomerID	FirstName	LastName	Address	City	State
19	Erin	Erin	28 Karrie Terrace	Los Angeles	CA
37	Allan	Cimo	24 Crestwood CT	New York	NY
40	Kelly	Costa	45 Sixth Ave	Philadelphia	PA
66	Arnold	Webster	53 Southern Blvd	Miami	FL

(There are more records in the result set than the ones shown in this image)
(11 row(s) returned)

179. Find unrelated records using a subquery and criteria

Find customers for whom there are no orders using date criteria

Discussion:

In the previous example, we learned how to identify customers without orders for all sales years in the database. This is excellent knowledge, but in actual business practice, we will need additional criteria to derive insightful information. For example, identify the customers who have not placed any orders in the last year, quarter, month, or week. Alternatively, we might want to know what customers from NY have not placed any orders in the last two months. In this example, we are looking for customers who have not placed any orders in 2021. We can use the vast arsenal of date functions from the respective chapter to extract any time period we need.

Code:

```
SELECT CustomerID, FirstName, LastName, Address, City, State
FROM Customers
WHERE CustomerID NOT IN
(SELECT CustomerID
FROM tbls_Orders
WHERE OrderDate BETWEEN #1/1/2021# AND #12/31/2021#)
```

Result:

CustomerID	FirstName	LastName	Address	City	State
2	Mary	Demania	12 Madison Ave	New York	NY
6	Michael	Demizio	23 Grove Rd	New York	NY
15	Pindar	Ames	23 Cornell Dr	New York	NY
19	Erin	Erin	28 Karrie Terrace	Los Angeles	CA

(There are more records in the result set than the ones shown in this image)
(36 row(s) returned)

SECTION 4 – RELATED RECORDS

180. Find related records using a subquery

Find customers who have placed orders

Discussion:

Related records are, for instance, customers who have placed orders last week, suppliers who have sent raw materials in the last two days, or products that sold last month. In this example, we are looking for customers who have placed at least one order throughout all the years we have in the database. We can add additional criteria to identify customers who place orders in certain periods such as years, quarters, or months.

Code:

```
SELECT CustomerID, FirstName, LastName, Address, City, State
FROM Customers
WHERE CustomerID
IN (SELECT CustomerID from tbls_orders)
```

Result:

CustomerID	FirstName	LastName	Address	City	State
1	John	Demarco	11 Lark Street	New York	NY
2	Mary	Demania	12 Madison Ave	New York	NY
3	George	Demers	23 New Scotland Ave	New York	NY
4	Phillip	Demetriou	22 Academy Road	New York	NY

(There are more records in the result set than the ones shown in this image)
(190 row(s) returned)

181. Find related records using a subquery and criteria

Find customers who placed orders during a specific quarter of the year

Discussion:

In this scenario, we are looking for customers who have placed orders in the 4th quarter of 2021. Notice that we use two date functions, datepart() and year(), to extract the quarter and year out of the OrderDate field. Using a subquery and two date functions, we extract exactly the information we need. This list of customers without orders can help in our marketing and promotional campaigns.

Code:

```
SELECT CustomerID, FirstName, LastName, Address, City, State
FROM Customers
WHERE CustomerID
IN (SELECT CustomerID from tbls_orders WHERE
DatePart('q' , OrderDate) = 4 AND  year(OrderDate) = 2021)
```

Result:

CustomerID	FirstName	LastName	Address	City	State
4	Phillip	Demetriou	22 Academy Road	New York	NY
5	Andrew	Demichele	14 Glandel Ave	New York	NY
7	Robert	Demaggio	34 Princeton Dr	New York	NY
8	Nicholas	Demaico	44 Notre Dame Dr	New York	NY

```
(There are more records in the result set than the ones shown in this image)
(74 row(s) returned)
```

DISCUSSION QUESTIONS

1. How do we call the records for which there are no primary key values for corresponding foreign key values?
2. How do we call the records for which there are no foreign key values for corresponding primary key values?
3. When referential integrity is off what kind of risk do we incur? End up with orphaned, duplicate, related or unrelated records?
4. If referential integrity is on, can we still end up with duplicate records in the database? Why yes or why not?
5. What techniques can we use to identify orphaned records in the database?
6. What do we mean by duplicate records? For two records to be duplicates do they need to have identical data?
7. If we have customers without orders is this a database integrity problem or a business problem?
8. If we have orders without customers is this a database integrity problem or a business problem?
9. What kind of action do we need to take when we find orphaned records in the database?
10. What kind of action do we need to take when we find unrelated records in the database?

HANDS-ON EXERCISES

Case 1

For each of the questions in this case create a new query in SQL view and name it as per the instructions in each question.

1. Accounts has notified IT that something is not right with the orders presented for payment. It looks like some of them are repeated entries and we risk paying them twice. They are asking you to check for duplicate records in the table tbls_Orders based on the values of the fields CustomerID, SalesRepID, and ShipperID. Your report should also include the number of instances of repeated records. Create a new query that satisfies the accounts receivable request and save it as Duplicates_Case1_Q1.

Your result should look like:

CustomerID	SalesRepID	ShipperID	NumberofDuplicates
1	4	1	2
3	4	1	3
3	1	1	2
4	5	3	2

```
(There are more records in the result set than the ones shown in this image)
(96 row(s) returned)
```

2. The accounts receivable people are happy with your report, but they want to make sure that what they do makes business sense. That is, it might be natural for the same customer to have ordered through the same salesperson and used the same shipping company multiple times. To account for this fact and make sure they identify only real duplicate records, they are asking you to check for duplicate records in the table tble_Orders based on the values of all fields. Your report should also include the number of instances of duplicate records. Create a new query that includes all fields from the tble_Orders table and satisfies the accounts receivable request. Save the query as Duplicates_Case1_Q2. (Hint: Do not include the OrderID in the list of fields in your code since it is the primary key and it will always have a unique value.)

Your result should look like:

CustomerID	SalesRepID	ShipperID	OrderDate	RequiredDate	ShippedDate	ShippingCost	#ofDuplicates
46	8	1	9/4/2022	9/19/2022	9/9/2022	39	2
71	3	1	4/1/2022	4/16/2022	4/6/2022	36	2
93	1	3	10/23/2020	11/7/2020	10/28/2020	46	2
99	10	2	10/14/2020	10/29/2020	10/19/2020	49	3
198	3	2	7/15/2020	7/30/2020	7/20/2020	36	2

(5 row(s) returned)

3. Human Resources called in and they say they are trying to calculate commissions for salespeople, but some orders refer to sales reps they cannot find in the database. Check to see why the HR people cannot find the sales representatives in the SalesReps table and why these sales reps have orders in the tbls_Orders table. Make a list of all orders for which no sales reps exist in the SalesReps table. Create a new query that includes all fields from the tbls_Orders table and satisfies the HR people request. Save it as Duplicates_Case1_Q3.

Your result should look like:

OrderID	CustomerID	SalesRepID	ShipperID	OrderDate	RequiredDate	ShippedDate	ShippingCost
1500	250	11	2	1/20/2020	2/4/2020	1/25/2020	49
1501	251	12	2	11/18/2020	12/3/2020	11/23/2020	40
1502	252	14	3	2/5/2021	2/20/2021	2/10/2021	36

(3 row(s) returned)

4. The sales director thinks that some of the salespeople are not very aggressive in the market, which means they miss commissions and the company is missing sales. He asks for a report that lists the salespeople without sales for the month of December 2022 using the tbls_Orders table. Create a new query that includes the fields FirstName, LastName, Title, City, and State from the SalesReps table and satisfies the sales director request. Save it as Duplicates_Case1_Q4.

Your result should look like:

FirstName	LastName	Title	City	State
George	Spicer	Account Manager	Boston	MA
Phillip	Zensons	Sales Representative	New York	NY
Michael	Bernstein	Sales Representative	New York	NY

(3 row(s) returned)

5. The sales director is now asking for a report of salespeople who actually had sales in the month of December 2022. Create a new query that includes the fields FirstName, LastName, Title, City, and State from the SalesReps table and satisfies the sales director request. Save it as Duplicates_Case1_Q5. Use the tbls_Orders table to check for placed orders.

Your result should look like:

FirstName	LastName	Title	City	State
John	Anderson	Sales Representative	Boston	MA
Mary	Teall	Sales Director	Boston	MA
Andrew	Simmons	Account Manager	New York	NY
Kenneth	Delaney	Assistant Manager	New York	NY

(There are more records in the result set than the ones shown in this image)
(7 row(s) returned)

Case 2

For each of the questions in this case create a new query in SQL view and name it as per the instructions in each question.

1. The salespeople are asking for a list of shipping companies which have not shipped any orders for us for the records we have in the tbls_Orders table. Create a query that includes the fields CompanyName, City, State, and Phone from the ShippingCompanies table and satisfies the salespeople request. Name the query as Duplicates_Case2_Q1.

Your result should look like:

CompanyName	City	State	Phone
US Postal Service	Philadelphia	PA	438-433-8998

(1 row(s) returned)

2. The salespeople are back asking for a report that lists the shipping companies we have not used in the shipping of our orders for the last six months of 2022. Use the tbls_Orders table. Create a query that includes the fields CompanyName, City, State, and Phone from the ShippingCompanies table and satisfies the salespeople request. Name the query as Duplicates_Case2_Q2. Why is the result the same as in question 1?

Your result should look like:

CompanyName	City	State	Phone
US Postal Service	Philadelphia	PA	438-433-8998

(1 row(s) returned)

3. The salespeople are now asking for a report that will list orders in the tbls_Orders table without any associated shipping companies. Create a query that includes the fields OrderID, ShipperID, OrderDate, ShippedDate, and ShippingCost from the tbls_Orders table and satisfies the salespeople request. Name the query as Duplicates_Case2_Q3. What is the meaning of 0 rows returned?

Your result should look like:

(0 row(s) returned)

4. The salespeople need a report that will list the shipping companies we used for the shipping of at least one order in the tbls_Orders table. Create a query that includes the fields CompanyName, City, State, and Phone from the ShippingCompanies table and satisfies the salespeople request. Name the query as Duplicates_Case2_Q4.

Your result should look like:

CompanyName	City	State	Phone
Federal Speed	Los Angeles	CA	451-237-4387
NHL	New York	NY	518-589-4990
United Postal	Boston	MA	546-437-3989

(3 row(s) returned)

5. The salespeople need a report that will list all the shipping companies which shipped our orders between the 10th and 31st of December 2022. Use order data from the tbls_Orders table. Create a query that includes the fields CompanyName, City, State, and Phone from the ShippingCompanies table and satisfies the salespeople request. Name the query as Duplicates_Case2_Q5.

Your result should look like:

CompanyName	City	State	Phone
Federal Speed	Los Angeles	CA	451-237-4387

(1 row(s) returned

CHAPTER 22
NULL VALUES IN DATASETS

There are three concepts we need to know to understand null values in full: First, a zero (0) value is not a null value. It means that there is a value, and it is zero. Second, a zero-length string, also called an empty string, is not a null value. In Access we designate an empty string by typing two double quotation marks with no space between them (""). It means that there should be a value, but there is none yet. Third, a null (*NULL*) value means that we do not know whether there should be a value or not. Zero-length strings and null values appear as empty cells in Access. We have no way of distinguishing between cells with null values and cells with empty strings in them; they both appear blank.

We will see how to deal with them but the best way to avoid problematic situations with nulls and zero-length strings is to prevent them altogether. When designing a new database, we can assign default values to fields that users might leave blank. For example, for a customer middle name, we can set a default value of "NA" when none is entered. For existing databases, we can run update statements to replace null and empty string values with default values.

Null values and zero-length strings will affect your calculations in aggregate functions, search expressions, union operations, and will leave doubts about the validity of your analytics. In this chapter, to verify the effects of null values and zero-length strings, we will work with a table called "tbls_products_n" which contains only ten records. Using only ten records, we will be able to see and verify our calculations and learn how to work with missing values effectively. Then, we can apply the same techniques on thousands of records.

182. Looking for nulls using the IS NULL Expression

Retrieve products whose stock keeping unit codes (SKUs) are null

Discussion:

We want to retrieve all products for which the SKU code is missing. Of course, with only ten products, we can just eye the table and tell right away that there are four SKU codes missing. Let us use code to retrieve them and see if the database agrees. We use the "IS NULL" expression in the WHERE clause and only two records appear in the result set. I have included a note in parenthesis in the ProductName field so that we know what SKUs contain zero length strings and what SKUs contain null values. Only two records appear in the result set because only two contain null SKUs. The other two records with blank SKUs contain zero-length strings.

Code:

```
SELECT ProductID, ProductName, ProductPrice, SKU
FROM tbls_products_n
WHERE SKU IS NULL
```

Result:

ProductID	ProductName	ProductPrice	SKU
71	Almonds (SKU is Null)		
72	Almonds Roasted (SKU is Null)		

(2 row(s) returned)

183. Looking for nulls and zero-length strings using one SQL statement

Retrieve products whose stock keeping unit codes (SKUs) are nulls or zero-length strings

Discussion:

In this example we use the "IS NULL" expression and an additional criterion in the WHERE clause to look for records in which the SKU is null or a zero-length string. Now four records with blank values appear!

Code:

```
SELECT ProductID, ProductName, ProductPrice, SKU
FROM tbls_products_n
WHERE SKU IS NULL or SKU = ""
```

Result:

ProductID	ProductName	ProductPrice	SKU
3	Banana Chips (SKU is Zero-Length)	30	
4	Berry Cherry (SKU is Zero-Length)	30	
71	Almonds (SKU is Null)		
72	Almonds Roasted (SKU is Null)		

(4 row(s) returned)

184. Looking for nulls using the IsNull() function

Display all products whose SKU is null

Discussion:

The IsNull() function provides additional functionality when looking for nulls. It will produce a true or false value for all the entries in the field we are inspecting. For every value in the SKU field, we will get a true or false response from the database. In Access, the value 0 means false, and the value -1 means true. In the following datasheet, we will get -1 for the two records with null values.

Code:

```
SELECT ProductID, ProductName, ProductPrice, IsNull(SKU) AS SKUCheck
FROM tbls_products_n
```

Result:

ProductID	ProductName	ProductPrice	SKUCheck
3	Banana Chips (SKU is Zero-Length)	30	0
4	Berry Cherry (SKU is Zero-Length)	30	0
5	California Original Pistachios	29	0
6	Choice Apricots	32	0
7	Cran Raisin Mix	31	0
8	Dried Blueberries	28	0
9	Dried Cranberries	35	0
10	Raw Sunflower Seeds	25	0
71	Almonds (SKU is Null)		-1
72	Almonds Roasted (SKU is Null)		-1

(10 row(s) returned)

185. Calculations with nulls and zero-length strings

Calculate product inventory subtotals where some values are null

Discussion:

In this example, we want to multiply the field ProductPrice with the QuantityPerUnit to calculate the value of our inventory by product. In the tbls_products_n table, there are missing entries for both the ProductPrice and the QuantityPerUnit fields.

Code:

```
SELECT ProductID, ProductName, ProductPrice, QuantityPerUnit, (productprice*quantityperunit) As Subtotal
FROM tbls_products_n
ORDER BY (productprice*quantityperunit) DESC
```

Result:

As you can see, for the records with null values for either one of the two multiplied fields, there will be no result. This will have consequences for our inventory calculations since at least for ProductID=72, we know that we do have 25 units on hand. Since their price is missing, the inventory report will be incorrect. To avoid this situation, we need to make it a habit to look for nulls and zero-length strings before we do any calculations.

ProductID	ProductName	ProductPrice	QuantityPerUnit	Subtotal
6	Choice Apricots	32	25	800
10	Raw Sunflower Seeds	25	25	625
9	Dried Cranberries	35	15	525
4	Berry Cherry (SKU is Zero-Length)	30	15	450
5	California Original Pistachios	29	15	435
7	Cran Raisin Mix	31	12	372
3	Banana Chips (SKU is Zero-Length)	30	12	360
8	Dried Blueberries	28	10	280
72	Almonds Roasted (SKU is Null)			
71	Almonds (SKU is Null)		25	

(10 row(s) returned)

186. Looking for nulls using the iif() function

Display the value "null" for products with null SKUs

Discussion:

The iif() function in this example will display the text value "null" for every null in the SKU field. If there is no null, it will display the actual SKU value. Two of the values in the SKUCheck field appear as blanks because they contain a zero-length string, and this empty string is displayed!

Code:

```
SELECT ProductID, ProductName, ProductPrice, IIf(IsNull([SKU]),"null", [SKU]) AS SKUCheck
FROM tbls_products_n
ORDER BY SKU
```

Result:

ProductID	ProductName	ProductPrice	SKUCheck
72	Almonds Roasted (SKU is Null)		null
71	Almonds (SKU is Null)		null
4	Berry Cherry (SKU is Zero-Length)	30	
3	Banana Chips (SKU is Zero-Length)	30	
9	Dried Cranberries	35	PDK-2347
6	Choice Apricots	32	PDK-2347
5	California Original Pistachios	29	PDK-2347

10	Raw Sunflower Seeds	25	PDKLS-1889
8	Dried Blueberries	28	PDKLS-1889
7	Cran Raisin Mix	31	PDKLS-1889

(10 row(s) returned)

187. Looking for zero-length strings using the iif() function

Display the value "zero-length" for products with zero-length SKU values

Discussion:

The iif() function in this example will display the text "zero-length" for every zero-length string ("") in the SKU field. If there is no zero-length string, it will display the actual SKU value. Two of the values in the SKUCheck field appear as blanks because they contain a null value and null values appear as blank values in Access.

Code:

```
SELECT ProductID, ProductName, ProductPrice, IIf([SKU] ="","zero-length", [SKU]) AS SKUCheck
FROM tbls_products_n
ORDER BY SKU
```

Result:

ProductID	ProductName	ProductPrice	SKUCheck
72	Almonds Roasted (SKU is Null)		
71	Almonds (SKU is Null)		
4	Berry Cherry (SKU is Zero-Length)	30	zero-length
3	Banana Chips (SKU is Zero-Length)	30	zero-length
9	Dried Cranberries	35	PDK-2347
6	Choice Apricots	32	PDK-2347
5	California Original Pistachios	29	PDK-2347
10	Raw Sunflower Seeds	25	PDKLS-1889
8	Dried Blueberries	28	PDKLS-1889
7	Cran Raisin Mix	31	PDKLS-1889

(10 row(s) returned)

188. Identify and indicate nulls and zero length strings using nested iif() functions

Display the word "null" and "zero-length" for products with null or zero-length SKUs respectively

Discussion:

Using the nested iif() function below, practically an iif() function within an iif() function, we identify all the null values and zero-length strings in the SKU field and we display the corresponding text in those cells as you can see in the image below.

Code:

```
SELECT ProductID, ProductName, ProductPrice, IIf(IsNull([SKU]),"NULL", IIf([SKU] = "","zero-length string"))
AS SKUCheck
FROM tbls_products_n
ORDER BY SKU
```

Result:

ProductID	ProductName	ProductPrice	SKUCheck
72	Almonds Roasted (SKU is Null)		NULL
71	Almonds (SKU is Null)		NULL
4	Berry Cherry (SKU is Zero-Length)	30	zero-length string
3	Banana Chips (SKU is Zero-Length)	30	zero-length string
9	Dried Cranberries	35	
6	Choice Apricots	32	
5	California Original Pistachios	29	
10	Raw Sunflower Seeds	25	
8	Dried Blueberries	28	
7	Cran Raisin Mix	31	

(10 row(s) returned)

189. Using sum() with null values

Calculate the total inventory value

Discussion:

When we use aggregate functions, we cannot see the empty field values to realize we have missing data. When aggregate functions encounter null values, they will leave them out of the calculations altogether and report only on known values.

In the tbls_products_n table, the products with productID 71 and 72 will be missing from the calculations. For productid=72, we have no quantity or price data, and we do not know if this is correct or not. For productid=71, we know that we have a quantity per unit = 25 but no price, and our results will be wrong. The best way to avoid these situations is to check the data for null and empty string values and make every effort to fill in the missing values.

Code:

```
SELECT SUM(productprice*quantityperunit) As Total
FROM tbls_products_n
```

Result:

Total
3847

(1 row(s) returned)

190. Using count() with null values

Count the number of products in the inventory correctly

Discussion:

As I have mentioned countless times in this book, our primary goal is to rid the database of nulls by replacing them with concrete values in our tables such as 'NA' for text fields or numbers for numeric ones. In this example, our goal is to calculate the number of products in our inventory table. If we apply the count() function on the SKU field, we will get eight records. This is because there are two null values in the SKU field that have not been counted!

Code:

```
SELECT Count(SKU) As CountSKUs
FROM tbls_products_n
```

Result:

CountSKUs
8

(1 row(s) returned)

Discussion:
My recommendation is to use count() or other arithmetic functions on fields that, by default, do not allow nulls in their values. For example, we could use count() on the ProductID field which is the primary key of the table.

Code:
```
SELECT Count(ProductID) As CountSKUs
FROM tbls_products_n
```

Result:

CountSKUs
10

(1 row(s) returned)

Discussion:
Another solution for correct counts is to use the count(*) function, which will return the actual number of records in the table independently of any null values in the field.

Code:
```
SELECT Count(*) As CountRecords
FROM tbls_products_n
```

Result:

CountSKUs
10

(1 row(s) returned)

191. Leaving nulls out of the result set

Find products for which the SKU code is not null

Discussion:
Use the IS NOT NULL expression to obtain a list of products that do not contain null values in the SKU field. The IS NOT NULL expression is not a panacea to null values problems. The real solution would be to use UPDATE statements to replace null values with concrete values such as 'NA' for text or numbers for numeric fields. As we have expected, the SQL statement returned eight records with non-null values for the SKU field.

Code:
```
SELECT ProductID, ProductName, ProductPrice, SKU
FROM tbls_Products_n
WHERE SKU IS NOT NULL
```

Result:

ProductID	ProductName	ProductPrice	SKU
3	Banana Chips (SKU is Zero-Length)	30	
4	Berry Cherry (SKU is Zero-Length)	30	
5	California Original Pistachios	29	PDK-2347
6	Choice Apricots	32	PDK-2347
7	Cran Raisin Mix	31	PDKLS-1889
8	Dried Blueberries	28	PDKLS-1889
9	Dried Cranberries	35	PDK-2347
10	Raw Sunflower Seeds	25	PDKLS-1889

```
(8 row(s) returned)
```

192. Permanently replace nulls using an update statement

Use UPDATE to replace null values in the SKU field

Discussion:

We can replace the null values in the SKU field by using the UPDATE statement with the WHERE clause and the IS NULL expression. As you can see from the result set, the database will replace the existing null values in the SKU field. We will create a copy of the tbls_products_n table before we apply the UPDATE statement.

Code:

```
SELECT *
INTO temp_tbls_Products_n
FROM tbls_Products_n
```

Result:

```
(10 row(s) affected)
```

Code:

```
UPDATE temp_tbls_Products_n SET SKU = 'NA'
WHERE SKU IS NULL
```

Result:

```
(2 row(s) affected)
```

193. Using the NZ() function to deal with null values

Calculate inventory replenishment amounts

Discussion:

Our task is to report how many units of a product we need so that we have enough to operate. We subtract from the reorder level the units we have on hand and the units we have already ordered. Null values will get in the way again. In this example with ten records in the table, we can easily check for null values, but with 10,000 product records, we will not be able to tell. If we try to perform these calculations while ignoring the presence of nulls, we will end up with the database unable to produce results for 40% of our products—four out of ten!

Code:

```
SELECT ProductID, (ReorderLevel-(UnitsInstock+UnitsOnOrder)) AS UnitsToOrder
FROM tbls_Products_n
```

Result:

ProductID	UnitsToOrder
3	5
4	5
5	
6	3
7	
8	2
9	
10	3
71	21
72	

(10 row(s) returned)

Using the nz() function, we can replace nulls with any values we want to. The nz() function has two arguments:

Nz(field, value of field if it is null)

For the "value of field if it is null" argument, we can put any value we want to like 0, 1, 2, etc. for numeric fields or "hi my name is John" for text fields. In this particular example, the nz() function will replace the null values of the fields unitsinstock and unitsonorder with zeros.

Code:

```
SELECT ProductID, (ReorderLevel-(nz(UnitsInstock,0)+nz(UnitsOnOrder,0))) AS UnitsToOrder
FROM tbls_Products_n
```

Result:

ProductID	UnitsToOrder
3	5
4	5
5	30
6	3
7	1
8	2
9	5
10	3
71	21
72	25

(10 row(s) returned)

DISCUSSION QUESTIONS

1. What is a null value?
2. Is a null value the same as a zero (0) value?
3. Is a null value the same as a zero-length string? What is the difference?
4. How can we designate a zero-length string?
5. If we look at data in a table, can we distinguish which cells contain null values?
6. What is the best strategy to avoid problematic situations with null values?
7. How can we avoid the presence of null values when we design a new database?
8. How can we eliminate null values from an existing database?
9. How do null values affect calculations with aggregate functions?
10. Why is it a good idea to use the IsNull() function?

HANDS-ON EXERCISES

Case 1

For each of the questions in this case create a new query in SQL view and name it as per the instructions in each question.

1. The marketing people have initiated a marketing campaign which includes repeated written letters to customers. They have many of those letters coming back with an "undeliverable" notice. It looks like the state is missing from many of the addresses in the database. They are asking you to help them identify who are the customers with missing states. Create a new query that includes the fields CustomerID, LastName, FirstName, City, State, and zip from the tbls_customers_n table and satisfies the marketing people request. Save the query as Nulls_Case1_Q1.

Your result should look like:

CustomerID	LastName	FirstName	City	State	zip
7	Demaggio	Robert	New York		12110
13	Vanderback	David	New York		89890
20	Zartons	Lisa	Los Angeles		94851
47	Woods	Patricia	Philadelphia		56789

(There are more records in the result set than the ones shown in this image)
(11 row(s) returned)

2. The marketing people are now asking for a list of customers with the following fields from the tbls_customers_n table: CustomerID, LastName, FirstName, City, State, and zip. For the state field they want the value to appear as "zState NA" wheever there is no state value. Sort descending on the state field. Create a new query that satisfies the marketing people request and name it Nulls_Case1_Q2.

Your result should look like:

CustomerID	LastName	FirstName	City	CustomerState	Zip
7	Demaggio	Robert	New York	zState NA	12110
13	Vanderback	David	New York	zState NA	89890
20	Zartons	Lisa	Los Angeles	zState NA	94851
47	Woods	Patricia	Philadelphia	zState NA	56789

(There are more records in the result set than the ones shown in this image)
(201 row(s) returned)

3. The marketing people need some statistics on the number of bad records they have. Specifically, they need to know how many states have values in the table. Use the count() function on the state field of the tbls_customers_n table to provide them with an answer. Create a new query that satisfies this request and save it as Nulls_Case1_Q3.

Your result should look like:

CountState
190

(1 row(s) returned)

4. The marketing people need the number of the total records they have in the table tbls_customers_n. Create a new query that satisfies this request and save it as Nulls_Case1_Q4.

Your result should look like:

CountState
201

(1 row(s) returned)

5. The marketing people finally need a list of customers for which the state field is not null. Create a new query that includes the fields CustomerID, LastName, FirstName, City, State, and Zip from the tbls_customers_n table and satisfies the marketing people request. Save it as Nulls_Case1_Q5.

Your result should look like:

CustomerID	LastName	FirstName	City	State	zip
1	Demarco	John	New York	NY	12189
2	Demania	Mary	New York	NY	12189
3	Demers	George	New York	NY	12189
4	Demetriou	Phillip	New Yor k	NY	12189

(There are more records in the result set than the ones shown in this image)
(190 row(s) returned)

Case 2

For each of the questions in this case create a new query in SQL view and name it as per the instructions in each question.

1. The inventory people think there are missing values for the quantity field in the table tbls_JoinOrdersProducts_n. They would like to know which are the records with no quantity entries. Create a new query that includes the fields ProductID, OrderID, UnitPrice, and Quantity from this table and satisfies the request. Save the query as Nulls_Case2_Q1.

Your result should look like:

ProductID	OrderID	UnitPrice	Quantity
23	5		
26	5		
3	6		
23	25		

(There are more records in the result set than the ones shown in this image)
(117 row(s) returned)

2. Seeing the result set, the inventory people notice that there are null values in the UnitPrice field as well. They need a new report that will count the null values in the UnitPrice field in the table tbls_JoinOrdersProducts_n. Save the query as Nulls_Case2_Q2.

Your result should look like:

NumberOfNulls
2411

(1 row(s) returned)

3. The inventory people are asking for aggregate calculations to plan for inventory replenishment. Specifically, they need to report the total number of orders, the total order amount, and the average order amount by ProductID. Create a new query on the table tbls_JoinOrdersProducts_n that satisfies the inventory people request. Save the query as Nulls_Case2_Q3.

Your result should look like:

ProductID	NumberOfOrders	AvgOrder	TotaAmount
1	29	51.6666666666667	930
2	41	51.2068965517241	1485
3	36	57.2222222222222	1545
4	35	67.4074074074074	1820

(There are more records in the result set than the ones shown in this image)
(70 row(s) returned)

4. The inventory people are back and are very politely indicating to you that the numbers you provided appear to be off according to some written records they have. Your mind immediately goes to null values. Check to see if there are any null values in the fields UnitPrice or Quantity. Create a new query that includes the fields OrderID, ProductID, UnitPrice, Quantity, and Discount from the tbls_JoinOrdersProducts_n table and shows the records with null values for the UnitPrice and Quantity fields. Save the query as Nulls_Case2_Q4.

Your result should look like:

ProductID	OrderID	UnitPrice	Quantity	Discount
23	2		4	0.15
23	5			0.15
26	5			0.15
69	5		3	0.2

(There are more records in the result set than the ones shown in this image)
(204 row(s) returned)

5. Now that you know you have 204 records with null values for the UnitPrice or Quantity field or both you need to recreate the report requested by the inventory people in question 3. This time you need to make sure you leave out null values from your calculations. Create a new query that satisfies the inventory people request and save it as Nulls_Case2_Q5.

Your result should look like:

ProductID	NumberOfOrders	AvgOrder	TotaAmount
1	18	51.6666666666667	930
2	29	51.2068965517241	1485
3	27	57.2222222222222	1545
4	27	67.4074074074074	1820

(There are more records in the result set than the ones shown in this image)
(70 row(s) returned)

CHAPTER 23
ANALYTICS WITH TEXT FUNCTIONS

It is now time to enter the amazing world of string functions. Text functions produce output (new attributes) that it is impossible to generate otherwise. For example, we can extract part of a field value from the beginning, end, or the middle of the field, or based on the position of a special character. We can uppercase or lowercase a string of characters or we can add or remove spaces or characters at will. They should be in the toolbox of every data professional since lack of such knowledge will affect database and table design where extra fields might be used when not needed. For a list of all the string functions available, please see the table at the end of this chapter.

194. Capitalize field values - ucase() function

Capitalize the first and last names of customers

Discussion:

The ucase() function takes just one argument, and it will capitalize the contents of the field on which it is applied. Ucase() will capitalize all the characters in the field, leaving any existing capital characters unchanged.

ucase(field name)

Code:

```
SELECT ucase(lastname) AS CustLastName, ucase(firstname) AS CustFirstName, City, State, Zip
FROM customers
```

Result:

CustLastName	CustFirstName	City	State	Zip
DEMARCO	JOHN	New York	NY	12189
DEMANIA	MARY	New York	NY	12189
DEMERS	GEORGE	New York	NY	12189
DEMETRIOU	PHILLIP	New York	NY	12189

(There are more records in the result set than the ones shown in this image)
(201 row(s) returned)

195. Capitalize fields values - format() function

Capitalize the first and last names of customers

Discussion:

The format() function is the third function we can use to manipulate the case of characters in a field. The general syntax of the format() function for text manipulation appears below. We will use the format() function again in date and number fields.

Format(field, constant)

Constant Value	Output
<	Force all characters to lowercase.
>	Force all characters to uppercase.

Code:

```
SELECT format(lastname, '>') AS CustLastName, format(firstname, '>') AS CustFirstName, City,
State, Zip
FROM customers
```

Result:

CustLastName	CustFirstName	City	State	Zip
DEMARCO	JOHN	New York	NY	12189
DEMANIA	MARY	New York	NY	12189
DEMERS	GEORGE	New York	NY	12189
DEMETRIOU	PHILLIP	New York	NY	12189

(There are more records in the result set than the ones shown in this image)
(201 row(s) returned)

196. Capitalize only the first character of a field - strConv() function

Capitalize the first letters of the first and last names of our customers

Discussion:

The strConv() takes two arguments from which the second is a constant. Its general syntax appears below:

strConv (field, constant)

The constant takes three values and depending on which the strConv() function will produce different output. The table below shows the three possibilities for the constant:

strConv (field, constant)

Constant Value	Output Result
1	Converts field value to uppercase characters.
2	Converts field value to lowercase characters.
3	Converts the first letter of every word in the field to uppercase.

In this example, we will use the value 3 for the constant because we want to capitalize only the first character of each word in the last and first name fields.

Code:

```
SELECT strconv(lastname, 3) AS CustLastName, strConv(firstname, 3) AS CustFirstName, City,
State, Zip FROM Customers
```

Result:

CustLastName	CustFirstName	City	State	Zip
Demarco	John	New York	NY	12189
Demania	Mary	New York	NY	12189
Demers	George	New York	NY	12189
Demetriou	Phillip	New York	NY	12189

(There are more records in the result set than the ones shown in this image)
(201 row(s) returned)

197. Lowercase field values - Lcase() function

Convert the first and last names of our customers to lowercase

Discussion:

The lcase() function takes only one argument, the field name, and results in converting all characters of a field value to lowercase. Its general syntax is:

Lcase(field name)

Code:

```
SELECT Lcase(lastname) AS CustLastName, Lcase(firstname) AS CustFirstName, City, State, Zip
FROM Customers
```

Result:

CustLastName	CustFirstName	City	State	Zip
demarco	john	New York	NY	12189
demania	mary	New York	NY	12189
demers	george	New York	NY	12189
demetriou	phillip	New York	NY	12189

(There are more records in the result set than the ones shown in this image)
(201 row(s) returned)

198. Count the number of characters in a field - len() function

Count the number of characters in the SKU field

Discussion:

The len() function counts the number of characters in a field. For example, if we work with extraction, transformation, and loading (ETL) tools, this function will provide us with the number of characters in the source fields instead of making guesses and ending up with truncated values. The len() function takes one argument, and its general syntax appears below:

Len(field name)

In this example, we count the number of characters in the SKU field of the Products table. Notice in the output that the result of the function for each record is different. We can then sort ascending or descending to display the shortest or lengthiest fields first.

Code:

```
SELECT ProductID, ProductName, len(sku) AS CountSKUChars
FROM Products
```

Result:

ProductID	ProductName	CountSKUChars
1	Almonds Hickory Smoked	10
2	Almonds Roasted and Salted	11
3	Banana Chips	11
4	Berry Cherry	8

(There are more records in the result set than the ones shown in this image)
(70 row(s) returned)

199. Extract a specific number of characters from the beginning of a field - left() function

Retrieve the first four characters of the SKU code

Discussion:

The left() function will extract a substring of a specific length of characters from a field. For example, we can use the left function to retrieve the first four characters of the SKU field in the Products table. The left() function takes two arguments—the field name and the number of characters we want to retrieve.

left(fieldname, number of characters to retrieve)

Code:

```
SELECT ProductName, left(sku,4) AS 4SKU
FROM Products
```

Result:

ProductName	4SKU
Almonds Hickory Smoked	PDKL
Almonds Roasted and Salted	PDKL
Banana Chips	PDKL
Berry Cherry	PDK-

(There are more records in the result set than the ones shown in this image)
(70 row(s) returned)

200. Find the position of a hyphen in a field - instr() function

Find the number of characters occurring before the "-" character in the SKUs field

Discussion:

In the Products table, we have an SKU field. This field's values contain letters, a hyphen, and some numbers like PDKLS-3483. The letter part of the code before the hyphen signifies some larger category on which we can create groupings. The problem is that the number of letters in the SKU code is not always the same for every record. Consequently, we need to extract the string part of the SKU regardless of the number of characters it contains. We can use the instr() function to determine the position of the hyphen in the string (PDKLS-3483). Its general syntax appears below:

instr(starting character, field, character to find)

In this example, we use inStr(1,sku,"-") to look for the "-" character in the SKU field starting from the first character.

Code:

```
SELECT ProductID, Productname, Sku, InStr(1,sku,'-') AS PartSKU
FROM Products
```

Result:

ProductID	Productname	Sku	PartSKU
1	Almonds Hickory Smoked	PDKLS-2332	6
2	Almonds Roasted and Salted	PDKLSD-2344	7
3	Banana Chips	PDKLSD-2347	7
4	Berry Cherry	PDK-2589	4

(There are more records in the result set than the ones shown in this image)
(70 row(s) returned)

201. Find the position of a blank space in a field - instr() function

Find the number of characters occurring before a blank space in the SKU field

Discussion:

For this example, I have created an additional problem for us: Some of the hyphens separating the letter code of the SKU from the number code are missing. We can use the instr() function to find the position of those blank spaces. Notice the WHERE clause, which is there so that the result set includes only SKU codes with spaces between letter and number codes and not those with hyphens or any other characters. Pay close attention to the result set. You will see that for the first three records the position of the blank is indicated to be at the first character. This is correct since for the first three records there is a blank to the left of the "A" letter. This is one additional problem that we might have with data, which we can identify with the instr() function and solve with the ltrim() function.

Code:

```
SELECT ProductID, Productname, Sku, InStr(1,sku,' ') AS PartSKU
FROM Products
WHERE InStr(1,sku,' ') <> 0
```

Results:

ProductID	Productname	Sku	PartSKU
41	Banana Bisquits	ADSE 2345	1
42	Chocolate Bisquits	ADST 2345	1
43	Cocoa Biscuits	ADSD 2345	5
44	Honey Biscuits	ADSL 2345	5
45	Mushroom Sauce	ADST 2345	5
46	Artichokes in white sauce	ADST 2345	5
47	Chocolate Chip Cookies	ADST 2345	5

(There are more records in the result set than the ones shown in this image)
(7 row(s) returned)

202. Extract the part of a field before a hyphen - instr() and left() functions

Extract the letter part of the SKU field

Discussion:

In this example, we extract a substring from within the text field. To do this, we use the left() and instr() functions together. First, we use the instr() function on the SKU field to obtain the numeric value of the exact position of the "hyphen" in the SKU field. Then, we use the left() function, which takes two arguments. The first is the field, and the second is the number of characters to be returned. If we apply the left() function on the string "Hello there" as Left("Hi There", 5), it will return "Hi th".

left(sku, InStr(1,sku,'-')-1)

What is the -1 doing in the instr() function? The instr() function will return the numeric position of the hyphen including the hyphen. Thus, we apply the instr() function minus one character so that we obtain the characters till the hyphen but not the hyphen itself.

Code:

```
SELECT Productname, Sku, left(sku, InStr(1,sku,'-')-1) AS PartSKU
FROM Products
```

Result:

Productname	Sku	PartSKU
Almonds Hickory Smoked	PDKLS-2332	PDKLS
Almonds Roasted and Salted	PDKLSD-2344	PDKLSD
Banana Chips	PDKLSD-2347	PDKLSD
Berry Cherry	PDK-2589	PDK

(There are more records in the result set than the ones shown in this image)
(70 row(s) returned)

203. Extract the part of a field before a space - instr() and left() functions

Extract the letter part of the SKU field just before a blank space

Discussion:

This time we extract the letter code of the SKU before a space within a string. Pay attention to the result set. The first three records contain no PartSKU values since there is a blank space right in the beginning of the field value.

Code:

```
SELECT Productname, Sku, left(sku, InStr(1,sku,' ')-1) AS PartSKU
FROM Products
WHERE InStr(1,sku,' ') <> 0
```

Result:

Productname	Sku	PartSKU
Banana Bisquits	ADSE 2345	
Chocolate Bisquits	ADST 2345	
Cocoa Biscuits	ADSD 2345	ADSD
Honey Biscuits	ADSL 2345	ADSL
Mushroom Sauce	ADST 2345	ADST
Artichokes in white sauce	ADST 2345	ADST
Chocolate Chip Cookies	ADST 2345	ADST

(There are more records in the result set than the ones shown in this image)
(70 row(s) returned)

204. Remove blank spaces from the beginning of a field - the Ltrim() function

Remove blank spaces from the beginning of the Productname field

Discussion:

The ltrim() function takes only one argument and it will eliminate any blank spaces from the beginning of the values of a field. In this example, we are not certain if there are blank spaces at the start of the field for some product names. We can simply use the ltrim() function to make certain there are none before we create any analytics. If there are no blank spaces, it will leave those values unchanged. In addition, blank spaces affect how other functions such as instr() work. We can use the ltrim() function to make sure we count correctly from the beginning of the field.

Code:

```
SELECT Ltrim(productname) AS LeftTrimmedName, sku
FROM Products
```

Result:

LeftTrimmedName	sku
Almonds Hickory Smoked	PDKLS-2332

Almonds Roasted and Salted	PDKLSD-2344
Banana Chips	PDKLSD-2347
Berry Cherry	PDK-2589

(There are more records in the result set than the ones shown in this image)
(70 row(s) returned)

205. Detect zero-length strings in fields

Discussion:

Zero-length strings also appear as empty cells in Microsoft Access. To enter a zero-length string in a field in Access use the expression "" (two double quotes). In the example below, we look for zero-length strings in the QualityRating field.

Code:

```
SELECT ProductName, IngredientType, QualityRating
FROM tbls_DataPreprocessing
WHERE QualityRating = ""
```

Result:

ProductName	IngredientType	QualityRating
Apple Cinnamon Raisin Cookies	All-Natural	
Cappuccino Almonds	All-Natural	
Coffee biscuits	All-Natural	
Chocolate Almonds	GMO-Free	
Crispy Pears	Organic	

(5 row(s) returned)

206. Find and eliminate leading blank spaces

Find leading blank spaces discussion:

To eliminate blank spaces at the beginning of field values we use the ltrim() function. Four items to keep in mind: First, by blank spaces we mean spaces produced by hitting the spacebar on the keyboard one or multiple times. Null values and zero-length strings apply to the whole field value. Second, we are not certain if there are blank spaces at the beginning of field values. If there are, they will mess up our analytics and we need to eliminate them. Third, leading blank spaces will affect how other functions such as instr() will work. Fourth, notice how the ltrim() function has been applied to all the records in the table, not only the ones with leading blank spaces. If there are leading blank spaces, it will eliminate them. If there are not, it will leave the field values unchanged.

Code to identify blank spaces at the beginning of field values

```
SELECT CustomerFirstName, CustomerLastName, City
FROM tbls_DataPreprocessing
WHERE City LIKE ' *'
```

Result:

Notice how the ' *' expression identifies all blank spaces independently of their number, that is, if we have one, two, or multiple blank spaces.

CustomerFirstName	CustomerLastName	City
Peter	Anderson	New York
July	Trassati	Los Angeles
Pindar	Crooney	Houston
Thomas	McMaster	Phoenix

(4 row(s) returned)

Code to eliminate blank spaces at the beginning of field values on the fly

```
SELECT CustomerFirstName, CustomerLastName, ltrim(City) AS LeftTrimmedCity
FROM tbls_DataPreprocessing
```

Result:

Notice how the ltrim() function applies to the city field for all records in the table.

CustomerFirstName	CustomerLastName	LeftTrimmedCity
Joanne	Riegert	Albany
Lisa	Read	Washington
Lisa	Read	Washington
Lisa	Read	Washington

(There are more records in the result set than the ones shown in this image)
(2000 row(s) returned)

Code to permanently eliminate blank spaces at the beginning of field values

```
UPDATE tbls_DataPreprocessing SET city = ltrim(city)
```

Result:

"You are about to update 2000 rows"

Notice how the ltrim() function will update the city field for all records in the table. There will be no more blank spaces at the beginning of the city field after you apply this piece of code.

207. Remove spaces from the end of a field – the Rtrim() function

Remove blank spaces from the end of the product name field

Discussion:

The Rtrim() function takes one argument, and its main job is to eliminate blank spaces from the end of a field. If there are no blank spaces, it will leave those field values unchanged. Blank spaces affect how other functions work, for example the right() function.

Code:

```
SELECT Rtrim(productname) AS RightTrimmedName, sku
FROM Products
```

Result:

RightTrimmedName	sku
Almonds Hickory Smoked	PDKLS-2332
Almonds Roasted and Salted	PDKLSD-2344
Banana Chips	PDKLSD-2347
Berry Cherry	PDK-2589

(There are more records in the result set than the ones shown in this image)
(7 row(s) returned)

208. Find and eliminate trailing blank spaces

Discussion:

In data preparation, it is important to eliminate blank spaces from the end of field values. The value "MA" is different from the value "MA__" and it might create issues in data aggregations. The Rtrim() function will eliminate blank spaces at the end of field values. If there are no blank spaces, it will leave the field values unchanged.

Code to identify blank spaces at the end of field values

```
SELECT CustomerFirstName, CustomerLastName, MembershipType
FROM tbls_DataPreprocessing
WHERE MembershipType LIKE '* '
```

Result:

Notice how the '* ' expression identifies all blank spaces independently of their number, that is, if we have one, two, or multiple blank spaces.

CustomerFirstName	CustomerLastName	MembershipType
Joanne	Riegert	Platinum
Barbara	Irving	Silver
Catherine	Davis	Silver
Fred	Weinberger	Gold

```
(4 row(s) returned)
```

Code to eliminate blank spaces at the end of field values on the fly

```
SELECT CustomerFirstName, CustomerLastName, rtrim(MembershipType) AS
RightTrimmedMembershipType
FROM tbls_DataPreprocessing
```

Result:

Notice how the rtrim() function applies to the MemberShipType field for all records in the table.

CustomerFirstName	CustomerLastName	RightTrimmedMembershipType
Joanne	Riegert	Platinum
Lisa	Read	Silver
Lisa	Read	Silver
Lisa	Read	Silver

```
(There are more records in the result set than the ones shown in this image)
(2000 row(s) returned)
```

Code to permanently eliminate blank spaces at the end of field values

```
UPDATE tbls_DataPreprocessing SET MembershipType = rtrim(MembershipType)
```

Result:

```
"You are about to update 2000 rows"
```

Notice how the rtrim() function will update the MembershipType field for all records in the table. There will be no more blank spaces at the end of the MembershipType field after you apply this piece of code.

209. Trim blank spaces both at the end and beginning of a field – trim() function

Remove blank spaces from the beginning and end of the product name field

Discussion:

The role of the trim() function is to eliminate blank spaces from the beginning and end of a field simultaneously. The trim() function takes only one argument.

Code:

```
SELECT trim(Productname) AS TrimmedName, sku
FROM Products
```

Result:

TrimmedName	sku
Almonds Hickory Smoked	PDKLS-2332
Almonds Roasted and Salted	PDKLSD-2344
Banana Chips	PDKLSD-2347
Berry Cherry	PDK-2589

(There are more records in the result set than the ones shown in this image)
(70 row(s) returned)

210. Insert one space before or after field values

Insert one blank space in the beginning and end of the product name field

Discussion:

This time, we have the opposite task. Instead of using the ltrim(), rtrim(), or trim() functions to remove blank spaces from the beginning, end, or both ends of a field respectively, we want to add spaces. To achieve this task, we use the concatenation character '+' to add a space in the beginning and end of the Productname field.

Code:

```
SELECT (' ' +productname + ' ') AS SpacedName, sku
FROM Products
```

Result:

SpacedName	sku
Almonds Hickory Smoked	PDKLS-2332
Almonds Roasted and Salted	PDKLSD-2344
Banana Chips	PDKLSD-2347
Berry Cherry	PDK-2589

(There are more records in the result set than the ones shown in this image)
(70 row(s) returned)

211. Insert any number of spaces before or after a field - space() function

Insert ten blank spaces in the beginning and end of the ProductName field

Discussion:

We achieve this task using the space() function. In the example below, we add ten blank spaces before and after the ProductName field:

Code:

```
SELECT (space(10)+ ProductName + space(10))  AS SpacedName, sku
FROM Products
```

Result:

SpacedName	sku
Almonds Hickory Smoked	PDKLS-2332
Almonds Roasted and Salted	PDKLSD-2344
Banana Chips	PDKLSD-2347
Berry Cherry	PDK-2589

(There are more records in the result set than the ones shown in this image)
(70 row(s) returned)

212. Retrieve a number of characters from the end of a field - right() function

Retrieve the last four characters of the SKU code

Discussion:

In this example, we retrieve the last four characters from the SKU field. The right() function takes two arguments—the field name and the number of characters we would like to retrieve.

right(fieldname, number of characters to retrieve)

Code:

```
SELECT ProductName, right(sku,4) AS SKU4
FROM Products
```

Result:

ProductName	SKU4
Almonds Hickory Smoked	2332
Almonds Roasted and Salted	2344
Banana Chips	2347
Berry Cherry	2589

(There are more records in the result set than the ones shown in this image)
(70 row(s) returned)

213. Retrieve a specific number of characters from any part of a field - mid() function

Retrieve four characters of the SKU field starting at character 2

Discussion:

The mid() function is practically an improved left() function. It takes three arguments. In this example, we retrieve four characters from the SKU field starting at character two.

Mid(field name, character to start, number of characters to get)

Code:

```
SELECT ProductName, SKU, mid(SKU, 2, 4) As TrimmedSKU
FROM Products
```

Result:

ProductName	SKU	TrimmedSKU
Almonds Hickory Smoked	PDKLS-2332	DKLS
Almonds Roasted and Salted	PDKLSD-2344	DKLS
Banana Chips	PDKLSD-2347	DKLS
Berry Cherry	PDK-2589	DK-2

(There are more records in the result set than the ones shown in this image)
(70 row(s) returned)

214. Repeat the first character a field - string() function

Retrieve the first character of the product name field repeated five times

Discussion:

The string() function will return the first character of a field value any number of times we want. It takes two arguments.

String(number of times character repeats, field name)

The string function might look simplistic and you might wonder about its purpose. We can use it in concatenated fields to create categories like AAA, BBB, CCC, etc. or we can use it in combination with other functions to repeat characters in a field. In this example, we repeat the first letter of the ProductName field five times.

Code:

```
SELECT ProductName, string(5, productname) As NewProductName, Sku
FROM Products
```

Result:

ProductName	NewProductName	Sku
Almonds Hickory Smoked	AAAAA	PDKLS-2332
Almonds Roasted and Salted	AAAAA	PDKLSD-2344
Banana Chips	BBBBB	PDKLSD-2347
Berry Cherry	BBBBB	PDK-2589

(There are more records in the result set than the ones shown in this image)
(70 row(s) returned)

215. Change field values dynamically - replace() function

Replace part of supplier's SKU codes dynamically

Discussion:

The replace() function can change field values in the query results without affecting the data in the table! For example, products with the SKU letter codes "PDK" need to be updated to "PDS". However, products with SKU codes PDKSs and PDKRs need to remain as they were. In addition, the number part of the SKU code needs to remain untouched. So, "PDK-2389" needs to become "PDS-2389". We need to isolate the exact letter code "PDK", replace it with PDS, and leave the trailing numbers untouched. This is a job for the replace function. Its basic syntax appears below:

replace(field name, string to search for, string to replace with, at what character to start)

For example, the expression replace(sku, 'pdk-', pds-') will replace "pdk-" with "pds-". Notice that the fourth argument (at what character to start) is optional, and if we leave it out, the replace function will start the evaluation at the first character of the field. We could start with any character, however.

Code:

```
SELECT ProductName, replace(sku, 'pdk-', 'pds-') As skuUpdated
FROM Products
WHERE left(sku, 4) = 'PDK-'
```

Result:

ProductName	skuUpdated
Berry Cherry	pds-2589
California Original Pistachios	pds-2347

(2 row(s) returned)

216. compare the length of two fields - strComp() function

Compare the length of the first and lastname fields for all customers

Discussion:

In this example, we compare the length of the FirstName and LastName fields. One way to do it is to use the len() function on both fields and compare the results. However, we can achieve the same task by using the strComp() function. The general syntax of the strComp() function appears below:

strComp(field1, field2)

The strComp() function will return (-1, 0, 1, or Null) according to the table below:

Comparison Result	Output
field1 is less than field2	-1
field1 is equal to field2	0
field1 is greater than field2	1
field1 or field2 is Null	Null

Code:

```
SELECT LastName, FirstName, strcomp(firstname, lastname) As CompResult
FROM Customers
```

Result:

LastName	FirstName	CompResult
Demarco	John	1
Demania	Mary	1
Demers	George	1
Demetriou	Phillip	1

(There are more records in the result set than the ones shown in this image)
(201 row(s) returned)

217. Reverse the order of characters in a field - strReverse() function

Reverse the order of characters in the SKU field in the products table

Discussion:

The strReverse() function takes one argument and its syntax is shown below. It will return a string in which the character order is reversed.

strReverse(field)

In this example, we apply it on the SKU field in the Products table, and we see from the output that the number part of the SKU now appears first. Of course, this happens dynamically, and the actual data in the table will not be affected.

Code:

```
SELECT ProductID, strReverse(sku) As ReverseSKU
FROM Products
```

Result:

ProductID	ReverseSKU
1	2332-SLKDP

2	4432-DSLKDP
3	7432-DSLKDP
4	9852-KDP

(There are more records in the result set than the ones shown in this image)
(70 row(s) returned)

DISCUSSION QUESTIONS

1. What function can we use to repeat the first character of a field multiple times?
2. What function do we use to reverse the sequence of field values?
3. When we use text functions do we create additional measures or descriptors?
4. How additional attributes created with text functions can help with the analytics effort of the company?
5. What function do we use to retrieve only the last four characters from a field?
6. How does the usage of text functions affect the design of the transactional database?
7. What function can we use to find the position of a character or blank space in a field?
8. What functions do we use to remove spaces from the beginning or the end of fields?
9. What function can we use to add spaces before or after a field value?
10. When we update field values using the replace() function are those updates permanent in the back-end table?

HANDS-ON EXERCISES

Case 1

For each of the questions in this case create a new query in SQL view and name it as per the instructions in each question.

1. The salespeople need to create mailing labels for customer letters. They want the first name of the customer capitalized for emphasis. Create a new query that contains the FirstName, LastName, City, State, and Zip fields from the customer table that satisfies the salespeople request. Save the query as TextFunctions_Case1_Q1.

Your result should look like:

CustFirstName	LastName	City	State	Zip
JOHN	Demarco	New York	NY	12189
MARY	Demania	New York	NY	12189
GEORGE	Demers	New York	NY	12189
PHILLIP	Demetriou	New York	NY	12189

(There are more records in the result set than the ones shown in this image)
(201 row(s) returned)

2. The marketing people need to send out letters to customers but they fear that some of the addresses are too long and they might exceed the space limit they have on a special pamphlet they are preparing. They are asking you to provide a list that shows the customers whose address exceeds twenty (20) characters. Create a new query that contains the FirstName, LastName, city, state, and zip fields from the Customers table and satisfies the salespeople request. Save the query as TextFunctions_Case1_Q2.

Your result should look like:

FirstName	LastName	city	state	zip
Kenneth	Crondos	Houston	TX	53289
Stephanie	Elser	San Jose	CA	36945
Cynthia	Papadopoulos	Phoenix	AZ	44895

(3 row(s) returned)

3. The marketing people are back asking for a list of customers for whom it is certain there are no blank spaces in front of the FirstName or LastName fields because any blank spaces interfere with the alignment of the

various paragraphs in the personalized brochures they are preparing. Create a new query that contains the FirstName, LastName, City, State, and Zip fields from the Customers table and satisfies the marketing people request. Save the query as TextFunctions_Case1_Q3.

Your result should look like:

TrimmedFirstName	TrimmedLastName	City	State	Zip
John	Demarco	New York	NY	12189
Mary	Demania	New York	NY	12189
George	Demers	New York	NY	12189
Phillip	Demetriou	New York	NY	12189

(There are more records in the result set than the ones shown in this image)
(201 row(s) returned)

4. The marketing people are very happy with the lists you are providing them with. They also need five blank spaces for all customers at the end of the Zip field. Create a new query that contains the FirstName, LastName, City, State, and Zip fields from the customers table and satisfies the marketing people request. Save the query as TextFunctions_Case1_Q4.

Your result should look like:

FirstName	LastName	City	State	SpacedZip
John	Demarco	New York	NY	12189
Mary	Demania	New York	NY	12189
George	Demers	New York	NY	12189
Phillip	Demetriou	New York	NY	12189

(There are more records in the result set than the ones shown in this image)
(201 row(s) returned)

5. The marketing people need a report that contains the FirstName, LastName, City, State, and Zip fields from the Customers table. However, for the customers in the state of NY they want the whole name of the state to appear as "New York" instead of the abbreviated "NY". Create a new query that satisfies the marketing people request without changing the state values in the back-end Customers table. Save the query as TextFunctions_Case1_Q5.

Your result should look like:

FirstName	LastName	City	FullStateName	Zip
John	Demarco	New York	New York	12189
Mary	Demania	New York	New York	12189
George	Demers	New York	New York	12189
Phillip	Demetriou	New York	New York	12189

(There are more records in the result set than the ones shown in this image)
(201 row(s) returned)

Case 2

For each of the questions in this case create a new query in SQL view and name it as per the instructions in each question.

1. The salespeople need a new product catalog that contains the ProductName and ProductUnitPrice fields from the table tble_products_strings. For the Product name field, they only need the portion of the name up until the dash to appear and not any weight information about the product. Create a new query that satisfies the salespeople request and save it as TextFunctions_Case2_Q1.

Your result should look like:

NewProductName	ProductUnitPrice
Almonds, Hickory Smoked	$35.00
Almonds, Roasted and Salted	$22.00
Banana Chips	$27.00
Berry Cherry	$30.00

(There are more records in the result set than the ones shown in this image)
(12 row(s) returned)

2. The salespeople need a product catalog to contain the ProductName and ProductUnitPrice fields from the tble_Products_Strings table but this time they want the "oz." notation to be replaced by "grams." Create a new query that satisfies the salespeople request and save it as TextFunctions_Case2_Q2.

Your result should look like:

NewProductName	ProductUnitPrice
Almonds, Hickory Smoked - 12 grams. Bag	$35.00
Almonds, Roasted and Salted - 18 grams. Bag	$22.00
Banana Chips - 20 grams. Bag	$27.00
Berry Cherry - in 8 grams. Bag	$30.00

(There are more records in the result set than the ones shown in this image)
(12 row(s) returned)

3. In the tble_Products_Strings table, the SupplierID field has the format XXX-XXX or XXXX-XXX with the first three or four numbers indicating the region of the supplier while the last three digits representing the product family the supplier is manufacturing. The production people need a list that includes the ProductName and SupplierID fields. For the SupplierID field they only need the region to appear. They do not want any dashes to appear at the end of the SupplierID field. Create a new query that satisfies the production people request and save it as TextFunctions_Case2_Q3.

Your result should look like:

NewSupplierID	ProductName
1111	Almonds, Hickory Smoked - 12 oz. Bag
1111	Almonds, Roasted and Salted - 18 oz. Bag
1111	Banana Chips - 20 oz. Bag
112	Berry Cherry - in 8 oz. Bag

(There are more records in the result set than the ones shown in this image)
(12 row(s) returned)

4. The inventory people need a report that includes the SupplierID and the total value of inventory in stock grouped by the region portion of the SupplierID. Create a new query that satisfies the inventory people request and save it as TextFunctions_Case2_Q4.

Your result should look like:

SupplierRegion	TotalValueInventoryInStock
1111	2779
1119	2674
112	3963
115	1609

(4 row(s) returned)

5. The inventory people need a report that will total the value of inventory on hand by product family. The product family is identified by the last three digits in the SupplierID field. Create a new query with the fields ProductFamily and TotalValueInStock from the tble_Products_Strings table that satisfies the inventory people request and save it as TextFunctions_Case2_Q5.

Your result should look like:

ProductFamily	TotalValueInStock
121	3404
122	1540
123	1554
141	1419
143	3108

(5 row(s) returned)

CHAPTER 24
ANALYTICS WITH DATE FUNCTIONS

Date functions enable us to perform multiple analytics tasks. First, we can extract the month from a date field and then summarize data by month. Practically, we supply our analytics platform with additional descriptors (attributes). These descriptors constitute for the company a source of competitive advantage. For example, if we use the datepart() function to summarize sales amounts by week of the year, we provide management the insight to direct resources and focus on the best weeks of the year. The result will not only be increased sales but also reduced operational expenses since the management will increase and decrease resources for sales, marketing, shipping, and other operations only for the period and the amounts needed.

Second, we can extract the quarters from a date range and create a crosstab query displaying summaries by quarter. Third, we can create projected order fulfillment cycle times by adding, let us say, two business days to the order date field and comparing our projections with the actual shipped dates for quality control. Fourth, we can use date functions as default field values for fields to record the exact date and time a record was inserted. Fifth, with date functions, we can convert date values such as 9/20/2025 to actual named values such as September 20, 2025. Sixth, we can combine date functions with aggregate functions for exceptional data calculations and summaries.

Our knowledge level on date functions will have a direct effect on the quality of our database design and analytics model since we can avoid date fields that we can create from existing date fields. As we go through the examples below, we will realize that date functions do not represent just additional knowledge; they constitute required knowledge for the analytics professional.

218. Retrieve orders between two dates

Discussion:
There are two ways to achieve this task. We can use the equality and inequality predicates or the BETWEEN operator. Remember the BETWEEEN operator is inclusive which means that boundary dates will be included in the result set.

Code (using BETWEEN AND):
```
SELECT OrderID, OrderDate, InvoiceAmount, PackagingType, PackageWeight
FROM Orders
WHERE OrderDate BETWEEN #1/1/2022# AND #6/30/2022#
ORDER BY OrderDate ASC
```

Code (using inequality and equality predicates):
```
SELECT OrderID, OrderDate, InvoiceAmount, PackagingType, PackageWeight
FROM Orders
WHERE OrderDate>=#1/1/2022# AND OrderDate<=#6/30/2022#
ORDER BY OrderDate
```

Result:

OrderID	OrderDate	InvoiceAmount	PackagingType	PackageWeight
351	1/14/2022	139	Cardboard	39.8
76	1/15/2022	281	Metal	6.8
854	1/15/2022	168	Paperboard	10.4
380	1/15/2022	187	Shrink film	35.2

(There are more records in the result set than the ones shown in this image)
(162 row(s) returned)

219. Retrieve orders outside of two dates

Discussion:

To retrieve orders outside of two dates we use equality and inequality predicates as in the code below. Notice how we use the OR operator when we want to define outside date ranges.

Code:

```
SELECT OrderID, OrderDate, InvoiceAmount, PackagingType, PackageWeight
FROM Orders
WHERE OrderDate<=#1/1/2022# OR OrderDate >=#6/30/2022#
ORDER BY OrderDate
```

Result:

OrderID	OrderDate	InvoiceAmount	PackagingType	PackageWeight
388	1/1/2020	92	Foil	15.1
754	1/3/2020	237	Shrink film	6.8
879	1/5/2020	61	Paperboard	30.3
32	1/6/2020	311	Foil	12.9

(There are more records in the result set than the ones shown in this image)
(838 row(s) returned)

220. Set default field values - the now() and date() functions

Discussion:

The now() and date() functions are often used for default values. This means that every time a record is inserted in the table, a time stamp will be entered by default in this field. The now() function will output the system date and time while the date() function only the date. Their syntax appears below:

now(field or value)   date(field or value)

Code with now():

```
SELECT now() as CurrentDateAndTime
```

Result:

CurrentDateAndTime
02/27/2025 11:15:51 AM

(1 row(s) returned)

Code:

```
SELECT date() as CurrentDate
```

Result:

CurrentDate
02/27/2025

(1 row(s) returned)

221. Retrieve the latest order by customer - the max() function

Discussion:

The salespeople are asking for a report that shows the latest order for each customer. Specifically, they want to see a list that contains the last name, first name, and latest order date for each customer. There is a plethora of solutions here, but we will go for the simplest one.

Solution 1:

We can identify the latest order using the max() function and the group by clause in the Orders table, but the problem is we will not see the customer first and last names:

Code 1:

```
SELECT CustomerID, max(OrderDate) As LatestOrder
FROM Orders
GROUP BY CustomerID
```

Result 1:

CustomerID	LatestOrder
1	11/7/2022
2	6/21/2022
3	10/25/2022
4	9/26/2022

(There are more records in the result set than the ones shown in this image)
(190 row(s) returned)

Solution 2 (practically wrong in most cases):

If we need the name of the customer to show we can use the max() function, an INNER JOIN and the GROUP BY clause. This solution is conceptually correct but practically wrong because in most cases we have multiple customers with the same last name. Even if you concatenate the customers' first and last names and use the group by clause on the concatenated name, you might still get wrong results because some customers will have the same first and last names. Notice that we already have 171 records returned from the 190 in the previous example. Of course, you can always group on multiple fields like LastName, FirstName, and CustomerID in which case the result will be correct.

Code 2 (wrong in most cases):

```
SELECT LastName, Max(Orders.OrderDate) AS MaxOfOrderDate
FROM Customers INNER JOIN Orders ON Customers.CustomerID = Orders.CustomerID
GROUP BY LastName
```

Result 2:

LastName	MaxOfOrderDate
Ackerman	10/28/2022
Ames	10/30/2021
Andersen	5/21/2022
Anderson	12/13/2022

(There are more records in the result set than the ones shown in this image)
(171 row(s) returned)

Solution 3 (Simple and correct solution)

In this example we use the group by clause on the first name, last name, and CustomerID fields combined. There is no way to mess up results since the CustomerID field is the primary key (PK) in the customer table and thus unique for each customer.

Code 3

```
SELECT Customers.CustomerID, Customers.LastName, Customers.FirstName,
Max(Orders.OrderDate) AS LatestOrderDate
FROM Customers INNER JOIN Orders ON Customers.CustomerID = Orders.CustomerID
GROUP BY Customers.CustomerID, Customers.LastName, Customers.FirstName
```

Result 3

CustomerID	LastName	FirstName	LatestOrderDate
1	Demarco	John	11/7/2022
2	Demania	Mary	6/21/2022
3	Demers	George	10/25/2022
4	Demetriou	Phillip	9/26/2022

(There are more records in the result set than the ones shown in this image)
(190 row(s) returned)

222. Calculate the number of days, months, quarters, or years between two dates.

Discussion:

We can calculate the number of time intervals (days, months, quarters, years) between two dates using the datediff(interval, date1, date2) function. As you can see from the code below, date2 is greater than date1 but Access will not complain even if it is the other way around; that is to calculate the number of days to a future date. Make sure you enclose the interval argument in quotes.

Code for days:

```
SELECT DateDiff('d', #5/15/2024#, #4/3/2026#)  As NumberOfDays
```

Result:

NumberOfDays
688

(1 row(s) returned)

Code for months:

```
SELECT DateDiff('m', #5/15/2024#, #4/3/2026#)  As NumberOfMonths
```

Result:

NumberOfMonths
23

(1 row(s) returned)

Code for quarters:

```
SELECT DateDiff('q', #5/15/2024#, #6/3/2026#)  As NumberOfQuarters
```

Result:

NumberOfQuarters
8

(1 row(s) returned)

Code for years:

```
SELECT DateDiff('yyyy', #5/15/2024#, #6/3/2026#)  As NumberOfYears
```

Result:

NumberOfYears
2

(1 row(s) returned)

223. Calculate order totals by year - the year() and datepart() functions

Discussion:

On many occasions, we want to extract the year out of a date field to create aggregate summaries of our data. One way to achieve this task is to use the year() function, which takes only one argument. Its general syntax is:

year(date)

In this example, we want to calculate order totals by year. We use the year() function to extract the year out of the OrderDate field in combination with the sum() aggregate function to calculate order totals.

Code:

```
SELECT year(OrderDate) AS Year, sum(unitprice*quantity) AS OrderTotal
FROM Qry_Invoices
GROUP BY year(OrderDate)
```

Discussion (datepart function):

We could also extract the year from a date field using the datepart() function. The datepart() function has two arguments. Its syntax appears below:

datepart(datepart, datefield)

The datepart argument indicates the date part we want to extract from the date field. For example, we would use 'yyyy' to extract the year or 'q' to extract the quarter. Check the table at the end of this chapter for a list of all possible values for the datepart argument of the datepart() function.

Code:

```
SELECT datepart('yyyy', OrderDate) AS Year, SUM(unitprice*quantity) AS OrderTotal
FROM Qry_Invoices
GROUP BY datepart('yyyy', OrderDate)
```

Result:

Year	OrderTotal
2020	51164
2021	45002
2022	44230

(3 row(s) returned)

224. Calculate order totals by quarter - the datepart() and format() functions

Discussion (with datepart):

The business goal is to create a quarterly sales report for the year 2022. To achieve this task, we need to use two date functions. First, we will use the year() function to extract the year from the OrderDate field and use this expression in the WHERE clause to limit results for 2022. Then, we use the datepart() function to group order totals by quarter. We could also use the format function to extract quarters, which is demonstrated in the second part of this example and the result is the same.

Code:

```
SELECT datepart('q', OrderDate)  AS Quarter, sum(unitprice*quantity) AS OrderTotal
FROM Qry_Invoices
WHERE year(OrderDate) = 2022
GROUP BY datepart('q', OrderDate)
```

Code:

```
SELECT format(OrderDate, 'q') AS Quarter, sum(unitprice*quantity) AS OrderTotal
FROM Qry_Invoices
WHERE year(OrderDate) = 2022
GROUP BY format(OrderDate, 'q')
```

Result:

Quarter	OrderTotal
1	9231
2	13879
3	8481
4	12639

(3 row(s) returned)

225. List orders within a specific year and month- the datepart() function

Discussion (month):

In this example we create a list of orders for a specific month and year. We use the datepart(datepart, datefield) function to extract the month from the OrderDate field and the year(datefield) function to extract the year. Notice the usage of "m" for the interval argument in the datepart() function. Check the table at the end of this chapter for a list of all possible values for the datepart argument of the datepart() function.

Code:

```
SELECT OrderID, OrderDate, InvoiceAmount, PackagingType, PackageWeight
FROM Orders
WHERE datepart('m', [OrderDate]) =6 AND year(Orderdate) = 2022
ORDER BY OrderDate
```

Result:

OrderID	OrderDate	InvoiceAmount	PackagingType	PackageWeight
170	6/1/2022	107	Box	9.6
959	6/1/2022	157	Box	24.4
30	6/2/2022	275	Shrink film	26
57	6/3/2022	172	Cardboard	20.4

```
(There are more records in the result set than the ones shown in this image)
(32 row(s) returned)
```

We can obtain the same result by leaving out the functions and use absolute date intervals.

Code:

```
SELECT OrderID, OrderDate, InvoiceAmount, PackagingType, PackageWeight
FROM Orders
WHERE OrderDate BETWEEN #2022/6/1# AND #2022/6/30#
ORDER BY OrderDate
```

226. Count orders by business day of the week – the datepart() function

Discussion:

In this example, we use the datepart(DatePart, Date) function to count orders by the business days of the week. By default, the week in Access starts on Sunday and consequently Monday will be the second (2) day, Tuesday the third (3), and Friday the sixth (6). The weekday 'w' argument will output the days of the week and then in the IN operator we filter for days 2 through 6, that is Monday through Friday. In the WHERE clause we also filter for a specific year and quarter.

Code:

```
SELECT datepart('w', orderdate) As BusinessDay, Count(OrderID) AS NumberOfOrders
FROM Orders
WHERE year(orderdate) = 2022 AND datepart('q', orderdate) = 2 AND datepart('w', orderdate) IN
(2,3,4,5,6)
GROUP BY datepart('w', orderdate)
```

Result:

BusinessDay	NumberOfOrders
2	15
3	13
4	13
5	12
6	16

```
(5 row(s) returned)
```

227. Count orders by day of the month - the datepart() function

Discussion:

We will use the datepart(datepart, datefield) function to respond. Check the table at the end of this chapter for a list of all possible values for the datepart argument of the datepart() function.

Code:

```
SELECT datepart('d',OrderDate) AS Day, Count(OrderID) AS NumberOfOrders
FROM Orders
WHERE year(OrderDate)=2022 AND datepart('m',OrderDate) = 6
GROUP BY datepart('d',OrderDate)
ORDER BY DatePart('d',OrderDate)
```

Result:

We only have twenty-one records because we did not have orders every single day of this month.

Day	NumberOfOrders
1	2
2	1
3	3
4	2

(There are more records in the result set than the ones shown in this image)
(21 row(s) returned)

228. Count orders by week - the datepart() function

Discussion:

In this example we calculate the number of orders by each of the 52 weeks of the calendar year. Notice from the code that we only have two output fields (Week and NumberofOrders) while we use the year([OrderDate]) field in the WHERE clause to limit the results within one year. This is a quick way to identify order numbers and look for seasonality effects in our sales patterns.

Code:

```
SELECT datepart('ww', OrderDate) AS Week, Count(OrderID) AS NumberOfOrders
FROM Orders
WHERE Year(OrderDate) =2022
GROUP BY datepart('ww', OrderDate)
```

Result:

Week	NumberOfOrders
3	4
4	6
5	11
6	4

(There are more records in the result set than the ones shown in this image)
(51 row(s) returned)

229. Count orders for Mondays - the datepart() function

Discussion:

We use the datepart(datepart, datefield) function twice to extract the month and the weekday from the OrderDate field. Then, we use the year() and datepart() functions in the WHERE clause to isolate the year, the quarter to the first quarter of the year, and the weekday to Monday since by default in Access the week starts on Sunday which is day 1. Then, we group the results by month and day to arrive at the desired outcome. This way we can count the orders for any day of the week and any period we would like. Check the table at the end of this chapter for a list of all possible values for the datepart argument of the datepart() function.

Code:

```
SELECT datepart('m', OrderDate) As Month, datepart('w', OrderDate) AS Day,  Count(OrderID) AS
NumberOfOrders
FROM Orders
WHERE year(OrderDate) = 2022  AND  datepart('q', OrderDate) = 1  AND datepart('w', OrderDate) =
2
GROUP BY datepart('m', OrderDate), datepart('w', OrderDate)
ORDER BY datepart('m', OrderDate)
```

Result:

Month	Day	NumberOfOrders
1	2	3
2	2	4
3	2	1

(3 row(s) returned)

230. Calculate order totals for the same week in different years - the year() and datepart() functions

Discussion:

The management is asking for a report of order totals for the week before Christmas for all the years for which we have data in the database. Practically, we are talking about week 50 of the year. For this request we first group order totals by year and then by week since we need to show the difference in sales for weeks 50 in every year. We use the year(datefield) function to extract the year out of the OrderDate field. We use the datepart(datepart, datefield) function to extract the week. Finally, we use the datepart() function in the WHERE clause to isolate results only for weeks that equal 50. This is some interesting time series analysis. Check the table at the end of this chapter for a list of all possible values for the datepart argument of the datepart() function.

Code:

```
SELECT year(OrderDate) AS CalendarYear, datepart('ww',OrderDate) AS CalendarWeek,
Sum(unitprice*quantity) AS OrderTotal
FROM Qry_Invoices
WHERE datepart('ww',OrderDate)=50
GROUP BY year(OrderDate), datepart('ww',OrderDate)
```

Result:

CalendarYear	CalendarWeek	OrderTotal
2020	50	932
2021	50	1025
2022	50	1056

(3 row(s) returned)

231. Calculate order totals by month name - the month(), monthname(), and datepart() functions

The management wants to have a look at the order and discount totals to check the discount percentages forwarded by the sales reps. There are three different ways to achieve this result depending on the date function we use. In all examples we use the year() function in the WHERE clause to limit results to 2022 and then a function to extract the month from the OrderDate field and group by month within 2022. Finally, notice that we use two calculated fields (OrderTotal and TotalDiscount) to calculate the order and discount totals for each month.

The month() function

The month() function has only one argument and displays months as numbers.

month(datefield)

Code:

```
SELECT month(OrderDate) AS [Month], sum(unitprice*quantity) AS OrderTotal,
Sum(([unitprice]*[quantity])*[Discount]) AS TotalDiscount
FROM Qry_Invoices
WHERE year(orderdate) = 2022
GROUP BY month(OrderDate)
```

Result:

Month	OrderTotal	TotalDiscount
1	2792	442.4
2	2944	453.5
3	3495	510.95
4	3872	566.85

(There are more records in the result set than the ones shown in this image)
(12 row(s) returned)

The monthname() function

The management is not very happy with our first report because the month numbers confused them, and they could not quickly discern the corresponding month name. They now ask us to provide them with another report showing actual month names. We achieve this using the datename() function.Notice how we use the month(orderdate) function in the ORDER BY clause to have the months appear in the correct order. For a full list of all the arguments for the datename function please refer to the end of this chapter.

Code:

```
SELECT monthname(month(OrderDate)) AS [Month], sum(unitprice*quantity) AS OrderTotal,
sum(([unitprice]*[quantity])*[Discount]) AS TotalDiscount
FROM Qry_Invoices
WHERE year(orderdate) = 2022
GROUP BY monthname(Month(OrderDate)), month(OrderDate)
ORDER BY month(OrderDate)
```

Result:

Month	OrderTotal	TotalDiscount
January	2792	442.4
February	2944	453.5
March	3495	510.95
April	3872	566.85

(There are more records in the result set than the ones shown in this image)
(12 row(s) returned)

The datepart() function

We can also use the datepart() function to achieve the same result except that we will get numerals instead of month names. In other words, the result will be identical with that of the month() function.The only real difference is that the month function is much simpler, and we do not need to remember the "m" argument of the datepart() function.

Code:

```
SELECT datepart('m', OrderDate) AS [Month], sum(unitprice*quantity) AS OrderTotal,
Sum(([unitprice]*[quantity])*[Discount]) AS TotalDiscount
FROM Qry_Invoices
WHERE year(orderdate) = 2022
GROUP BY datepart('m', OrderDate), month([OrderDate])
ORDER BY datepart('m', OrderDate)
```

Result:

Month	OrderTotal	TotalDiscount
1	2792	442.4
2	2944	453.5
3	3495	510.95
4	3872	566.85

(There are more records in the result set than the ones shown in this image)
(12 row(s) returned)

The format() function

Finally, we can use the format() function with the 'mm' argument to put a leading zero in front of the month for sorting purposes.

Code:

```
SELECT format(OrderDate, 'mm')  AS [Month], sum(unitprice*quantity) AS OrderTotal,
sum(([unitprice]*[quantity])*[Discount]) AS TotalDiscount
FROM Qry_Invoices
WHERE year(orderdate) = 2022
GROUP BY format(OrderDate, 'mm')
ORDER BY format(OrderDate, 'mm')
```

Result:

Month	OrderTotal	TotalDiscount
01	2792	442.4
02	2944	453.5
03	3495	510.95
04	3872	566.85

(There are more records in the result set than the ones shown in this image)
(12 row(s) returned)

232. Aggregate data by day of the week - the datepart() function

Discussion:

The goal here is to count the number of orders by day of the week , that is, how many orders did we have on Mondays, how many on Tuesdays, how many on Wednesdays etc. Notice how we use the day of the week argument "dw" in the DatePart(datepart, datefield) function to isolate the days of the week and then group by them. Remember that by default the week starts on Sunday = 1 in Access.

Code:

```
SELECT datepart('w',OrderDate) AS Day, Count(OrderID) AS NumberOfOrders
FROM Orders
WHERE year(OrderDate)=2022
GROUP BY DatePart('w',[OrderDate])
```

Result:

Day	NumberOfOrders
1	46
2	45
3	46
4	45

(There are more records in the result set than the ones shown in this image)
(7 row(s) returned)

233. Aggregate data by day of the week displaying the name of the day - the weekdayname() function

We can obtain the actual names of the weekdays using the weekdayname() function. Its syntax appears below:

Weekdayname (date, [abbreviation], [first day of the week])

Date: it can be any date field or date value.
Abbreviation: true or false. True means the name of the day will be abbreviated such as "Wed". False means the whole day name will be returned.
First day of the week: 1 if Sunday is the first day of the week, 2 if Monday is the first day. It can take additional values if we want to designate another day as the first day of the week.

Code:

```
SELECT weekdayname(datepart('w',OrderDate), false, 1) AS Day, Count(OrderID) AS
NumberOfOrders
FROM Orders
WHERE (((Year([OrderDate]))=2022))
GROUP BY weekdayname(datepart('w',OrderDate), false, 1)
```

Day	NumberOfOrders
Friday	46
Monday	45
Saturday	46
Sunday	46
Thursday	39
Tuesday	46
Wednesday	45

(7 row(s) returned)

234. Aggregate data by day of the year - the datepart() function

Discussion:

In this example, we calculate the number of orders by the day of the year. We have 365 days per year and by using the "y" datepart argument we can isolate the number of orders by the day of the year. Very useful data for time series analysis throughout the year. Notice from the result set that from 365 days of the year we had orders only on 222 days.

Code:

```
SELECT datepart ('y', OrderDate) AS Day, Count(OrderID) AS NumberOfOrders
FROM Orders
WHERE year(OrderDate)=2022
GROUP BY datepart('y',OrderDate)
ORDER BY datepart('y',OrderDate)
```

Result:

Day	NumberOfOrders
14	1
15	3
16	1
17	1

(There are more records in the result set than the ones shown in this image)
(213 row(s) returned)

235. Create a crosstab report of sales by week - the datepart() and format() functions

Discussion (with datepart):

The management asks for a report listing total sales by week within a six-month period and within a specific year. To create this crosstab query, we need to use three date functions in combination. First, we use the month() function to extract the month number from the OrderDate field and use it as a criterion in the WHERE clause. Notice how the IN operator is used within the WHERE clause to get the first six months of the year. Since, however, we have multiple years of sales in the database, we need to include a criterion in the WHERE clause to isolate the year we want. We use the year function on the OrderDate field to limit results to 2022. Finally, in the PIVOT part of the crosstab query, we use the datepart() function with the 'ww' argument to produce a column for each week. As you can see from the result set, we can now examine detailed total product sales by week for a period of 27 weeks within the six-month period that we defined in our WHERE clause.

Code:

```
TRANSFORM Sum([unitprice]*[quantity]) AS OrderTotal
SELECT ProductName
FROM Qry_Invoices
WHERE month(OrderDate) IN (1,2,3,4,5,6) AND year(OrderDate) = 2022
GROUP BY ProductName
PIVOT datePart('ww',OrderDate)
```

Result:

ProductName	3	4	5	6	7	8	9	10	11	12	13	14	15	16	17	18	19	20	21	22	23	24	25	26	27
All-Purpose Marinade						56		42									84					28			
Almonds Hickory Smoked		75								15			75			60	60	90							30
Almonds Roasted and Salted															75			90			60	90			75
Apple Cinnamon Raisin Cookies		60										48													
Artichokes in white sauce					60														45				45		30
Banana Biscuits	8	24	24		24				16				8		96										
Banana Chips		60												90			30						75	30	
Berry Cherry			60								60				80	20			60						

```
(There are more records in the result set than the ones shown in this image)
(70 row(s) returned)
```

Discussion (with format):

We could use the format function to achieve the same result but notice in the result set that the weeks are not in order this time.

Code:

```
TRANSFORM Sum(unitprice*quantity) AS OrderTotal
SELECT ProductName
FROM Qry_Invoices
WHERE month(orderdate) IN (1,2,3,4,5,6) AND year(orderdate) = 2022
GROUP BY ProductName
PIVOT format([OrderDate], 'ww')
```

Result:

ProductName	10	11	12	13	14	15	16	17	18	19	20	21	22	23	24	25	26	27	3	4	5	6	7	8	9
All-Purpose Marinade	42									84					28									56	
Almonds Hickory Smoked			15			75			60	60	90							30		75					
Almonds Roasted and Salted								75			90			60	90			75							
Apple Cinnamon Raisin Cookies					48															60					
Artichokes in white sauce												45				45		30					60		
Banana Bisquits		16				8		96											8	24	24		24		
Banana Chips							90			30						75	30			60					
Berry Cherry				60				80	20			60									60				

```
(There are more records in the result set than the ones shown in this image)
(70 row(s) returned)
```

236. Create a crosstab report of sales by day of the month - the day(), datepart(), and month() functions

Discussion (day function):

The management is asking for a report of daily product sales for May in 2022. We will use three date functions—two for criteria and one to pivot our results. We will use the month() and year() functions to isolate the year and the month in the WHERE clause and the day() function to pivot product sales by day. Notice that only days with product sales appear as columns in the result set.

Code:

```
TRANSFORM sum(unitprice * quantity) AS OrderTotal
SELECT ProductName
FROM Qry_Invoices
WHERE month(OrderDate) = 5 AND year(orderdate) = 2022
GROUP BY ProductName
PIVOT day(OrderDate)
```

Discussion (datepart function):
We can achieve the same result using the datepart() function with the 'd' (day) argument. For a full list of possible arguments for the datepart() function, see the table at the end of this chapter.

Code:

```
TRANSFORM sum(unitprice * quantity) AS OrderTotal
SELECT ProductName
FROM Qry_Invoices
WHERE month(OrderDate) = 5 AND year(orderdate) = 2022
GROUP BY ProductName
PIVOT datepart('d',OrderDate)
```

Result:

ProductName	1	2	3	4	5	6	7	10	11	14	15	16	17	19	20	21	22	23	24	27	29	30	31
All-Purpose Marinade							84																
Almonds Hickory Smoked			30			30			60	30													
Almonds Roasted and Salted									90												60		
Artichokes in white sauce																45							
Banana Chips		30																					
Berry Cherry											40		20										
Biscuits with Cream		75																					
California Original Pistachios													15	30	75								

```
(There are more records in the result set than the ones shown in this image)
(51 row(s) returned)
```

237. Create a crosstab report of sales by day of the week. The weekday() and weekdayname() functions

Discussion (weekday function):
The management is asking for a report of product sales by day within the 25th week of the year 2022. First, we will use the datepart() and year() functions in the WHERE clause to limit results to the particular year and week. Then, we will use the weekday() function to display product sales by day within the week. The general syntax of the weekday() function appears below. It takes two arguments, datefield and firstdayofweek, and the second argument is optional. The firstdayofweek argument defines the first day of the week. We can choose any day between Sunday and Saturday as the table indicates below. In this example, we left the second argument blank, which defaults the first day of the week to Sunday. In the result set, you can see the sales by product and day of the week.

weekday (datefield, [firstdayofweek])

Argument value	First day of week
1	Sunday (default)
2	Monday
3	Tuesday
4	Wednesday
5	Thursday
6	Friday
7	Saturday

Code:

```
TRANSFORM sum(unitprice * quantity) AS OrderTotal
SELECT ProductName
FROM Qry_Invoices
WHERE datePart('ww', OrderDate) = 25 AND year(OrderDate) = 2022
GROUP BY ProductName
PIVOT weekday([OrderDate])
```

Result:

ProductName	1	2	3	4	5	6	7
Artichokes in white sauce				45			
Banana Chips				75			
Biscuits with Cream			90	15			
Caramel Brownie	15						
Chocolate Almonds				60			
Chocolate Chip Cookies					16		
Chocolate Chunk Cookies							192
Chocolate Fudge		75					

(There are more records in the result set than the ones shown in this image)
(20 row(s) returned)

Discussion (weekdayname function)

The previous example is fine, but it will confuse management and anybody else who tries to understand what day of the week corresponds to numbers 6 or 7. To solve this problem, we can use the weekdayname() function to provide the actual day name. As you can see in the result set, the names of the days appear now as column headings.

Code:

```
TRANSFORM Sum([UnitPrice]*[Quantity]) AS OrderTotal
SELECT ProductName
FROM Qry_Invoices
WHERE datePart('ww',[OrderDate]) = 25 AND year(OrderDate) = 2022
GROUP BY ProductName
PIVOT weekdayname(weekday([OrderDate]))
```

Result:

ProductName	Friday	Monday	Saturday	Sunday	Thursday	Tuesday	Wednesday
Artichokes in white sauce							45
Banana Chips							75

Biscuits with Cream						90	15
Caramel Brownie				15			
Chocolate Almonds							60
Chocolate Chip Cookies					16		
Chocolate Chunk Cookies			192				
Chocolate Fudge		75					

(There are more records in the result set than the ones shown in this image)
(20 row(s) returned)

238. Anniversaries: Past anniversaries - the LIKE operator

Discussion:

In this example, we want to retrieve orders which occurred on 10/20 of each year in our order history. An easy and flexible way to achieve this is by using the LIKE operator. Notice how we placed the asterisk in the year part of the date.

Code:

```
SELECT OrderID, CustomerID, OrderDate
FROM Orders
WHERE OrderDate Like '10/20/*'
```

Result:

OrderID	CustomerID	OrderDate
308	196	10/20/2020
329	88	10/20/2021
606	25	10/20/2022

(3 row(s) returned)

239. Anniversaries: Future anniversaries - the dateadd() function

Discussion:

In this example we are looking for the future dates on which our sales representatives complete 20 years of service. We achieve this using the dateadd(datepart, number, date field) function which takes three arguments. We use the 'yyyy' datepart argument to add 20 years to the DateOfHire field. For a full list of the options for the datepart argument see the dateadd() table at the end of this chapter.

Code:

```
SELECT FirstName, LastName, dateadd('yyyy', 20 , dateofhire) AS Anniversary20yr
FROM SalesReps
```

Result:

FirstName	LastName	Anniversary20yr
John	Anderson	1/1/2021
Mary	Teall	6/12/2041
George	Spicer	5/15/2024
Phillip	Zensons	6/10/2041

(There are more records in the result set than the ones shown in this image)
(10 row(s) returned)

240. Anniversaries: upcoming employee birthdays

Discussion:

In this example, we generate a list of employees who have birthdays in the month of April. We achieve this by using the datepart (datepart, datefield) function twice; first to show the day of the employee's birthday and second to isolate the month of the year as you can see in the WHERE clause.

Code:

```
SELECT FirstName, LastName, Title, datepart('d', dateofbirth) As DayOfBirth
FROM SalesReps
WHERE datepart('m', dateofbirth) = 4
```

Result:

FirstName	LastName	Title	DayOfBirth
John	Anderson	Sales Reppresentative	15
George	Spicer	Account Manager	4
Phillip	Zensons	Sales Reppresentative	3
Gerald	Williams	Sales Reppresentative	1

(4 row(s) returned)

241. Anniversaries: Calculate time elapsed such as employment length - the datediff() function

Discussion:

In this example, we calculate the number of employment years for our employees. We use the datediff(datepart, start date, end date) function to calculate the elapsed time between the employee's date of hire and today's date. We use the 'yyyy' option to display the interval in years and the date() function to obtain today's date from which we will subtract the date of hire.

Code:

```
SELECT FirstName, LastName, datediff('yyyy', DateOfHire, date()) AS YearsEmployed
FROM SalesReps
```

Result:

FirstName	LastName	YearsEmployed
John	Anderson	23
Mary	Teall	3
George	Spicer	20
Phillip	Zensons	3

(There are more records in the result set than the ones shown in this image)
(10 row(s) returned)

242. Anniversaries: Calculate Employee Age

Discussion:

The goal here is to calculate the ages of our employees. We do this using the datediff(datepart, start date, end date) function which subtracts the start date from the end date and provides the difference in years, months, quarters or in any other period we need. Refer to the end of this chapter for all possible interval settings for the datediff() function. In this example, we see the age in years using the 'yyyy' option.

Code:

```
SELECT FirstName, LastName, Title, datediff('yyyy', DateOfBirth, date())  As Age
FROM SalesReps
```

Result:

FirstName	LastName	Title	Age
John	Anderson	Sales Reppresentative	44
Mary	Teall	Sales Director	24
George	Spicer	Account Manager	41
Phillip	Zensons	Sales Reppresentative	26

(There are more records in the result set than the ones shown in this image)
(10 row(s) returned)

243. Cycle times: Calculate order processing times - the datediff() function

Discussion:

Customer service has reported to management that customers are complaining about shipping. Specifically, they complain that it takes a lot of time to receive their orders after they complete the ordering process. Management is trying to determine the cause and they need our help. They want to know if the problem is internal as a result of packaging and payment processing or if the problem is external as a result of the shipping company. They suspect the problem is internal, and they tell us to produce a report that lists how many days it takes for an order to ship from the time it has been received.

We do this using the datediff() function. The datediff() function takes three arguments and the general syntax of the function appears below. The datepart argument is a string that will determine in what interval we want to obtain the difference between the start date and end date. For instance, we might want to calculate the difference in days, weeks, months, or years. Please refer to the end of this chapter for a full list of values for the datepart argument. As you can see from the code below, we calculate the difference between OrderDate and ShippedDate in days. In other words, how many days elapsed between receiving and shipping an order? The results are not good at all. It takes a full five days to get the orders out from our factory for the month of September 2022.

datediff(datepart, start date, end date)

Code:

```
SELECT OrderID, datediff('d', OrderDate, ShippedDate) AS CycleTime
FROM Orders
WHERE year(OrderDate) = 2022 AND month(OrderDate) = 9
```

Result:

OrderID	CycleTime
25	5
68	5
111	5
167	5

(There are more records in the result set than the ones shown in this image)
(20 row(s) returned)

244. Policies: Establish policies on shipping dates - the dateadd() function

Discussion:

Management is not very happy to see that it takes five days to ship an order. This means that customers will receive their orders in about ten to fifteen days total. This is unacceptable because we are in the food industry, and our products need to arrive fresh. So, management asks for our help again to produce a timetable that will list the expected shipping dates for orders. Management has determined that it should take two days at most for any order to ship, and they have stated that this policy will be strictly enforced. We can produce target shipping dates using the dateadd() function. It takes three arguments, and its general syntax appears below:

dateadd(datepart, number, date field)

The datepart argument is a string like 'd', 'm', or 'yyyy' determining the time interval we want to add. For instance, if we want to add days to a date, we use the "d" value. If we want to add years, we use the 'yyyy' value for the datepart argument. For a full list of the values for the datepart argument, please refer to the table at the end of this chapter. The number argument is the actual number of time intervals we want to add. If we want to add 15 days, we use the number 15. Finally, the date field argument is the date field to which we want to add a number of days, months, or years. In the code below, we add 2 days to the OrderDate field:

Code:

```
SELECT OrderID, dateadd('d', 2, OrderDate) AS PolicyShipmentDate
FROM Orders
WHERE year(OrderDate) = 2022 AND month(OrderDate) = 9
```

Result:

OrderID	PolicyShipmentDate
25	9/13/2022
68	9/5/2022
111	9/25/2022
167	10/2/2022

(There are more records in the result set than the ones shown in this image)
(20 row(s) returned)

Date Functions	
Syntax	**Return value**
now(datefield)	Returns the date and time of the computer.
date(datefield)	Returns the date of the computer without the time.
time(datefield)	Returns the time of the computer.
timer(datefield)	Returns the number of seconds elapsed since midnight.
dateadd (datepart , number , datefield)	Returns a date to which a datepart interval such as year, quarter, month etc. has been added.
datediff (datepart, datefield1, datefield2)	Returns a number of time intervals between two specified dates.
datepart(datepart, datefield, [firstdayofweek], [firstweekofyear])	Returns a date part, for example 1 for the quarter or 89 for the day of the year.
year(datefield)	Returns the year portion of a date field value, for example 2025.
format(datefield, datepart, [firstdayofweek], [firstweekofyear])	Returns a date part, for example 4 for the quarter or 2025 for the year.
formatdatetime(datefield, namedformat)	Returns a date or time formatted according to the value of the namedformat argument. See table below for all possible values of the namedformat argument.
month(datefield)	Returns the month portion of a date field value, for example, 11 for November.
weekday(datefield, [firstdayofweek])	Returns the number of the day of the week as a of a date field value, for example 2 for Monday. The default value for the first day of the week is 1 for Sunday. We can set what is the first day of the week. The possible output values are 1-7.
weekdayname(datepart, [abbreviate], [firstdayofweek])	Returns the actual name of the day of the week as a of a date field value, for example Monday.
day(datefield)	Returns the day of the month of a date field value such as 29. The possible output values are 1-31.
hour(datefield)	Returns the hour part of a date field value. The possible output values are 0 to 23.
minute(datefield)	Returns the minute part of a date field value. The possible output values are 0 to 59.
second(datefield)	Returns the second part of a date field value. The possible output values are 0 to 59.

Source: https://support.microsoft.com/en-us/office/Expressions-684295d0-97c2-443c-8e0a-8c6b635bec56#ID0EAABAAA=Date_time&ID0EBBD=Date_time

datepart(), datename(), dateadd(), and datediff() argument settings	
Setting	Description
yyyy	Year
q	Quarter
m	Month
y	Day of year
d	Day
w	Weekday
ww	Week
h	Hour
n	Minute
s	Second

Source: https://support.microsoft.com/en-us/office/datepart-function-26868a79-5505-4e5a-8905-6001372223fa

formatdatetime() namedformat argument settings		
Constant	**Value**	**Description**
vbGeneralDate	0	If there is a date part, display it as a short date. If there is a time part, display it as a long time.
vbLongDate	1	Display a date using the long date format specified in your computer's regional settings.
vbShortDate	2	Display a date using the short date format specified in your computer's regional settings.
vbLongTime	3	Display a time using the time format specified in your computer's regional settings.
vbShortTime	4	Display a time using the 24-hour format (hh:mm).

Source: https://support.microsoft.com/en-us/office/formatdatetime-function-aef62949-f957-4ba4-94ff-ace14be4f1ca

DISCUSSION QUESTIONS

1. In business analytics, when we use date functions to create new fields, are we creating new measures or new descriptors?
2. How do these new descriptors offer the company a competitive advantage?
3. What date functions can we use to extract the month out of a date field?
4. What date function we use to retrieve the month name (such as January) instead of the number (such as 1)?
5. Why deep knowledge of date functions leads to better database design?
6. Why do we want to use date functions as default values in table fields?
7. What are the functions we can use to extract quarters from date fields?
8. What function can we use to extract the day of the year from a date field?
9. What is the purpose of the datediff() function? How many arguments does it take?
10. What function can we use to add date intervals, for example months, to a date field?

HANDS-ON EXERCISES

Case 1

For each of the questions in this case create a new query in SQL view and name it as per the instructions in each question.

1. The accounts director is asking for report that will list the Order totals for all the years for which we have data in the database. Create a new query on the tble_dates table with the fields "Year" and "OrderTotal" that satisfies the director's request and save it as Dates_Case1_Q1. Do not take into consideration any given discounts.

Your result should look like:

Year	OrderTotal
2020	51164
2021	45002
2022	44230

(3 row(s) returned)

2. The accounts director needs a report that shows the sum of order amounts by month for the year 2022. Create a new query on the tble_Dates table with the fields "Month" and "OrderTotal" that satisfies the director's request. Do not take into consideration any given discounts and make sure the director sees month names and not month numbers. In addition, month names should be in the correct order starting in January and ending in December. Save your query as Dates_Case1_Q2.

Your result should look like:

Month	OrderTotal
January	2792
February	2944
March	3495
April	3872
May	5508
June	4499
July	2612
August	2563
September	3306
October	4212
November	4059
December	4368

`(12 row(s) returned)`

3. The accounts director now needs a pivot report that will show the total shipping cost by CustomerCity and month in the year 2022. Create a new query on the tble_dates table that satisfies the director's request and save it as Dates_Case1_Q3.

Your result should look like:

CustomerCity	2022
Albany	803
Boston	1447
Chicago	2024
Dallas	1894
Denver	1288

`(There are more records in the result set than the ones shown in this image)`
`(15 row(s) returned)`

4. The accounts director is back asking for a report that will list the total order amount by quarter in the year 2022. Do not take into consideration any given discounts. Quarters should be displayed in the correct order, that is, 1,2,3, and 4. Create a new query on the tble_dates table that satisfies the director's request and save it as Dates_Case1_Q4.

Your result should look like:

Quarter	OrderTotal
1	9231
2	13879
3	8481
4	12639

`(4 row(s) returned)`

5. The accounts receivable director is really amazed by the pieces of information you provide him. He now needs a report that will list the quantity of products sold by sales representative and quarter in the year 2022. Create a new query on the tble_dates table that satisfies the director's request and save it as Dates_Case1_Q5.

Your result should look like:

SalesRepLastName	1	2	3	4
Anderson	1098	1287	1520	983
Baker	961	1532	698	1575
Bernstein	1123	1047	603	1349
Delaney	869	1055	996	1564

```
(There are more records in the result set than the ones shown in this image)
(10 row(s) returned)
```

Case 2

For each of the questions in this case create a new query in SQL view and name it as per the instructions in each question.

1. The sales department is asking for a report that will show the Total Order Amount by customer state and by week for April 2022. Do not take into consideration any given discounts. Create a new query on the tble_dates table that satisfies the salespeople request and save it as Dates_Case2_Q1. HINT: April 2022 had five weeks.

Your result should look like:

CustomerState	14	15	16	17	18
AZ					40
CA		344	90	112	35
CO				219	
DC		146		56	288
FL			94	101	100

```
(There are more records in the result set than the ones shown in this image)
(9 row(s) returned)
```

2. The sales department is impressed with your data analytics, and they are now asking for the Total Order Amount by week 50 in the years 2020, 2021, and 2022. Do not take into consideration any given discounts for your calculations. Create a new query on the tble_dates table that satisfies the salespeople request and save it as Dates_Case2_Q2.

Your result should look like:

Year	Week	TotalOrderAmount
2020	50	932
2021	50	1025
2022	50	1056

```
(3 row(s) returned)
```

3. The salespeople are asking for a report that will list the total order amount by city for the months of January, May, and September in the year 2022. Sort results by total order amount so that bigger amounts show first. Do not take into consideration any given discounts for your calculations. HINT: we are looking for totals by city for the three months together and not for totals by city and by month. Create a new query on the tble_dates table that satisfies the salespeople request and save it as Dates_Case2_Q3.

Your result should look like:

CustomerCity	TotalOrderAmount
New York	2600
Los Angeles	1219
San Jose	1076
Dallas	923

(There are more records in the result set than the ones shown in this image)
(15 row(s) returned)

4. The shipping director set a new rule that all orders should arrive to the customer within ten days of the order date. She needs a report that includes the OrderID, CustomerLastName, OrderDate, and the RequiredArrivalDate fields from the tble_dates table where the RequiredArrivalDate field is ten days after the OrderDate field. She will compare these results with what actually happened. Create a new query that satisfies the director's request and save it as Dates_Case2_Q4.

Your result should look like:

OrderID	CustomerLastName	OrderDate	RequiredArrivalDate
42	Stoll	4/19/2021	4/29/2021
43	Demichele	5/6/2020	5/16/2020
43	Demichele	5/6/2020	5/16/2020
43	Demichele	5/6/2020	5/16/2020

(There are more records in the result set than the ones shown in this image)
(2411 row(s) returned)

5. The HR director is asking for a report that will list the name of the sales representatives and the number of years they are with the company. Create a new query on the tble_dates table that satisfies the director's request and save it as Dates_Case2_Q5.

Your result should look like:

SalesrepLastName	NumberOfYears
Anderson	25
Baker	18
Bernstein	33
Delaney	29

(There are more records in the result set than the ones shown in this image)
(10 row(s) returned)

CHAPTER 25
UPDATING ROWS IN LARGE DATASETS

Update statements are powerful tools for the advanced user, administrator, and developer. They provide astonishing flexibility to complete tasks in minutes for which we would otherwise need hours. For example, we might have a database of 1000 suppliers and a few thousand products associated with each supplier. Every week, due to promotional campaigns, pricing strategies, or replenishment costs, our suppliers might change their prices and since their products constitute our own raw materials, we need to update our own prices as well. After all, the only constant in business is change. Consequently, we must be ready for lightning speed updates to our operational data.

Our suppliers will never update their product prices at the same time and at the same percentage rates. This scenario is valid only for theoretical books. What really happens is that suppliers will send us a price update when their business operations dictate it, and this update will most probably be different from everyone else's. We respond to such scenarios by employing flexible update statements which we can reuse at will. This chapter starts with very simple examples and ends up with powerful conditional updates for data manipulation.

Pay attention: we cannot undo the results of update statements. Consequently, my advice and my own policy are to first use a SELECT statement to check the records to be updated and then, run the update itself. This is common industry practice. We never run an update statement in the blind. The general syntax of an update statement is shown below:

```
UPDATE table
SET fieldvalue1 = value1, fieldvalue2 = value2, fieldvalue3 = value3...
[WHERE condition]
```

We can also run updates on queries (updateable ones). We can construct a dataset having data from multiple tables and run the update against the query. We can also update a table based on the values of another table using subqueries. Update statements are highly efficient for operations. Before we delve into examples, let us make sure we understand what cascade updates are and how they work.

245. What are cascade updates, how to use them, and what they mean

There are cases in which we must update the values of primary keys in our tables. Usually, these changes are mandated by entities external to the organization, such as the government. For example, up until now, we might have used the social security number of an employee as the primary key for the employees' table. As a result, SSN functioned as the foreign key for all related tables for that employee (sales, HR records etc.). Now, the government steps in and says that we cannot do that anymore. This means that we have to change the SSN value for the employee in the employees table, and, most importantly, we need to change all of its occurrences in related tables. So, if this employee worked for us for 10 years, he might have 260 paystub records in the HR table. We might have thousands of related records that we need to update for this employee.

Doing so manually is an impossible task, especially if we have several thousand employees. This is where cascade updates come in. Cascade updates will allow us to change the value of the primary key in the primary table, and the database will automatically change all occurrences of the foreign key in related tables. Let us go through a simple graphical example using a customer database to see how cascade updates work.

Customers	
CustID	Name
1	John
2	Mary
3	George
4	Stacy

Orders		
OrderID	CustID	OrderDate
1	2	9/10/2022
2	2	10/10/2022
3	1	11/10/2022
4	3	11/11/2022

Products_Orders		
OrderID	ProductID	Quantity
1	2	2
2	2	5
3	1	3
4	2	4

Products	
ProductID	ProductName
1	A
2	B
3	C
4	D

In the figure above, let us assume that we need to change Mary's primary key value from 2 to 222. First, we need to turn cascade updates on for the relationship between customers and orders (technical explanation follows shortly). Then, we can change the primary key value 2 to value 222 in the customers table. The database will ask us to confirm the action, and once the updates are completed, this is how the same tables will look:

Customers	
CustomerID	Name
1	John
222	Mary
3	George
4	Stacy

Orders		
OrderID	CustomerID	OrderDate
1	222	9/10/2022
2	222	10/10/2022
3	1	11/10/2022
4	3	11/11/2022

Products_Orders		
OrderID	ProductID	Quantity
1	2	2
2	2	5
3	1	3
4	2	4

Products	
ProductID	ProductName
1	A
2	B
3	C
4	D

Notice how the database automatically changed all the references of CustomerID = 2 to 222 in the Orders table. Still, I strongly recommend having cascade updates turned off except when you want to make changes to primary key values. This is a precaution in case the value of a primary key is changed by accident. To set cascade updates on for a relationship is straightforward following the steps below:

1. Click on the "Database Tools" tab. Then, in the group "Relationships", click on "Relationships".

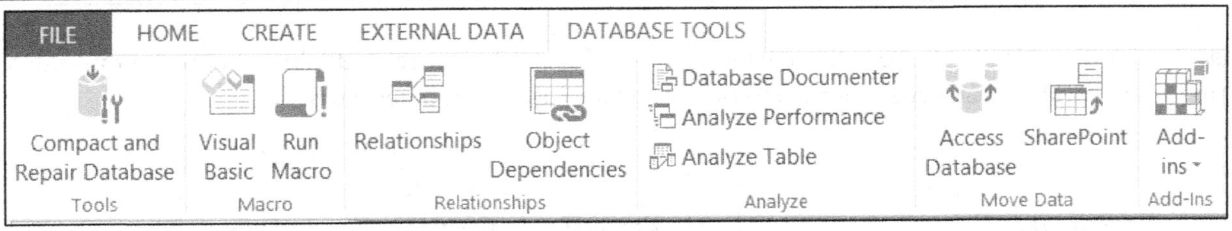

This will open up the relationships window as shown below:

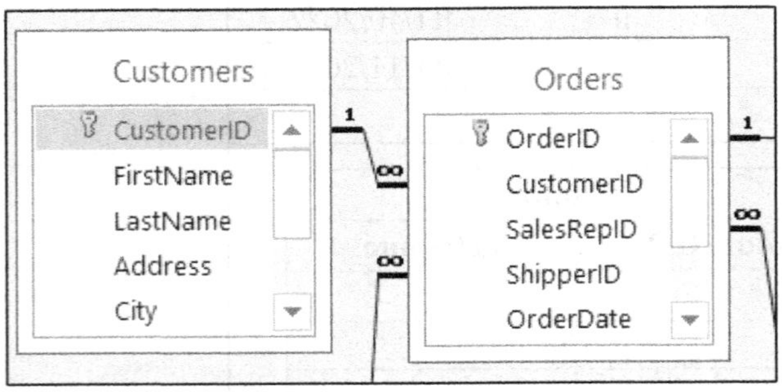

2. Double click on the relationship line between customers and orders. The following screen will appear. Click on "Cascade Update Related Fields" and click "OK".

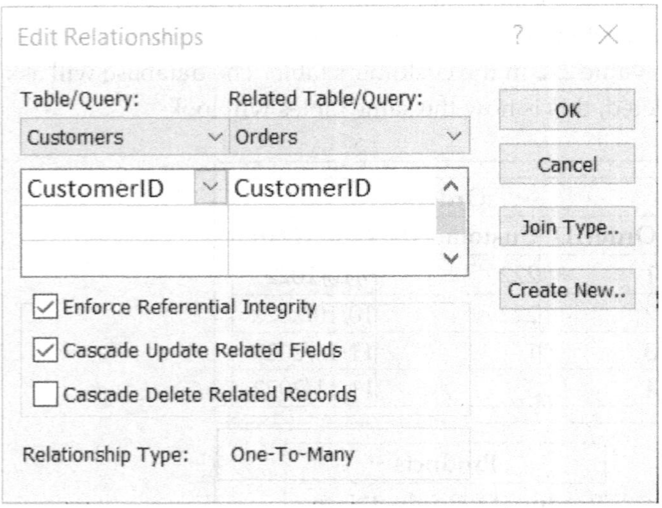

Now, we are ready to open the customer table and change the value of the primary key for any customer. Our change will be propagated throughout the database where the database finds a foreign key value, in this case a CustomerID value, which is equal to the primary key we changed. Remember to edit the relationship again and turn off "Cascade Updates" once the records are updated.

246. Update a single field value in a single record

Update the address field for a single customer

Discussion:

The goal is to update the address field for one customer. Notice the criteria in the query. They must uniquely identify the customer we want to update. We use a SELECT statement to make certain that we do not have another customer with the same first and last names and then we will apply the update statement.

SELECT Code:

```
SELECT *
FROM tbls_customers_upd
WHERE lastname = 'Demizio' AND firstname = 'Michael'
```

Result:

```
(1 row(s) returned)
```

UPDATE Code:

```
UPDATE tbls_customers_upd
SET Address = '12 Lark Street'
WHERE lastname = 'Demizio' AND firstname = 'Michael'
```

Result:

```
(1 row(s) affected
```

247. Update multiple field values in a single record

Update the address and city fields for a single customer

Discussion:

Now we want to update both the address and the city fields for a customer. The criteria remain the same but notice how the two fields we are updating are separated by a comma in the SET part of the code.

SELECT Code:

```
SELECT *
FROM tbls_customers_upd
WHERE lastname = 'Demizio' AND firstname = 'Michael'
```

Result:

```
(1 row(s) returned)
```

UPDATE Code:

```
UPDATE tbls_customers_upd
SET Address = '12 Lark Street', city = 'Albany'
WHERE lastname = 'Demizio' AND firstname = 'Michael'
```

Result:

```
(1 row(s) affected
```

248. Update one field in multiple records

Update the zip code of customers in a specific city

Discussion:

This time we will update zip code values for customers in the city of Denver in the state of Colorado. It might look simple, but we need to pay attention that the city of Denver does not exist in any other state. If it does, we need to add one more criterion in the WHERE clause to identify the state as well. Always run a SQL statement in advance to make sure your operation will affect the records you intend it to affect.

SELECT Code:

```
SELECT *
FROM tbls_customers_upd
WHERE city = 'Denver'
```

Result:

```
(13 row(s) returned)
```

UPDATE Code:

```
UPDATE tbls_customers_upd
SET zip = '22215'
WHERE city = 'Denver'
```

Result:

```
(13 row(s) affected
```

249. Update multiple fields in multiple records

Update city, zip, and address values of customers in Dallas, Texas

Discussion:

Because of erroneous data entry, customers that show up from Denver, Colorado are actually from Tucson, Arizona. Consequently, we have to update their zip, city, and state information.

SELECT Code:

```
SELECT *
FROM tbls_customers_upd
WHERE city = 'Denver'
```

Result:

```
(13 row(s) returned)
```

UPDATE Code:

```
UPDATE tbls_customers_upd
SET zip = '22730', city = 'Tucson', state = 'AZ'
WHERE city = 'Denver'
```

Result:

```
(13 row(s) affected
```

250. Update records using calculations

Increase product prices by a percentage

Discussion:

One of our suppliers has sent us updated prices for raw materials and as a result we need to increase our own product prices by 5% for the products from that supplier. In the WHERE clause, instead of the supplier name, we will use the supplier ID to identify the correct supplier. Notice that we work with the query "Qry_SupplierPrices" which combines the information of suppliers and their products.

SELECT Code:

```
SELECT *
FROM Qry_SupplierPrices
WHERE SupplierID = 1
```

Result:

```
(10 row(s) returned)
```

UPDATE Code:

```
UPDATE Qry_SupplierPrices
SET ProductPrice = ProductPrice * (1+0.05)
WHERE SupplierID = 1
```

Result:

```
(10 row(s) affected
```

251. Update records conditionally using the switch() function

Update product prices using different update conditions for every supplier

Discussion:

As you might expect, in everyday work scenarios, our suppliers, customers, or partners do not set up meetings to send us uniform and standardized information just so that we can have a nice time with our operations. Instead, they send us their own percentage increases and not at the same time. So, what can we do to take care of this business fact in minutes instead of making it an operational nightmare? We can combine the powers of the update statement and the switch() function. As you can see below, our suppliers sent us percentage updates ranging from 2% all the way up to 15%. Using one update statement with the switch() function we obtain the following: First, we can take care of all the updates in minutes. Second, the statement is so clean that it is reusable the next time we need to do the same job. Third, suppose that some of our suppliers have not sent us any updates. We can leave the statement below as is and update the ProductPrice with itself as is the case with supplierID=5 where nothing is updated.

SELECT Code:

```
Select
SWITCH (
supplierid=1,    ProductPrice*(1.1) ,
supplierid=2,    ProductPrice*(1.05),
supplierid=3,    ProductPrice*(1.1) ,
supplierid=4,    ProductPrice*(1.05) ,
supplierid=5,    ProductPrice ,
supplierid=6,    ProductPrice*(1.02) ,
supplierid=7,    ProductPrice *(1.03),
supplierid=8,    ProductPrice*(1.05) ,
supplierid=9,    ProductPrice*(1.15) ,
supplierid=10,   ProductPrice*(1.1) ,
)
As UpdatedPrice
from Qry_SupplierPrices
```

Result:

```
(70 row(s) returned)
```

UPDATE Code:

```
UPDATE Qry_SupplierPrices
SET ProductPrice =
SWITCH (
supplierid=1,    ProductPrice*(1.1) ,
supplierid=2,    ProductPrice*(1.05),
supplierid=3,    ProductPrice*(1.1) ,
supplierid=4,    ProductPrice*(1.05) ,
supplierid=5,    ProductPrice ,
supplierid=6,    ProductPrice*(1.02) ,
supplierid=7,    ProductPrice *(1.03),
supplierid=8,    ProductPrice*(1.05) ,
supplierid=9,    ProductPrice*(1.15) ,
supplierid=10,   ProductPrice*(1.1) ,
)
```

Result:

```
(70 row(s) affected)
```

252. Update records in a table using criteria from another table or query

Update the Products table using criteria from the Suppliers table

Discussion:

In this example we update prices in the tbls_products_upd table with criteria from the Suppliers table. Specifically, we update product prices by 20% from suppliers who are in Boston and Denver. The problem is that the tbls_products_upd table does not contain the city field for suppliers and we need to use a subquery to satisfy this request. The subquery will retrieve supplier IDs from the Suppliers table and will update the corresponding product prices in the tbls_products_upd table.

SELECT Code:

```
Select * from tbls_products_upd
WHERE SupplierID IN
(SELECT SupplierID FROM Suppliers
WHERE city= 'Boston' or city = 'Denver')
```

Result:

```
(26 row(s) returned)
```

UPDATE Code:

```
UPDATE tbls_products_upd
SET ProductPrice = ProductPrice * (1+0.20)
WHERE SupplierID IN
(SELECT SupplierID FROM Suppliers
WHERE city= 'Boston' or city = 'Denver')
```

Result:

```
(26 row(s) affected
```

DISCUSSION QUESTIONS

1. What is the primary goal of update statements?
2. Can we undo the result of an update statement if we change our mind?
3. What is a good safety strategy to follow before we use an update statement?
4. What is the role of cascade updates in relational databases?
5. Why it is a good idea to keep cascade updates off and use them only when needed?
6. Can you provide an example in which it makes sense to use cascade updates?
7. Can we update multiple values in a single record with a single SQL statement?
8. Can we update multiple values in multiple records by using a single SQL statement?
9. What function can we use to update records based on multiple conditions?
10. What technique can we use to update records in one table using criteria from another table?

HANDS-ON EXERCISES

Case 1

For each of the questions in this case create a new query in SQL view and name it as per the instructions in each question.

1. The inventory people want to change the UnitsOnOrder quantity from 0 to 5 for the Almonds, Roasted and Salted product with ProductID=2. Create a new query on the table tbls_products_upd that satisfies the inventory people request and save it as Updates_Case1_Q1.

Your result should look like:

```
(1 row(s) affected)
```

2. The inventory people now want to change the ProductPrice and UnitsInStock to 32 and 30 respectively for the product Banana Chips with ProductID = 3. Create a new query on the table tbls_products_upd that satisfies the inventory people request and save it as Updates_Case1_Q2.

Your result should look like:

```
(1 row(s) affected)
```

3. The replenishing department just called in and notified us that we need to add five dollars to the price of all products from the supplier with SupplierID = 5. Create a new query on the table tbls_products_upd that satisfies this request and save it as Updates_Case1_Q3.

Your result should look like:

```
(8 row(s) affected)
```

4. The purchasing department just called and informed us that we need to make the following changes for the supplier with SupplierID = 3. Create a new query on the table tbls_products_upd that satisfies this request and save it as Updates_Case1_Q4.

   a) Change the QuantityPerUnit to 35.
   b) Add 12 dollars to the price of each of the products.
   c) Change the ReorderLevel to 15.

Your result should look like:
```
(7 row(s) affected)
```

5. The purchasing department called in and informed us that the supplier with SupplierID = 5 increased their prices by 7.5%. Now we need to increase our own prices by the same amount. Create a new query on the table tbls_products_upd that satisfies this request and save it as Updates_Case1_Q5.

Your result should look like:
```
(8 row(s) affected)
```

Case 2

For each of the questions in this case create a new query in SQL view and name it as per the instructions in each question.

1. HR called in and said that the city for employee John Anderson is wrong and it needs to be changed to "Los Angeles". Create a new query on the tbls_salesreps_upd table that satisfies the HR request and save it as Updates_Case2_Q1.

Your result should look like:
```
(1 row(s) affected)
```

2. HR called in again and said that for the employee Gerald Williams the zip code needs to be updated to 83044 and the date of hire to 5/10/2022. Create a new query on the tbls_SalesReps_upd table that satisfies the HR request and save it as Updates_Case2_Q2.

Your result should look like:
```
(1 row(s) affected)
```

3. The salespeople are asking for a ten dollar increase to the price of all products with a ProductPrice lower than $30. Create a new query on the table tbls_products_upd that satisfies this request and save it as Updates_Case2_Q3.

Your result should look like:
```
(28 row(s) affected)
```

4. The purchasing people called in and reported that some of our suppliers changed their prices. Now we need to change our own prices as follows:
For supplierid=1 the price should go up by 20%
For supplierid=3 the price should go up by 10%
For supplierid=7 the price should go up by 4%
For supplierid=9 the price should go up by 8%

Create a new query on the tbls_products_upd table that satisfies the purchasing people request and save it as Updates_Case2_Q4. You need to be able to do all the updates using a single query.

Your result should look like:
```
(70 row(s) affected)
```

5. The salespeople are asking us to decrease prices by $4 of the products in the tbls_products_upd table for which the price in the JoinOrdersProducts table equals or exceeds $32. Create a new query that satisfies the salespeople request and save it as Updates_Case2_Q5.

Your result should look like:

```
(4 row(s) affected)
```

CHAPTER 26
DELETING ROWS IN LARGE DATASETS

DELETE statements remove one or multiple records in one operation. Instead of deleting table rows manually, we use delete statements with criteria. The general syntax of a delete statement appears below, and while it looks simple, it can become an amazing tool when coupled with criteria and subqueries.

```
DELETE
FROM table
WHERE criteria
```

As with update statements, we cannot undo the results of DELETE statements. Thus, once we delete a set of records, there is no way to get them back. Consequently, we should have a solid backup strategy just in case we make a mistake. In this chapter, we will see how to move records to other tables before deleting them. Furthermore, it is professional practice to run a SELECT statement first to determine if the result contains the records we want to delete and then, run the delete statement. Before we run any code in this chapter, we should learn about the role of cascade deletes.

253. What are cascade deletes, how to use them, and how they operate

In order to understand cascade deletes, let's work with the record of a customer from five years ago who is no longer in business. We want to delete this customer from the database so that it does not come up in our query results. We could simply go to the customers table and try to delete this record. However, if there are any associated orders with this customer, the database will not allow us to delete the customer, since we would end up with orphaned records in the Orders table. Referential integrity rules do not allow this to happen, and we would not be able to delete the customer.

To delete this customer manually, we should first delete all the orders associated with this customer. However, since we also have a many-to-many relationship between Orders and Products, we first need to go to the JoinOrdersProducts table and delete the respective records of order items for that customer. In a visual example, if we want to delete the customer Mary with CustomerID = 2 from the database, we need to do the following in the order provided:

1. Delete from the JoinOrdersProducts table the two records with OrderIDs 1 and 2. For example, the order with OrderID 1 contains the product with ProductID 2.
2. Delete from the Orders table the orders with Orderid = 1 and 2 since they belong to Mary.
3. Finally, delete Mary's record with CustomerID = 2 from the Customers table.

Customers	
CustomerID	**Name**
1	John
2	Mary
3	George
4	Stacy

Orders		
OrderID	**CustomerID**	**OrderDate**
1	2	9/10/2025
2	2	10/10/2025
3	1	11/10/2025
4	3	11/11/2025

Products	
ProductID	**ProductName**
1	A
2	B
3	C
4	D

JoinOrdersProducts		
OrderID	**ProductID**	**Quantity**
1	2	2
2	2	5
3	1	3
4	2	4

Even in this simple scenario, deleting a customer is an involved process. Imagine the scenario where you have thousands of customers with tens of thousands of associated orders. It would be impossible to remove customers manually. Cascade deletes allow us to delete customers in the primary table, and the database will delete all related records to those customers in all related tables. In this example, if cascade deletes were on for the relationship between Customers and Orders and the relationship between Orders and JoinOrdersProducts, when we delete Mary from the Customers table, the database will automatically delete all of Mary's references in the Orders and JoinOrdersProducts tables at once. To turn cascade deletes on, follow these steps:

This is where cascade deletes come in. By using cascade deletes, we can delete a customer in the primary table, and the database itself will delete all references to that customer in all related tables. In this example, if cascade deletes are on, when we delete Mary from the customers table, the database will automatically delete all of Mary's references in the Orders and ProductOrders tables reliably and at once. To turn cascade deletes on, follow these steps:

1. In the ribbon, click on the "Database Tools" tab. Then, in the group "Relationships", click on "Relationships".

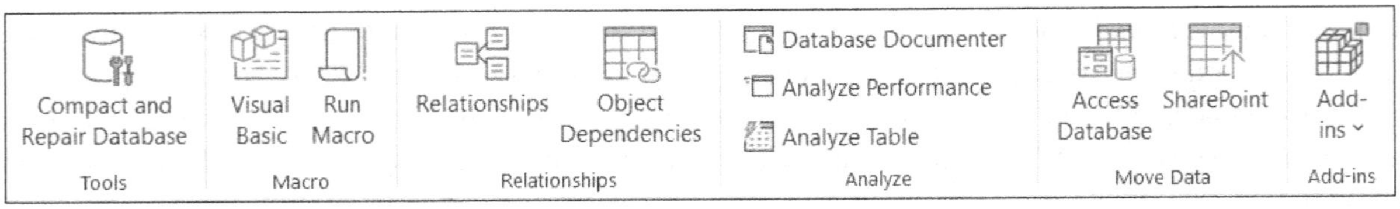

2. This will open up the Relationships window. Double click on the relationship line between Customers and Orders.

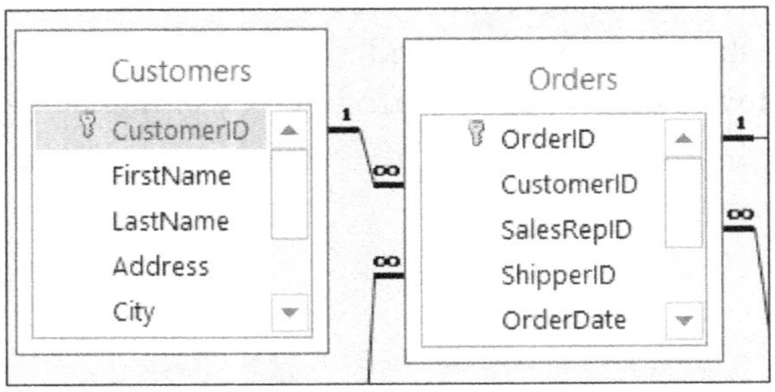

3. The following screen will appear. Click on "Cascade Delete Related Fields" and click "OK".

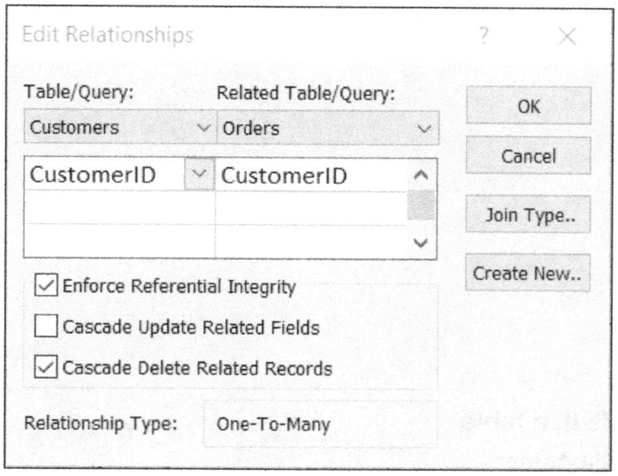

4. Repeat step two for the relationship between Orders and JoinProductsOrders to enable cascade deletes as well.

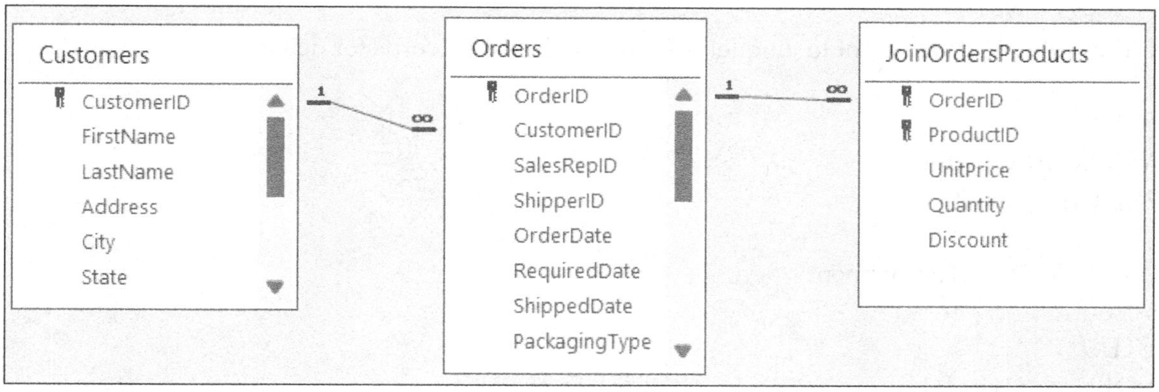

5. At this point, if we open the Customers table and delete Mary's record, all of Mary's orders in the Orders table will be deleted and all related records in the JoinOrdersProducts table will be deleted as well.

In this chapter we will be working on the tbls_orders_del table, which is just a copy of the Orders table in which we can delete records at will.

254. Delete a single record in a table

Delete a specific customer's order

Discussion:

In this example we delete a single record from the tbls_orders_del table. Notice how we use the OrderID as the criterion in the WHERE clause. The OrderID is the primary key of the tbls_orders_del table and it will uniquely identify the record for deletion. Always run a SELECT statement beforehand to make sure you are deleting what you intend to delete.

Step 1: Run a SELECT statement

Code:

```
SELECT *
FROM tbls_orders_del
WHERE OrderID = 20
```

Step 2: Run the DELETE statement

Code:

```
DELETE
FROM tbls_orders_del
WHERE OrderID = 20
```

Result:

```
(1 row(s) affected
```

255. Delete multiple records in a table

Delete all orders for a specific customer

Discussion:

In this example, we want to delete all orders for customerid= 2, i.e., Mary. To achieve this task, we will use the CustomerID field in the WHERE clause, which is the primary key for the customers table and the foreign key in the orders table.

Step 1: Run a SELECT statement to uniquely identify and verify records for deletion.

Code:

```
SELECT *
FROM tbls_orders_del
WHERE CustomerID = 2
```

Step 2: Run the DELETE statement

Code:

```
DELETE
FROM tbls_orders_del
WHERE CustomerID = 2
```

Result:

```
(4 row(s) affected
```

256. Delete records within a certain date range

Delete multiple orders from multiple customers within a date range

Discussion:

This is an example of how we can use date criteria to delete orders within a specified date range.

Step 1: Run a SELECT statement

Code:

```
SELECT *
FROM tbls_orders_del
WHERE OrderDate BETWEEN #2022/10/15# AND #2022/10/17#
```

Step 2: Run the DELETE statement

Code:

```
DELETE
FROM tbls_orders_del
WHERE OrderDate BETWEEN #2022/10/15# AND #2022/10/17#
```

Result:

```
(2 row(s) affected
```

257. Delete duplicate records while controlling if you want to delete the earliest or the latest ones

Delete earliest or latest duplicate customer orders

Discussion:

Let us discuss the setup of this example in detail. First, in the table tbls_orders_del, records with OrderID 1001, 1002, and 1003 are duplicates. Specifically, the record with OrderID = 1 is identical to 1001, the record with OrderID = 988 is identical to 1002, and the record with OrderID = 990 is identical to 1003. Keep in mind that these records have identical field values but different primary keys values.

The burning question is which records should we delete, the earliest ones or the latest ones? We know that a record with a lesser OrderID value was entered before a record with a higher OrderID value since the primary key is an auto increment. In the following example, we discuss both alternatives in detail. The four steps to follow appear below:

Step 1: Run a SELECT statement to uniquely identify and verify records for deletion.

The SQL statement below will SELECT the records with smaller OrderID values. Notice we use a subquery to obtain what we need. In the main SELECT statement, we select all orders from the tbls_orders_del table that do not belong in the subquery. The subquery itself will fetch the duplicate records with the maximum OrderID values (1001, 1002, and 1003). The main SELECT statement will fetch what is left from the six duplicated records, i.e., 1, 988, and 990. We can also use the NOT IN operator instead of the "<>" inequality predicate to obtain the same results. The function max() is used in the subquery to identify duplicates with maximum primary key values. Then, the main SELECT statement will fetch all duplicates not in the subquery.

Code:

```
SELECT OrderID, CustomerID, OrderDate, RequiredDate, InvoiceAmount, PackagingType
FROM tbls_orders_del AS T2
WHERE OrderID <>
(SELECT Max(OrderID)
FROM tbls_Orders_Del AS T1
WHERE T2.CustomerID = T1.CustomerID AND T2.SalesRepID = T1.SalesRepID AND T2.ShipperID
= T1.ShipperID AND T2.OrderDate = T1.OrderDate)
```

Result:

OrderID	CustomerID	OrderDate	RequiredDate	InvoiceAmount	PackagingType
1	139	11/11/2020	11/21/2020	31	Box
988	145	3/26/2021	4/5/2021	296	Plastic
990	160	5/22/2022	6/1/2022	31	Cardboard

```
(3 row(s) returned)
```

This SQL statement will select the latest duplicate records:

Code:

```
SELECT OrderID, CustomerID, OrderDate, RequiredDate, InvoiceAmount, PackagingType
FROM tbls_orders_del AS T2
WHERE OrderID <>
(SELECT Min(OrderID)
FROM tbls_orders_del AS T1
WHERE T2.CustomerID = T1.CustomerID AND T2.SalesRepID = T1.SalesRepID AND T2.ShipperID
= T1.ShipperID AND T2.OrderDate = T1.OrderDate)
```

Result:

OrderID	CustomerID	OrderDate	RequiredDate	InvoiceAmount	PackagingType
1001	139	11/11/2020	11/21/2020	31	Box
1002	145	3/26/2021	4/5/2021	296	Plastic
1003	160	5/22/2022	6/1/2022	31	Cardboard

```
(3 row(s) returned)
```

Step 2: Run the DELETE statement

Code:

```
DELETE  tbls_orders_del
FROM tbls_orders_del AS T2
WHERE OrderID <>
(SELECT Min(OrderID)
FROM tbls_orders_del AS T1
WHERE T2.CustomerID = T1.CustomerID AND T2.SalesRepID = T1.SalesRepID AND T2.ShipperID
= T1.ShipperID AND T2.OrderDate = T1.OrderDate)
```

Result:

```
(3 row(s) affected
```

258. Use SELECT INTO to back up records before deleting them

Create a temporary table to back up customers' orders before deleting them

Discussion:

In this example, we delete records from the tbls_orders_del table but just in case we need these records later on, we back them up on the fly in a new table using the SELECT INTO statement. Alternatively, we can append the deleted records in a historical table using the INSERT INTO statement.

Code:

```
SELECT * INTO TempTable1
FROM tbls_orders_del
WHERE OrderDate
BETWEEN #2022/8/15# AND #2022/9/15#
```

Result:

```
(17 row(s) affected)
```

Code:

```
DELETE
FROM tbls_orders_del
WHERE OrderDate
BETWEEN #2022/8/15# AND #2022/9/15#
```

Result:

```
(17 row(s) affected)
```

259. Delete records in a table based on the values in a different table

Delete records in tbls_orders_del table using criteria from the Customers table

Discussion:

This time, we have a request from management to delete all orders in the city of Los Angeles for a customer whose last name is "Orlando". The problem is we do not have a city field or a last name field in the tbls_orders_del table. To achieve this task, we use a subquery to delete records in the tbls_orders_del table using criteria from the Customers table.

Step 1: Run a SELECT statement to uniquely identify and verify records for deletion.

Code:

```
SELECT OrderID, CustomerID, OrderDate, ShippedDate, InvoiceAmount
FROM tbls_orders_del
WHERE CustomerID IN
(SELECT CustomerID FROM Customers
WHERE city= 'Los Angeles' AND lastname = 'Orlando')
```

Result:

OrderID	CustomerID	OrderDate	ShippedDate	InvoiceAmount
202	153	4/8/2021	4/13/2021	184
215	153	8/3/2020	8/8/2020	326
237	153	5/15/2022	5/20/2022	161
414	153	3/20/2020	3/25/2020	213

```
(There are more records in the result set than the ones shown in this image)
(6 row(s) returned)
```

Step 2: Run the DELETE statement

Code:

```
DELETE
FROM tbls_orders_del
WHERE CustomerID IN
(SELECT CustomerID FROM Customers
WHERE city= 'Los Angeles' AND lastname = 'Orlando')
```

Result:

```
(6 row(s) affected)
```

260. Delete records in a table based on calculations performed in a different table

Delete Orders with total sales above $400

Discussion:

In this example, we delete orders with a grand total of more than $400. We do not have order totals in the tbls_orders_del table. We do not have order totals in any table, correctly from a database design perspective, since we can calculate them. In the JoinOrdersProducts table we do have the price and quantity for each product in each order. We will calculate the total amount per order in the JoinOrdersProducts table and then use these calculated amounts as criteria to delete orders from the tbls_orders_del table.

A sample dataset from the JoinOrdersProducts table appears below. Notice the pairs of OrderIDs and ProductIDs so that you know what product is included in what order. To be able to comply with the request of management, we first need to calculate order subtotals by multiplying unitprice*quantity. Once we have the order subtotals for each product in each order, then we calculate order totals, that is the amount sold for all products in each order. To do this, we use the SUM() function and the GROUP BY clause. Finally, since we only want order totals which exceed $400, we use the HAVING clause with "> 400" as the criterion. Please note that we use HAVING instead of WHERE since HAVING is applied after the records are grouped while WHERE is applied before any records are grouped.

Table JoinOrdersProducts

OrderID	ProductID	UnitPrice	Quantity	Discount
1	61	15	2	0.2
2	23	15	4	0.15
2	24	15	1	0.2
2	32	15	3	0
2	70	15	6	0.15

(There are more records in the result set than the ones shown in this image)
(2411 row(s) returned)

Step 1: Run a SELECT statement to uniquely identify and verify records for deletion.

```
SELECT OrderID, CustomerID, OrderDate, ShippedDate
FROM tbls_orders_del
WHERE OrderID IN(
SELECT Sum((unitprice * quantity) * (1-Discount)) AS TotalOrder
FROM JoinOrdersProducts
GROUP BY OrderID
HAVING Sum((unitprice * quantity) * (1-Discount)) > 400 )
```

Result:

OrderID	CustomerID	OrderDate	ShippedDate
446	28	12/14/2022	12/19/2022
473	160	1/4/2021	1/9/2021
477	121	10/31/2020	11/5/2020

(3 row(s) returned)

Step 2: Run the DELETE statement

```
DELETE
FROM tbls_orders_del
WHERE OrderID IN(
SELECT Sum((unitprice * quantity) * (1-Discount)) AS TotalOrder
FROM JoinOrdersProducts
GROUP BY OrderID
HAVING Sum((unitprice * quantity) * (1-Discount))  > 400 )
```

Result:

```
(3 row(s) affected)
```

DISCUSSION QUESTIONS

1. Can we undo the actions of delete statements if we delete the wrong records?
2. What is a good strategy to follow before we use a delete statement?
3. What is the role of cascade deletes in relational databases?
4. Is the Cascade Delete property related to a table or the relationship between two tables?
5. Why it is a good idea to keep cascade deletes off and use them only when needed?
6. Provide a business example in which it makes sense to use cascade deletes.
7. If we have duplicate records in a table, how can we delete the earliest or latest ones?
8. How can we delete all duplicate records in a table using a single SQL statement?
9. What SQL command can we use to backup records in a different table before we delete them from the current one?
10. How can we delete records in a table using criteria from a different table?

HANDS-ON EXERCISES

Case 1

For each of the questions in this case create a new query in SQL view and name it as per the instructions in each question.

1. The inventory people want you to delete from the table tble_products_del the product "Dried Blueberries". Create a new query that satisfies the department's request and save it as Deletes_Case1_Q1.

Your result should look like:

```
(1 row(s) affected)
```

2. Now, the inventory people need you to delete from the tble_products_del table all the products with prices between $15 and $19. Create a new query that satisfies the department's request and save it as Deletes_Case1_Q2.

Your result should look like:

```
(8 row(s) affected)
```

3. The inventory people are very happy with your work. Now, they want you to delete additional records from the tble_products_del table but they need a backup copy of it before they proceed. Create a new query that creates a backup copy of the tble_products_del table and save it as Deletes_Case1_Q3. Save the backup table as TempProductsDEL.

Your result should look like:

```
(61 row(s) affected)
```

4. The management of the company decided to suspend operations with suppliers from Dallas after a government directive for potential pollutants in their products. They want you to delete all the products in the tble_products_del table from suppliers in the city of Dallas. Create a new query that satisfies the management's request and save it as Deletes_Case1_Q4.

Your result should look like:

```
(4 row(s) affected)
```

5. Prices in the northeast went out of control and the management decided to replace the suppliers there with others from the southeast of the country. Create a new query that deletes all products in the tble_products_del table from suppliers in the states of NY and MA and save it as Deletes_Case1_Q5.

Your result should look like:
```
(54 row(s) affected)
```

Case 2

For each of the questions in this case create a new query in SQL view and name it as per the instructions in each question.

1. The sales department called in and said that the customer Lisa Zartons from Los Angeles does not exist, and they ask you to remove her orders from the tble_orders_del table. Create a new query that satisfies this request and save it as Deletes_Case2_Q1.

Your result should look like:
```
(9 row(s) affected)
```

2. The sales department sent us a message that the processed orders from the sales representative with ID=2 and shipping cost = 21 were a mistake and we need to delete them from the tble_orders_del table. Create a new query that satisfies the salespeople request and save it as Deletes_Case2_Q2.

Your result should look like:
```
(8 row(s) affected)
```

3. The salespeople want us to delete all orders with an order date before 12/31/2021 from the table tble_orders_del since they only clutter the database. Create a new query that satisfies the HR request and save it as Deletes_Case2_Q3.

Your result should look like:
```
(674 row(s) affected)
```

4. The sales manager called in and is asking us to delete all orders from tble_orders_del that were put in by sales reps from the city of Dallas. Create a new query that satisfies this request and save it as Deletes_Case2_Q4. HINT: You need to use a subquery to achieve this result.

Your result should look like:
```
(51 row(s) affected)
```

5. The shipping people are asking us to delete all orders from tble_orders_del placed between 1/1/2022 and 1/31/2022 through any shipping company in the city of Boston. Create a new query that satisfies this request and save it as Deletes_Case2_Q5.

Your result should look like:
```
(6 row(s) affected)
```

CHAPTER 27
JOINING DATA SETS

The power of joins is a hidden jewel in the world of analytics. Some professionals stay away from a comprehensive understanding of joins because they perceive them as being complicated; they are not! Practical applications of joins constitute the only way someone could convince me to use them. By the way, you are not learning joins for SQL. To work with data in Tableau, Power BI, Qlik, SAS, Cognos, Python, R, Machine Learning, and AutoML prediction models, data warehouses, Data Lakes, Lakehouses, and many other popular analytics tools and platforms, you must understand how they work and what exactly they produce. This is exactly what we do in this chapter.

In relational databases, we keep data in separate tables. We keep supplier information in the Suppliers table, customers in the Customer table, and orders in an Orders table. This is what we call the physical structure or design of the database. This is done so that normalization rules apply in the database to conduct our business transactions (orders, quotations, invoices). However, we are interested in the conceptual invocations in the relational database. That is, we would like to generate and send out information, such as invoices, in a way that makes sense to our customers and to us. In this respect, joins are links we establish among tables with the goal of retrieving related pieces of information in ways that make business sense.

In this chapter, we explore the use of inner joins, left joins, right joins, full joins, cross joins, natural joins, and self joins. Among them, inner joins are the ones most used in practice. Left joins are useful in certain business scenarios, while right joins can check the integrity of the database and identify orphaned records. The rest of them have specific applications, as we shall see shortly.

261. Inner Joins

Retrieve customers who have orders

Discussion:

In a one-to-many relationship between customers and orders, an inner join will list customers who have orders. If there are any customers without orders, they will not appear in the result set. If there are any orders without associated customers, they will not appear either. Only records from the two tables for which there are matching CustomerID PK-FK values will be returned.

Our supervisor asks for a list of customers who have placed at least one order. The Customers table might include people who have asked for quotations, leads, or other people that have not placed an order before. We need to retrieve customers who have orders. We achieve this result using an inner join.

Create a Query in Design View

Create a query in design view and add the Customers and Orders tables. There is a one-to-many relationship between Customers and Orders. Add the fields LastName and FirstName, from the Customers table and OrderDate and ShippingCost from the Orders table to the query.

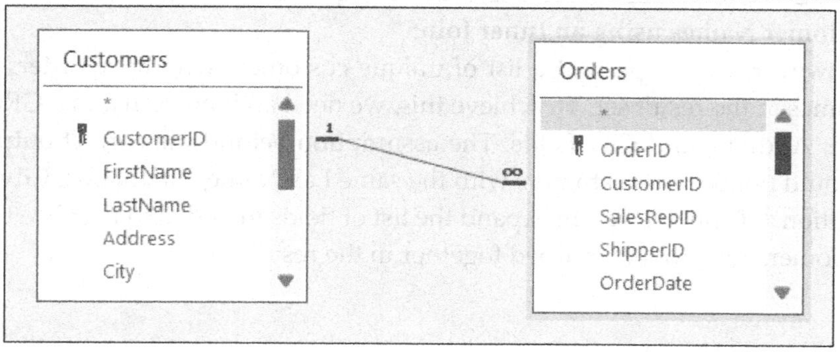

Right-click on the relationship line between Customers and Orders and click on "Join Properties". If you do not see the "Join Properties" dialog box, make sure you right click on the relationship line. The following dialog box comes up. By default, the database will join the two tables through an inner join which will output records from both tables which have a common CustomerID value, that is, an identical value of the CustomerID Primary Key in the Customers table and the CustomerID Foreign Key in the Orders table.

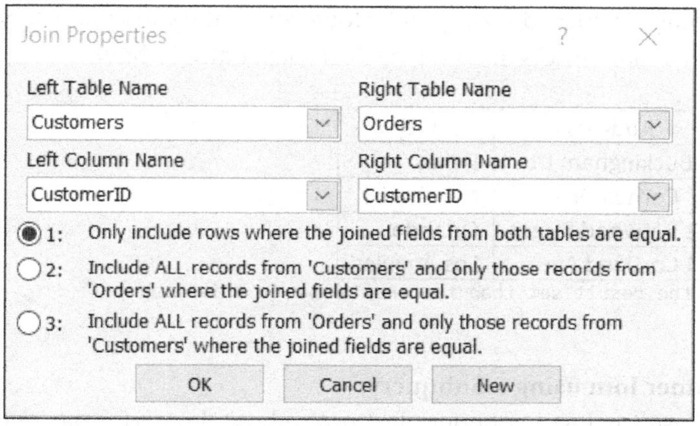

The SQL code for the inner join appears below:

Code:

```
SELECT FirstName, LastName, OrderDate, ShippingCost
FROM Customers
INNER JOIN Orders ON Customers.CustomerID = Orders.CustomerID
```

Result:

Notice that the database returned 1000 records. This is because there are 1000 cases in which the CustomerID in the Customers table has an associated CustomerID in the Orders table. This is happening because one customer can have multiple orders. That is why the same customer name appears multiple times. The eleven customers in the Customers table without a CustomerID FK value in the Orders table will not appear in the result set.

FirstName	LastName	OrderDate	ShippingCost
John	Demarco	6/10/2022	14
John	Demarco	6/9/2020	20
John	Demarco	11/7/2022	14
John	Demarco	3/23/2022	29

```
(There are more records in the result set than the ones shown in this image)
(1000 row(s) returned)
```

Retrieve Unique Customer Names using an Inner Join:

The initial request, however, was to present a list of unique customers who have orders. We do not need any repeated customer names in the result set. To achieve this, we need an inner join and a GROUP BY clause on the LastName, FirstName, Address, and City fields. The assumption behind the correct output of the GROUP BY clause is that there should not be two customers with the same LastName, FirstName, City, and Address values, which is a fair assumption. Of course, we can expand the list of fields included in the GROUP BY clause to ensure that two separate customers will not be grouped together in the result set.

Code:

```
SELECT FirstName, LastName, Address, City
FROM Customers
INNER JOIN Orders ON Customers.CustomerID = Orders.CustomerID
GROUP BY FirstName, LastName, Address, City
ORDER BY LastName
```

Result:

Notice the number of customers returned is only 190. However, in the Customers table, there are 201 customers. So, 11 customers have not had any orders at all for the historical data we have.

FirstName	LastName	Address	City
Nicholas	Ackerman	5 Buckingham Dr	Dallas
Pindar	Ames	23 Cornell Dr	New York
Thomas	Andersen	52 Betwood Street	Orlando
Joseph	Anderson	34 Cortland Ave	Los Angeles

```
(There are more records in the result set than the ones shown in this image)
(190 row(s) returned)
```

Achieve the result of an Inner Join using a Subquery:

We can achieve the same result using a subquery but notice how the performance goes down, that is we wait more for the query to execute. Also, the sort order is different.

Code:

```
SELECT FirstName, LastName, Address, City
FROM Customers
WHERE CustomerID
IN (SELECT CustomerID from Orders)
```

Result:

FirstName	LastName	Address	City
John	Demarco	11 Lark Street	New York
Mary	Demania	12 Madison Ave	New York
George	Demers	23 New Scotland Ave	New York
Phillip	Demetriou	22 Academy Road	New York

```
(There are more records in the result set than the ones shown in this image)
(190 row(s) returned)
```

262. Left Outer Joins

Retrieve Customers whether they have orders or not

Discussion:

In a one-to-many relationship between the tables Customers and Orders, a left join will output all customers from the Customers table and any related orders from the Orders table based on matches of the CustomerID field. If there are any customers without orders, they will still appear in the result set. If there are any orders without associated customers, they will not appear in the result set. For customers without orders, it will return blank values for fields from the Orders table such as the OrderDate and ShippingCost fields.

Our supervisor asks for a list of customers from the Customers table whether or not they have placed an order. The Customers table might include people who have asked for quotations, leads, or other people that have not placed an order before. We need to retrieve all customers with or without orders. We achieve this result using a LEFT join.

Create a Query in Design View

Create a new query in design view, add the tables Customers and Orders, and then add the fields LastName, and FirstName from the Customers table and OrderDate and ShippingCost from the Orders table.

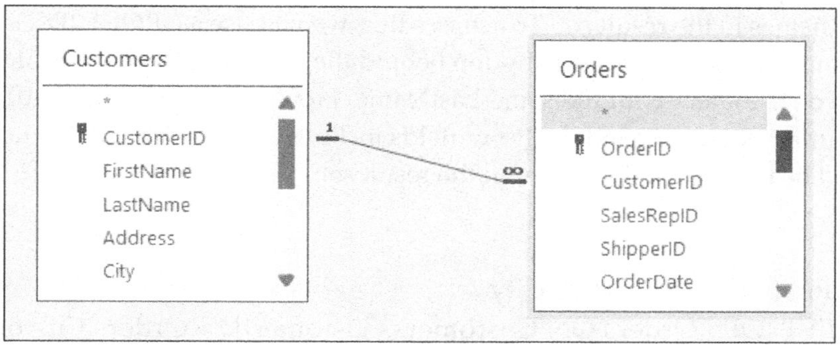

Right-click on the relationship line between Customers and Orders and click on "Join Properties". If you do not see the "Join Properties" dialog box, make sure you right click on the relationship line. Change the join type to "**Include ALL records from "Customers" and only those records from "Orders" where the joined fields are equal**."

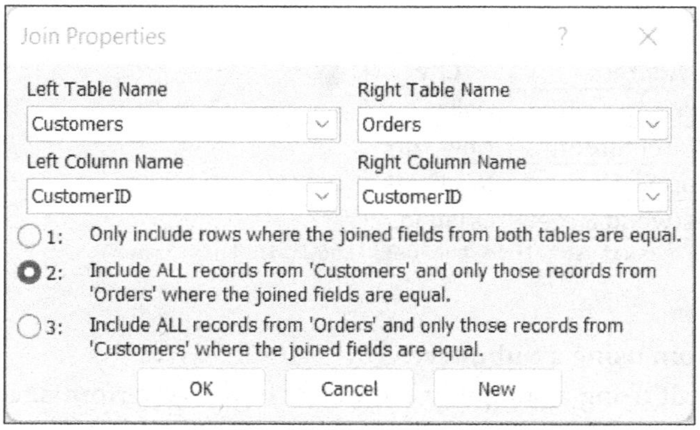

The SQL code for the left join appears below:

Code:

```
SELECT LastName, FirstName, OrderDate, ShippingCost
FROM Customers LEFT JOIN Orders ON Customers.CustomerID = Orders.CustomerID
```

Result:

Notice that the database returned 1011 records. This is because there are 1000 records for which the CustomerID in the Customers table has an associated CustomerID in the Orders table. In addition, there are 11 customers in the Customers table without an associated CustomerID in the Orders table, but they will still appear in the result set because this is a left join.

LastName	FirstName	OrderDate	ShippingCost
Demarco	John	6/10/2022	14
Demarco	John	6/9/2020	20
Demarco	John	11/7/2022	14
Demarco	John	3/23/2022	29

```
(There are more records in the result set than the ones shown in this image)
(1011 row(s) returned)
```

Retrieve Unique Customer Names using a Left Join:

The initial request was to present a list of unique customers who might have orders or not. We do not want to see repeated customer names in the result set. To achieve this, we will use a GROUP BY clause on the LastName, FirstName, Address, and City fields. The assumption behind the correct output of the GROUP BY clause is that there should not be two customers with the same LastName, FirstName, City, and Address values, which is a fair assumption. Of course, we can expand the list of fields included in the GROUP BY clause to ensure that two separate customers will be not grouped together in the result set.

Code:

```
SELECT LastName, FirstName, Address, City
FROM Customers LEFT JOIN Orders ON Customers.CustomerID = Orders.CustomerID
GROUP BY FirstName, LastName, Address, City
ORDER BY LastName
```

Result:

Notice that 201 customer records are included in the result set which is the total number of records in the Customers table:

LastName	FirstName	Address	City
Ackerman	Nicholas	5 Buckingham Dr	Dallas
Allen	Alfred	29 Water Street	New York
Ames	Pindar	23 Cornell Dr	New York
Andersen	Thomas	52 Betwood Street	Orlando

```
(There are more records in the result set than the ones shown in this image)
(201 row(s) returned)
```

Achieve the result of a Left Join using a Subquery:

We can achieve the same result using a subquery but notice how the performance goes down, that is we wait more for the query to execute. Also, the sort order is different.

Code:

```
SELECT FirstName, LastName, Address, City
FROM Customers
WHERE CustomerID
IN (SELECT CustomerID from Orders) OR CustomerID NOT IN (SELECT CustomerID from Orders)
```

Result:

FirstName	LastName	Address	City
John	Demarco	11 Lark Street	New York
Mary	Demania	12 Madison Ave	New York
George	Demers	23 New Scotland Ave	New York
Phillip	Demetriou	22 Academy Road	New York

```
(There are more records in the result set than the ones shown in this image)
(201 row(s) returned)
```

263. Right Outer Joins

Retrieve all orders including those without customers

Discussion:

In a one-to-many relationship between the tables Customers and Orders, a Right Join will output all orders from the Orders table and any related customers from the Customers table based on matches of the CustomerID field in both tables. If there are any orders without customers, they will still appear in the result set. If there are any customers without orders, they will not appear in the result set. For orders without associated customers, it will return blank values for fields from the Customers table such as the FirstName and LastName fields. If you see fields from the Customers table that are blank, these are orphaned records. This means that we have orders without customers, and the integrity of our database is compromised.

Our supervisor asks for a list of orders from the Orders table whether or not they have associated customers in the Customers table. The Orders table should only include orders which have associated customers in the Customers table but we never know and a RIGHT JOIN will display all orders with or without customers.

Create a Query in Design View

Create a query in design view and add the Customers and Orders tables. There is a one-to-many relationship between Customers and Orders. Add the fields OrderDate and ShippingCost from the Orders table and LastName and FirstName from the Customers table.

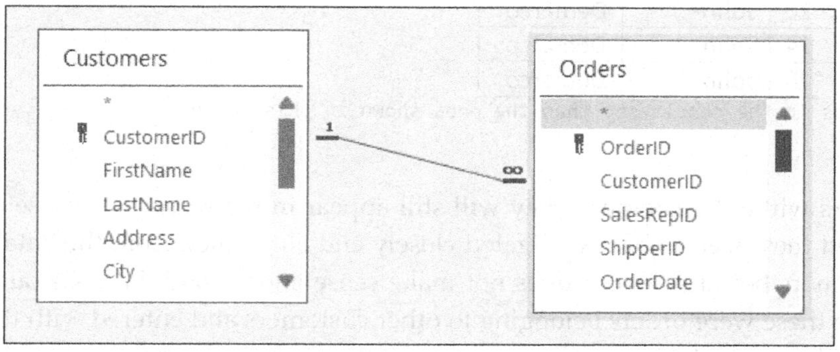

Right-click on the relationship line between Customers and Orders and click on "Join Properties". If you do not see the "Join Properties" dialog box, make sure you right click on the relationship line. The following dialog box comes up. Change the join type to **"Include ALL records from "Orders" and only those records from "Customers" where the joined fields are equal."**

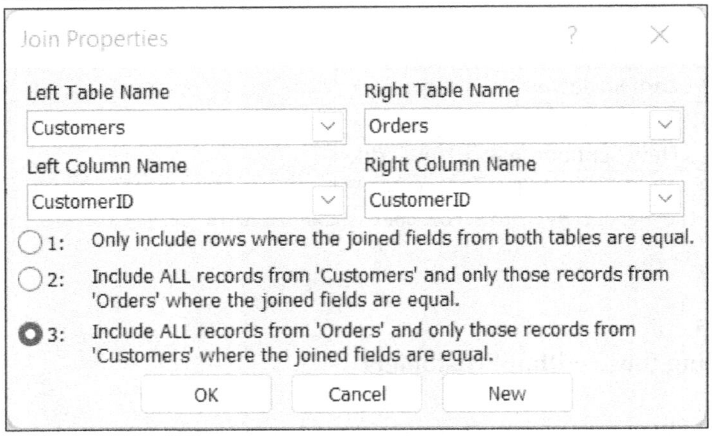

The SQL code for the Right JOIN appears below:

Code:

```
SELECT OrderDate, ShippingCost, FirstName, LastName
FROM Customers
RIGHT JOIN Orders ON Customers.CustomerID = Orders.CustomerID
```

Result:

Notice that the database returned 1000 records. This is because there are 1000 cases in which the CustomerID in the Orders table has an associated CustomerID in the Customers table. This is happening because one customer can have multiple orders. That is why the same customer name appears multiple times. The eleven customers in the Customers table without a CustomerID FK value in the Orders table will not appear in the result set.

OrderDate	ShippingCost	FirstName	LastName
6/10/2022	14	John	Demarco
6/9/2020	20	John	Demarco
11/7/2022	14	John	Demarco
3/23/2022	29	John	Demarco

```
(There are more records in the result set than the ones shown in this image)
(1000 row(s) returned)
```

If there are any orders without customers, they will still appear in the result set. These orders are considered orphaned records, and they need to be investigated closely and eliminated from the database. We cannot have orders without customers because first, it does not make sense and second, because our database integrity is compromised. Maybe these were orders belonging to other customers and entered with the wrong CustomerID as the foreign key while referential integrity was not on. If this is the case, change the value of the CustomerID field in the Orders table to associate them with existing customers in the Customers table. If we cannot find any customers to associate with the orphaned orders, we must delete them from the database.

Retrieve Unique Order records using a RIGHT JOIN:

The initial request was to present a list of unique orders which might have customers or not. To achieve this, we will use a GROUP BY clause on the OrderID, OrderDate, ShippingCost, LastName, and FirstName fields. The assumption behind the correct output of the GROUP BY clause is that there should not be two orders with the same OrderID, OrderDate, and ShippingCost fields which is a correct assumption since the OrderID by itself is more than enough as the Primary Key of the table (by default its values are unique).

Code:

```
SELECT OrderID, OrderDate, ShippingCost, FirstName, LastName
FROM Customers
RIGHT JOIN Orders ON Customers.CustomerID = Orders.CustomerID
GROUP BY OrderID, OrderDate, ShippingCost, LastName, FirstName
ORDER BY OrderID
```

Result:

Notice that the Orders table contains 1000 orders and also notice that the result of the query returned 1000 records. Also, if we scroll through the result set, we will not notice any customers with blank first or last names. The conclusion is that there are no orphaned records in the relationship, that is there are no orders without customers.

OrderID	OrderDate	ShippingCost	FirstName	LastName
1	11/11/2020	16	Joanne	Riegert
2	7/30/2020	19	Lisa	Read
3	7/4/2020	14	Gerald	Moore
4	12/19/2021	28	Catherine	Davis

(There are more records in the result set than the ones shown in this image)
(1000 row(s) returned)

Achieve the result of a RIGHT JOIN using a Subquery:

We can achieve the same result using a subquery but notice how the performance goes down, that is we wait more for the query to execute.

Code:

```
SELECT OrderID, OrderDate, ShippingCost
FROM Orders
WHERE CustomerID
IN (SELECT CustomerID from Customers) OR CustomerID NOT IN (SELECT CustomerID from Customers)
```

Result:

OrderID	OrderDate	ShippingCost
1	11/11/2020	16
2	7/30/2020	19
3	7/4/2020	14
4	12/19/2021	28

(There are more records in the result set than the ones shown in this image)
(1000 row(s) returned)

264. Full Outer Joins

List all customers and all orders

Discussion:

In a one-to-many relationship between the tables Customers and Orders, a full outer join will output all records from both tables. All customers from the Customers table and all orders from the Orders table will be listed regardless of any matching between the CustomerID PKs and FKs. Specifically, if some customers do not have orders or if some orders do not have associated customers, they will still be listed in the result set.

Our supervisor asks for a list of all customers from the Customers table and all orders from the Orders table. We achieve this result using a Full Outer Join.

Create a Query in Design View

Create a query in design view and add the Customers and Orders tables. There is a one-to-many relationship between Customers and Orders. Add the fields LastName and FirstName from the Customers table and OrderDate and ShippingCost from the Orders table.

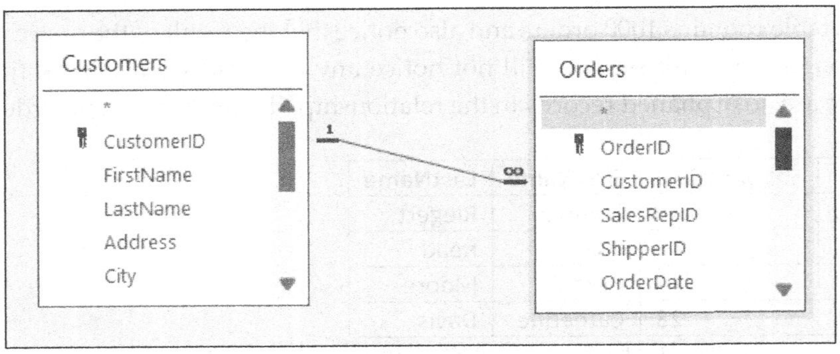

Right-click on the relationship line between Customers and Orders and click on "Join Properties". If you do not see the "Join Properties" dialog box, make sure you right click on the relationship line. The following dialog box comes up with an inner join by default. As you can see, there is no way to graphically set up a Full Outer Join, and consequently, we will use code.

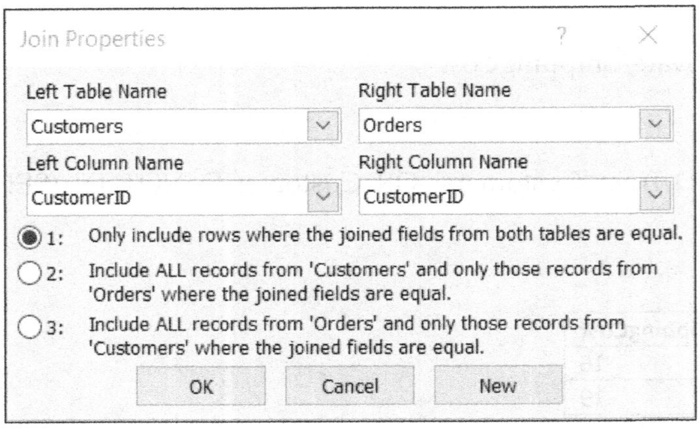

Emulate a Full Join using Union

To emulate a Full Join, we will use the UNION operator since Access does not support Full JOINs using code either. In this case we assume that there are no duplicate records and there are no orphaned records, that is there are no CustomerIDs in the Orders table without associated CustomerIDs in the Customers table. Both are true in our database.

```
SELECT LastName, FirstName, OrderDate, ShippingCost
FROM Customers
Left JOIN Orders
ON Customers.CustomerID = Orders.CustomerID
UNION
SELECT LastName, FirstName, OrderDate, ShippingCost
FROM Customers
```

Right JOIN Orders
ON Customers.CustomerID = Orders.CustomerID

Result:

LastName	FirstName	OrderDate	ShippingCost
Ackerman	Nicholas	8/5/2020	32
Ackerman	Nicholas	8/13/2020	23
Ackerman	Nicholas	7/29/2021	29
Ackerman	Nicholas	3/27/2022	25

```
(There are more records in the result set than the ones shown in this image)
(1011 row(s) returned)
```

The database returned 1011 records. 1000 records have been returned because there are 1000 orders with an associated CustomerID in the Customers table. An additional 11 records have been returned because there are eleven customers without an associated CustomerID in the Orders table. If there were any orders without associated customers, they too would appear in the result set.

265. Cross Joins

Derive the Cartesian product of two tables

Discussion:

A cross join, also called a Cartesian product, will join every record in one table with every record in the other table. In the database, the Suppliers table contains ten (10) records and the Products table contains seventy (70) records. A cross join between the two will result in seven hundred records. Each supplier will be joined to every single product which means there will be seventy rows per supplier. The syntax for a cross join is:

SELECT * from TABLE1, TABLE2

Code:

SELECT CompanyName, ContactName, City, ProductName, IngredientType FROM Suppliers, Products

Result:

Notice that the fields CompanyName, ContactName, and City come from the Suppliers table while the ProductName and IngredientType come from the Products table.

CompanyName	ContactName	City	ProductName	IngredientType
Home of Snacks	Pedro Adkins	Boston	Almonds Hickory Smoked	GMO-Free
American Foods	John Marrey	Boston	Almonds Hickory Smoked	GMO-Free
American Imports	Maria Hopkins	Boston	Almonds Hickory Smoked	GMO-Free
America's Greatest Snacks	Andrew Daves	New York	Almonds Hickory Smoked	GMO-Free

```
(There are more records in the result set than the ones shown in this image)
(700 row(s) returned)
```

266. Cross Joins with the WHERE clause

Create the Cartesian product of specific fields

Discussion:

In this example, we cross join the SalesReps and Suppliers tables but only for salesreps who reside in the city of Boston. Notice how we define the table name for each field in each table, since we have the same field name for City in both tables.

Code:

```
SELECT salesreps.LastName as SalesRepLastName, salesreps.FirstName as SalesRepFirstName,
salesreps.City as SalesRepCity, suppliers.CompanyName as SupplierCompanyName, suppliers.City
as SupplierCity
FROM
Suppliers, Salesreps
where salesreps.city = 'Boston'
```

Result:

SalesRepLastName	SalesRepFirstName	SalesRepCity	SupplierCompanyName	SupplierCity
Anderson	John	Boston	Home of Snacks	Boston
Teall	Mary	Boston	Home of Snacks	Boston
Spicer	George	Boston	Home of Snacks	Boston
Anderson	John	Boston	American Foods	Boston

(There are more records in the result set than the ones shown in this image)
(30 row(s) returned)

267. Natural Joins (emulated)

List suppliers and sales reps from the same city

Discussion:

A natural join will connect two tables on a common field which is different from the standard primary key – foreign key (PK, FK) combination. The standard way of joining the tables Customers and Orders is to use the CustomerID field which is the primary key in the Customers table and the foreign key in the Orders table.

In this example we want a list of sales representatives and suppliers who reside in the same city. Such a list is very useful because it will give us the "load" of sales reps in each city. That is, it will enable us to see how many suppliers are serviced by each sales rep in each city. Depending on the results, we might want to reallocate the workload of the sales reps to optimize their performance. In the code below notice how we define the table name for each field from each table, since we have the same field name in both tables. In addition, notice how we use the WHERE clause.

Code:

```
SELECT salesreps.LastName as salesrepsLastName, salesreps.City as SalesrepsCity,
suppliers.CompanyName as SuppliersCompanyName, suppliers.city as SuppliersCity
FROM Suppliers inner join Salesreps
ON Suppliers.City = SalesReps.City
```

Result:

salesrepsLastName	SalesrepsCity	SuppliersCompanyName	SuppliersCity
Anderson	Boston	American Imports	Boston
Anderson	Boston	American Foods	Boston
Anderson	Boston	Home of Snacks	Boston
Teall	Boston	American Imports	Boston

(There are more records in the result set than the ones shown in this image)
(38 row(s) returned)

268. Self Joins

What is a self join and how to use it

Discussion:

In all the examples to this point, we have joined two separate tables. In a self join, we join a table to itself. In this example, we will use the tbls_products_joins table twice to demonstrate how a self-join works.

The business rationale behind this example is that each product consists of multiple components, but it can also be a component to other products. Notice how a product can consist of one or two components, while others have no components. Notice the hierarchical relationship between products here. A product might have multiple components and one of its components might have subcomponents. For example, product D consists of products E and C. Product C in turn consists of products D and H. Product H consists of product E. At the same time, we see that products A and I do not have any subcomponents at all. To capture these relationships among rows in the same table we use self joins.

tbls_products_joins

ProductID	ProductName	Comp1	Comp2
1	A		
2	B		3
3	C	4	8
4	D	5	3
5	E	6	4
6	F	3	2
7	G		4
8	H		5
9	I		

tbls_products_joins

ProductID	ProductName	Comp1	Comp2
1	A		
2	B		3
3	C	4	8
4	D	5	3
5	E	6	4
6	F	3	2
7	G		4
8	H		5
9	I		

269. Self Joins with Inner Joins

Show products which have components

Discussion:

Even in self joins, it is important to select the correct join type such as inner join, left join, or right join to list the records we need. In this example, we use an inner join to connect the ProductID and Comp1 fields to see how many products have a first component. For this example, we present the design of the query to visualize the inner join between the two tbls_products_joins tables. Since in the code we cannot use the same table name twice, we employ p1 and p2 for the tbls_products_joins table. As you can see from the result set, only products which have a first component show up in the result set.

Design:

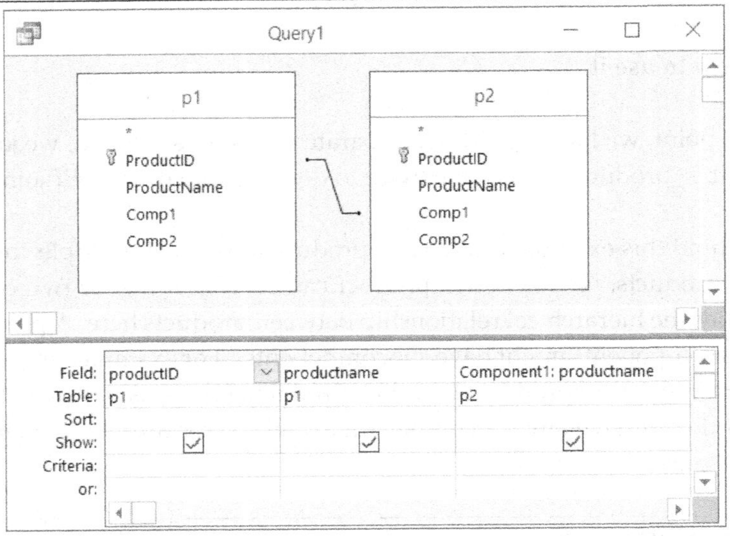

Code:

```
SELECT p1.productID, p1.productname, p2.productname as Component1
FROM  tbls_products_joins AS p1 inner JOIN
tbls_products_joins AS p2 ON p2.Comp1 = p1.ProductID
```

Result:

productID	productname	Component1
4	D	C
5	E	D
6	F	E
3	C	F

(4 row(s) returned)

270. Self Joins with Left Joins

Show all products whether they have components or not

Discussion:

In this example, we use a left join to connect the ProductID and Comp1 fields to list all products whether they have a first component or not. We present the design of the view to visualize the left join between the two tbls_products_joins tables. We still use the p1 and p2 names for the tbls_products_joins table. As you can see from the result set, all products will appear in the result set whether or not they have a first component.

Design

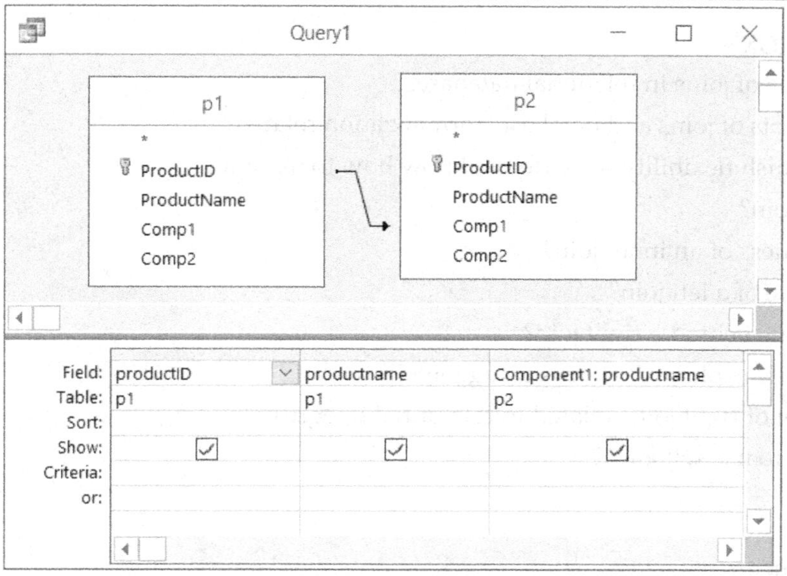

Code:

```
SELECT p1.productID, p1.productname, p2.productname as Component1
FROM  tbls_products_joins AS p1 left JOIN
tbls_products_joins AS p2 ON p2.Comp1 = p1.ProductID
```

Result:

productID	productname	Component1
1	A	
2	B	
3	C	F
4	D	C
5	E	D
6	F	E
7	G	
8	H	
9	I	

(9 row(s) returned)

DISCUSSION QUESTIONS

1. What is the purpose of joins in relational databases?
2. Why are the concepts of joins and database normalization related?
3. Why do we relinquish flexibility if we do not know how to use joins?
4. What is a natural join?
5. What is the usefulness of an inner join?
6. What is the purpose of a left join?
7. What is the rationale behind a right join?
8. How can we identify orphaned records using joins?
9. How is the concept of right joins related to referential integrity?
10. When do we need to use self joins?

HANDS-ON EXERCISES

Case 1

For each of the questions in this case create a new query in SQL view and name it as per the instructions in each question.

1. The sales director needs a list of sales representatives who have orders in the orders table. Create a new query that contains the FirstName, LastName, and Address fields and satisfies the director's request. Use a subquery to achieve this task. Save the query as Joins_Case1_Q1.

Your result should look like:

FirstName	LastName	Address
John	Anderson	32 Colonial Street
Mary	Teall	14 Highland Ave
George	Spicer	90 Lenox Ave
Phillip	Zensons	32 Camberland Street

```
(There are more records in the result set than the ones shown in this image)
(10 row(s) returned)
```

2. You need to achieve the same task as in question 1 but using a join this time. Create a new query and save it as Joins_Case1_Q2.

Your result should look like:

FirstName	LastName	Address
Andrew	Simmons	16 Greenway Street
George	Spicer	90 Lenox Ave
Gerald	Williams	192 Tampa Ave
Jason	Vanderback	22 Woodville Ave

```
(There are more records in the result set than the ones shown in this image)
(10 row(s) returned)
```

3. The sales director needs a report that lists sales reps and their respective order information. He wants the report to include all sales reps whether they have orders or not. Specifically, from the SalesReps table he needs to see the LastName, FirstName, and Address fields, while from the Orders table he would like to see the OrderDate and RequiredDate fields. Create a new query that satisfies the director's request and name it Joins_Case1_Q3.

Your result should look like:

LastName	FirstName	Address	OrderDate	RequiredDate
Anderson	John	32 Colonial Street	8/15/2021	8/25/2021
Anderson	John	32 Colonial Street	4/19/2021	4/29/2021
Anderson	John	32 Colonial Street	5/6/2020	5/16/2020
Anderson	John	32 Colonial Street	10/16/2021	10/26/2021

```
(There are more records in the result set than the ones shown in this image)
(1000 row(s) returned)
```

4. This time the sales director needs a report that will list all orders and their related salesreps information. Specifically, from the SalesReps table he needs to see the LastName, FirstName, and Address fields, while from the Orders table he would like to see the OrderDate and RequiredDate fields. Create a new query that satisfies the director's request and name it Joins_Case1_Q4.

Your result should look like:

LastName	FirstName	Address	OrderDate	RequiredDate
Anderson	John	32 Colonial Street	8/15/2021	8/25/2021
Anderson	John	32 Colonial Street	4/19/2021	4/29/2021
Anderson	John	32 Colonial Street	5/6/2020	5/16/2020
Anderson	John	32 Colonial Street	10/16/2021	10/26/2021

```
(There are more records in the result set than the ones shown in this image)
(1000 row(s) returned)
```

5. The sales director wants you to check if there are any orders without an associated sales rep. As a result, she wants a list of orphaned records in the Orders table, if there are any. You must use a join to achieve this task. Create a new query that satisfies the director's request and name it Joins_Case1_Q5.

Your result should look like:

```
(0 row(s) returned)
```

Case 2

For each of the questions in this case create a new query in SQL view and name it as per the instructions in each question.

1. The sales director needs a list of suppliers who have products in our inventory. Create a new query that includes the CompanyName, ContactName, and ContactTitle fields from the Suppliers table and satisfies the director's request. You need to use a join to achieve your goal and the supplier names must appear only once in the result set. Use the tbls_products_joins table to create the join. Save it as Joins_Case2_Q1.

Your result should look like:

Notice that although we have ten suppliers in the suppliers table, only seven appear in the result set.

CompanyName	ContactName	ContactTitle
American Foods	John Marrey	Purchasing Manager
American Imports	Maria Hopkins	Sales Manager
America's Greatest Snacks	Andrew Daves	Sales Manager
BayLine Farms	Lisa Anderson	Sales Representative

```
(There are more records in the result set than the ones shown in this image)
(7 row(s) returned)
```

2. The inventory director needs a list of suppliers and their respective product information. She wants to see suppliers whether or not they have products in the inventory. Create a new query that includes the CompanyName, ContactName, and ContactTitle fields from the Suppliers table and the ProductName, ProductPrice, and UnitsInStock fields from the tble_products_joins table. You need to use a join to achieve your goal and the result set should be sorted by ProductName ascending. Save the query as Joins_Case2_Q2. Notice that there are three suppliers with no related product information.

Your result should look like:

CompanyName	ContactName	ContactTitle	ProductName	ProductPrice	UnitsInStock
Old York Foods	Julia Ford	Sales Manager			
Nature's Food	Tony Lebrant	Purchasing Director			
Cape Cod Snacks	George Casey	Accounting Manager			
Home of Snacks	Pedro Adkins	Sales Manager	Almonds, Hickory Smoked	35	40
Home of Snacks	Pedro Adkins	Sales Manager	Almonds, Roasted and Salted	22	32
BayLine Farms	Lisa Anderson	Sales Representative	Apple Cinnamon Raisin Cookies	27	15

```
(There are more records in the result set than the ones shown in this image)
(52 row(s) returned)
```

3. The inventory director got word that there is a discrepancy in the tble_products_joins table. Specifically, she was told that some products do not have associated supplier information making replenishing impossible. Consequently, the director is asking for a report that will list the CompanyName, ContactName, and ContactTitle fields from the Suppliers table and the ProductName, ProductUnitPrice, and UnitsInStock fields from the tble_Products_Joins table. She needs to see all product information whether or not they have an associated supplier. You need to use a join to achieve your goal and the result set should be sorted by CompanyName ascending. Save the query as Joins_Case2_Q3. Notice there are four products without associated supplier information.

Your result should look like:

CompanyName	ContactName	ContactTitle	ProductName	ProductPrice	UnitsInStock
			Chunky Pretzels	22	43
			Chocolate Coconut Bar	26	37
			Cappuccino Almonds	35	32
			Chocolate Covered Apples	37	42
American Foods	John Marrey	Purchasing Manager	Chocolate Raspberries	29	39
American Foods	John Marrey	Purchasing Manager	Chocolate Fudge	41	31
American Foods	John Marrey	Purchasing Manager	Chocolate Blueberries	24	28
American Foods	John Marrey	Purchasing Manager	Chocolate Almonds	25	21

```
(There are more records in the result set than the ones shown in this image)
(53 row(s) returned)
```

4. There are four products in the tble_products_joins table without associated supplier information in the Suppliers table. There are two logical possibilities: Some of the four products have a SupplierID value that does not exist in the Supplier table or some of the four products have a NULL value in their SupplierID field, or both. Your task is to identify the products with a SupplierID value which does not exist in the SupplierID field in the Suppliers table. Use a subquery to achieve your result. Create a new query and save it as Joins_Case2_Q4a.

Your result should look like:

ProductName	SupplierID	ProductPrice	UnitsInStock	ReorderLevel
Cappuccino Almonds	11	35	32	30
Chocolate Coconut Bar	11	26	37	45

```
(2 row(s) returned)
```

Your task now is to identify the products in the tble_products_joins table which have a NULL value in their SupplierID field. Create a new query and save it as Joins_Case2_Q4b.

Your result should look like:

ProductName	SupplierID	ProductPrice	UnitsInStock	ReorderLevel
Chocolate Covered Apples		37	42	40
Chunky Pretzels		22	43	45

(2 row(s) returned)

5. Continuing from question 4, your task is to create a list of products in the tble_products_joins table that do not have an associated supplier in the Suppliers table. It does not matter if they have a NULL value or a specific value in their SupplierID field. Create a new query that includes the fields ProductName, SupplierID, ProductPrice, and QuantityPerUnit, and save it as Joins_Case2_Q5. HINT: Specify the tble_Products_Joins.SupplierID field including the table name in the SQL statement because the same field exists in the Supplier table, and you might get an error from the database engine.

Your result should look like:

ProductName	SupplierID	ProductPrice	QuantityPerUnit
Cappuccino Almonds	11	35	30
Chocolate Covered Apples		37	35
Chunky Pretzels		22	30
Chocolate Coconut Bar	11	26	15

(4 row(s) returned)

CHAPTER 28
SUBQUERIES FOR DYNAMIC INFERENCES

A subquery is a query within a query. Subqueries are used to achieve results in a single step instead of using multiple queries. They are highly useful in manipulating records from multiple tables and providing intricate results. Specifically, they can search for records in a table using criteria from another table, identify records in a table with no related records in another table, find orphaned records, find duplicate records, create dynamic search lists, produce dynamic aggregations, update or delete records in one table using criteria from other tables, build cross tabulations, relate tables on fields other than the primary keys, create dynamic aggregations, and a multitude of other tasks. Subqueries must constitute fundamental knowledge for a data analyst or data scientist. Let us explore the above scenarios through practical examples.

271. Search for records in one table using criteria from another table

Discussion:
In this example, we use IN with two date functions to retrieve customers with orders in the fourth quarter of 2021. We are looking for records in the Customers table using criteria from the Orders table.

Code:
```
SELECT FirstName, LastName, Address, City, Zip
FROM Customers
WHERE CustomerID IN
(Select CustomerID FROM Orders WHERE
DatePart('q',[OrderDate]) = 4 AND Year(OrderDate)=2021)
```

Result:

FirstName	LastName	Address	City	Zip
Robert	Demaggio	34 Princeton Dr	New York	12110
Paul	Demarist	89 Mercer Street	New York	12110
Jim	Devito	102 Lexington Ave	New York	89890
David	Vanderback	91 Fifth Ave	New York	89890

```
(There are more records in the result set than the ones shown in this image)
(60 row(s) returned)
```

272. Search for unrelated records in one table using criteria from another table

Discussion:
In this example, we retrieve customers without orders in the first six months of 2022. Notice how we use the NOT IN predicate.

Code:

```
SELECT FirstName, LastName, Address, City, Zip
FROM Customers
WHERE CustomerID NOT IN
(SELECT CustomerID
FROM tbls_orders
WHERE OrderDate BETWEEN #2022/1/1# AND #2022/6/30#)
```

Result:

FirstName	LastName	Address	City	Zip
John	Demarco	11 Lark Street	New York	12189
George	Demers	23 New Scotland Ave	New York	12189
Phillip	Demetriou	22 Academy Road	New York	12189
Andrew	Demichele	14 Glandel Ave	New York	12189

(There are more records in the result set than the ones shown in this image)
(86 row(s) returned)

273. Find orphaned records using a subquery

Find orders without customers

Discussion:

In this instance, we are looking for orders without customers, that is, orphaned records. If we find any orders without customers, we need to delete these orders from the database and check the referential integrity settings for the one-to-many relationship between Customers and Orders. We use the table tbls_Orders where I put some orphaned records for demonstration purposes. As you can see from the result set, three orphaned records are found.

Code:

```
SELECT OrderID, CustomerID, OrderDate, ShippingCost
FROM tbls_orders
WHERE CustomerID
NOT IN (SELECT CustomerID FROM Customers)
```

Result:

OrderID	CustomerID	OrderDate	ShippingCost
1500	250	1/20/2020	49
1501	251	11/18/2020	40
1502	252	2/5/2021	36

(3 row(s) returned)

274. Find duplicate records using a subquery

Find duplicate records in a table

Discussion:

Our goal is to identify all duplicate records in the tbls_Orders table. Keep in mind that these records have identical field values and identical primary keys values. So, they are exact duplicates. If you need to find duplicate records based on the values of one, two, or multiple fields, consult the chapter on Duplicate records. As you can see from the result set in this example, there are 11 duplicate records in this table.

Code:

```
SELECT *
FROM tbls_Orders WHERE OrderID IN(
SELECT OrderID
FROM tbls_Orders
GROUP BY OrderID
HAVING count(*)>1)
ORDER BY OrderID
```

Result:

OrderID	CustomerID	SalesRepID	ShipperID	OrderDate	RequiredDate	ShippedDate	ShippingCost
8	71	3	1	4/1/2022	4/16/2022	4/6/2022	36
8	71	3	1	4/1/2022	4/16/2022	4/6/2022	36
45	93	1	3	10/23/2020	11/7/2020	10/28/2020	46
45	93	1	3	10/23/2020	11/7/2020	10/28/2020	46

```
(There are more records in the result set than the ones shown in this image)
(11 row(s) returned)
```

275. Find unrelated records using a subquery

Find customers without any orders

Discussion:

This time, we will use NOT EXISTS to find customers who have not submitted any orders at all. Practically, we are looking for customers in the Customers table without any related orders in the Orders table. This is not a problem when it comes to database integrity. It is just a business fact. The "C" and "O" designations are just abbreviations for the Customers and Orders tables respectively. You can write the SQL statement without using these abbreviations.

Code:

```
SELECT FirstName, LastName, Address, City, State, Zip
FROM Customers C
WHERE NOT EXISTS (SELECT CustomerID FROM Orders O WHERE C.CustomerID =
O.CustomerID)
```

Result:

FirstName	LastName	Address	City	State	Zip
Erin	Erin	28 Karrie Terrace	Los Angeles	CA	94851
Allan	Cimo	24 Crestwood CT	New York	NY	45357
Kelly	Costa	45 Sixth Ave	Philadelphia	PA	56789
Arnold	Webster	53 Southern Blvd	Miami	FL	88987

```
(There are more records in the result set than the ones shown in this image)
(11 row(s) returned)
```

276. Create dynamic aggregations (working on one table)

Find products with prices above the average product price

Discussion:

In this example, we are looking for products with above average prices. We want the database to calculate the average price per product, compare every product price to the average price, and display only those products which exceed the average price. It looks like a lot for a single SQL statement, but it is possible. The essence of this SQL statement is in the WHERE clause where we ask the ProductPrice to be bigger than the average ProductPrice using the inequality predicate ">" and the aggregate function avg().

Code:

```
SELECT ProductName, ProductPrice
FROM Products
WHERE (ProductPrice) > (SELECT avg(ProductPrice) FROM Products)
ORDER BY ProductPrice DESC
```

Result:

ProductName	ProductPrice
Coffee biscuits	50
Pepper Cheese Box	50
Pizza croutons	49
Chocolate Chip Cookies	49

(There are more records in the result set than the ones shown in this image)
(30 row(s) returned)

277. Create dynamic aggregations with EXISTS (working with two tables)

List order information with shipped invoices above $500

Discussion:

This time, we need to retrieve orders with a total of over $500. Our problem however is that we need to list order information from the Orders table while making calculations in the JoinOrdersProducts table where we keep product prices and quantities. We can achieve this task using a subquery with EXISTS and GROUP BY, which will run very fast as well.

The crucial part of this piece of code is in the GROUP BY clause. We need to group by OrderID in the subquery since in the JoinOrdersProducts table, the same OrderID appears multiple times because there might be multiple products in the same order. However, we want our subquery to produce only one OrderID per order. In addition, we use the HAVING clause because we do not know beforehand what orders have a total of $500 or more. By using the HAVING clause, we are telling the database to first calculate the order totals through the sum() function, group the results by order, and then, apply the filter HAVING (Sum([unitprice]*[quantity]))>500). After all the above actions are complete, the WHERE clause will run.

Code:

```
SELECT OrderID, OrderDate, RequiredDate, ShippedDate, ShippingCost
FROM orders O
WHERE EXISTS
(SELECT OrderID, Sum([unitprice]*[quantity])
FROM JoinOrdersProducts P
WHERE O.OrderID = P.OrderID
GROUP BY orderid
HAVING Sum([unitprice]*[quantity]) > 500)
```

Result:

OrderID	OrderDate	RequiredDate	ShippedDate	ShippingCost
308	10/20/2020	10/30/2020	10/25/2020	21
354	4/28/2022	5/8/2022	5/3/2022	24
404	11/23/2020	12/3/2020	11/28/2020	16
609	5/9/2021	5/19/2021	5/14/2021	13
944	9/18/2020	9/28/2020	9/23/2020	24

(5 row(s) returned)

278. Return single values from calculations

Find the latest shipped order from the orders table

Discussion:

In this example, we return the latest order we shipped using the max() function.

Code:

```
SELECT OrderID, CustomerID, OrderDate, ShippingCost
FROM Orders
WHERE ShippedDate = (SELECT max(ShippedDate) FROM Orders)
```

Result:

OrderID	CustomerID	OrderDate	ShippingCost
156	103	12/26/2022	21

(1 row(s) returned)

279. Create temporary tables using subqueries, UNION, and SELECT INTO

Combine records from the customers and suppliers tables and create a temp table

Discussion:

In this case we generate a combined list of names and addresses from our customers and suppliers tables and we output the result in a new table. We use a subquery, UNION, and SELECT INTO to achieve this result. Notice how we use single quotes ('') in the SQL statement for the suppliers since in that table, there are no first and last name fields.

Code:

```
SELECT LastName, FirstName, Address, City, State, Zip INTO tempPeopleTable
FROM
(SELECT LastName, FirstName, Address, City, State, Zip
FROM Customers
UNION
SELECT ContactName, '' , Address, City, State, Zip
FROM Suppliers)
```

Result:

"You are about to paste 211 row(s) into a new table

280. Update records in one table using criteria from another table

Update product prices in the products table using criteria from the suppliers table

Discussion:

Management has decided to increase product prices from suppliers in Boston and Dallas due to transportation costs. Practically, we will update prices in the Products table using criteria from the Suppliers table. We will also use filtering criteria within the subquery statement.

Code:

```
UPDATE tbls_Products_upd
SET ProductPrice = ProductPrice * (1.2)
WHERE SupplierID IN
(SELECT SupplierID FROM Suppliers
WHERE City= 'Boston' or City = 'Dallas')
```

Result:

"You are about to update 36 row(s)."

281. Delete records in one table using criteria from another table

Delete orders from the Orders table using criteria from the Customers table

Discussion:

Our task is to delete orders from customers in the cities of Los Angeles and Orlando. In essence, the subquery will retrieve the CustomerIDs of these customers from the Customers table and then the main query will use these CustomerIDs to delete their orders in the tbls_Orders_del table. Always remember to run a SELECT statement first before deleting records.

Code:

```
DELETE
FROM tbls_Orders_del
WHERE CustomerID IN
(SELECT CustomerID FROM Customers
WHERE City = 'Orlando' OR City = 'Los Angeles')
```

Result:

"You are about to delete 218 row(s) from the specified table."

282. Relate two tables on fields other than the primary and foreign keys using EXISTS

Find customers who reside in the same city as that of sales representatives

Discussion:

Our supervisor asks for a list of customers who live in the same city as our sales representatives. So, if we have a sales representative in Orlando, our supervisor wants us to identify all the customers residing in that city. To achieve this, we create a relationship between the Customers and SalesReps tables based on the city field using the subquery below.

Code:

```
SELECT FirstName, LastName, Address, City, State, Zip
FROM Customers
WHERE exists
(SELECT *
FROM SalesReps
WHERE Customers.City = SalesReps.City)
```

Result:

FirstName	LastName	Address	City	State	Zip
John	Demarco	11 Lark Street	New York	NY	12189
Mary	Demania	12 Madison Ave	New York	NY	12189
George	Demers	23 New Scotland Ave	New York	NY	12189
Phillip	Demetriou	22 Academy Road	New York	NY	12189

```
(There are more records in the result set than the ones shown in this image)
(54 row(s) returned)
```

283. Crosstab calculations in one table using criteria from another table

Create a crosstab report that shows the number of orders by customer

Discussion:

We would like to create a report that lists the number of orders by customer name and year. The issue we face is that order data is in the Orders table and the customer first and last names are in the Customers table. We can dynamically connect the two tables using multiple subqueries equivalent to the columns we want to create for the Year field. Practically, in the code below, we calculate the number of orders from the Orders table as they relate to each customer in the Customers table.

Code:

```
SELECT LastName, FirstName,
(SELECT Count(*) FROM Orders O WHERE O.CustomerID = C.CustomerID AND (year(OrderDate) = 2020) ) AS [2020],
(SELECT Count(*) FROM Orders O WHERE O.CustomerID = C.CustomerID AND (year(OrderDate) = 2021) ) AS [2021],
(SELECT Count(*) FROM Orders O WHERE O.CustomerID = C.CustomerID AND (year(OrderDate) = 2022) ) AS [2022]
FROM Customers AS C
ORDER BY LastName
```

Result:

LastName	FirstName	2020	2021	2022
Ackerman	Nicholas	2	1	2
Allen	Alfred	0	0	0
Ames	Pindar	0	5	0
Andersen	Thomas	0	2	2
Anderson	Joseph	3	1	1

```
(There are more records in the result set than the ones shown in this image)
(201 row(s) returned)
```

284. Cross tabulate data using subqueries

Create a crosstab report of invoice amounts by payment type

Discussion:

In this example, we create a query that will display the sum of invoice amounts by payment type and year. It is practically a crosstab query but we use pure SQL code which will work with any relational database unlike the TRANSFORM and PIVOT commands which will work only with Access. Of course, we will have to use the respective conditional function that works with that database, for example case() instead of switch().

Code:

```
SELECT PaymentType,
SUM (SWITCH (year(OrderDate) = 2022, InvoiceAmount)) AS 2022,
SUM (SWITCH (year(OrderDate) = 2021, InvoiceAmount)) AS 2021,
SUM (SWITCH (year(OrderDate) = 2020, InvoiceAmount)) AS 2020
FROM Orders
GROUP BY PaymentType
```

Result:

PaymentType	2022	2021	2020
COD	7056	9066	12201
Credit	19965	21061	25638
CryptoCurrency	4161	3714	4901
Debit	8481	9529	8826
EBT	9319	12140	8988
Mobile	10008	9672	10498
Paper Check	6717	6850	5977

(7 row(s) returned)

DISCUSSION QUESTIONS

1. What is a subquery?
2. Name two scenarios in which we can use subqueries.
3. Why is it so useful from a business perspective to be able to use subqueries to find related records?
4. Can we use a WHERE clause in the main query and a WHERE clause in the subquery in the same SQL statement?
5. Can we use subqueries to identify orphaned records?
6. Using subqueries can we identify duplicate records or identical records?
7. What kind of questions are answered by subqueries which return single values?
8. Why subqueries are so useful with dynamic aggregations on one table?
9. What is the reason for using subqueries to create dynamic aggregations involving multiple tables?
10. What is the usefulness of subqueries in creating temporary tables? Why not use SELECT INTO only?

HANDS-ON EXERCISES

Case 1

For each of the questions in this case create a new query in SQL view and name it as per the instructions in each question.

1. The sales reps got word that there are orders in the tble_Orders table without associated salespeople in the SalesReps table. This results in lost commissions for them. They ask you to identify these orders so that they can get the appropriate commissions. Create a new query that includes the fields OrderID, SalesRepID, OrderDate, and ShippingCost from the tble_Orders table and satisfies the sales reps request. Save the query as Subqueries_Case1_Q1.

Your result should look like:

OrderID	SalesRepID	OrderDate	ShippingCost
957	11	9/4/2022	26
958	11	8/20/2021	21
959	11	6/1/2022	12
960	11	1/22/2021	25

(There are more records in the result set than the ones shown in this image)
(9 row(s) returned)

2. Management is asking for a list of suppliers with offices in the same cities as the ones where our sales representatives live. Create a new query that includes the fields CompanyName, ContactName, Address, City, and State from the Suppliers table and satisfies the management request. The result should show records for the state of MA only. Save the query as Subqueries_Case1_Q2.

Your result should look like:

CompanyName	ContactName	Address	City	State
Home of Snacks	Pedro Adkins	22 Taft Street	Boston	MA
American Foods	John Marrey	30 Maplewood Ave	Boston	MA
American Imports	Maria Hopkins	10 Silver Street	Boston	MA

```
(3 row(s) returned)
```

3. The sales director is back asking for a list of orders from the tble_orders table for which the shipping cost is greater than the average shipping cost of all the orders in this table. Create a new query that includes the fields OrderID, CustomerID, OrderDate, and ShippingCost from the tble_orders table and satisfies the sales director's request. Save the query as Subqueries_Case1_Q3.

Your result should look like:

OrderID	CustomerID	OrderDate	ShippingCost
4	165	12/19/2021	28
9	194	4/19/2021	26
11	3	6/7/2020	27
13	53	2/10/2022	32

```
(There are more records in the result set than the ones shown in this image)
(505 row(s) returned)
```

4. The sales director needs a similar report as in question 3, but one that only shows the number of orders for which the shipping cost is greater than the average shipping cost of all the orders in the tble_orders table. Create a new query that satisfies the sales director's request. Save the query as Subqueries_Case1_Q4.

Your result should look like:

NumberOfOrders
505

```
(1 row(s) returned)
```

5. The sales director is finally asking for a list of products with sales above $3,000 without taking into consideration any discounts. Create a query that includes the fields ProductName, ProductWeight, IngredientType, and ProductPrice from the products table and satisfies the sales director's request. Save the query as Subqueries_Case1_Q5. HINT: Quantities and prices for products sold are stored in the JoinOrdersProducts table.

Your result should look like:

ProductName	ProductWeight	IngredientType	ProductPrice
Chocolate Covered Apples	9 oz	Organic	37
Dark Chocolate Apricots	9 oz	All-Natural	46
Crispy Pears	7 oz	Organic	33
Chocolate Chunk Cookies	2 lb	Organic	48

```
(There are more records in the result set than the ones shown in this image)
(9 row(s) returned)
```

Case 2

For each of the questions in this case create a new query in SQL view and name it as per the instructions in each question.

1. The sales manager needs a list of sales reps from the SalesReps table with orders in the months of January, February, March, April, May, and June 2022 from the table tble_orders. Create a new query that includes the FirstName, LastName, Title, and Department fields from the SalesReps table and satisfies the sales manager request. Save the query as Subqueries_Case2_Q1.

Your result should look like:

FirstName	LastName	Title	Department
John	Anderson	Sales Reppresentative	Sales
Mary	Teall	Sales Director	Sales
George	Spicer	Account Manager	Sales
Phillip	Zensons	Sales Reppresentative	Sales

```
(There are more records in the result set than the ones shown in this image)
(10 row(s) returned)
```

2. The sales manager is back and this time she is asking for a list of salespeople from the SalesReps table without any orders in the month of June 2022 in the tble_orders table. Create a new query that includes the FirstName, LastName, Title, and Department fields from the SalesReps table and satisfies the sales manager request. Save the query as Subqueries_Case2_Q2.

Your result should look like:

FirstName	LastName	Title	Department
George	Spicer	Account Manager	Sales
Jim	Baker	Account Manager	Marketing

```
(2 row(s) returned)
```

3. The accounts receivable people need to know the details of the latest orders that were input in the system according to the order date in the tble_orders table. Create a new query that includes the fields OrderID, CustomerID, OrderDate, and ShippingCost from the tble_orders table and satisfies the accounting people request. Save the query as Subqueries_Case2_Q3.

Your result should look like:

OrderID	CustomerID	OrderDate	ShippingCost
573	65	12/29/2022	19
777	109	12/29/2022	29

```
(2 row(s) returned)
```

4. The inventory people need a list of orders for which the shipping cost is greater than the average shipping cost of all orders in the tble_orders table. Create a new query that includes the OrderID, CustomerID, OrderDate, and ShippingCost fields and satisfies the inventory people request. Sort results by OrderID ascending. Save the query as Subqueries_Case2_Q4.

Your result should look like:

OrderID	CustomerID	OrderDate	ShippingCost
4	165	12/19/2021	28
9	194	4/19/2021	26
11	3	6/7/2020	27
13	53	2/10/2022	32

```
(There are more records in the result set than the ones shown in this image)
(505 row(s) returned)
```

5. The sales manager needs a final report. She needs a crosstab report from the tble_Orders table that shows the number of orders by sales representative name (first name and last name must show in the result) for the years 2020, 2021, and 2022. You must use a pure SQL subquery (no PIVOT command) to obtain your result. Create a new query that satisfies the sales manager request and save it as Subqueries_Case2_Q5.

Your result should look like:

SalesRepName	2020	2021	2022
John Anderson	37	40	33
Mary Teall	33	30	29
George Spicer	38	35	39
Phillip Zensons	31	32	36

```
(There are more records in the result set than the ones shown in this image)
(10 row(s) returned)
```

CHAPTER 29
DATA TYPE CONVERSION FUNCTIONS

Type conversion functions constitute a must-have tool for the data analytics professional. A lot of your time is spent accessing and synthesizing data from multiple sources. In many cases you will have to convert attribute and measure data types from the source system(s) to an analytics platform such as a data warehouse or Data Lake. For example, you might have to convert a date from a text data type in Excel to a date data type in the destination database. This is where you will need the type conversion functions in this chapter.

The type conversion functions at our disposal are:

FUNCTION	RETURN TYPE	RANGE FOR *EXPRESSION* ARGUMENT
CBool	Boolean	Any valid **string** or numeric expression.
CByte	Byte	0 to 255.
CCur	Currency	-922,337,203,685,477.5808 to 922,337,203,685,477.5807.
CDate	Date	Any valid date expression.
CDbl	Double	-1.79769313486231E308 to -4.94065645841247E-324 for negative values; 4.94065645841247E-324 to 1.79769313486232E308 for positive values.
CDec	Decimal	+/-79,228,162,514,264,337,593,543,950,335 for zero-scaled numbers, that is, numbers with no decimal places. For numbers with 28 decimal places, the range is +/-7.9228162514264337593543950335. The smallest possible non-zero number is 0.0000000000000000000000000001.
CInt	Integer	-32,768 to 32,767; fractions are rounded.
CLng	Long	-2,147,483,648 to 2,147,483,647; fractions are rounded.
CSng	Single	-3.402823E38 to -1.401298E-45 for negative values; 1.401298E-45 to 3.402823E38 for positive values.
CStr	String	Returns for CStr depend on the *expression* argument.
CVar	Variant	Same range as **Double** for numerics. Same range as **String** for non-numerics.

Source:https://support.microsoft.com/en-us/office/type-conversion-functions-8ebb0e94-2d43-4975-bb13-87ac8d1a2202

We will start with the conversion functions CByte(), CInt(), CLng(), CSng(), and CDbl(). All of these functions relate to the number data type, and we use them for two purposes: First, to change numeric data from one format to another such as to change a numeric field from an integer to a double size. Second, to convert text data to numeric data. For instance, suppose a developer created a table and assigned the "Quantity" as a text field. If we later need to make calculations on this field, we first need to convert it into a numeric data type.

Let us assume we have a table field called "PartWeight": Although the data type is number, you can see from the figure below that we have various choices for its size. Shifting dynamically between these choices of Byte, Integer, Long Integer, Single, Double, or Decimal is exactly the job for conversion functions like CByte(), CInt(), CLng(), CSng(), and CDbl().

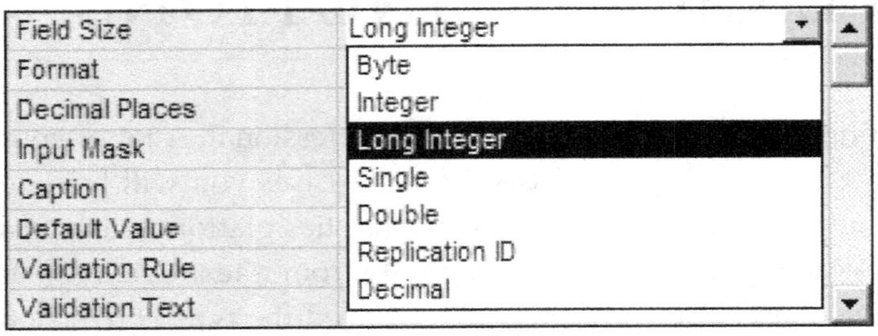

285. The CByte() function

Convert numbers to the size of a byte

Discussion:

The CByte() function will convert any numbers, such as those with decimals, to a number between 0 and 255, which is one byte according to extended ASCII. Let us suppose we have a field or a number that we want to convert to a byte.

Code:

```
SELECT cbyte(245.2346) as Number_Byte
```

Result:

Number_Byte
245

(1 row(s) returned)

If we try to use cbyte() on a number bigger than 255, we get an overflow error, and the conversion is not possible.

Code:

```
SELECT cbyte(289.2346) as Number_Byte
```

Result:

"overflow"

Finally, we can dynamically use the cbyte() function on a column without affecting the table design as per the code below:

Code:

```
SELECT cbyte(unitprice) as ByteNumber
FROM JoinOrdersProducts
```

Result:

ByteNumber
15
15
15
15

(There are more records in the result set than the ones shown in this image)
(2411 row(s) returned)

286. The CInt() function

Convert numbers to an integer size

Discussion:

An integer size will hold numbers between -32,768 to 32,767 with no decimals. Consequently, if we want to convert the number 3900.2345 to an integer value, we can write:

Code:

```
SELECT cint(3900.2345) as Number_Integer
```

Result:

Number_Integer
3900

(1 row(s) returned)

287. The CLng() function

Convert expressions to long integer numbers

Discussion:

A long integer size will hold numbers between -2,147,483,648 to 2,147,483,647 with no decimals. If we want to convert the number 50,234.2345 to a long integer value, we will write clng(50234.2345). Notice that we cannot convert to a simple integer in this case since this number exceeds the integer's capabilities.

Code:

```
SELECT clng(50234.2345) as Number_Long
```

Result:

Number_Long
50234

(1 row(s) returned)

288. The CSng() and CDbl() functions

Convert numbers to Single or Double sizes

Discussion:

We can use the Single and Double number sizes when working with high precision floating numbers. Both single and double sizes are high precision field sizes, and we can store a lot of detail using them. Specifically, we can use the Single size for floating values between -3.4 x 10^{38} and +3.4 x 10^{38}. Single number field sizes can have up to 7 digits. We can use the double size for floating values between -1.797 x 10^{308} and +1.797 x 10^{308}. Double number field sizes can have up to 15 digits. Let us go through two examples working with the number 1500345.45349345. Notice this number has 15 digits in total.

If we convert it to a single number, we write:

Code:
```
SELECT csng(1500345.45349345) as Number_Single
```

Result:
Notice the resulting number contains only 7 digits, and the decimal has been rounded to one digit.

Number_Single
1500345.5

```
(There are more records in the result set than the ones shown in this image)
(1 row(s) returned)
```

If we convert the same number to a double, we write:

Code:
```
SELECT cdbl(1500345.45349345) as Number_Double
```

Result:
As you can see, when converting to a double number, we do not lose any of the digits either before or after the decimal since double numbers can hold up to fifteen digits.

Number_Double
1500345.45349345

```
(1 row(s) returned)
```

289. The CBool() function

Compare customer first and last name values
Discussion:
The cbool() function will return a true or false value. To demonstrate its usefulness, let us assume that a coworker comes to our office and says that something is wrong with the mailing labels they are producing. On certain occasions, the last and first name fields print the same. Obviously, someone typed in the same value as both first and last name in the database. We can use the cbool() function to find the records for which this occurs.

Code:
```
SELECT CustomerID, cbool([LastName]=[FirstName]) As TrueFalse
FROM customers
```

Result:
Whenever you see 0, it means the result is false, or, in other words, the last and first names have different values since you checked for equality. If you see -1, the result is true, which means that the first and last names have identical values. As you scroll through the records, you will notice that you get a -1 for CustomerID = 19.

CustomerID	TrueFalse
1	0
2	0
3	0
4	0

(There are more records in the result set than the ones shown in this image)
(201 row(s) returned)

This is a cause for investigation. For record 19, the last and first names are the same!

290. The cCur() function

Convert numbers to currency

Discussion:

If we open the JoinOrdersProducts table in design view, we notice that the UnitPrice and Quantity fields are of the number data type and integer size. We want to create a report that shows their multiplication as currency to show order subtotals. We accomplish this task by using the ccur() conversion function. Notice the dollar sign in front of the OrderSubtotal values.

Code:

```
SELECT OrderID, CCur(UnitPrice*Quantity) as OrderSubtotal
FROM JoinOrdersProducts
```

Result:

OrderID	OrderSubtotal
1	$30.00
2	$60.00
2	$15.00
2	$45.00

(There are more records in the result set than the ones shown in this image)
(2411 row(s) returned)

291. The CDate() function

Convert text to dates

Discussion:

We might have date data in text format like "November 21 2022" or "21 November 2022". To convert these text values to a date format and store them in a date field, we use the cdate() function.

Code:

```
SELECT cdate("November 21 2022") as DateType
```

You will achieve the same result if you use:

```
SELECT cdate("21 November 2022") as DateType
```

Result:

DateType
11/21/2022

(1 row(s) returned)

Of course, we can combine the cdate() conversion function with a date function like year() to concurrently extract the year out of our text data.

Code:
SELECT year(cdate("November 21 2022")) as FormattedDate

Result:

FormattedDate
2022

```
(There are more records in the result set than the ones shown in this image)
(1 row(s) returned)
```

292. The CStr() function

Convert numeric data to text

Discussion:

Let us assume that the previous DBA used the number data type to store zip codes. Zip codes as numbers might behave oddly in situations where we need to concatenate them, for example with address numbers. The best way is to convert them to text before proceeding with any concatenation. In any case, we only use the number data type for a field if we expect to perform calculations with this field. Consequently, zip codes or phone numbers should be text fields. The cstr() function will convert anything to a string (text) value.

Code:
SELECT cstr(12456) As ZipCode

Result:

ZipCode
12456

```
(There are more records in the result set than the ones shown in this image)
(1 row(s) returned)
```

DISCUSSION QUESTIONS

1. Why is it a good idea to use type conversion functions?
2. Why is it better to change a field data type using conversion functions rather than forcing a change in the design of the table?
3. How many digits can we have in a single number and how many in a double number?
4. Can we use type conversion functions to change text data to numeric data and vice versa?
5. What will happen if we try to convert a number bigger than 255 using the Cbyte() function?
6. What is the range of numbers an integer data type can hold?
7. What type conversion function do we use to return a true or false value?
8. What is the type conversion function we use to designate data as currency?
9. What is the usefulness of the Cstr() type conversion function?
10. If we have imported date data from a flat file and we want to convert it to a date data type what function do we use?

HANDS-ON EXERCISES

Case 1

For each of the questions in this case create a new query in SQL view and name it as per the instructions in each question.

1. The inventory people want the UnitPrice field values to appear without decimals. They do not want any changes in the original data in the tble_Orders_Conversion table. Create a new query that contains the SalesRepName, OrderDate, UnitPrice, and Quantity fields from the tble_Orders_Conversion table as well as a new field named NewUnitPrice that should be an integer. Save the query as DataTypeConversions_Case1_Q1.

Your result should look like:

SalesRepName	OrderDate	Quantity	UnitPrice	NewUnitPrice
Anderson	May 21 2023	6	15.015	15
Anderson	May 21 2023	4	15.09	15
Anderson	May 21 2023	6	8.02	8
Anderson	May 21 2023	1	15.02	15

```
(There are more records in the result set than the ones shown in this image)
(20 row(s) returned)
```

2. The marketing people need to send out letters to customers and they need to time those letters based on the values in the order date field. However, when they try to use the dates in the order date field they have trouble because the values are in plain text. Create a new query that contains the fields SalesRepName, OrderDate, UnitPrice, Quantity, and a new field named NewOrderDate from the tble_Orders_Conversion table that should be a date value in the format mm/dd/yyyy. Save the query as DataTypeConversions_Case1_Q2.

Your result should look like:

SalesRepName	OrderDate	UnitPrice	Quantity	NewOrderDate
Anderson	May 21 2023	15.015	6	5/21/2023
Anderson	May 21 2023	15.09	4	5/21/2023
Anderson	May 21 2023	8.02	6	5/21/2023
Anderson	May 21 2023	15.02	1	5/21/2023

(There are more records in the result set than the ones shown in this image)
(20 row(s) returned)

3. The marketing people need to retrieve the year value out of the order date field because they want to perform calculations based on year totals. Create a new query that contains the same fields as in question 2 and modify the NewOrderDate field to show only the year. Save the query as DataTypeConversions_Case1_Q3.

Your result should look like:

SalesRepName	OrderDate	UnitPrice	Quantity	NewOrderDate
Anderson	May 21 2021	15.015	6	2023
Anderson	May 21 2021	15.09	4	2023
Anderson	May 21 2021	8.02	6	2023
Anderson	May 21 2021	15.02	1	2023

(There are more records in the result set than the ones shown in this image)
(20 row(s) returned)

4. The inventory people need a list of customers that shows who pays above $40 for shipping cost and who below 40. Create a new query that contains the FirstName, LastName, State, and another field named "SC40" that shows the category in which the customer belongs. Save the query as DataTypeConversions_Case1_Q4.

Your result should look like:

FirstName	LastName	State	SC40
July	Grady	CA	0
Scott	Mahoney	FL	-1
Luis	Trindan	NY	-1
Luis	Trindan	NY	-1

(There are more records in the result set than the ones shown in this image)
(20 row(s) returned)

5. The salespeople want to calculate order totals for customers. However, when they try to multiply the UnitPrice field with the Quantity field they get errors. Convert the UnitPrice and Quantity fields into appropriate formats so that the salespeople can perform their calculations. Create a new query that contains the FirstName, LastName, UnitPrice, and Quantity fields from the tble_Orders_Conversion table as well as two fields named NewUnitPrice and NewQuantity on which the appropriate conversion functions are used. Name the query DataTypeConversions_Case1_Q5.

Your result should look like:

FirstName	LastName	UnitPrice	NewUnitPrice	Quantity	NewQuantity
July	Grady	15.015	$15.02	6	6
Scott	Mahoney	15.09	$15.09	4	4
Luis	Trindan	8.02	$8.02	6	6
Luis	Trindan	15.02	$15.02	1	1

```
(There are more records in the result set than the ones shown in this image)
(20 row(s) returned)
```

Case 2

For each of the questions in this case create a new query in SQL view and name it as per the instructions in each question.

1. The salespeople need to change the ProductUnitPrice field to extend new prices to customers but they have trouble doing those changes because the ProductUnitPrice field is of the text data type. They also need to make the decimal points disappear from this field. Create a new query that contains the ProductName, QuantityPerUnit, CatalogLastUpdated, and a new field called NewPrice of the integer data type from the tble_Products_Conversion table that satisfies the salespeople request. Save the query as DataTypeConversions_Case2_Q1.

Your result should look like:

ProductName	QuantityPerUnit	CatalogLastUpdated	NewPrice
Almonds, Hickory Smoked - 12 oz. Bag	12.00	November 13 2024	35
Almonds, Roasted and Salted - 18 oz. Bag	12.00	December 10 2024	22
Banana Chips - 20 oz. Bag	12.00	January 14 2024	23
Berry Cherry in 8 oz. Bag	15.00	January 18 2024	30

```
(There are more records in the result set than the ones shown in this image)
(15 row(s) returned)
```

2. The salespeople need to create a report using the CatalogLastUpdated date field but they have difficulty since the field data type is text. Create a new query that contains the ProductName, QuantityPerUnit, and a new field called NewCatalogLastUpdated from the tble_Products_Conversion table that satisfies the salespeople request. The CatalogLastUpdated field should have the format mm/dd/yyyy. Save the query as DataTypeConversions_Case2_Q2.

Your result should look like:

ProductName	QuantityPerUnit	NewCatalogLastUpdated
Almonds, Hickory Smoked - 12 oz. Bag	12.00	11/13/2024
Almonds, Roasted and Salted - 18 oz. Bag	12.00	12/10/2024
Banana Chips - 20 oz. Bag	12.00	1/14/2024
Berry Cherry in 8 oz. Bag	15.00	1/18/2024

```
(There are more records in the result set than the ones shown in this image)
(15 row(s) returned)
```

3. Continuing with the request in question 2 the salespeople need to extract the year out of the CatalogLastUpdated field. Create a new query with the same fields as in question 2 from the tble_Products_Conversion table. Convert the CatalogLastUpdated field to a date field as you did in question 2 and then extract the year out of this field. Save the query as DataTypeConversions_Case2_Q3.

Your result should look like:

ProductName	QuantityPerUnit	NewCatalogLastUpdated
Almonds, Hickory Smoked - 12 oz. Bag	12.00	2024
Almonds, Roasted and Salted - 18 oz. Bag	12.00	2024
Banana Chips - 20 oz. Bag	12.00	2024
Berry Cherry in 8 oz. Bag	15.00	2024

(There are more records in the result set than the ones shown in this image)
(15 row(s) returned)

4. The inventory people need a report that shows which products require replenishment and which ones do not. Specifically, they need to know for which products the sum of the quantity per unit and the units on order is less than the reorder level and for which products is greater. Create a new query that contains the ProductName and another field, named ProductCategory, that shows the category in which the product belongs according to the criteria above. Save the query as DataTypeConversions_Case2_Q4.

Your result should look like:

ProductName	ProductCategory
Almonds, Hickory Smoked - 12 oz. Bag	0
Almonds, Roasted and Salted - 18 oz. Bag	0
Banana Chips - 20 oz. Bag	0
Berry Cherry in 8 oz. Bag	0

(There are more records in the result set than the ones shown in this image)
(15 row(s) returned)

5. The salespeople need the ProductUnitPrice field to be of the currency data type and the UnitsInStock and UnitsOnOrder of the integer data type. Create a new query that contains the ProductName field and three new fields one for the price named NewPrice, one for the units in stock named NewUnitsInStock, and one for the units on order named NewUnitsOnOrder from the tble_Products_Conversion table. Save the query as DataTypeConversions_Case2_Q5.

Your result should look like:

ProductName	NewPrice	NewUnitsInStock	NewUnitsOnOrder
Almonds, Hickory Smoked - 12 oz. Bag	$35.01	30	5
Almonds, Roasted and Salted - 18 oz. Bag	$22.02	15	0
Banana Chips - 20 oz. Bag	$23.02	25	0
Berry Cherry in 8 oz. Bag	$30.01	35	0

(There are more records in the result set than the ones shown in this image)
(15 row(s) returned)

CHAPTER 30 IMPUTING DATA

Business operational data such as customer orders, invoices, quotations, inventory levels, and shipping addresses contain missing values either by mistake or simply because the data was not available. It is a primary task for the data professional to eliminate or replace missing data in the dataset. The choice to eliminate the records with missing data is the easiest but comes with perils because all or some of the deleted observations might be critical for the development and validity of the business model we develop such as a Time Series Machine Learning Prediction Model. The second choice, to keep the rows with the missing values in the dataset dictates that we substitute the missing values with specific values. This is the process of data imputation, a data preprocessing technique, which we can implement using multiple way which we explore in this chapter.

In this chapter we work with the tbls_Impute table which contains null values in the fields PackagingType, UnitsInStock, QuotationAmount, QuantityPerUnit, and MaterialCost. The PackagingType is a text field and the rest of them are numeric fields.

293. Identify missing values in multiple columns in the dataset

Discussion:

In MS Access, there is no functionality like in Python, to look for missing values in all columns of the dataset at once. We need to look for them using criteria for every column in which we want to look for missing values. For text columns we use the IS NULL expression which looks for blank entries as well as the LIKE "" expression which looks for zero-length strings. For numeric columns we use the IS NULL expression.

Code:

```
SELECT  DataRowID, PackagingType, UnitsInStock, QuotationAmount, QuantityPerUnit,
MaterialCost
FROM tbls_Impute
WHERE PackagingType Is Null OR PackagingType LIKE "" OR UnitsInStock IS NULL OR
QuotationAmount IS NULL OR QuantityPerUnit IS NULL OR MaterialCost IS NULL
```

As you can see from the result set, we have multiple missing values in these columns. I have placed all the rows with the missing values at the top of the table dataset so that we can visualize them quickly and easily for the purposes of this chapter.

Result:

DataRowID	PackagingType	UnitsInStock	QuotationAmount	QuantityPerUnit	MaterialCost
2	Plastic			26	74
3	Plastic	38			
4			320		
5			260	30	
6	Bio-Plastic	24	280		81
7				32	81
8	Bio-Plastic	23			
9				35	
10	Cardboard	41	54		
11				26	89
12					
13	Box	38	277		
15	Box	49	303		
16		25	453	12	

(16 row(s) returned)

294. Count missing values in dataset columns

Discussion:

In this example, we count the number of missing values in each column. We need to define the columns in the code and I understand that this is a tedious process with respect to Python. Still, once you have written the code you can use it in seconds and you can manipulate the code and the results extremely fast. Notice how we check for both null values and zero-length strings in the column "PackagingType"

Code:

```
SELECT
sum(iif(PackagingType IS NULL, 1, 0)) AS PackagingType_Null,
sum(iif(PackagingType LIKE "", 1, 0)) AS PackagingType_ZeroLength,
sum(iif(UnitsInStock IS NULL, 1, 0)) AS UnitsInStock_Null,
sum(iif(QuotationAmount IS NULL, 1, 0)) AS QuotationAmount_Null,
sum(iif(QuantityPerUnit IS NULL, 1, 0)) AS QuantityPerUnit_Null,
sum(iif(MaterialCost IS NULL, 1, 0)) AS MaterialCost_Null
FROM tbls_Impute
```

Result:

Packaging Type_Null	PackagingType _ZeroLength	UnitsInStock _Null	QuotationAmount _Null	QuantityPerUnit _Null	MaterialCost _Null
5	2	7	7	8	10

(16 row(s) returned)

295. Impute columns with a constant

Discussion:

In the "PackagingType" column there are in total seven missing values. Five of them are null values and two of them are zero-length strings (""). All seven of them appear as blank values although they are of a different kind. All rows with blank values are at the top of the dataset so that you can easily locate them. In text columns, we must look for nulls and zero-length strings at the same time. In numeric columns we can only look for nulls or any other values that do not comply with the business requirements.

In the "PackagingType" column, the Rows with DataRowIDs of 4, 5, 9, 11, 16 contain null values. Rows with DataRowIDs of 7,12 contain zero-length strings.

Code to visualize missing values in the PackagingType field:

```
SELECT  DataRowID, PackagingType
FROM tbls_Impute
WHERE PackagingType Is Null OR PackagingType LIKE ""
```

Result:

DataRowID	PackagingType
4	
5	
7	
9	
11	
12	
16	

(7 row(s) returned)

Code to Replace Missing Values with a constant:

```
UPDATE tbls_Impute
SET PackagingType = 'Shrink film'
WHERE PackagingType Is Null OR PackagingType LIKE ""
```

Result:

(7 row(s) updated)

296. Impute with Random Values

Discussion:

In this example, we work on a column with numeric values. Most of the data preprocessing tasks in machine learning involve numbers. In the "UnitsInStock" column, the Rows with DataRowIDs of 2, 4, 5, 7, 9, 11, 12 contain null values.

Code to visualize missing values in the UnitsInStock field:

```
SELECT DataRowID, UnitsInStock
FROM tbls_Impute
WHERE UnitsInStock IS NULL
```

Result:

DataRowID	UnitsInStock
2	
4	
5	
7	
9	
11	
12	

```
7 row(s) returned)
```

Discussion on imputing with random values:
We want to impute with random numbers that make sense, for example, within the range of the max and min values in UnitsInStock. Let us identify the boundaries:

SELECT max(UnitsInStock) FROM tbls_Impute = 50
SELECT min(UnitsInStock) FROM tbls_Impute = 12

We will use the above boundaries but with the code below you have full freedom to assign your own custom boundaries for random number generation:
SYNTAX: int((MaxValue – MinValue + 1) * rnd(YourField) + MinValue)

Code to generate random numbers within two boundaries:

```
SELECT int((50 - 12 + 1) * rnd (DataRowID) + 12) As RandomUnitsInStock
FROM tbls_Impute
```

Result:
Random numbers are generated between the values of 12 and 50

Code to update the missing values with random numbers within two boundaries:

```
UPDATE tbls_Impute
SET UnitsInStock =   int((50 - 12 + 1) * rnd (DataRowID) + 12)
WHERE UnitsInStock IS NULL
```

Result:

```
(7 row(s) updated)
```

297. Impute with the Mean

Discussion:
In this example, we impute missing values in the QuotationAmount field using the mean (average) of the values in the column. The QuotationAmount values for DataRowIDs = 2, 3, 7, 8, 9, 11, 12 are null.

Code to visualize missing values in the QuotationAmount field:

```
SELECT DataRowID, QuotationAmount
FROM tbls_Impute
WHERE QuotationAmount IS NULL
```

Result:

DataRowID	QuotationAmount
2	
3	
7	
8	
9	
11	
12	

(7 row(s) returned)

Code to calculate the mean:

```
SELECT avg(QuotationAmount) AS Mean
FROM  tbls_Impute
```

Result:

Mean
277

Code to update the missing values with the mean:

```
UPDATE tbls_Impute
SET QuotationAmount =  277
WHERE QuotationAmount IS NULL
```

Result:

(7 row(s) updated)

298. Impute with Logical Rules

Discussion:

In this example, we use the swift() function to set logical rules for imputing missing values. The rows with DataRowIDs = 3, 4, 6, 8, 10, 12, 13, 15 contain missing values for the QuantityPerUnit field.

Code to visualize missing values in the QuantityPerUnit field:

```
SELECT DataRowID, QuantityPerUnit
FROM tbls_Impute
WHERE QuantityPerUnit IS NULL
```

Result:

DataRowID	QuantityPerUnit
3	
4	
6	
8	
10	
12	
13	
15	

(8 row(s) returned)

The business requirements are:

1. If the ContainerType field value is "Plastic Bag" then impute missing values using the mean of the QuantityPerUnit field.
2. If the ContainerType field value is "Paper Bag" then impute missing values using an expression that multiplies the mean of the QuantityPerUnit field * 1.2.
3. If the ContainerType field value is "Plastic Container" then impute missing values using a constant, in this case the number 28.
4. If the ContainerType field value is "Paper Box" then impute missing values using a random value between 10 and 35.
5. If the ContainerType field value is "Flexible Pouch" then impute missing values using a random value between 15 and 20.

Code to calculate the mean in the QuantityPerUnit field:

```
SELECT avg(QuantityPerUnit) AS Mean FROM  tbls_Impute
```

Result:

26.0908634538153

Code to update missing values with logical rules:

```
UPDATE tbls_Impute
SET QuantityPerUnit =
SWITCH(
ContainerType = 'Plastic Bag',   26,
ContainerType = 'Paper Bag',   26*1.2,
ContainerType = 'Plastic Container',  28,
ContainerType = 'Paper Box',   int((35 - 10 + 1) * rnd(DataRowID) + 10),
ContainerType = 'Flexible Pouch',    int((20 - 15 + 1) * rnd(DataRowID) + 15),
)
WHERE QuantityPerUnit IS NULL
```

Result:

```
(8 row(s) updated)
```

Code to check the result of the update statement:

```
SELECT DataRowID, ContainerType, QuantityPerUnit
FROM tbls_Impute
WHERE DataRowID IN (3, 4, 6, 8, 10, 12, 13, 15)
```

Result:

As you can see, all the missing values have been replaced according to the business requirements

DataRowID	ContainerType	QuantityPerUnit
3	Plastic Bag	26
4	Paper Bag	31
6	Plastic Container	28
8	Flexible Pouch	18

10	Plastic Bag	26
12	Plastic Container	28
13	Paper Box	16
15	Paper Bag	31

(8 row(s) returned)

299. Delete rows with missing values

Discussion:

The company for which we consult asked us to remove rows with missing values. This is their strategy and we will implement it. We use multiple OR operators to achieve the result since in MS Access there is no other efficient way using SQL.

Code:

Before running a DELETE statement always check its effect using a SELECT statement. The fields included in this statement all include missing values except the Primary Key field DataRowID.

```
SELECT DataRowID, PackagingType, UnitsInStock, QuotationAmount, QuantityPerUnit,
MaterialCost
FROM tbls_Impute
WHERE PackagingType Is Null OR PackagingType LIKE "" OR UnitsInStock IS NULL OR
QuotationAmount IS NULL OR QuantityPerUnit IS NULL OR MaterialCost IS NULL
```

Result:

DataRowID	PackagingType	UnitsInStock	QuotationAmount	QuantityPerUnit	MaterialCost
2	Plastic			26	74
3	Plastic	38			
4			320		
5			260	30	
6	Bio-Plastic	24	280		81
7				32	81
8	Bio-Plastic	23			
9				35	
10	Cardboard	41	54		
11				26	89
12					
13	Box	38	277		
15	Box	49	303		
16		25	453	12	

(8 row(s) returned)

Discussion:

Now, we use the DELETE statement to delete the records with null values. Remember, for text fields like Packaging type, you need to look for zero-length strings as well.

Code:

```
DELETE
FROM tbls_Impute
WHERE PackagingType Is Null OR PackagingType LIKE "" OR UnitsInStock IS NULL OR
QuotationAmount IS NULL OR QuantityPerUnit IS NULL OR MaterialCost IS NULL
```

Result:
```
(14 row(s) will be deleted)
```

300. Delete columns with missing values

Discussion:

On some occasions, the data team might decide to simply delete the columns with missing data. This is the process of dimensionality reduction in Machine Learning and it is commonly used to remove variables (columns) that are either problematic with many irrelevant or missing values or simply not needed for the specific algorithmic model.

Code:
```
ALTER TABLE tbls_Impute
DROP COLUMN MaterialCost, PackagingType
```

Result:
```
Both columns have been deleted. There is no warning for this action.
```

CHAPTER 31 SAMPLING DATA

Data sampling is a fundamental technique in analytics because in many cases it is not feasible to work with the entire dataset (the whole population of observations). It would be impossible to develop a prediction model working with tens of millions of observations since the cycle of developing, testing, and deploying the model would take amounts of time that would make the project impractical from a business perspective. When sampling data our priority is to obtain a subset that is representative of the characteristics of the whole dataset. For example, if we construct a sample dataset of salaries and the average salary for the sample is 110K while the average salary for the entire dataset is 50K, then our sample is useless for conclusions with respect to the population.

Two major techniques: Probability Sampling and **Non-Probability Sampling**.
The two major sampling techniques are Probability Sampling (or Random Sampling) and Non-Probability Sampling.

A. PROBABILITY SAMPLING TECHNIQUES

In Probability Sampling, observations are selected completely at random. There are four different techniques to create samples of random observations.

Simple Random Sampling (SRS)

Every observation has an equal chance of being selected. It is the equivalent of a hundred people buying a lottery ticket. Each one of them can win at random.

Systematic sampling

In systematic sampling, we select rows at a fixed interval such as every ten rows. We do not need to start from row 1, we can start at any record number such as the 1st, 15th, 25th, etc. The sampling interval will depend on the records in the dataset and the sample size we want to obtain. For instance, if we have a dataset of 1000 records and we want to obtain a sample of 100 records we can sample every 10 records. We need to pay attention to the presence of seasonality and cyclical events especially in time series data so that we do not select the peaks or bottoms of those seasonal or cyclical values. The dataset should be randomly ordered for this sampling method to be valid.

Stratified Sampling

We split the population data into groups based on specific, pre-determined attribute values. We are the ones that define the criteria. For example, we can create groups (strata) for our inventory products based on attributes such as weight, substance, price, quality rating, and container type. Then, we take a random sample from each stratum in proportion to its size in the population. For example, if 95% of our products use container type A and 5% use container type B, then 95% of our sample dataset should consist of products with container type A and 5% of container type B. Stratified sampling allows for a more accurate representation of the population as it ensures that all strata are included in the final sample dataset and are adequately represented. After we have defined the strata, we use simple random sampling to obtain rows from each stratum. Finally, the random samples from all strata are combined to obtain the final sample dataset

Clustered Sampling

In clustered sampling, the dataset observations are divided into multiple groups or clusters according to the values of a feature (field). For example, using the Products table, we can create clusters based on the product quality rating. In this field, we have values such as excellent, acceptable, very good, top-rated, and need-to-improve. From these clusters we randomly select some and their observations are combined to form the sample dataset. Pay attention, we do not select a set of random records from each cluster but rather a random subset of the clusters themselves with all the records they contain. We call this process a one-stage cluster sampling. We can also use two-stage clustered sampling, in which the clusters are randomly selected but then from each cluster we also select a set of random observations. Finally, we have multiple stage clustered sampling which we usually use with hierarchies such as geography. For example, in the products table we can form clusters based on the values of the product container. If we have seven product container values such as plastic, paper, etc. seven clusters will be created. Then, we select a random number of those clusters, for example three. The next stage is: for each product container value, we form subgroups based on the Stock Keeping Unit (SKU). Then, we randomly select some of the SKU clusters such as four. The next stage is: within each SKU group we form subgroups based on the product quality rating. Then, we randomly select some of the quality rating groups, for instance, three. Since this is the last stage, from the three quality rating groups, we also select random records to construct the final dataset.

B. NON-PROBABILITY SAMPLING TECHNIQUES

In non-probability sampling, observations are not selected randomly but in a subjective, personal way by the researcher. Although there is a high bias associated with non-probability sampling, the convenience and ease of use of its methods make these techniques very popular among researchers and data professionals.

Convenience sampling

A common, easy, and usually low budget sampling technique where a sample is constructed from a group of readily available participants. For example, the customers who enter the store and being asked to answer a few questions or complete a survey. These customers are selected subjectively because first they entered the store and second because they agreed to answer the survey questions. There is no randomness here, responses will be collected from the subjects who are willing to provide them. Still, it is one of the most commonly used techniques in research and the reason lies in the inherent simplicity of the technique. Convenience sampling is associated with very high bias and it is not adequate for generalizations.

Quota Sampling

This technique divides a set of observations into segments according to the values of one or more attributes. For example, we can segment the Orders table based on the values of the PackagingType, PaymentType, and InvoiceAmount fields. The PackagingType field contains values such as "Box", "Plastic", "Bio-Plastic", and "Cardboard". The PaymentType field contains values such as "COD", "Credit", and "Paper Check". The InvoiceAmount field contains a range of numeric values. The data professional or researcher segments and selects data in a personal and subjective way using quotas for specific attribute values i.e. (attribute: PackagingType – Attribute Value: Box) . For example, the researcher might select observations using the following fields and respective values:

Data Segmentation Step 1:
1. PackagingType: 30% of the records to be of type "Box"
2. PackagingType: 25% of the records to be of type "Plastic"
3. PackagingType: 30% of the records to be of type "Bio-Plastic"
4. The researcher leaves out all other attribute values for the PackagingType field.

After the above filtering criteria, a dataset has been created.

Data Segmentation Step 2:
Using the dataset resulting from step 1:
1. 50% of the records should be of Payment Type "Credit"
2. 30% of the records should be of Payment Type "COD"
3. 20% of the records should be of Payment Type "Paper Check"

After the above filtering criteria, a dataset has been created.

Data Segmentation Step 3:
Using the dataset resulting from step 2:
1. 30% of the records should have an InvoiceAmount between $1 and $150.
2. 20% of the records should have an InvoiceAmount between $151 and $300.
3. 50% of the records should have an InvoiceAmount above $301.

After step 3, a final dataset has been created.

As we can see from the above example, the segmentation of the records by the researcher has not been random but subjective. There is no "correct" or "step-by-step method" when segmenting records using quotas; it is up to the researcher to use any segmentation steps and criteria they deem effective for their project goals.

Snowball sampling

This technique is usually associated with qualitative research with human subjects in which few people are initially available and it is based on referrals to augment or "snowball" the number of participants. For example, a study might need to understand the factors affecting drug abuse among people from a certain area or population. It is obvious that not that many subjects will be available or willing to participate in surveys because this is a very sensitive topic. Consequently, the researcher will identify a few people who are willing to talk and then these people will refer others within their community who might be willing to take the survey. This process continues with more referrals added every time to the study and the sample size increases or "snowballs" until the desired sample size is reached. The main advantage of snowball sampling is its ability to reach members of communities that would be close to impossible reaching by using other methods.

Purposive sampling

Employing this technique, data professionals select from a dataset records that contain fields with values of high interest for their project. Likewise, researchers select participants with special characteristics that are of high relevance to their studies. The selection is purposeful, non-random, and focused on observations or people who can contribute the most to the project or study. Some common applications of this technique are in projects in which expert opinions are required, the study of very specific subgroups of a population, the study of outlier observations, or the study of a very specific medical case, weather phenomenon, or other case in which the number of available cases is limited.

301. Simple Random Sampling – sample with specific number of records and all fields

Discussion:

In this example we retrieve at random 100 records from the tbls_Sampling table. Notice that we use the asterisk to retrieve all the columns from the table. We use the rnd() function on the values of the DataRowID which is the Primary Key field of the table. Every time we run this piece of code, it will produce different results. Also, remember that the TOP operator always applies to the field in the ORDER BY clause, in this case DataRowID, to produce random records. The field or fields included in the SELECT statement do not have any connection or influence on the TOP operator, they just produce the fields included in the result set.

Code:

```
SELECT TOP 100 *
FROM  tbls_Sampling
ORDER BY rnd (DataRowID)
```

Result:

DataRowID	FirstName	LastName	ProductName	SKU
114	Andrew	Demichele	Dried Blueberries	PDKLS-2347
531	Arnold	Cormack	Chocolate Covered Cherries	EPDA-2345
1697	Angelo	Lareous	Chocolate Fudge	DKLS-4732
1600	George	Vandyke	Chocolate Raspberries	PDKLS-2347

```
(100 row(s) returned)
(There are more records in the result set than the ones shown in this image)
(There are more fields in the result set than the ones shown in this image)
```

302. Simple Random Sampling – sample with specific number of records and fields

Discussion:

In this example we retrieve at random 100 records from the tbls_Sampling table but we select specific columns for the result set. The TOP operator applies to the field in the ORDER BY clause, in this case DataRowID, to produce random records. The field ProductName and all the other fields in the SELECT statement are irrelevant as to what records will be retrieved at random, they only produce the columns in the result set.

Code:

```
SELECT TOP 100 ProductName, SKU, QualityRating, BoxType
FROM  tbls_Sampling
ORDER BY rnd (DataRowID)
```

Result:

ProductName	SKU	QualityRating	BoxType
Pepper Cheese Box	PDKL-2389	Very Good	Long
Buttermilk Muffins	KTRT-4589	Excellent	Side Loading
Coconut Flavour Cream Wafers	ASDT-3456	Very Good	Long
Berry Cherry	PDK-2589	Top-Rated	Side Loading

```
(100 row(s) returned)
(There are more records in the result set than the ones shown in this image)
```

303. Systematic Sampling: sample every nth records starting from the nth record

Discussion:

To achieve systematic sampling, we will use the mod (modulo) operator. This operator divides two numbers and returns the remainder of the division. For example, if we divide 10 by 3, the remainder is 1. The number 10 is the dividend, the number 3 is the divisor, and 0 is the modulo. Some more examples:

20 MOD 4 = 0
20 MOD 6 = 2
10 MOD 6 = 4
10 MOD 4 = 2
10 MOD 5 = 0

The expression we use to obtain our systematic sample is:

(Dividend Mod Divider) = remainder value

Dividend = the auto-increasing primary key field or any other sequential, auto-increasing field in the table.
Divider = the row interval used to retrieve a record.
Remainder value = the record number at which we want to start the sampling.

For example:
(DataRowID Mod 10) = 1 will select every tenth record starting with the first record.
(DataRowID Mod 20) = 5 will select every twentieth record starting with the fifth record.

Let us check both examples below. Allow time for the queries to run as sampling is a resource consuming process.

Code:

```
SELECT DataRowID, ProductName, SKU, QualityRating, BoxType
FROM tbls_Sampling
WHERE (DataRowID Mod 10) = 1
```

Result:

DataRowID	ProductName	SKU	QualityRating	BoxType
1	Dried Light Red Tart Cherries	EPDA-2345	Top-Rated	Cube
11	Roasted & Salted Cashews	PDKL-2389	Acceptable	Multi-Height
21	Honey Biscuits	ADSL 2345	Acceptable	Side Loading
31	Honey Biscuits	ADSL 2345	Acceptable	Telescopic
41	Roasted & Salted Almonds	PDKL-2389	Need to Improve	Telescopic

```
(200 row(s) returned)
(There are more records in the result set than the ones shown in this image)
(There are more fields in the result set than the ones shown in this image)
```

Code:

```
SELECT DataRowID, ProductName, SKU, QualityRating, BoxType
FROM tbls_Sampling
WHERE (DataRowID Mod 20) = 5
```

Result:

DataRowID	ProductName	SKU	QualityRating	BoxType
5	Fried Jalapenos	EPDA-2345	Very Good	Long
25	Coffee biscuits	ASDT-3456	Acceptable	Cube
45	Banana Chips	PDKLSD-2347	Very Good	Long
65	Raspberry brownie bar	KTRT-4589	Acceptable	Cube
85	Peanut Butter Creme Cookies	ASDT-3456	Excellent	Tall

304. Stratified Sampling with Proportionate number of random records using subqueries

From the theory section of this chapter, we know that in stratified sampling we partition the population dataset into groups or strata using the values of one or more attributes. In this example, we create strata based on the ContainerType" field. We use DISTINCT to retrieve the unique values in this field.

Code:

```
SELECT DISTINCT ContainerType
FROM tbls_Sampling
```

Result:

ContainerType
Flexible Pouch
Paper Bag
Paper Box
Plastic Bag
Plastic Container

(5 row(s) returned)

From the five container types we will create a corresponding number of groups. However, we want the number of sample records from each group to be proportioned to the number of records in each group. To calculate the number of records in each group:

Code:

```
SELECT ContainerType, Count (DataRowID)  AS NumProducts
FROM tbls_Sampling
GROUP BY ContainerType
```

Result:

ContainerType	NumProducts
Flexible Pouch	458
Paper Bag	437
Paper Box	382
Plastic Bag	438
Plastic Container	285

(5 row(s) returned)

From each of the above five strata, we will retrieve 10% of the records at random. To achieve this result, we use:

Code:

```
SELECT  S.*
FROM tbls_Sampling AS S
WHERE S.DataRowID IN (
SELECT TOP 10 PERCENT P.DataRowID
FROM tbls_Sampling AS P
WHERE P.ContainerType = S.ContainerType
ORDER BY Rnd (P.DataRowID))
```

Result:

DataRowID	FirstName	LastName	ProductName	SKU
3	Lisa	Read	Roasted No-Salt Almonds	PDKL-2389
23	Catherine	Davis	Apple Cinnamon Raisin Cookies	KTRT-4589
42	Fred	Weinberger	Banana Bisquits	ADSE 2345
48	Erin	Rogers	Chocolate Covered Cherries	EPDA-2345
54	Diane	Darek	Green Sauce	EPDA-2345

(208 row(s) returned)
(There are more records in the result set than the ones shown in this image)
(There are more fields in the result set than the ones shown in this image)

305. Stratified Sampling with Specific number of records using UNION

In this example, we will partition the population dataset into groups or strata, using the values in the "MembershipType" field. Unlike in the previous example in which we have used proportions, in this example we will retrieve a fixed number of random records from each stratum.

Identify the strata

To identify the strata in the "MembershipType" field, we use DISTINCT to retrieve the unique values in this field.

Code:

```
SELECT DISTINCT MembershipType
FROM tbls_Sampling
```

Result:

MembershipType
Gold
Platinum
Silver

(3 row(s) returned)

We will create three different strata from the unique values in the "MembershipType" field. We want the number of sample records from each group to be a fixed number such as ten, twenty, or fifty. We also want the retrieved records to be randomly chosen. Let us first calculate the number of records in each stratum to see if we have any large differences in their numbers:

Code:

```
SELECT MembershipType, Count (DataRowID)  AS NumRecords
FROM tbls_Sampling
GROUP BY MembershipType
```

Result:

MembershipType	NumRecords
Gold	705
Platinum	557
Silver	738

(3 row(s) returned)

We see that the number of records in each stratum does not vary widely. From each of the above strata, we will retrieve twenty records at random. To achieve this result, we first need to create a query for each stratum and then combine the results using a UNION query. Some sources suggest doing the opposite: create a UNION query and include the three SQL statements below. The best approach in MS Access is to create three separate queries:

```
SELECT TOP 20 FirstName, LastName, City, State, MembershipType, DataRowID
FROM tbls_Sampling
WHERE MembershipType = 'Gold'
ORDER BY rnd(DataRowID)
```

Save this query as Qry_Customer_Gold.

```
SELECT TOP 20 FirstName, LastName, City, State, MembershipType, DataRowID
FROM tbls_Sampling
WHERE MembershipType = 'Platinum'
ORDER BY rnd(DataRowID)
```

Save this query as Qry_Customer_Platinum.

```
SELECT TOP 20 FirstName, LastName, City, State, MembershipType, DataRowID
FROM tbls_Sampling
WHERE MembershipType = 'Silver'
ORDER BY rnd(DataRowID)
```

Save this query as Qry_Customer_Silver.

Code:

```
SELECT * FROM  Qry_Customer_Gold
UNION ALL
SELECT  * FROM Qry_Customer_Platinum
UNION ALL
SELECT  * FROM Qry_Customer_Silver
```

Result:

This result shows the first five rows of the gold customers. Your result will show different customers because the records are selected at random every time the query runs.

FirstName	LastName	City	State	MembershipType	DataRowID
Lisa	Luigi	Houston	TX	Gold	1159
Alfred	Tranton	Washington	DC	Gold	233
Fred	Weinberger	Orlando	FL	Gold	904
Thomas	Ming	Boston	MA	Gold	472
Jean	Dudek	Chicago	OH	Gold	1358

(60 row(s) returned)
(There are more records in the result set than the ones shown in this image)

306. Clustered Sampling

In clustered sampling, we partition observations based on the values of a specific attribute or a set of attributes. In this example, we partition the tbls_Sampling table into clusters, using the values in the "City" field. What is different with clustered sampling is that from all the available clusters we randomly select some of them and from those randomly selected clusters, we select all available observations to form the sample dataset.

Identify the clusters

To identify the clusters in the "City" field, we use DISTINCT to retrieve the unique values frpm this field.

Code:

```
SELECT DISTINCT City
FROM tbls_Sampling
```

Result:

City
Albany
Boston
Chicago
Dallas
Denver
Houston
Los Angeles
Miami
New York
Orlando
Philadelphia
Phoenix
San Diego
San Jose
Washington

(15 row(s) returned)

Let us calculate the number of records for each city to see if we have any imbalances in the city clusters, that is, if observations for one city are too many or two few in the dataset.

Code:

```
SELECT City, Count (DataRowID)  AS NumRecords
FROM tbls_Sampling
GROUP BY City
```

Result:

City	NumRecords
Albany	49
Boston	81
Chicago	165
Dallas	145
Denver	101

Houston	124
Los Angeles	348
Miami	95
New York	252
Orlando	78
Philadelphia	80
Phoenix	111
San Diego	144
San Jose	81
Washington	146

(15 row(s) returned)

Obtain the random clusters and their records

We see that we have fifteen clusters for the "city" field. In this specific example, we can manually select some of the cities and combine their records to form the final sample dataset. However, with high-cardinality attributes (fields with large number of unique values), in the range of thousands or hundreds of thousands of unique values, we need a way to randomly select the desired number of clusters from the thousands of available ones. The most reliable way to achieve clustered sampling in MS Access is to create two queries.

STEP 1: Randomly select a specific number of clusters (cities in this example)

Code:

```
SELECT TOP 5 City
FROM tbls_Sampling
ORDER BY rnd (DataRowID) * DataRowID
```

Save this query as Qry_Random_City

STEP 3: Obtain the sample dataset from the random clusters

Keep in mind the result of this code will be the combination of records from the five randomly selected cities (clusters) we have obtained in the previous query which we use as the criterion in the subquery below.

Code:

```
SELECT * FROM tbls_Sampling
WHERE City IN (SELECT City FROM Qry_Random_City)
```

Result:

The cities in the result below will be different when you run the code each time

DataRowID	FirstName	LastName	ProductName	SKU	Address	City
473	Thomas	Ming	All-Purpose Marinade	EPDA-2345	150 8th Ave	Boston
1651	Patricia	Madsen	Choice Apricots	PDKLS-2347	39 Cambria Street	Boston
1652	Patricia	Madsen	Roasted & Salted Almonds	PDKL-2389	39 Cambria Street	Boston
1653	Patricia	Madsen	Traditional Swedish Cookies	PDKL-2389	39 Cambria Street	Boston

(623 row(s) returned)
(There are more records in the result set than the ones shown in this image)
(There are more columns in the result set than the ones shown in this image)

Verify the clustering result

We are not done yet. We need to verify the results of the clustering code to see if they make sense. In this example, yours will be different due to randomness, the randomly selected cities are Albany, Miami, New York, San Jose, and Washington. From our calculation of the number of records by city we know that the number of records for Albany = 49, Miami = 95, New York = 252, Jan Jose = 81, and Washington = 146. The total number should be 623 according to our clustering code. We count and indeed the two numbers from the clustering code and the counting by city are the same.

REFERENCE CHAPTER 32
CREATE, EDIT, AND DELETE TABLES

In this chapter, we will work with three DDL statements: CREATE TABLE, ALTER TABLE, and DROP TABLE. We use the CREATE statement to create new tables, the ALTER statement to modify existing ones, and the DROP statement to delete tables. The basic structure of the three statements appear below:

```
CREATE TABLE "tablename" (
fieldname1 datatype (size),
fieldname2 datatype (size),
fieldname3 datatype (size)
)
```

```
ALTER TABLE "tablename"
[ADD] [ALTER] [DROP] COLUMN fieldname datatype(size)
```

```
DROP TABLE "tablename"
```

307. Create a simple table using SQL

Discussion:
This is a simple example of creating a table using SQL in MS Access. The Access help file says that we need to use data definition queries to create objects. Actually, we can enter this code in the SQL view of a select query, and it will work. The table in this example contains only six text fields and is bare without any primary keys defined, NULL handling, or indexes.

Code:

```
CREATE TABLE Customer1 (
[LastName] text(50),
[MiddleName] text(50),
[FirstName] text(50),
[Address] text(100),
[State] text(2),
[Zip] text(5))
```

Result:
As soon as you run the SQL statement a new Customer1 table is created in the objects pane in Access on the left part of the screen.

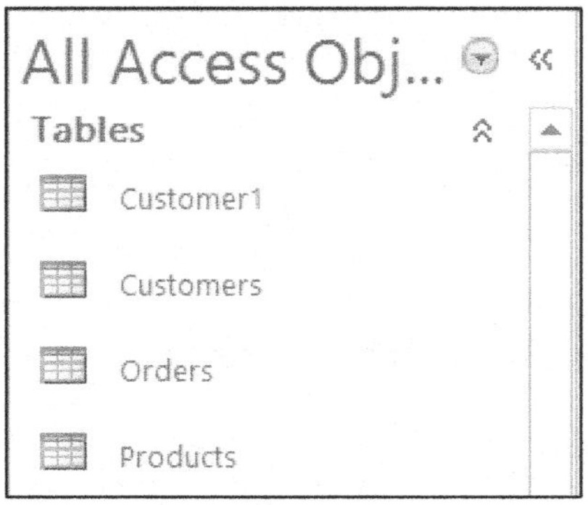

Right click on the name of the "Customer1" table and select "**Design View**". The design of the new table along with its fields appears below.

Field Name	Data Type
LastName	Short Text
MiddleName	Short Text
FirstName	Short Text
Address	Short Text
State	Short Text
Zip	Short Text

308. Create a table using SQL, and populate it with data on the fly

Discussion:

In most of our work tasks, we do not just create a table. We might also insert some data at the same time. Creating a table and populating it on the fly is possible using the SELECT INTO statement. In this example, we create the table customer2, and we populate it with data from the Customers table.

Code:

```
SELECT * INTO Customer2
FROM Customers
```

Result:

Click "Yes" in the dialog box below to create the Customer2 table.

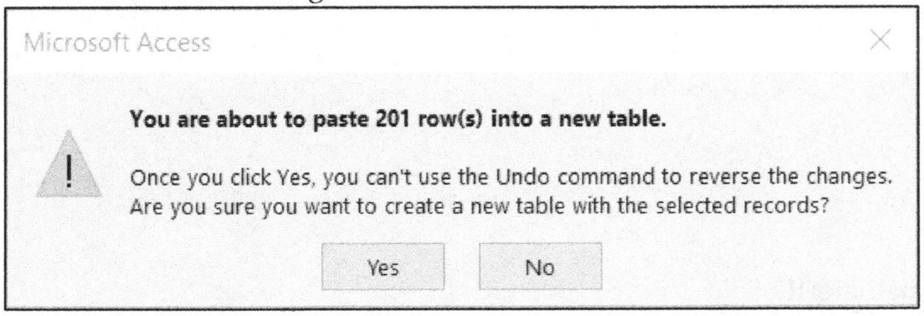

309. Create a table using SQL, and populate it with specific rows and columns

Discussion:

In this example, we create the table Customer3 and we populate it with only three fields and 14 records from the Customers table.

Code:

```
SELECT LastName, FirstName, Address INTO Customer3
FROM Customers
WHERE city = 'Boston'
```

Result:

Double click on the name of the Customer3 table to open it. It will look like the following image.

Customer3

lastname	firstname	address
Cormack	Arnold	31 2nd Street
Currier	Carolyn	58 Holmes CT
Davis	Catherine	87 Coral Street
Geisler	Cristopher	93 Kate Street
Johnson	Colleen	84 Aramingo Road
Jones	Pamela	58 William Street
Madsen	Patricia	39 Cambria Street
Manson	Stephen	15 Martha Street
McGrath	Chris	49 Emerald Road
Ming	Thomas	150 8th Ave
Miller	James	18 Allen Street
Powers	Gerald	125 Frankford Ave
Sterling	Fred	10 Clearfield Street
Strack	Joanne	88 Joyce Street

Record: 1 of 14 No Filter Searc

310. Create a table defining its primary key

Discussion:

In this scenario, we create a table with a primary key of data type "Number" and two simple text fields. Notice the primary key picture on the left of the CustomerID field in the table design view in the picture below:

Code:

```
CREATE TABLE Customer4 (
[CustomerID] number Primary key,
[LastName] text(50),
[FirstName] text(50))
```

Result:

Notice the key icon in front of the CustomerID field.

Customer4

Field Name	Data Type
CustomerID	Number
LastName	Short Text
FirstName	Short Text

311. Create a table defining a field as the primary key and an autonumber data type

Discussion:

In this scenario, we create a table with the primary key of data type "AutoNumber" and two simple text fields.

Code:

```
CREATE TABLE Customer5 (
[CustomerID] Counter Primary key,
[LastName] text(50),
[FirstName] text(50))
```

Result:

Customer5

	Field Name	Data Type
🔑	CustomerID	AutoNumber
	LastName	Short Text
	FirstName	Short Text

312. Create table with a field that does not accept nulls

Discussion:

On some occasions, we want to create a table with a field that will not accept null or empty values. Null values are different from zero-length strings or zeros. Check the chapter on Nulls for a full discussion of null values). To avoid nulls for a field, we simply make the field required. In other words, we force users to enter a value, or they will not be able to save the record in the database. We can do this with the following code, which makes the LastName field required.

Code:

```
CREATE TABLE Customer6 (
[CustomerID] Counter PRIMARY KEY,
[LastName] text(50) NOT NULL,
[FirstName] text(50),
[Address] text(50))
```

Result:

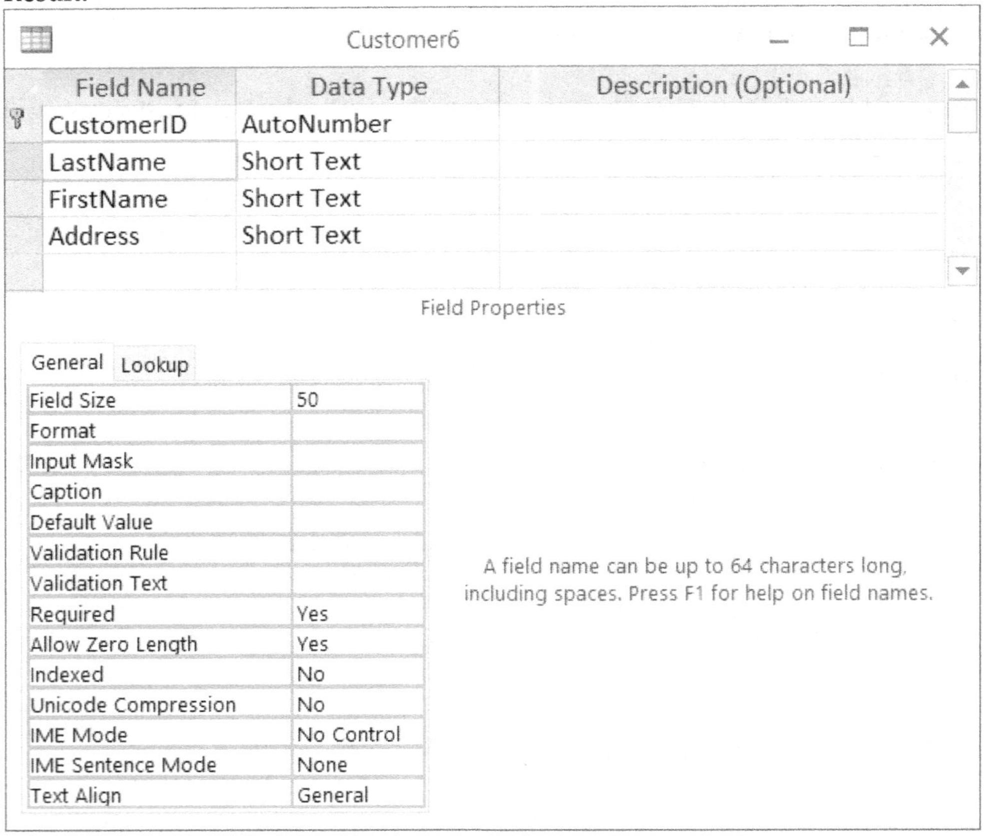

313. Create a table with the primary key consisting of two fields

Discussion:

We must know how to create concatenated keys, that is, primary keys consisting of two or more fields. This knowledge is imperative for creating join tables in many to many relationships. In this example, we create the tbls_ProductsOrders table whose primary key will consist of the combination of the values of the ProductID and OrderID fields.

Code:

```
CREATE TABLE tbls_ProductsOrders (
[ProductID] number,
[OrderID] number,
PRIMARY KEY (ProductID, OrderID))
```

Result:

Notice how the key icon is in front of both fields.

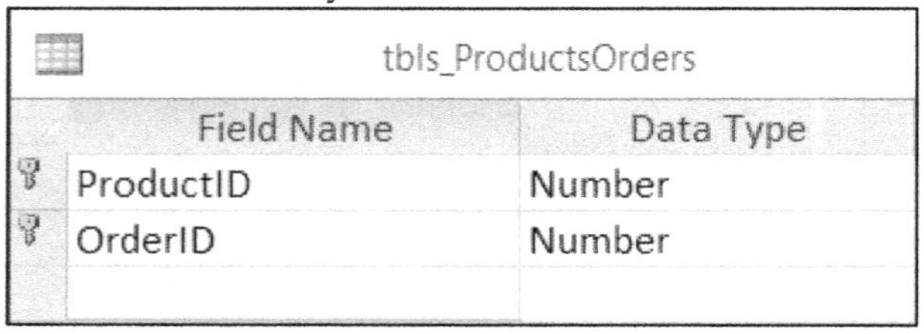

314. ALTER table: add a column

Discussion:

In this example, we add the City field to the Customer1 table.

Code:

```
ALTER TABLE Customer1
ADD COLUMN City TEXT(25)
```

or if you would like to make it a required field:

```
ALTER TABLE Customer1
ADD COLUMN City TEXT(25) NOT NULL
```

Result:

Customer1

Field Name	Data Type
LastName	Short Text
MiddleName	Short Text
FirstName	Short Text
Address	Short Text
State	Short Text
Zip	Short Text
City	Short Text

315. ALTER table: delete a column

Discussion:

We can delete a field from a table using the DROP statement. In this example, we delete the "City" field from the Customer1 table.

Code:

```
ALTER TABLE Customer1
DROP COLUMN City
```

Result:

Customer1

Field Name	Data Type
LastName	Short Text
MiddleName	Short Text
FirstName	Short Text
Address	Short Text
State	Short Text
Zip	Short Text

316. ALTER table: change an existing text column to accept more characters

Discussion:

In this example, we change the size of the LastName field from 50 to 80 characters. Notice that the data type of the LastName field is already text. We can also change the data type or the name of the field, if we wish, using the ALTER COLUMN statement.

Code:

```
ALTER TABLE Customer1
ALTER COLUMN LastName TEXT(80)
```

Result:

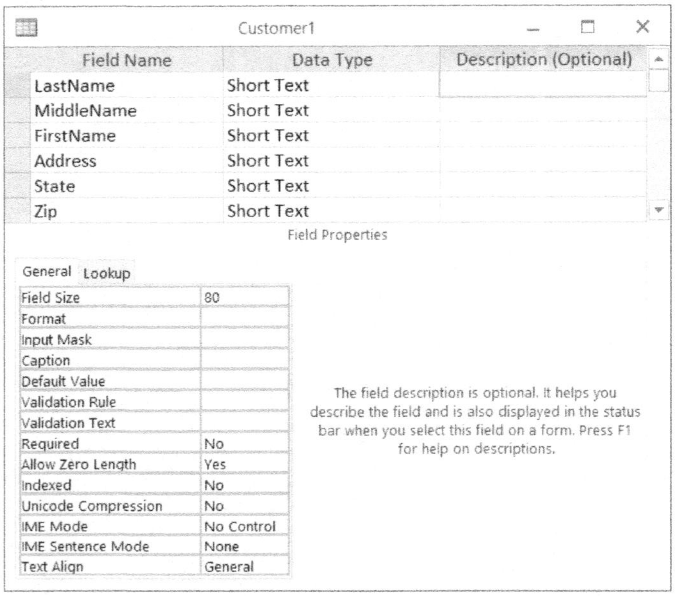

317. ALTER table: Change the data type of an existing field

Discussion:

In this example, we modify the address field of the Customer2 table from text to long text. This means that the field will be able to store up to 1 GB of data. Access forms and reports though will be able to display only the first 64000 characters. For the LONGTEXT data type we do not specify the number of characters.

Code:

```
ALTER TABLE Customer2
ALTER COLUMN Address LONGTEXT
```

Result:

Customer2

Field Name	Data Type
CustomerID	AutoNumber
FirstName	Short Text
LastName	Short Text
Address	Long Text
City	Short Text
State	Short Text
Zip	Short Text
Country	Short Text

318. Delete Table

Discussion:

We can use SQL to delete tables using the DROP statement. In this example, we delete the Customer1 table. We must pay attention, however, when we delete tables using the DROP statement because there is no warning or undo action for it. The table will be deleted permanently from the database.

Code:

```
DROP TABLE Customer1
```

Result:

The table customer1 has been deleted from the database.

DISCUSSION QUESTIONS

1. What type of SQL do we use when we create tables? DDL or DML?
2. What DDL keyword do we use to create a table?
3. Do we need to enclose field names in brackets in DDL statements?
4. Can we use DDL to alter the structure of an existing table? What is the keyword used?
5. Can we create and populate a table using a single DDL statement?
6. What DDL statement do we use to delete a table?
7. What keyword do we use to define a field as an AutoNumber?
8. What keyword do we use to define a field as the primary key?
9. What is the SQL keyword we use so that a field does not accept null values?
10. Can we use DDL to change the size of an existing field?

REFERENCE CHAPTER 33 CREATE, EDIT, DELETE RELATIONSHIPS

An essential skill in relational databases is the ability to create relationships among tables (entities). After 30 years of work in this field, I can attest that this process is more art than science. There are neither rigid rules to follow nor guidelines to cover all of the situational scenarios we will encounter. We need to have solid technical knowledge on the subject, a thorough understanding of the business processes involved, amazing communication skills (top factor), and experience. When it comes to technical knowledge, we should understand the role of primary keys, foreign keys, composite keys, natural keys, referential integrity, one-to-many, and many-to-many relationships. This is what we do in this chapter.

319. Why and how to create a one-to-many relationship

Create a one-to-many relationship between customers and orders

In this example, we create a relationship between the Customers and Orders tables. The business logic is that each customer can have multiple orders while one order definitely belongs to one customer only. This is the case for a one-to-many relationship. This one-to-many relationship is depicted graphically in the figure below. I have included data values on purpose to actually show how records from one table relate to records in the other table. This is because when we talk about relationships among tables, we are actually talking about record relations.

CUSTOMERS	
CustomerID	**Name**
1	John
2	Mary
3	George
4	Stacy

ORDERS		
OrderID	**CustomerID**	**OrderDate**
1	2	9/10/2025
2	2	10/10/2025
3	1	11/10/2025
4	3	11/11/2025

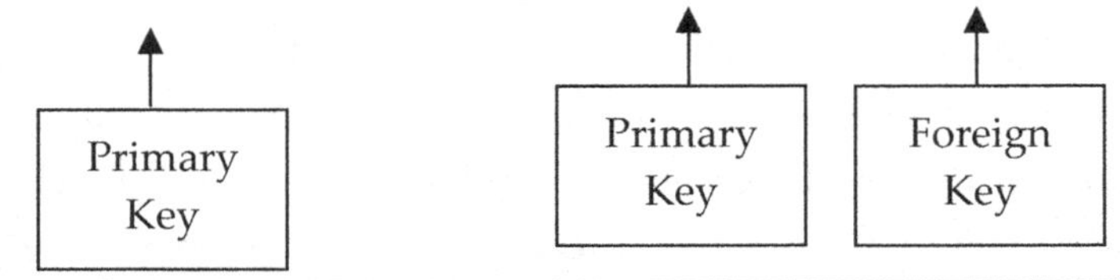

The steps for creating a one-to-many relationship between two tables are the following:

1. Assign a primary key to both tables if they do not already have one. In this example, the primary key for the Customers table is "CustomerID", and the primary key for the Orders table is "OrderID".

2. Make sure your primary key is not a "natural" key like a social security number, or a driver's license number. The data types for the primary keys in both tables should be of the "Auto Number" data type.
3. Create a field in the Orders table and name it "CustomerID." The "CustomerID" field in the Orders table is the "Foreign key" of the table. The data type of the "CustomerID" field in the Orders table should be a number so that it can be joined with the CustomerID in the Customers table.
4. Click on the "Database Tools" tab on the ribbon. In the "Relationships" group, click on the relationships button. The relationships window will appear. In the "relationships" group again click on the "Add Tables" button." The "Show Table" dialog box opens. Add the tables Customers and Orders.

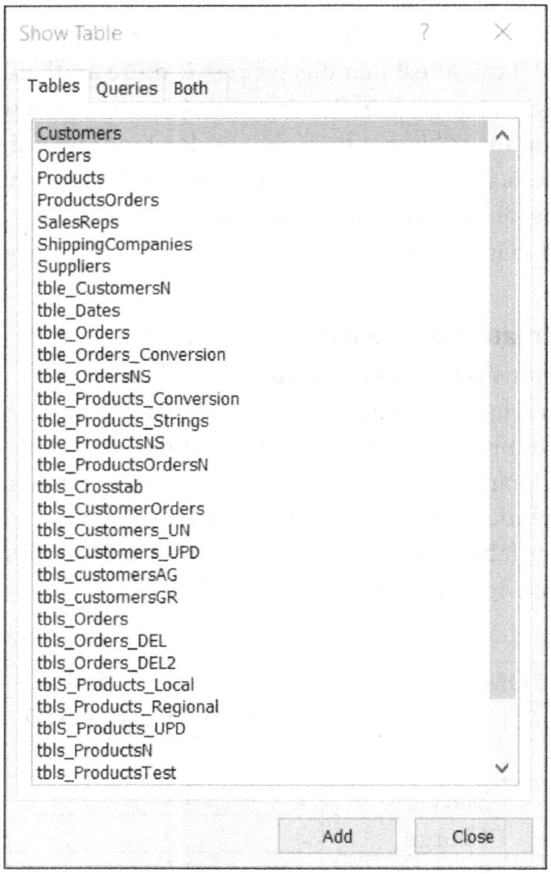

5. The relationships window in Access shows the entity relationship diagram (ERD) of the database. In the ERD, all related tables appear along with the field names and the primary and foreign keys. The ERD allows us to understand the design of the database, and it is the place in which we can create, edit, and delete relationships. In this case, we will create a new relationship between Customers and Orders.

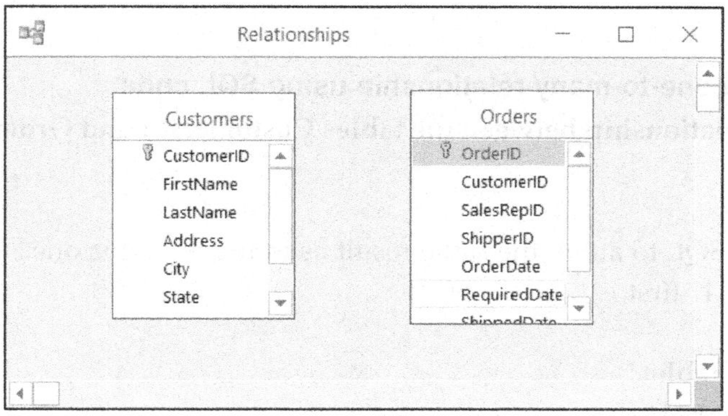

6. Click on the CustomerID field in the Customers table and drag it on the CustomerID field in the Orders table. The "Edit Relationships" window will come up.

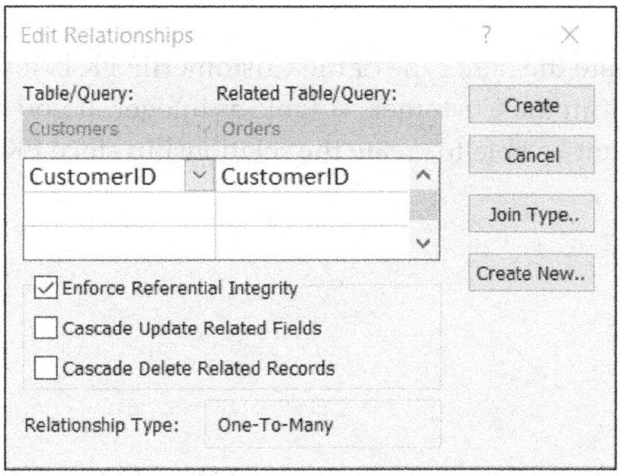

7. We can just click "Create", and our relationship is ready. However, in this case, we will also click on "Enforce Referential Integrity" so that our database remains in good state when inserting new records and deleting existing ones. When referential integrity is on, first, we will not be able to add an order in the Orders table without a corresponding customer in the Customers table. Second, we will not be able to delete a customer from the Customers table for whom there are orders in the Orders table. We will have to first delete the orders for that customer and then delete the customer. For a full understanding of referential integrity and its important implications, read the corresponding section in this chapter.

8. Finally, our Entity Relationship Diagram (ERD) will look like this:

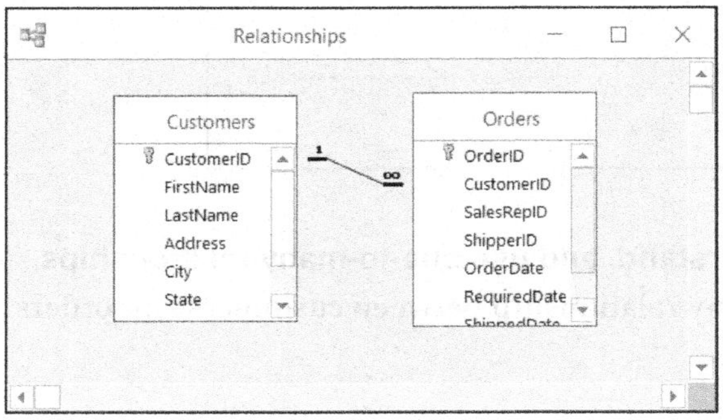

320. How to create a one-to-many relationship using SQL code

Create a one-to-many relationship between the tables Customers41 and Orders41

Discussion:

In this example, we use SQL to attain the same result as in the previous one. We will create the tables Customers41 and Orders41 first.

Create the Customers41 table:

```
CREATE TABLE Customers41 (
[CustomerID] Counter Primary key,
[LastName] text(50),
[FirstName] text(50))
```

Create the Orders41 table:

Pay attention here: we designate the data type of the CustomerID FK below as integer since Access designates the CustomerID PK in the Customers41 table as integer. If you designate the CustomerID FK as simply "number" you will not be able to create the relationship since PK and FK data types need to be the same.

```
CREATE TABLE Orders41 (
[OrderID] Counter Primary key,
[CustomerID] integer,
[ShippedDate] Date)
```

Create the one-to-many relationship between Customers41 and Orders41:

```
ALTER TABLE Orders41
ADD CONSTRAINT FK_CustomerID
FOREIGN KEY (CustomerID)
REFERENCES Customers41 (CustomerID)
```

Result:

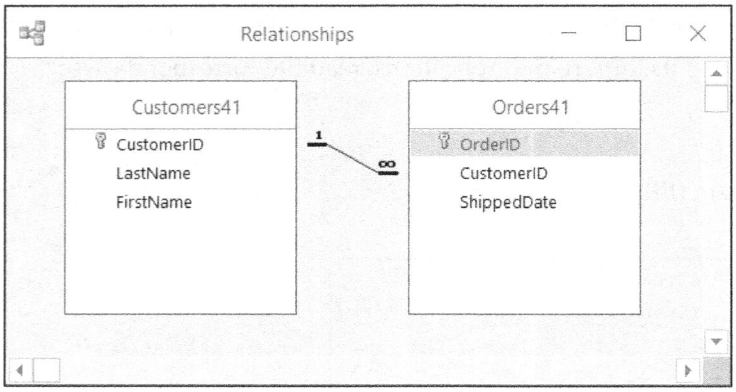

321. How to read, understand, and use one-to-many relationships

The meaning of one-to-many relationship between customers and orders

Knowing how to create a one-to-many relationship is fine but the essential objective is to actually understand its meaning, be able to apply it, and take advantage of its many possibilities. Let us understand what is happening in our two related tables of Customers and Orders.

First, when looking at the foreign key values (CustomerID) in the Orders table, we notice that only John, Mary, and George have orders. Second, we see that John and George have one order each, while Mary has two orders. Third, we see that Stacy does not have any orders at all, so we might want to initiate a marketing effort for her. Fourth, when we look at the Orders table and examine order number 3 (with OrderID = 3), we immediately understand that this order belongs to John because the corresponding foreign key value is 1. If we look up this value in the Customer table, we find that the corresponding customer name is John. This is the way relational databases work and are able to retrieve related records from two or more tables.

CUSTOMERS	
CustomerID	**Name**
1	John
2	Mary
3	George
4	Stacy

↑ Primary Key (CustomerID)

ORDERS		
OrderID	**CustomerID**	**OrderDate**
1	2	9/10/2025
2	2	10/10/2025
3	1	11/10/2025
4	3	11/11/2025

↑ Primary Key (OrderID) ↑ Foreign Key (CustomerID)

322. Why and how to create a many-to-many-relationship

Create a many-to-many relationship between orders and products

Our task now is to create a database to manage our customers, orders, and products. We already know how to create a one-to-many relationship between customers and orders. Now, we need to create a relationship between orders and products. Whenever we design a database, the setup of relationships is the cornerstone of the process. We do have an ally in this process, which is our logic.

In this respect, we examine and draw conclusions on the relation of each table to the other or of relations among entities because this is how we refer to tables in database parlance. From the orders point of view, we conclude that each order in the Orders table can contain more than one product. It is only logical that a customer can order multiple products in one order. From the products point of view, we conclude that each product can participate in more than one order. It is also logical that we can sell the same product to multiple customers. When this is the case, we need to establish a many-to-many relationship between Orders and Products.

To create a many-to-many relationship between the Orders and Products tables, we need to create a join table between them like the JoinOrdersProducts table in this example. The primary key of the join table will be the combination of the primary keys of the tables we join in a many-to-many relationship. In other words, the primary key of any join table in a many-to-many relationship is a composite key consisting of two fields. As we already know, the values of a primary key in a relational table must always be unique, and this uniqueness is expressed in this case by the combination of the values of OrderID and ProductID.

For example, in the figure below, the value (1,2) of the first record in the JoinOrdersProducts table is different from the value (2,2) in the second record. This is how we obtain uniqueness of primary key values of join tables in many-to-many relationships.

Customers	
CustomerID	**Name**
1	John
2	Mary
3	George
4	Stacy

Orders		
OrderID	**CustomerID**	**OrderDate**
1	2	9/10/2017
2	2	10/10/2017
3	1	11/10/2017
4	3	11/11/2017

Products	
ProductID	**ProductName**
1	A
2	B
3	C
4	D

JoinOrdersProducts		
OrderID	**ProductID**	**Quantity**
1	2	2
2	2	5
3	1	3
4	2	4

To create a many-to-many relationship, we follow these steps:

1. Make sure that the two tables you are about to join in a many-to-many relationship have primary keys.
2. Create a new table whose name is the combination of the names of the two tables that you would like to join and add "Join" at the front—in this case "JoinOrdersProducts." You can follow any other naming convention you prefer as long as you can remember that this is a join table and it joins the tables Orders and Products.
3. In the join table "JoinOrdersProducts", create two fields: ProductID and OrderID. The data types of both OrderID and ProductID should be "Number". This is because we need to join these fields with the corresponding keys in the Orders and Products tables, and we cannot join two fields with dissimilar data types. Your table should look like this:

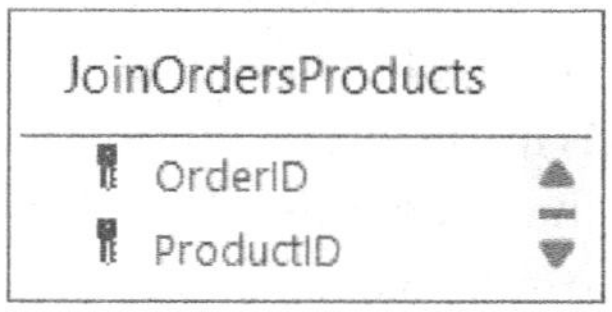

4. We are not done yet. Let us assume that a customer orders two units of product (A) and three units of product (B). This customer orders multiple quantities of the same product in the same order. In addition, we might want to extend different discounts for different products in the same order. How can we accomplish this? The answer is to include additional fields in the JoinOrdersProducts table. Our final table will look like this:

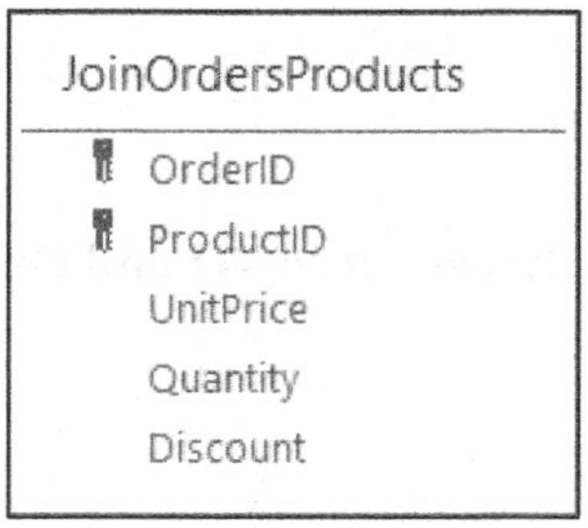

5. The final step is to join the Orders table to the JoinOrdersProducts table by dragging the OrderID field from the Orders table on the OrderID field in the JoinOrdersProducts table. We do the same by dragging the ProductID field from the Products table on the ProductID field in the JoinOrdersProducts table. Our relationships window will now look like the figure below:

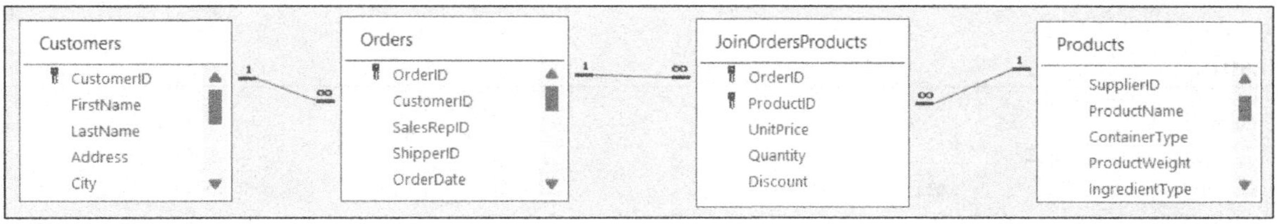

323. How to create a many-to-many relationship using pure SQL code

Create a many-to-many relationship between the tables Orders41 and Products41

Discussion:
In this example, we use SQL code to create a many-to-many relationship between the tables Orders41 and Products41.

Create the Orders41 table:

```
CREATE TABLE Orders41 (
[OrderID] Counter Primary key,
[CustomerID] integer,
[ShippedDate] Date)
```

Create the Products41 table:

```
CREATE TABLE Products41 (
[ProductID] Counter Primary key,
[ProductName] text (50))
```

Create the JoinOrdersProducts41 table:
This is the join table we need to establish the many-to-many relationship between Customers41 and Orders41. We designate the data type of the OrderID and ProductID fields as integers since the CustomerID PK in the Customers41 table and the OrderID PK in the Orders41 table are integers. The last line of the code designates the combination of the OrderID and ProductID values as the PK of the JoinOrdersProducts41 table.

```
CREATE TABLE JoinOrdersProducts41 (
[OrderID] integer,
```

[ProductID] integer,
PRIMARY KEY (OrderID, ProductID))

Create a one-to-many relationship between Orders41 and OrdersProducts41:
ALTER TABLE JoinOrdersProducts41
ADD CONSTRAINT FK_OrderID
FOREIGN KEY (OrderID)
REFERENCES Orders41 (OrderID)

Create a one-to-many relationship between Products41 and OrdersProducts41:
ALTER TABLE JoinOrdersProducts41
ADD CONSTRAINT FK_ProductID
FOREIGN KEY (ProductID)
REFERENCES Products41 (ProductID)

Result:

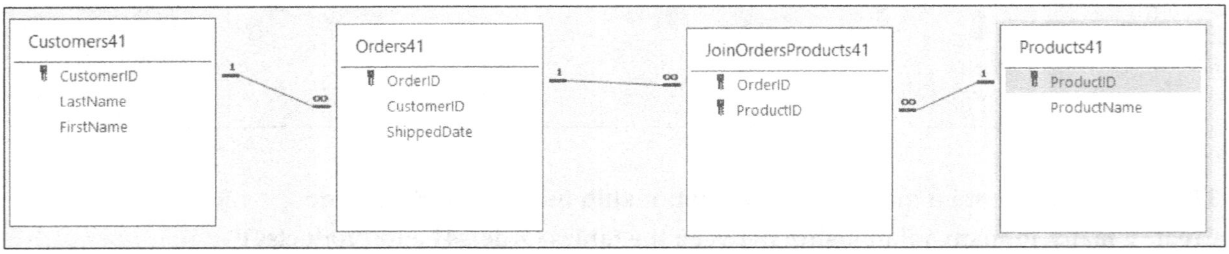

324. How to "read", understand, and use a many-to-many relationship

The meaning of many-to-many relationship between orders and products

The important goal when working with relationships is to understand what we are doing and not so much the process of doing it. If we do not remember the series of clicks to achieve the task, we can always resort to a handy reference. However, if we do not understand how many-to-many relationships work, we will not be able to use them or, at the very least, cannot take full advantage of them.

Let us examine the meaning of a many-to-many relationship from A to Z. The figure below depicts a many-to-many relationship between the Orders and Products tables. Let us answer a couple of questions:

What specific products were included in John's order?
To answer this question, we should go to John's record in the Customers table. There, we see that John's primary key value is 1 (PK=1). Then, we proceed to the Orders table, which is joined with the Customers table through a one-to-many relationship. There, we see that John appears in the third record of the table where CustomerID = 1. In database parlance, this translates to foreign key value = 1 or FK=1. Next, we see that the corresponding OrderID value for FK=1 is 3 (OrderID =3). From there, we are looking for OrderID = 3 in the JoinOrdersProducts table. The corresponding ProductID value is 1. Next, we go to the Products table and see that ProductID = 1 corresponds to product A. Since the quantity for the pair (3,1) in the JoinOrdersProducts table is 3, we can finally answer that John ordered three units of product (A). This is how relational databases use associations (relationships) to store and retrieve data.

Customers	
CustomerID	Name
1	John
2	Mary
3	George
4	Stacy

Orders		
OrderID	CustomerID	OrderDate
1	2	9/10/2025
2	2	10/10/2025
3	1	11/10/2025
4	3	11/11/2025

Products	
ProductID	ProductName
1	A
2	B
3	C
4	D

JoinOrdersProducts		
OrderID	ProductID	Quantity
1	2	2
2	2	5
3	1	3
4	2	4

What specific products were included in Mary's orders?
Mary's PK is 2. For FK = 2 in the Orders table, the corresponding PK values are 1 and 2. We now know that Mary placed two orders. For OrderID 1 and 2 in the JoinOrdersProducts table, the corresponding ProductIDs are 2 and 2. The quantities are 2 and 5. Therefore, we know right away that Mary ordered seven product Bs in two separate orders. We also note that Mary has a pattern of ordering only product Bs, which allows us to direct our marketing efforts.

325. What is referential integrity, how to apply it, and what it means

The meaning and implications of referential integrity in table relationships

Referential Integrity is a vague concept in the data world. Some data professionals will turn this option on because it is a good "thing" to do even though they do not fully understand its implications. Referential integrity in relational databases means that relationships among joined tables remain consistent. Of course, as is the case with all definitions, we do not understand much. Let us approach it from a practical perspective. First, we set referential integrity on table relationships, not the tables themselves.

Here is how we do it. Let's say we want to create a one-to-many relationship between Customers and Orders. To achieve this, we drag the CustomerID field (PK in the Customers table) on the CustomerID field in the Orders table (FK in the Orders table). The relationships window then opens up as we can see below:

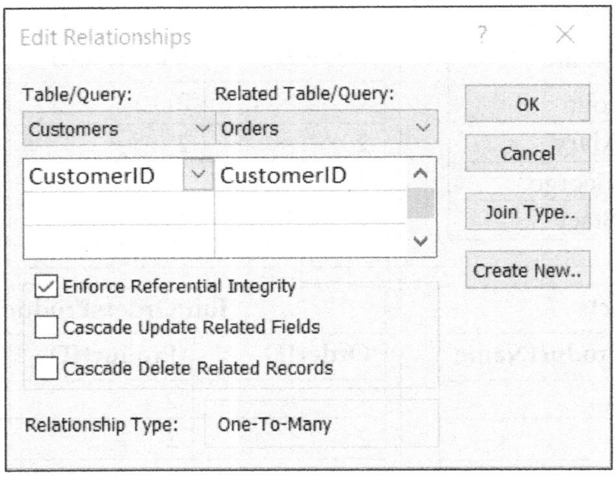

Click on the Referential Integrity check box. In some cases, you might find that the database does not allow you to apply referential integrity. You should immediately look for orphaned records in the table in the many part of the relationship which means we have CustomerID (FK) values in the Orders table without corresponding CustomerID values (PKs) in the Customers table. In short, we have orders without corresponding customers. In this book, we have devoted a whole chapter to orphaned and unrelated records because it is a crucial topic in any database work.

Once referential integrity is on, it has several effects: First, the database will not allow us to enter an order in the Orders table without a corresponding customer in the Customers table. If we have an order from a new customer, we have to enter that customer's data in the Customers table first and then, the order data in the Orders table.

Second, if we try to enter an order in the Orders table with a CustomerID value (FK value) that does not exist in the Customers table the database will produce an error message that a related record is required in the Customers table.

Third, in Access, if we try to enter an order in the Orders table leaving the CustomerID FK field blank (FK value null) this will be ok for the database but very bad for the integrity of our data since we will not know who this order belongs to. In this case, referential integrity will not be enforced. The solution is to make the CustomerID field (FK field) in the Orders table required as shown in the figure below:

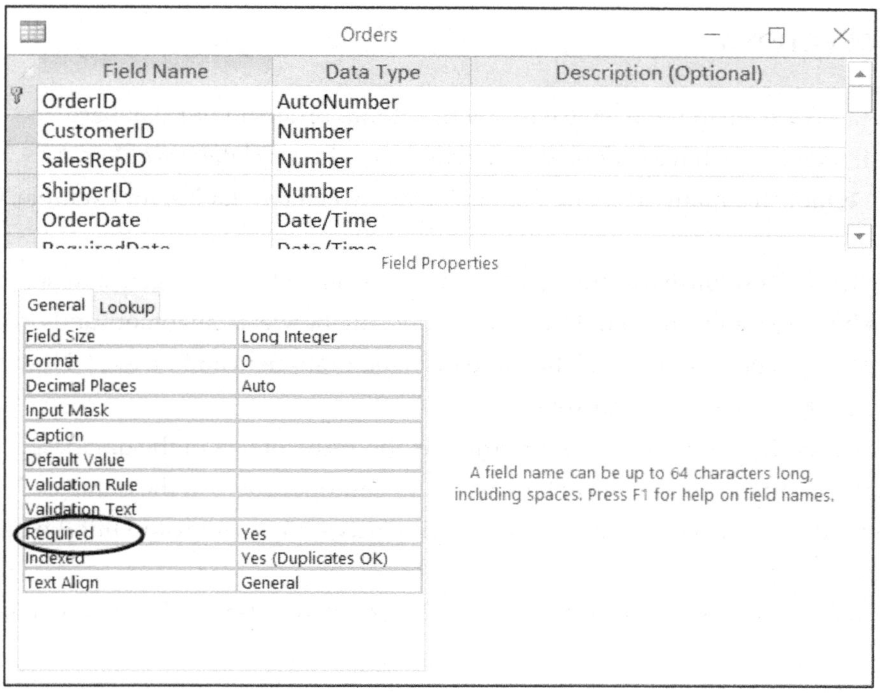

Fourt, the database will not allow us to delete a customer who has orders in the database. To delete such a customer, we first need to delete all the orders associated with him or her and then delete the customer. If we try to delete a customer with existing orders, the following message will appear.

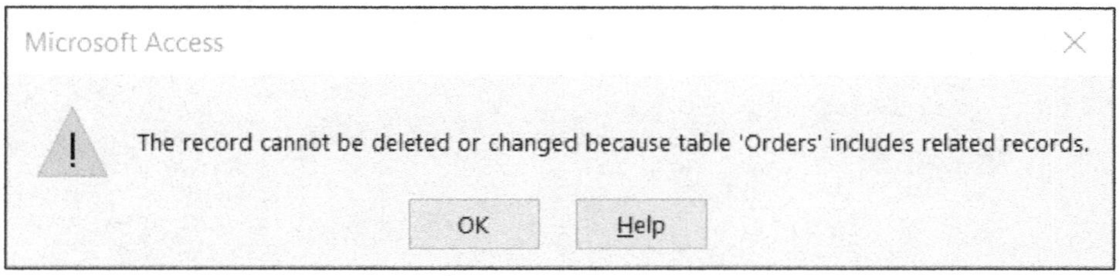

If we want to delete a customer and his/her existing orders in one step, we can click on "Cascade Deletes". This option helps the professional delete all related data about a customer in the database, but it is very dangerous to leave permanently on because users can delete customers and their related data by mistake. Check the chapters on "Update" and "Delete" statements for full details on their use since they are an important productivity tool for data professionals.

DISCUSSION QUESTIONS

1. In what scenario are we in if we have customers without orders in our database?
2. What does it mean if we have orders without customers in our database?
3. How do we establish a many-to-many relationship between two tables, for example, Orders and Products?
4. Why do we have to establish a many-to-many relationship between singers and songs?
5. Why do we have to establish a one-to-many relationship between customers and orders?
6. How do we setup a one-to-many relationship between customers and orders? How many primary keys we need? How many foreign keys?
7. If referential integrity is on, can we enter orders without customers in the database?
8. If referential integrity is on, can we enter customers without orders in the database?
9. What does it mean if we try to apply referential integrity for a relationship but the database does not allow us to do so?
10. If referential integrity is on, can we delete a customer with existing orders in the database?

REFERENCE CHAPTER 34
CREATE, EDIT, AND DELETE INDEXES

The use of indexes is crucial in analytics projects. First, they will speed up searches on our dimensional attributes, text fields, in data warehouses, data lakes, and lakehouses. Second, they will work great with WHERE and ORDER BY clauses in any relational database used for transaction processing, staging server, or as the basis of an analytics platform such as a data mart. However, they will slow down INSERT and UPDATE statements since every insert or update needs to be saved in both the table and the index. Third, they should be avoided in small tables with few records; they work better in large tables with thousands of records. Fourth, it is good practice to create indexes on fields used repeatedly in searches.

Unique and non-unique indexes
In addition, indexes can be set up as unique or non-unique and they can function as constraints disallowing duplicate values for the indexed field or fields. For example, if we set up a unique index on the last name field, all the last names in the table must have unique values. Primary keys are automatically indexed when created, and these indexes are set up as unique.

Composite indexes
We can also create multi-field indexes that will index the combination of values from multiple fields instead of just indexing the values of each individual field. For example, we can create a multi-field unique index on both the last and first name fields that will accept duplicate values for the individual's last or first name fields but will not accept duplicate values for their combinations. Let us go through some examples to demonstrate the points we mentioned in practice.

326. Create a table and setup a unique index

Optimize customer searches on the last name field
Discussion:
Since we expect heavy searching activity on the LastName field, we need to create an index to accelerate these searches. In this example, we create a new table and a unique index on the LastName field. That is, we do not allow duplicate values on the LastName field which means two customers cannot have the same last name.

Code:
```
CREATE TABLE tblCustomer21 (
[CustomerID] Counter Primary key,
[LastName] text(50),
[FirstName] text(50),
[Address] text(50),
CONSTRAINT indLastName UNIQUE (LastName))
```

Result:

In the figure below, the LastName field is indexed and, at the same time, does not accept duplicates due to the unique index we created on this field.

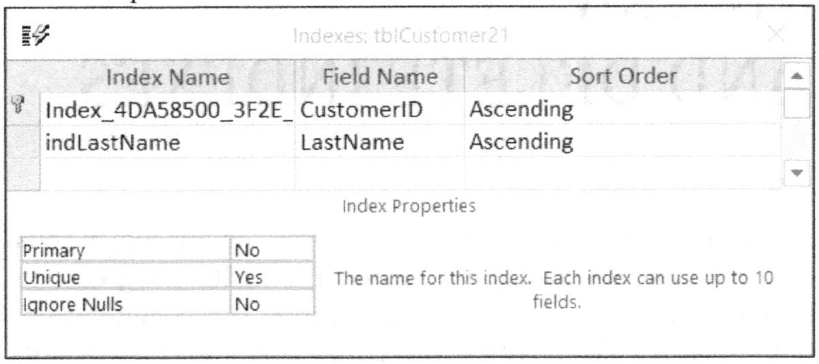

To see the index you have just created, open the table in design view and in the "Show/Hide" group click on "Indexes".

327. Create a non-unique index

Add a non-unique index for the first name field in the customer table

Discussion:

In this example, the index indFirstName is non-unique. This means we allow duplicate values for the FirstName field. That means, we can have two "Johns" or two "Marys" in the table, but they definitely have to have different last names as defined by the indLastName, which is a unique index in the previous example.

Code:

```
CREATE INDEX indFirstName ON tblCustomer21 (FirstName)
```

Result:

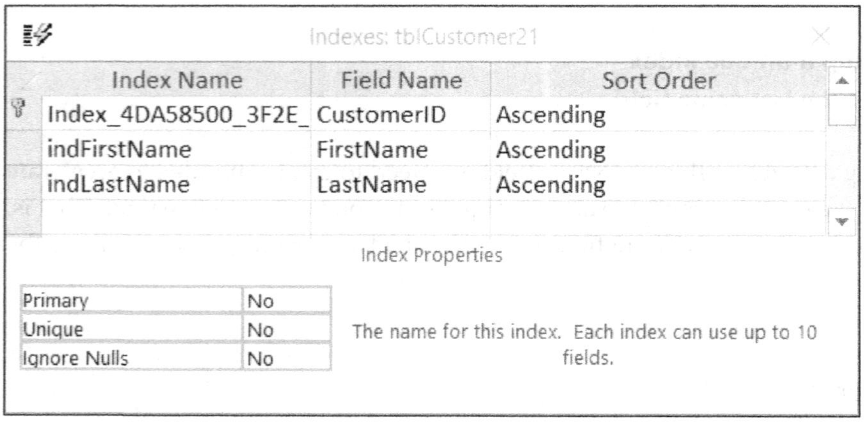

To see the index you have just created, open the table in design view and in the "Show/Hide" group click on "Indexes".

328. Create a unique index in an existing table

Add a unique index for the last name field in the existing customer table

Discussion:

As we can see from the figure in the previous example, the indFirstName index is non-unique, and it does not ignore nulls. What is the exact meaning of a unique index? What is the meaning of an index ignoring or not ignoring nulls?

First, by a unique index, we mean that no duplicate values are allowed for that field. We know that unique values are not allowed for fields that have been designated as primary keys. However, by defining a unique index, we can disallow duplicate values for a field that is not a primary key. For example, if we are working with the LastName field, and we create a unique index on it, we cannot have two customers in our table with the same last name. If we try to enter two customers with the same last name, the database will not allow it. The SQL code below will create a unique index on a field in an existing table. Let us create the table first:

Code:

```
CREATE TABLE tblCustomer22 (
[CustomerID] Counter Primary key,
[LastName] text(50),
[FirstName] text(50),
[Address] text(50))
```

Code:

```
CREATE UNIQUE INDEX indLastName ON tblCustomer22 (LastName)
```

Result:

As we can see from the figure below, the indLastName is a unique index now. However, this is not always a desirable scenario since there might be multiple customers with the same last name. How can we setup index constraints so that we allow multiple customers to have the same last name or the same first name, but disallow multiple customers to have the same last and first names at the same time? Let us see the next example with multiple-field or composite indexes.

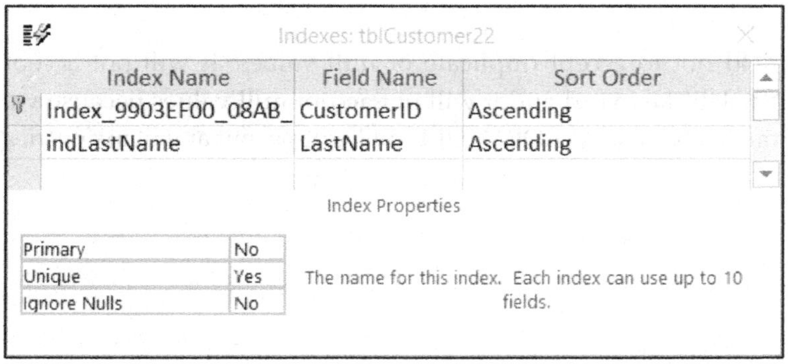

To see the index you have just created, open the table in design view and in the "Show/Hide" group click on "Indexes".

329. Create multiple-field indexes to avoid duplicates

Add a unique composite index for the last and first name fields

Discussion:

When working with customers, we want to make sure that no duplicate customer records exist in our database. At the same time, it is logical that many customers might have the same last name, and many of them will have the same first name.

With a composite unique index on the last and first name fields, our database will accept values such as Smith John and Smith Tracy. However, if we try to enter another Smith John in the database, we will get a message that such an entry violates existing indexing rules and it will not be accepted.

Code:

```
CREATE UNIQUE INDEX indLastFirst ON tblCustomer22 (LastName, FirstName);
```

Result:

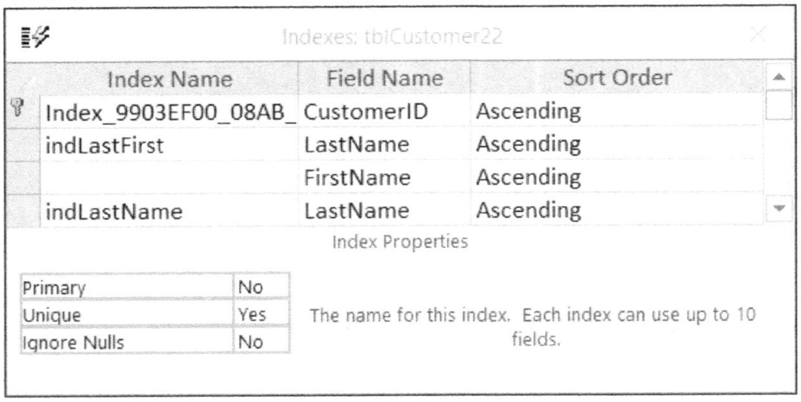

To see the index you have just created, open the table in design view and in the "Show/Hide" group click on "Indexes".

330. Create an index on a field so that it does not accept null values

Add a unique index for the last name field that will not allow null values

Discussion:

In this scenario, we want the indexed field not to accept duplicate or null values. It will not accept duplicate values because we use the "UNIQUE" keyword and it will not accept null values because we use the "DISALLOW NULL" keyword. Practically, "DISALLOW NULL" will not permit any blank entries in the last name field.

Code:

```
CREATE TABLE tblCustomer23 (
[CustomerID] Counter Primary key,
[LastName] text(50),
[FirstName] text(50),
[Address] text(50))
```

Code:

```
CREATE UNIQUE INDEX indLastName ON tblCustomer23 (LastName) WITH DISALLOW
NULL
```

Result:

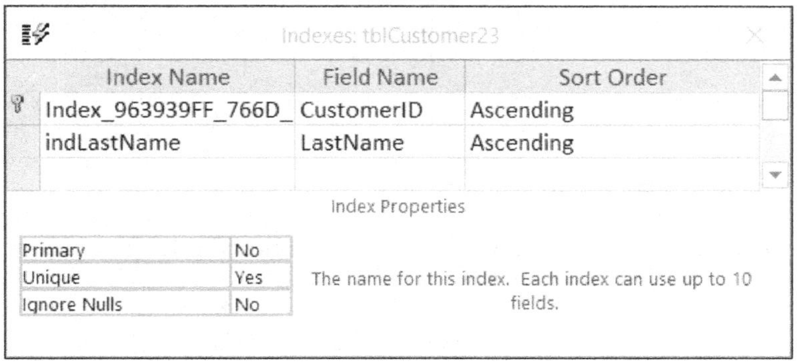

To see the index you have just created, open the table in design view and in the "Show/Hide" group click on "Indexes".

331. Create an index that ignores nulls

Create an index on lastname that ignores null last name values

Discussion:

By default, when we create an index for a field, this index will include the field's null values in the indexed entries. We might, however, want null entries to be excluded from the index and only entries with data to be included. This is not the same as setting a field not to accept nulls. In this example, the keyword "WITH IGNORE NULL" will simply exclude null values from the index list. That is, a list of last names will be created and kept in the database as an index and this list will not have any blank entries in it.

Code:

```
CREATE TABLE tblCustomer24 (
[CustomerID] Counter Primary key,
[LastName] text(50),
[FirstName] text(50),
[Address] text(50))
```

Code:

```
CREATE UNIQUE INDEX indLastName ON tblCustomer24 (LastName) WITH IGNORE
NULL
```

Result:

As you can see from the result set, the "Ignore Nulls" property is set to "yes."

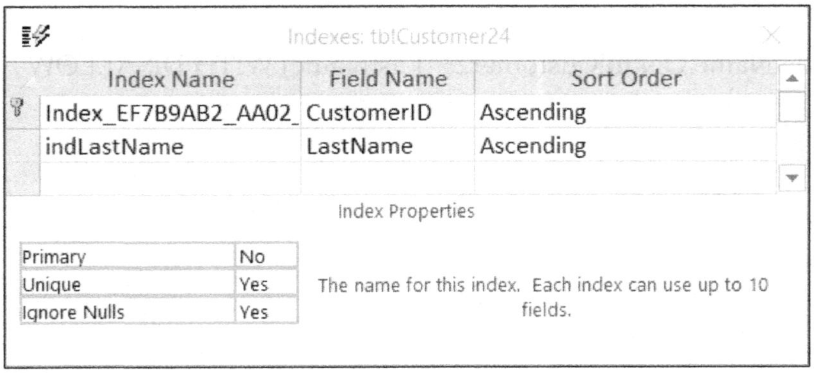

To see the index you have just created, open the table in design view and in the "Show/Hide" group click on "Indexes".

332. Delete Indexes

Delete the "indLastName" index from the customer table using SQL

Discussion:

In the previous example, we have created an index on the LastName field for the tblCustomer24 table and we named it indLastName. Now, we will delete this index using the DROP statement.

Code:

```
DROP INDEX indLastName ON tblCustomer24
```

Result:

The index "indLastName" has been deleted from the tblCustomer24 table. No feedback will be given from Access.

DISCUSSION QUESTIONS

1. What are the reasons for which we use indexes?
2. On what fields does it make sense to use indexes?
3. What does it mean to use indexes as constrains?
4. How can we use an index to disallow nulls in a field?
5. How can we avoid duplicate values in a field by using indexes?
6. What are the consequences of indexes on inserts and updates?
7. How can we avoid duplicate values in multiple fields by using indexes?
8. What are the consequences of indexes on the WHERE and ORDER BY clauses?
9. Where does it make sense to use indexes? Small or large tables?
10. How can we setup indexes to ignore null values?

APPENDIX I
THE SAMPLE DATABASE

The Entity Relationship Diagram (ERD) of the database is shown below:

1. There is a one-to-many relationship between Customers and Orders.
2. There is a many-to-many relationship between Orders and Products with the table JoinOrdersProducts functioning as the join table. The table JoinOrdersProducts contains the details of each particular order and what products it contains. Its primary key is the combination of the primary keys of the Orders and Products tables.
3. As you can see from the ERD, there are also one-to-many relationships between the ShippingCompanies and Orders tables, Suppliers and Products, and SalesReps and Orders. The SalesReps table is the employees table, i.e. the salespeople.

The tables you see in the ERD diagram are the main tables in the database. There are additional tables so that you can work on the examples without affecting the main tables. All of the secondary tables have the prefixes "tbls" or "tble" and you can work on them at will, deleting or updating data without affecting the main tables of the database. Just in case something goes wrong, you can always download the database again as you please.

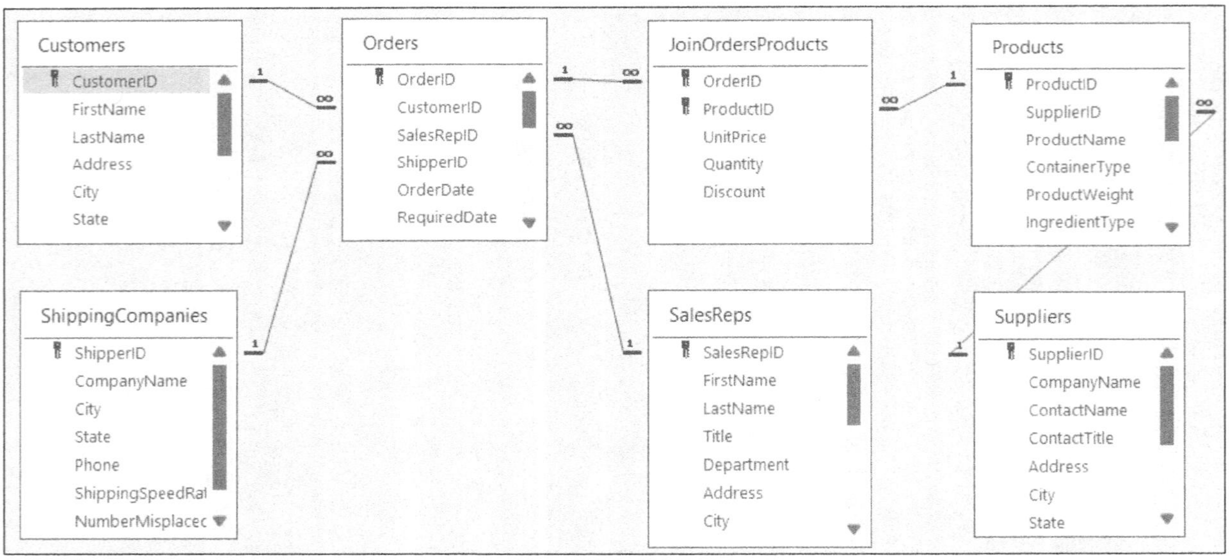

INDEX OF TERMS